URBAN
RESIDENTIAL PATTERNS

URBAN
RESIDENTIAL PATTERNS

AN INTRODUCTORY REVIEW

☆

R. J. JOHNSTON

PRAEGER PUBLISHERS
New York · Washington

BOOKS THAT MATTER

Published in the United States of America in 1972
by Praeger Publishers, Inc., 111 Fourth Avenue,
New York, N. Y. 10003

© G. Bell and Sons, Limited, 1971

Library of Congress Catalog Number: 71-172079

Printed in Great Britain

TO
T. W. FREEMAN

Preface

THIS BOOK emerges out of seven years work on intra-urban residential patterns which was originally stimulated by reading Emrys Jones' book *A Social Geography of Belfast*. No new research findings are reported; as the title indicates, the book is a review, presenting an ordered résumé of a large body of relevant research. The subject is one which indicates the strong dependence of much of geography on the theories of other social scientists, as the framework for the chapters indicates. The book is aimed at both student and researcher. For the former, it is hoped to give an appreciation of the findings of this research field and a structure within which knowledge on urban residential patterns can be ordered; for the latter, the aim is to present a critical appraisal of the present 'state of the art', to suggest further hypotheses which require testing. Like all reviews, it is not complete (between the times of writing and publishing, for example, Cambridge University Press have brought out Duncan Timms' *The Urban Mosaic: Towards a Theory of Residential Differentiation*): hopefully, all the salient literature up to late 1970 has been covered.

During these years of work I have received assistance from many sources. Initial study of the topic was undertaken at Monash University as part of a Ph.D., and I am grateful to Basil Johnson and Murray Wilson for their help with that project. For the last four years I have been at the University of Canterbury and I am grateful to Barry Johnston for his encouragement. Some of the ideas discussed here have been outlined to the academic public earlier, in published and conference papers, and I wish to express my thanks to the many

7

individuals who have debated them with me. Finally, I wish to express my debt to T. W. Freeman, to whom I am pleased to dedicate this book. He it was who encouraged me in my undergraduate and early graduate career, who supervised my first stuttering attempts at research, who helped me to present my thoughts verbally (unfortunately, I have never approached the heights of prose that he has always straddled). His constant encouragement of my work has been most gratifying, and I hope that he finds the results of these ten years acceptable.

In preparing this work I have received much valuable assistance. To Maureen Brunel, Judy Robertson and Fay Booker I am indebted for many hundreds of pages of typing, much of it from an almost illegible hand: to John Macdonald I am grateful for much technical advice in preparation of the illustrations, while thanks go to Claire McMichael and Pat Matthews for drawing these, and to Graham Mitchell for his photographic work. Barry Johnston, Jim Forrest and Eric Woolmington read and commented on the manuscript in draft form, and I am exceedingly grateful to them for their time and considerable assistance. To Mr. M. H. Varvill of G. Bell and Sons I am grateful for his interest in and assistance with this book. And finally, my thanks go to my wife Rita, in apology for those many silent evenings which I spent scribbling away in my armchair, and in gratitude for her encouragement and the environment in which this book was written; and to Chris and Lucy, whose efforts to divert my attention were not successful often enough, my apologies and thanks for helping me remain sane.

November, 1970   R. J. Johnston

Contents

		page
Preface		7
Figures		10
Tables		12
Acknowledgements		14
Introduction		15
I	Divisions of society	19
II	Residential differentiation	38
III	Models of residential patterns	64
IV	The changing social topography	119
V	Life styles, the family cycle and residential location	197
VI	Residential patterns of minority groups	242
VII	Residential mobility and residential patterns	293
VIII	The changing residential mosaic: towards an integrated model	330
Bibliography		355
Index		377

Figures

		page
III. 1	Movement of migrant groups within the city of Chicago	70
III. 2	Different zonal patterns	73
III. 3	Application of time and cost distance concepts	74
III. 4	Concentric zonal pattern, as applied to Chicago	75
III. 5	Schematic diagrams of the sectoral and zonal distribution of dwelling rents in American cities during the 1930s	82
III. 6	Multiple nuclei and sector conceptualisations of urban land use patterns	84
III. 7	Changing distribution of fashionable residential areas in six American cities	85
III. 8	Simplified cross-section through a city: filtering process	98
III. 9	Simplified cross-section through a city: family cycle location process	108
III. 10	Schematic diagrams of a growing city: distribution of migrant groups	113
IV. 1	Schematic diagram of zonal and sectoral distribution of sample collectors' districts, Melbourne 1961	142
IV. 2	Changing distribution of high-status residential areas, Melbourne	148
IV. 3	Changing distribution of high-status residential areas, Christchurch, 1951–64	151
IV. 4	Classification of high-status residential areas, Christchurch, 1951–64	152
IV. 5	Schematic diagram of elements in residential pattern of New Zealand cities	156
IV. 6	Pattern of social areas in Sunderland	159
IV. 7	Schematic representations of fashionable neighbourhoods, Belfast	162

page

IV. 8 Schematic representations of residential areas in industrial cities of northern England   164

IV. 9 Social areas in Greater London, 1951   166

V. 1 Demographic areas of Wellington   205

V. 2 Population age structures, Kansas City   208

V. 3 The changing age structure of Auckland   209

V. 4 The distribution of apartment construction, Toronto, 1952–62   217

V. 5 Relationships among population density, density gradient, city size, central density, time, and distance from the city centre   226

VI. 1 Transects showing distribution of minority groups, Chicago   248

VI. 2 Distribution of Negroes, Chicago, 1920–50   252

VI. 3 Process of invasion and succession   253

VI. 4 Classification of Negro residential areas, Chicago, 1950   255

VI. 5 Changing distribution of Dutch households in Kalamazoo   276

VI. 6 Distribution of coloured and Irish immigrants in Birmingham   286

VI. 7 Distribution of migrant groups, Melbourne, 1961   288

VII. 1 Schematic representation of household migration, Philadelphia   299

VII. 2 Sectoral mental map of an urban resident   319

VII. 3 Residence–workplace relationships   328

VIII.1 Distribution of social areas, Melbourne, 1961   338

VIII.2 Residential location process   345

VIII.3 Integrated spatial model of urban residential areas, based on Chicago   347

Tables

			page
I.	1	Inter-generational social mobility in Britain	28
I.	2	Intra-generational social mobility: Oakland, California	29
II.	1	Residential separation of occupation groups: Chicago, 1950	43
II.	2	Residential concentration: Melbourne, 1961	46
II.	3	Residential separation of migrant groups: Chicago, 1930–50	51
II.	4	Population distribution by social areas: San Francisco 1940	54
II.	5	Factorial ecology: Toledo, 1950	57
IV.	1	Gradients in the growth of the city: Chicago, c. 1920	120
IV.	2	Centralisation of occupation groups: Chicago and Cleveland	123
IV.	3	Zonal and sectoral patterns of occupation groups: Johannesburg and Pretoria, 1960	126
IV.	4	Residential distribution of educational classes: USA, 1960	131
IV.	5	Residential distribution of income groups: USA, 1960	133
IV.	6	Changing educational class distribution: Detroit, 1940–60	135
IV.	7	Redistribution of educational classes: metropolitan areas, 1950–60	136
IV.	8	Changes in zonal patterns: urbanised areas, 1950–60	137
IV.	9	Zonal and sectoral patterns in urban residential structure: Melbourne, 1961	144
IV. 10		Zonal patterns within sectors: Melbourne, 1961	145
IV. 11		Processes of change in high-status residential areas: Christchurch, 1951–64	153

TABLES

page

IV.12	Variables used in Anderson's analysis	174
IV.13	The changing educational status of the US population	179
IV.14	Neighbourhood status and migration: Providence, 1955–60	183
IV.15	Middle income housing costs: Boston	189
IV.16	Assignment of 1960 housing stock: Los Angeles	191
V.1	Zonal patterns of life style and family status: Melbourne, 1961	200
V.2	Hypothesised patterns in the Hoover–Vernon model of urban area differention	212
V.3	Tests of Hoover–Vernon model: Los Angeles, 1940–60	214
V.4	Land values in Chicago	223
V.5	Land values in Christchurch	224
V.6	San Francisco's social space: 1950	230
V.7	Attitudes of middle class suburban housewives in England	238
VI.1	The distribution of minority groups in Chicago	249
VI.2	Zonal patterns of Negro residential areas: Chicago, 1950	256
VI.3	Distribution of Negro in-migrants: ten cities, 1960	259
VI.4	Factorial ecology: Toledo, Ohio, 1960	268
VI.5	Zonal patterns in the Negro community: Chicago	269
VI.6	The changing structure of the Negro ghetto: Chicago, 1940–50	271
VI.7	The Russian community in Minneapolis,	280
VI.8	Indices of residential dissimilarity: Auckland, 1966	289
VII.1	Intra-area moves: Philadelphia, 1955–56	298
VII.2	Number of residences per ten years of residence: Norristown	304
VII.3	Retrospective and subsequent mobility: Los Angeles	305
VII.4	Desired and actual mobility: Philadelphia, 1955	308
VII.5	Moves among social areas: Rhode Island, 1955–60	312
VII.6	Inter- and intra-community migration: Cedar Rapids, 1966–67	315
VII.7	Major factors in home choice: Newcastle, N.S.W., 1964	323
VIII.1	Spatial patterns within the city: Toronto, 1951–61	333
VIII.2	Profits of social areas: Melbourne, 1961	337

Acknowledgements

I wish to thank all those who have kindly granted me permission to quote from their works or to reproduce their maps or diagrams. Acknowledgement has been made at the appropriate points in my text and full particulars of the sources used will be found in the bibliography at the end of this book. I am, indeed, most grateful for their assistance.

R.J.J.

Introduction

'NOB HILL', ghetto, Skid Row and Chinatown are some of the descriptive terms applied to various neighbourhoods in cities of the English-speaking world. They express the areal separation of various social, economic, demographic, ethnic and migrant groups which produces a mosaic of different neighbourhoods that together form the modern city. Such a mosaic often seems to have a definite pattern: ghettoes, for example, almost invariably are close to the city centre but upper class residential districts usually shun close contact with commercial and industrial land uses. The pattern is rarely stable, however. New areas are constantly being added, while older residential districts commonly decay, both socially and in their building fabric, although some may be rejuvenated. Thus the present slum may have been a desirable middle class neighbourhood twenty years ago, and in a few decades the present 'Nob Hills' may be the sites of urban renewal projects.

Within the usually fairly slow process of neighbourhood change, other alterations often occur more rapidly. Billboards and pages of newspaper advertisements give adequate testimony to the rate of property turnover and population movement. In the United States, for example, about one-fifth of the population change their residence each year and almost three-quarters move during a five-year period. Such mobility is often associated with neighbourhood change, but similar migration rates occur while an area retains its social personality, the characteristics of in-movers and out-movers being the same.

The patterns and processes of migration and neighbourhood change are topics which fall well within the geographer's orbit. Two traditional lines of geographical inquiry are into areal differentiation—the investigation of variability in the character of places (Hartshorne, 1939)—and sequent occupance—which relates to the changing use of a place or area (Whittlesey, 1929). Research into neighbourhood differentiation within a city clearly falls within the first topic, and the characteristics of residential area change are classic examples of the second.

In recent years a number of strong trends has resulted in additional approaches to geographic methodology. One of these has been the study of spatial pattern or geometry, and formed the organisation framework of Haggett's (1965) *Locational Analysis in Human Geography*. Study of the city's residential mosaic falls easily into this mould. As well as areal differentiation of the population groups, there may also be regularities in the actual and relative locations of various types of neighbourhood. Added to this, geographers are now placing at the core of their subject not only the traditional static patterns of areal differentiation, several of which at various dates give evidence on sequent occupance, but also the movement patterns which connect the myriad of specialised districts (Crowe, 1938). Thus, population movements are part of the interaction processes which Ullman (1953) claimed were fundamental to geographic study, and neighbourhood change with its associated migrations fits the diffusion concept now central to many research efforts (Brown, 1968).

Although it can be argued that the changing residential pattern of cities is an apt target for their research, geographers have given the topic relatively little attention. Partly this reflects a long-held view that not the characteristics of the population but only the features of places should be studied (Vidal de la Blache, 1913: Sauer, 1931). People and place must both be studied in the investigation of urban neighbourhoods, and it is perhaps because of this that geographers have concentrated on other aspects of the urban scene until recently, notably its economic and commercial structure (Berry, 1965). Most texts in urban geography devote very little space to residential areas, therefore: an exception is Dickinson's (1964)

City and Region, which uses few recent sources, however. Those interested in the topic must search elsewhere; most information can be gained from the branch of sociology known as human ecology (for example in Schnore, 1965, and Thomlinson, 1969), and to a lesser extent in economics.

The amount of geographical research on urban residential areas is increasing rapidly at present, and the residential mosaic is becoming an important subject in the teaching of urban geography. In view of these trends, the present volume attempts to give an introductory review of the literature on residential patterns, aimed at researcher and student alike. Little of the material is new, but most of it has not been brought together and discussed within a single volume, so it is hoped that not only the content but also the organisational framework will be of value.

The approach to the subject in this book is nomothetic. In line with recent trends, geography is viewed here not as a vehicle for elucidating the particular features of unique places but as a search for regularities and order in man's spatial organisation of the earth's surface. This requires the application of one or both of the two generally recognised scientific methodologies—deductive and inductive. In fact, most works combine both, as in this book. Full application of these approaches is limited, however, since an introductory review depends on already completed works for its information. Thus, high-order generalisations would not be possible from this work, even if the subject matter suggested them, but sufficient has been done on most topics here to allow some general conclusions.

With a subject still in its infancy like this one, an aim at universal coverage, discussion and generalisation would be presumptuous, as indeed Schnore (1968) has recognised for this very topic. Hence the concentration on cities in countries where the English language is dominant, partly for linguistic convenience but also because of a relatively common cultural base which should produce fewer complications than exist in areas where two or more major cultures are in contact (on these see McGee, 1967). This collection draws almost entirely on urban studies in the United States—where such work is most advanced and plentiful—Great Britain, Canada, Australia and

New Zealand, the last two providing many of the case studies because they have been the locale for most of the writer's research.

To understand why there is residential separation of groups within urban societies it is necessary to know, first, what the groups are and how they come about, and, second, why they choose to live in relatively mutual exclusion. The early chapters of this book therefore present an introductory analysis of the bases for social differentiation and areal segregation. Chapter I discusses three major ways in which an economically developed urban society is divided, and is followed in Chapter II by an outline of reasons why members of these divisions should choose to occupy separate parts of the city. The latter part of that chapter presents empirical evidence on the existence of such areal differentiation, thus setting the scene for the remainder of the book.

The main interest of this book is in the residential *pattern* of cities, so the first chapters present only a brief introduction to the reasons for differentiation. The rest of the book is concerned with the central theme. Chapter III outlines the basic constructs and hypotheses concerning the patterns, in some detail since full discussions of the various models is usually lacking in geographical studies. In addition, the main models have been formulated outside geography, so they are given a very full treatment, as are the comments of their contemporary critics.

Chapter III provides a statement of the major hypotheses concerning urban residential patterns, and material is presented to test these in the next four, dealing successively with the three main divisions of society and then the patterns of residential mobility. These consider the residential mosaic as independent forces, but of course all three operate together on the decision-makers whose choice of where to live produces the final pattern. Thus an attempt is made in the final chapter to integrate the various findings to date and so give a single model of the residential areas of the city. Such a statement is, necessarily, extremely tentative and marks completion of only one of the first steps in the long search for a true functional understanding of the city.

CHAPTER I

Divisions of Society

URBANISATION AND industrialisation are closely associated. Although it is possible for cities to develop without industries and for industries to exist outside cities, nevertheless the degree of population concentration into urban centres is generally very closely associated with levels of economic development (Schnore, 1961).

Neither industrialisation nor urbanisation can be considered as the cause of the other. Instead they operate together as mutually reinforcing variables. Rapid urbanisation would not occur without industrialisation, but urbanisation itself can lead to industrialisation, through the chain of cumulative causation which has been demonstrated by Myrdal (1957) and Pred (1965). Lampard has thus claimed that 'The growth of the modern city and the march of the industrial revolution are joint products of a single cultural strand—specialization' (Lampard, 1955, 91).

The role of specialisation or the division of labour in producing both industrialisation and urbanisation can be stated as follows (the argument is drawn from Lampard's presentation):

1. Economic advancement largely results from increases in productive efficiency, which reduce the real costs of output.

2. Higher productivity requires more specialised individual effort, which yields economies in time, effort and resources. The person who performs only a small task, therefore, will—all other things being equal—be more productive than one engaged in several functions.

3. Increasing specialisation between parts leads to their

greater interdependence. The subsistence farmer may produce all of his needs and so be completely independent of all other persons, but the locksmith has no need for the vast majority of his products and must exchange these with other producers in order to survive.

4. Interdependence requires contact, which is hampered by distance, for it takes time and costs money to transport goods.

From this, 'city growth is simply the concentration of differentiated but functionally-integrated specialisms in rational locales', since 'Specialization of functions makes inevitably for specialization of areas . . . Areal differentiation is, in fact, the spatial corollary of functional specialization and logically serves the same end—economy' (Lampard, 1955, 92). Early specialisation merely differentiates between types of farmers who meet at market places to exchange products, where craftsmen also foregather to sell tools and purchase foods. Thus a system of numerous small market centres develops which are but little differentiated (Lampard, 1963, 242). What Lampard (1965) has termed incessant urbanisation, or continued rapid urban growth and population concentration, only occurs with the development of much more specialised functions and the emergence of the factory system. Factories of themselves produce population concentrations, and encourage even greater exchange, initiating the growth of a large, urban entrepreneurial class.

The twin roles of specialisation in industrial and urban development have been charted by Lampard (1968), Pred (1966), and others. But the focus of the present book is not urbanisation *per se*, rather only one aspect of it: the patterns of areal differentiation in the residential segments of urban areas. Nevertheless, such differentiation is a reflection of social differentiation as shown in the following chapters, and this social differentiation is itself also a concomitant of functional specialisation. Thus the present chapter outlines the nature of the social divisions which emerge during economic development as a backcloth for the later discussions of their reflection in the landscape.

The Prerequisites of Specialisation

Functional and areal division of labour does not simply emerge from an ability of subsistence cultivators to produce a surplus. Although the potential for a surplus which will allow for a division of labour (basically into productive and non-productive) is a prerequisite for specialisation, some form of organisation is necessary to institute the surplus (Keyfitz, 1965). Thus the first cities were not the products of surpluses, but resulted from the superimposition of an organisation—usually priestly or military, or both—which demanded the surplus (Wheatley, 1967). This was the earliest division of labour, outside the divisions of age, sex, and seniority within family units, and it was brought forth by organisation.

Many aspects of societal organisation are important to economic development. Moore (1963, 93–97), for example, has indicated the necessity of monetary and fiscal systems, administrative systems, political stability, property rights, and channels for property transfers. In addition, he suggested the need for motivation or achievement orientation (as in Max Weber's (1930) Protestant ethic), which would involve full participation of individuals within the society, labour mobility, and perhaps strong nationalistic feelings also.

The Concomitants & Consequences of Specialisation

Specialisation results in economic development, therefore, and the concentration of population in urban centres. In addition it leads to many changes in societal structure. Economically it draws subsistence agriculturalists, pastoralists, hunters and gatherers into an exchange economy, in its initial stages. Even more importantly, as it progresses it continually removes more and more people from primary occupations, placing them in the secondary (manufacturing) and tertiary (distributive and administrative) sectors so that, in general, the economically most advanced countries have the lowest proportions of their population engaged in agriculture (Moore, 1966). This primary-secondary-tertiary transition is usually associated with Colin Clark's book *The Conditions of Economic Progress* (1940), in which he charted changing employment structures alongside indices of economic development, but his ideas are largely irrelevant in the presently termed 'developing' countries, where tertiary industries usually dominate the other two (see Mehta, 1961).

But Clark's scheme only outlined the broad economic repercussions of economic development. Within each industry, specialisation becomes more and more intense, and tasks more skilled and narrow. There is a professionalisation of work, and the need for labour mobility between occupations as machines replace men in the more routine tasks (Moore, 1963, 99).

With increased productivity, individuals and families are released from the Malthusian spectre. This may lead to the decay of the family as a basic social unit, for its role as an economic bulwark becomes less necessary. Individualism develops with such autonomy, with consequences on such things as mate selection, parent-child relationships, kinship bonds, the separate roles of males and females, and mental disorders resulting from emotional disturbances. In general, there is what two anthropologists have termed an increase in societal scale (Wilson and Wilson, 1945). Individuals within societies at various levels of economic development show the same degree of dependence on others, but the greater the level of development the more widely dispersed is the reliance on others. In primitive societies contacts are with only a few, well-known kin, but in highly developed urbanised societies they are many, and more frequently impersonal.

This differentiation was formalised in Tönnie's concepts of *gemeinschaft* and *gesellschaft*, or community and association, and the anonymity and presumed consequent mental disorders of the urban, community-less associations were decried by many early twentieth-century observers, who glorified what they saw as the benefits of the 'folk society'. The decline of community resulted from urbanisation, and the consequent life style (urbanism) was characterised as producing:

> the weakening of kinship bonds, family life and neighborliness, and the development of impersonality, superficiality, anonymity and transitoriness in personal relations . . . the process of urbanization is essentially a process of disorganization (Lewis, 1965, 496).

The classic and seminal statement of this point of view was Louis Wirth's (1938) essay 'Urbanism as a Way of Life'. He defined cities in terms of their population size, density, and heterogeneity and deduced the following consequences of these three as (the tabulation is taken from Shevky and Bell, 1955, 7–8; see also Morris, 1968, 16–19):

1. THE EFFECTS OF SIZE

a. The greater the number of interacting people, the greater the potential differentiation.

b. With dependence spread over more people, there is less dependence on particular individuals.

c. There is association with more people, but knowledge, especially intimate knowledge, of fewer.

d. Most contacts become impersonal, superficial, transitory and segmental.

e. There is more freedom from the physical and emotional controls of intimate groups.

f. There is association with a number of groups, but no allegiance to a single group.

2. THE EFFECTS OF DENSITY

a. A tendency to differentiation and specialisation.

b. The separation of workplace and residence.

c. The functional segregation of areas.

d. The segregation of people, creating a residential mosaic.

3. THE EFFECTS OF HETEROGENEITY

a. Without common background and knowledge, emphasis is placed on visual recognition and symbolism.

b. With no common value sets or ethical systems money tends to become the sole measure of worth.

c. Formal controls of society replace the informal controls of the group.

d. Life has an economic basis, mass production needing product and demand standardisation.

e. The growth of mass political movements.

In terms of the interest of this book in urban residential patterns, the effects of density seem most important. But these are not independent of the others; for example, the social segregation in 2d follows the monetary valuation of everything (3b) and the need for visual symbols (3a), among other things.

Many of Wirth's deductions have been strongly criticised (see Morris, 1968), and some are definitely not accepted; Lewis, for example, has demonstrated that very strong, tightly-knit communities have continued to exist within Mexican cities, particularly among the lower socio-economic classes. Nevertheless, although Wirth's statements mostly remain as hypotheses rather than theory, they seem to represent many aspects of urban life in the societies studied here. Communities have not entirely disappeared with city growth, however, and the aim of the book is to map spatial patterns of such groups. The question is raised as to how many such communities exist in urban areas, and how the society is split to produce them.

HOW MANY DIVISIONS?

A myriad of social and economic changes thus cause, accompany and result from industrialisation and urbanisation. They may all be part of a single dimension of economic progress, or alternatively could be divided into several, relatively independent, aspects of the same process. A major deductive attempt to determine the number of ways in which urban society is divided (Shevky and Bell, 1955) has suggested three, which can be briefly classified as:

1. Socio-economic status.
2. Family status and life style.
3. Geographical mobility and minority groups.

Whether these three separate dimensions exist, and are the only ones within society, has not been fully tested. A theory of social change was used as an axiom for developing a method of studying social areas, and while the latter aspect has proven empirically correct to a large degree, its linkage with the theory has not been satisfactorily displayed. Nevertheless, since the present book is mainly concerned with social areas within cities, since there is no superior theory, and since the dimensions have at least proven empirically valid, the Shevky-Bell construct is used as the basis for discussions of societal patterns.

Socio-economic Status

Traditional societies contain hierarchies of social status, power and prestige which are often unrelated to work patterns and the individual's societal function. Industrialised societies, on the other hand, are largely stratified by occupations, giving hierarchies of skill, income and prestige. Such stratifications are generally termed class structures, and a person's class situation represents his position within the occupational system (Runciman, 1969, 47). The usual ordering of an urban class system, as shown by the US Census classification of occupations, is:

Professional, technical and kindred workers.
Managers, proprietors and officials (except farm).
Sales workers.
Clerical and kindred workers.
Craftsmen, foremen and kindred workers.
Operatives and kindred workers.
Service workers, except in private households.
Labourers, except farm and mine.

The British and other censuses use similar schemas. In general, the ordering of occupations shown here is reflected in the incomes received and the amount of education needed to attain the various levels. Thus, occupation, education and income are often used interchangeably as measures of socio-economic status.

Why should such stratification develop, and why are occupational differences translated into classes through the uneven distribution of rewards (mainly income)? Early attempts to answer these questions have been termed the functionalist theory (Davis 1942; Davis and Moore, 1945). These two authors argued that an occupation's position in the class structure results from its functional importance and the differential scarcity of personnel, so that (Wesolowski, 1962):

1. Social stratification is functionally necessary, because 'some [jobs] require special talent of training and some are functionally more important than others. Also, it is essential that the duties of the positions be performed with the diligence

that their importance requires' (Davis and Moore, 1945, 243). Thus, society makes an uneven distribution of material rewards to match the functional importance of various occupations.

2. Stratification, and the concomitant rewards, is necessary because stimuli are needed to induce people to undertake the functionally more demanding and important positions.

3. The stratification mechanism ensures that the right people are located in each occupation.

The alternative approach to the functionalists is the conflict, or coercion, theory. The functional approach is seen to account for occupational differentiation, but not for the stratification of incomes into a status ranking. The coercion theory states that 'The origin of inequality is . . . to be found in the existence in all human societies of norms of behaviour to which sanctions are attached' (Dahrendorf, 1969, 34). Both positive (rewards) and negative (punishments) sanctions are imposed, and are used by the dominant group to produce a system of social ranking. Since a dominant group is unlikely to place itself anywhere but at the top of such a hierarchy, the present class structure indicates who has imposed the sanctions: 'The distribution of rewards in a society is a function of the distribution of power, not of system needs' (Lenski, 1966, 20).

It is unnecessary to go further into the origins of socio-economic stratification for the purpose of this book. However, it should be noted that sociologists conceive of not one but three dimensions of social inequality—class, status and power. As already indicated, class relates to position in the economic system. 'Status . . . is concerned with social estimation and prestige, and although it is closely related to class it is not synonymous with it' (Runciman, 1969, 48). This is shown by many prestige rankings of occupations, which are very similar in different societies of comparable economic development (Inkeles and Rossi, 1956): among the variations between class and status are the relatively high esteem to clerical work compared to better paid artisan occupations. Finally, 'The holders of power in a society need not be the most highly rewarded of its citizens, or even the most highly esteemed . . . [although] the connexion between class-situation and power-situation is usually demonstrable enough' (Runciman, 1969, 50). Thus, the dimension of socio-economic status, or class, has a number of slight deviations from it, knowledge of which may be important for the unravelling of residential patterns (see, for example, pages 44 and 177).

Class perpetuation is a general characteristic of social stratification in traditional societies, which comprise systems of (almost completely) closed castes and estates. A notable and often mentioned feature of economic development, on the other hand, is the growing porosity of class barriers. Good data to substantiate this statement are rare, however, and Smelser and Lipset (1966, 20) have been forced to conclude that 'There is a puzzling lack of association between indicators of economic development and measures of social mobility'. In the same volume, Duncan (1966) suggested there were no basic changes in mobility rates for Indianapolis between 1910 and 1940. Nevertheless, there is considerable movement between classes in industrialised societies.

Two forms of social mobility are generally recognised. The first, inter-generational mobility, is usually indexed by the difference in class position between father's and son's occupation. Glass and Hall (1954) studied this in Britain, and their results (such as Table I.1) indicated that there were more sons entering their fathers' occupations than would have occurred under conditions of 'perfect mobility' in which class origin was no constraint on occupational choice.

Of more interest to this study of residential patterns is the investigation of intra-generational mobility. Analysis of data for Oakland, California by Lipset and Bendix (1959), for example, showed that most males had been employed at class levels other than their present one at some period during their working life (Table I.2). A high percentage of all respondents had owned their own businesses, at least for a short period, and among those in professional occupations at the time of the survey 26 percent had worked in low-status white-collar jobs, 22 percent in semi-skilled occupations, and 17 percent in unskilled. Despite the 'rags to riches' (or 'small town school to President') stories, however, and the egalitarian pronouncements in many societies, birth is still an important determinant

TABLE I.1

INTER-GENERATIONAL SOCIAL MOBILITY IN BRITAIN

A. Percent of Sons by Father's Occupation

STATUS OF:	SON	1	2	3	4	5	6	7
FATHER	1	39	15	20	6	14	5	1
	2	10	27	23	12	21	5	2
	3	3	10	19	19	36	7	6
	4	2	4	11	21	43	12	6
	5	1	2	7	12	47	17	12
	6	—	1	4	9	39	31	15
	7	—	1	4	8	36	23	27

B. Percent of Fathers by Son's Occupation

STATUS OF:	SON	1	2	3	4	5	6	7
FATHER	1	48	12	8	2	1	1	—
	2	15	25	10	4	2	1	1
	3	12	22	20	14	9	4	5
	4	11	13	18	24	16	11	7
	5	14	23	34	40	50	43	45
	6	—	4	6	9	12	24	17
	7	—	2	4	7	10	15	25

Key to Occupations: 1. Professional and higher administrative; 2. Managerial; 3. Inspectors, Supervisors, high status non-manual; 4. *Ibid.*, low status non-manual; 5. Skilled manual, routine non-manual; 6. Semiskilled 7. Unskilled.

Source: Glass and Hall, 1954.

of class. Life chance is strongly influenced by status of parents in many cases so that, as Lipset and Bendix's tables indicated, most individuals either remain in the same class as their parents, or move up or down only a single step.

Industrialised societies are therefore stratified into classes, and there is movement between the various strata. Occupation, income and education are generally regarded as the best indicators of socio-economic class, but they are not completely synonymous. In addition, there are hierarchies of status and power which, while very close to it, do not exactly conform to that of class. Definition of various strata is not clear-cut, therefore, and in addition there is considerable evidence to suggest that the common class names are merely convenient taxonomic devices for dividing what is essentially a continuum.

TABLE I.2

INTRA-GENERATIONAL SOCIAL MOBILITY:
OAKLAND, CALIFORNIA

Percent with Percent of Career spent in Present Occupation

PRESENT OCCUPATION	80–100	50–79	50–
Professional	70	9	22
Semi-Professional	47	32	21
Own Business	11	31	57
Upper White Collar	14	21	65
Lower White Collar	18	33	49
Sales	26	24	50
Skilled	22	35	43
Semiskilled	22	29	49
Unskilled	18	21	61
All Manual	65	21	14
All Non-manual	58	23	19
TOTAL	22	29	50

Source: Lipset and Bendix, 1959, 161.

Family Status & Life Style

The family plays an important economic as well as social role in traditional, agrarian societies with few trading contacts. Self-sufficient, subsistence farming is the norm in the most primitive, and its organisation by large, extended family groups allows of some scale economies and division of labour. Perhaps more importantly, the larger group provides a better base for assistance in time of stress (such as harvest failure), and thus the extended family-oriented society tends to remain as the basic building block during early stages of economic development.

With industrialisation, the economic functions of the extended family decline (especially within the higher socio-economic classes). Work takes place outside the family, most households exist at well above the Malthusian limits, and in many societies the welfare state systems provide the cushions for times of stress. Individuals need to be flexible in searching for their socio-economic and geographical niches within society: often this can be best achieved away from close kinship networks which usually are traditional in their attitudes, closed to many socio-economic changes, parochial in their locational patterns, and believe in group rather than individual owner-ship of property (Goode, 1963, 242–243).

Not only is there a transition from home-based to extra-familial work with industrialisation, but also a trend to greater employment of females, who are over-represented in service and clerical occupations in the developed 'Western' societies. These occupations are mainly associated with the later stages of economic development with their more complex organisa-tions, and thus also with large cities.

Industrialisation is accompanied by the development of alternative family patterns to the extended, therefore, and by the increased participation of women in urban occupations. The declining importance of the family as an economic unit tends to reduce its power as a social unit (not only in 'advanced' societies, but also in the lower strata of the 'developing' where unemployment is rife: see Peattie, 1969). Family disorganisa-tion and collapse is more common (as shown by divorce and separation rates), and people can choose to live outside the family system entirely. Indeed, Bell (1958b) has suggested that individuals (and married couples) can choose between the following three life styles in an economically developed country:

1. Familism, in which child-rearing is the dominant feature and the whole way of life is centred on children. This life style is closest to the traditional one, though it usually does not involve extended family relationships to anything like the same extent (this statement applies particularly to certain socio-economic status groups, as discussed later). In addition, couples are more able to determine the size of their families, according to the degree to which they want to participate in the other two life styles.

2. Careerism, in which the members are mainly oriented towards the goal of vertical social mobility, and devote the major portion of their time and energy to this end. Many choosing this life style may never marry, but, of those who do, most will marry at an older age than is average, and many will have no children. Those who do have children will both have

them later in their married life than average and have fewer than average, so that the children will impede the vertical mobility as little as possible.

3. Consumerism, in which members opt for the 'good life', preferring to expend their time, money and energy 'eating, drinking and being merry'.

These three are, of course, not necessarily mutually exclusive, and most people choose some combination of two or three. Often one life style dominates, and this can lead to differences between households who have apparently made the same choice. For example, of two families with similar incomes who choose a similar combination of familism and consumerism, one may express the latter through car purchase while the other spend their whole consumerism segment on a month's annual holiday. Such differences could be reflected in choice of living area.

As well as the life style choice, there are two regular transitions which also affect individual actions. The first of these is age, which is associated with recreation and leisure patterns (Chapin and Brail, 1969), but more important is the family cycle. After the pre-marriage period, a number of stages such as the following is usually suggested (Foote *et al*, 1960):

Pre-child
Child Bearing
Child Rearing
Child Launching
Post-Child
Widowhood

In some of these stages, notably the pre-child, and, to a lesser extent, the last two, behaviour may be comparable to that in one or both of the careerism and consumerism life style choices, as it will be for the non-married not living at the parental home.

The general view is that the various changes in family structure are the results of economic development, but Goode (1963) has hypothesised that progress towards a conjugal family system was the independent rather than the dependent variable in Western modernisation. He suggested the importance of the Protestant, especially the Puritan, ethic in capitalism and industrialism, pointing out that it was the threat of unemployment and low wages which produced English worker resistance to the industrial revolution, not defence of the extended family system. In any case, the extended family system has not entirely disappeared, even among the vertically mobile middle classes (Litwak, 1960a, 1960b), although it has been considerably modified.

Geographical Mobility & Minority Groups

The rapid urbanisation of the industrial revolution period in Europe, North America and, to a lesser extent, Australasia resulted not from high levels of natural increase but from very large migrations into the larger urban areas from small towns and the countryside. Indeed, during the nineteenth century high urban mortality rates often meant that rates of natural increase were lower in the cities than the rural areas. Thus, there were massive flows of migrants to swell the cities, many of them forced off the land by unemployment and many more attracted by the city's potential for personal economic and social advance. Davis (1965) has shown that to maintain an annual population growth rate of 3 percent per annum, an in-migration rate of 4–4·5 percent per annum was required, so that the latter process contributed as much as 60 percent of the total urban growth. As a result, a large proportion of urban residents was not born there: in London in 1881 it was 37 percent, and was over 60 percent in some inner quarters (Booth, 1889–1902, Poverty Vol. 3, 150–166).

A detailed study of migration to late nineteenth-century London by Ravenstein (1885) produced a number of generalisations about the migration process, which were later validated for a number of countries (Ravenstein, 1889) and still are relevant today. He showed that migration was mainly in a series of steps away from rural areas through small and large towns to cities and metropoli, and that the majority of moves covered only short distances. Migration was, and still is, a highly selective process, especially with regard to age, with the result that the rapidly growing places experienced massive influxes of relatively young and unskilled persons from the countryside, recently removed from the close ties of kinship and community which existed there.

In addition to this intra-national population redistribution, the heterogeneity of city populations in many countries was added to by considerable flows of international migrants. Many of these were escaping from political, religious, or economic oppression in Europe and were particularly attracted to the egalitarian young nations of the 'New World'. Often they moved in community groups, rather than as households or individuals, into an almost completely alien urban environment. Problems of communication between these persons and their hosts were often immense, leading to distrust, prejudice and isolation on both sides, which was only gradually overcome through processes of assimilation, by which the various cultural differences and rivalries slowly disappear. (Note that this is not synonymous with the rarer process of integration, in which the alien group retains its cultural separateness but participates fully in the national community. In most of the countries studied here, assimilation or 'Anglo-Conformity' has been preferred by the majority.) Assimilation is not a simple, unidimensional process, but involves a number of sub-processes, of which Gordon (1964) has identified seven. The minority groups must break from their traditional life styles and develop a sense of belonging with the host society (*identificational assimilation*); they must participate in the minute structures of the larger community, its cliques and institutions (*structural assimilation*); they must be prepared to form permanent relationships outside their community through intermarriage (*marital assimilation*); and must enter civic and political life other than as representatives of the minority (*civic assimilation*). Most important, and perhaps also most difficult, they must change their culture patterns (including religious beliefs and practices) to those of the host society (*cultural or behavioural assimilation*). And, at the same time, there must be a removal among the host society of both prejudice (*attitude receptional assimilation*) and discrimination (*behaviour receptional assimilation*) against the minority.

Clearly, many groups will not pass through all of these

stages for many decades, if at all; retaining, for example, their own religious attitudes. Thus, Gordon showed that while cultural assimilation had occurred for most groups within the United States, and was always likely to be the first form of assimilation to emerge, none of the others may ever develop, so that this condition of 'acculturation only' may continue indefinitely (Gordon, 1964, 77). Once structural assimilation has occurred, however, all of the other types follow naturally.

The need for assimilation is clearly more likely for inter- than intra-national migrants, both because of the greater likelihood that those who travel long distances will do so in groups, and also because cultural differences are likely to be less between different parts of a single country. (The latter point becomes more relevant with increasing economic development as rural-urban and regional economic and social inequalities disappear.) Given the large numbers of migrants in the cities, however, (for example, in 1961 Sydney's population of 2,183,388 included 178,484 born in Great Britain; 20,481 in Germany; 20,697 in Greece; 11,624 in Hungary; 43,788 in Italy; 15,143 in Malta; 15,627 in the Netherlands; 12,371 in Poland; and 11,063 in Yugoslavia) it is clear that assimilation is a major social process within such areas.

TESTING THE DIMENSIONAL MODEL

One of the major problems in applying a model of society is that of testing its validity, so it is difficult to know whether three dimensions of socio-economic status, family status, and minority groups are both accurate and sufficient. For example we know that classes exist, although there are considerable differences in their definition; we know that people vary in their chosen life styles; and we know that many cities contain a number of unassimilated or only partly assimilated migrant groups. But are these divisions of society independent of each other, or are they all part of a uni-dimensional continuum? Alternatively, are they sufficient to encompass all of the variations in population characteristics within a city? Answers to these questions have been based on assumptions concerning some of the consequences of societal differentiation, particularly one that

34

Diverse population elements inhabiting a compact settlement thus tend to become segregated from one another in the
degree in which their requirements and modes of life are
incompatible with one another and in the measure in which
they are antagonistic to one another. Similarly, persons of
homogeneous status and needs unwittingly drift or con-
sciously select, or are forced by circumstances, into the same
area (Wirth, 1938, 15).

The rationale behind such an assumption is discussed in the
next chapter.

Given that such residential segregation does exist, and is
a result of societal differentiation, then analysis of population
distributions within cities has suggested both that the three
dimensions suggested by Shevky and Bell do exist, and that
they are generally sufficient to account for most of the segregation. (In some analyses sub-dimensions have emerged, such as,
for example, the separation of life styles and family status, and
of various migrant groups from each other.) The techniques
employed in such analyses have shown that the various dimensions (and their component measures) are largely uncorrelated.
This has been interpreted as indicating meaningful as well as
statistical independence, but Coleman (1964) and Janson
(1969) have argued against such interpretation (see also
Johnston, 1971a). This point will be made several times in the
present book, arguing that the various divisions may not be
independent in determining the choice of residential location.

One major problem in the application of Shevky and Bell's
theory of societal change has been in the measures which they
selected to represent the various dimensions. This is particularly so with the family status construct, which they claimed
is reflected in population age and sex structure, in house
structure, dwelling tenure, and persons per household, but
which they measure by the proportion of adult women who
go out to work, the proportion of single-family dwelling units,
and an index of fertility. There is considerable evidence that
the latter is related to socio-economic status also (Powers, 1966;
Davis and Blake, 1956), although some studies have suggested
that the association may be curvilinear with the greatest
fertility in the highest and lowest socio-economic status groups.

Also, the chosen fertility measure (the number of children under 5 years per 1,000 females aged 15–44) is sensitive to age structure differences and may reflect variations between socio-economic classes in similar age groups over such phenomena as average age at marriage, child-spacing, and number of children. Finally, Udry (1964) has shown temporal variations in fertility which do not conform to the general theory of social change.

Recent research has suggested that the two dimensions of socio-economic status and family status become independent as a consequence of economic development. This can be discerned, for example, from two studies of residential differentiation in twenty American cities in 1940 (Schmid, 1950) and 1950 (Schmid, McCannell and van Arsdol, 1958). Comparison between the two dates showed a strong negative association of −0·47 between fertility and socio-economic status (mean rent) at the former, but a minor positive correlation of +0·12 at the latter. For Rome in 1951, McElrath (1962) found a significant relationship between class and fertility (with a correlation of −0·676 between the latter and occupation), and Abu-Lughod's analysis of Cairo in both 1947 and 1960 produced a dimension 'that is to be interpreted as a "style of life" vector in which class and family patterns are inextricably linked' (Abu-Lughod, 1969, 205: see also Clignet and Sween, 1969, and Berry and Rees, 1969).

McElrath (1968) has put together the results of a number of such studies referring to cities at different levels of economic development (Accra, Ghana: Kingston, Jamaica: Rome, Italy: 10 US Cities (van Arsdol, Camilleri and Schmid, 1958a): San Francisco, USA). His work on Accra had shown that only migration status (geographical mobility) of the three Shevky and Bell dimensions was a major social differentiator, with family status inconsistent, dependent and weak. Proceeding up the scale of economic development, he found:

1. Social rank emerged as a societal dimension in the early stages (being observed in Accra and Kingston).
2. Social rank became increasingly independent of family status with economic advance.

3. Family status became independent of social rank at an early stage of development (in Kingston but not Accra).

4. The independence of family and socio-economic status was greatest in the United States.

5. In the most advanced economies there were variations between cities in the amount of independence, with the two main dimensions most separate in the largest cities.

The conclusion regarding city size would probably have been repeated at other levels if data for more than one city in Ghana, Jamaica and Italy had been presented, but it seems that some general theory of social change has emerged from the application of social area analysis to various levels of economic development, given the assumption concerning residential segregation. (Note that the form of analysis can be used within societies to test the degree of group assimilation: see Johnston, forthcoming.) Finally, Udry and Butler have hypothesised that as a society increases in scale, its sub-areas become more functionally specialised and differentiated and sub-areas become more homogeneous within, but more differentiated from, one another (Udry and Butler, 1968, 5).

Like most of the other tests reported here, this hypothesis assumed that the tendency for residential segregation actually existed and could be linked with the theory of social change. The first part of the hypothesis was validated, especially with regard to sub-area age and occupational structures, but there was no clear evidence of declining within-area heterogeneity in the four cities studied during the period 1940–1960.

Industrialisation leads to the social and economic differentiation of urban populations, therefore, through such agents as the ascription of values to occupations, alternative life styles which become available, and the movement of people into cities. Most of the various forms of differentiation can be subsumed under three major dimensions, usually termed socio-economic status, family status and migrant status. It has been suggested that residential segregation takes place in cities of the 'developed' world along these three dimensions, and so they form the basis for most of the discussion in the rest of this book.

37

CHAPTER II

Residential Differentiation

THE PRECEDING discussion suggested that economic development in 'Western' urban societies is accompanied by three parallel societal changes, in patterns of socio-economic status, in patterns of life styles, and in the large-scale movement of groups from place to place. Geographical interest in these dimensions of change arises because they produce patterns of areal differentiation in the distribution of populations, at all scales. Thus Berry has shown a demographic dimension in economic development at both inter-and intra-national levels (Berry, 1961, 1969), and several studies have indicated differences between cities in their population profiles which parallel variations in their economic functions (Moser and Scott, 1961). Such areal differentiation also occurs within individual cities in which members of various population groups are congregated. The present chapter outlines some of the more salient reasons for this residential differentiation, as an introduction to later discussions of the spatial patterns which this produces.

THE SOCIO-ECONOMIC STATUS OF NEIGHBOURHOODS

Location of residence within a city has been used in several American studies as a criterion to determine a person's socio-economic status within an urban community (for example, in Warner *et al*, 1960). This factor has not usually been given as much weight in developing a status index as, for example, a person's occupation or income, but its inclusion suggests the importance of living in the 'right' area for residents who are conscious of their position in society.

Why should address be an important status symbol? The modern large city, according to Wirth (1938), is a large, densely peopled area of unlike individuals, most of whom have no direct or even indirect contact with each other. In small communities, everyone is known to (if not by) everybody else, and each individual can assess the status of all others within that society. No external status symbols are needed there, but this is not the case in larger towns and cities, where relative anonymity is the situation in which most people live (on the minimum size of such places see Jones, 1962 and Barber and Bourne, 1969). In cities, people know only a small proportion of their fellow-citizens, so in order to demonstrate their position within the society—in particular, to allow an immediate appraisal of this by strangers—a public status symbol is needed. (This assumes that individuals desire status-display: all of the societies considered have their non-conformists, but it is accepted here that a majority wish to advertise, or conceal, their status. This view is modified in a later section.)

The need for a public status symbol excludes many of the nuances of life style which can only be known to a few, and also items for which the price range is not very great so that similar grades are available to a broad range within the class spectrum (clothes and motor cars are in this category in many countries). A dwelling meets such requirements, though not entirely. Possession of an expensive home is, in itself, not enough. Few city streets, apart from the main thoroughfares, are regularly traversed by most people, so the dwelling itself would only be visible to a few, and not a valid status symbol.

Not only must one live in a certain sort of dwelling, but this must be located in certain streets or districts within the city.

> Unless you have a sound social position, do not live north of North Avenue or west of North State Street, and be careful of your choice of blocks. If you must live at a hotel live at . . . A disapproved neighborhood or hotel goes to prove that you are undesirable . . . the exigencies of the social game demand that 'society' lives in certain neighborhoods (Zorbaugh, 1929, 57–63).

Areas are known to contain dwellings of a certain type and value, so that one's status can be determined from one's address.

Further explanation of differentiation in neighbourhood characteristics is based on a spatial explanation which is becoming increasingly common in geographical work. Distance is a barrier whose scaling involves costs, both in time and money, and thus it limits interaction: the greater the distance between two places or individuals, on average, the smaller is the contact between them (Olsson, 1965). The time and cost involved may not be so important to people that they locate to minimise them, but distance is a common constraint, leading, for example, to people shopping at the nearest centre offering the goods which they require or migrating to the nearest town with the wanted economic and social facilities.

The pattern of residences within a city will influence the interaction patterns, therefore. In a stratified society, people mostly wish to have social contacts with their peers or betters, and close social relations with lower-status individuals are generally frowned on. Mixing only with one's social equals is thus facilitated if these people all live in the same area. Formal and informal associations mostly operate at the neighbourhood level, and residential clustering occurs so that people can attend the 'right' church. Even in highly mobile societies, informal gatherings such as coffee mornings are closely constrained in their membership by distance, as Whyte's (1960) interesting maps and Bracey's (1964) discussions have indicated.

While distance is a constraint on social interaction, however, it does not always result in the development of very close spatial cliques. Some people are relatively free of the constraint, and these appear to be those with high personal mobility (not only car ownership, but also no children to mind, etc.) Thus Mowrer (1958; see also Cox, 1969, Gans, 1961) suggested that in the early period of a suburban development such spatial cliques develop, partly as mutual aid societies, but with time these partly dissolve and are replaced by groupings based on community of interest (such as occupation). Similarly, Smith, Form and Stone (1954) showed that while a large number of their respondents' best friends lived in the same district, few lived in the same block (see Moore and Brown, 1969). Finally, Zorbaugh wrote of a lack of neighbourliness on Chicago's Gold Coast: indeed as elsewhere in the city, one does not know one's neighbors. The Gold Coast, then, can scarcely be called a community. It is simply the fashionable place for the location of one's house, an abode for the social season (Zorbaugh, 1929, 65–68).

For lower-class people, however, the status factor may be less important than the interaction one. In Britain, for example, there is little home visiting among this class and most social contact is in the street or public place (such as a corner shop or an inn): proximity is clearly important for such patterns of social contact (Mogey, 1956). In many situations, actual location within a neighbourhood is related to participation (Herbert and Rodgers, 1967); for example, residents of end-of-corridor flats in large blocks have been found to be socially isolated (Caplow and Forman, 1950).

Kinship ties often require spatial propinquity of residence for the members of family groups. Even in the most advanced societies there are often many groups with such strong kinship ties—in contradiction to the earlier suggestions of Wirth (1938) and the Chicago school; see Lewis (1965). Such groups most frequently develop in the vertically non-mobile upper (Baltzell, 1966) and lower (Vereker and Mays, 1961) classes of an urban society. Their functioning has been described in both Britain (Young and Willmott, 1962) and America (Fried, 1967), and authors have also described the development of 'grief' conditions among people separated from such communities (Fried and Gleicher, 1961, Fried, 1963).

A final reason suggested for residential clustering of class groups is also based on the distance factor. In a theoretical model of urban social structures, Beshers (1962) noted that a consequence of a class system is the desire of its members to prolong it. He suggested that the system can only persist through marriage, with offspring—especially daughters—expected by parents to marry either within or above their own class. This retains the system and enables the individual family to maintain its own position. Arrangement of marriages could achieve this end, but in more open societies it can only be done by education, authoritarian parental control, or restriction of contacts. The latter, suggested as the basic mechanism

41

by Beshers, operates through the influence of distance on interaction.

Clearly this is a very much over-simplified model, but a number of researchers have indicated tendencies for betrothal of relatively near neighbours, although the number of potential mates increases with distance (Katz and Hill, 1958). This need not indicate a causal relationship, however. If classes cluster in residential space, and individuals tend to choose a mate within their own class, then the distance factor is merely a coincidence of this. Many people suggest that they chose a neighbourhood because there were 'nice children for the kids to play with' or 'daughter will meet the right sort of boy at the local youth club', but these may be very minor reasons for clustering. Indeed, Ramsøy has suggested that most researchers have not determined how the three elements of the pattern—residential segregation, endogamy, and choice of a spouse from nearby— are related; for her Oslo data she asked:

> Is it the *workplace* which brings together men and women doing the same type of work, is it the *family*, urging, manipu- lating or encouraging its offspring to find a 'suitable', i.e. socially equal, mate, or is it the *neighborhood*, putting into daily contact persons belonging to the same socio-economic stratum (Ramsøy, 1966, 779).

Her results were contradictory, however; people tended to marry their social equals and their near-neighbours but, despite clear residential segregation in Oslo, the distance and status elements were uncorrelated.

Some Empirical Findings

Whatever the precise mechanism(s), there should be patterns of residential differentiation associated with those of social stratification, and this has been testified to in a number of studies. These have used the following two indices of differ- ences between two spatial distributions, which vary between o and 100 and indicate the percentage redistribution necessary before two groups are similarly distributed over a set of districts:

1. The index of residential segregation, which indicates the percentage difference between one group's distribution and that of the rest of the population.

2. The index of residential dissimilarity, which indicates the percentage difference between the distributions of two component groups of a population.

The size and boundaries of the areas used affect the results (see Duncan, Cuzzort and Duncan, 1961, and Taeuber and Taeuber, 1965b, 195–245), but similar results to those presented

TABLE II.1

RESIDENTIAL SEPARATION OF OCCUPATION
GROUPS: CHICAGO, 1950

OCCUPATION GROUP	INDICES OF DISSIMILARITY								INDEX OF SEGREGATION
	1.	2.	3.	4.	5.	6.	7.	8.	
1. Professional		13	15	28	35	44	41	54	30
2. Managerial	13		13	28	33	41	40	52	29
3. Sales Workers	15	13		27	35	42	38	54	29
4. Clerical	28	28	27		16	21	24	38	13
5. Craftsmen, Foremen	35	33	35	16		17	35	35	19
6. Operatives	44	41	42	21	17		26	25	22
7. Service Workers	41	40	38	24	35	26		28	24
8. Labourers	54	52	54	38	35	25	28		35

Source: Duncan and Duncan, 1955, 497–498.

here have been produced for a large number of separate studies, thereby suggesting their generality.

The pioneer study by Duncan and Duncan (1955) was of Chicago, and concerned the distributions of eight occupational groups. The indices of segregation for these formed a U-shaped distribution, with greatest residential separation among the upper and lower classes (Table II.1); labourers and professionals were most segregated, and clerical workers were least. Middle-class families were fairly evenly distributed through Chicago, therefore, being found in most kinds of neighbourhood. Indices of dissimilarity showed that the degree of residential mixing of groups was related to their social similarity. Thus there was little difference (only 13 percent) between the distributions of professionals and managerial workers, or between service workers and labourers (28 percent), but a 54 percent difference between the highest and lowest strata (professionals and labourers). This same pattern has been found in many places (for example by Uyeki, 1964; Collison and Mogey, 1959; and Timms, 1965).

There were two deviations from the general relationship between social and spatial distance in the Chicago matrix. Firstly, clerical workers had a much more different distribution from the group above them in the class structure than from the group below (Table II.1). This suggested considerable residential mixing of this middle class group (only males were considered) with the lower classes, and relatively little mixing with the upper-middle classes. Income differentials seemed to account for this. The white-collar clerical workers on average earned less than the highest status blue-collar class (the craftsmen and foremen), but the residential patterns suggested that, despite their lower incomes, the clerical workers were more status conscious and were prepared to devote more of their income on the 'right' housing than were their blue-collar counterparts. The second deviation was lower dissimilarity between service workers and professionals and managers than between the latter groups and the higher status operatives. Presumably this was because about 20 percent of the service workers were janitors and caretakers, many of whom would live at their place of employment.

Evidence has been provided, therefore, that social classes live relatively separately from each other in urban areas, and several hypotheses have been suggested which would account for this. No mention has been made of how the segregation is operated, however. The usual way is via the property market. Upper-class groups set prices for land and homes in their neighbourhoods which are beyond the incomes of all other groups lower in the class structure, and this is repeated down through the occupational hierarchy. People who can afford to live in lower status districts prefer not to, because it would not be socially acceptable; such attitudes operate throughout the class structure, so that, for example, there are differences in location between the respectable and non-respectable working-class areas (Elias, 1965). Thus, although to some extent the upper classes determine where they want to live, the middle classes choose from what is left over and the lower classes take the rest, there are differences within the broad classes as the Duncan and Duncan matrix showed. Some groups protect themselves by covenants which prevent certain, usually cheaper, types of buildings, while others almost 'force' families away from districts by isolating them from the local social network.

FAMILY STATUS, THE LIFE CYCLE, & NEIGHBOURHOOD TYPES

Differences in life style and position in the family cycle should also produce residential separation of households because of variations in the type of accommodation required. For families with children, spacious living is usually desirable free from problems of neighbours and certain aspects of the urban environment. Home ownership is usually preferred by such families as a form of security. Many people outside the family cycle, on the other hand, orient their lives outside the home. Spacious living is not very desirable, a flat or apartment is often the preferred dwelling style, and such households often prefer renting with its relative lack of constraints on freedom of movement.

American experience has shown that apartment living is more common among young adults than among those in the various stages of the family cycle. Home ownership is also less prevalent in the earlier stages of the cycle and among households outside this average sequence, but as families expand, Chicago data have shown correlations with increasing home ownership, single-family home occupancy, and tenure of newly-built units (Duncan and Hauser, 1960). Proportions in these categories decline as family size contracts in the later stages of the cycle, though not to the same degree. This is because older families are more stable and tend to stay put rather than move to smaller dwellings, so that despite the fact that

> With respect to desiring to give up a single home for a multiple dwelling, it is the 'married but without children at home' group that most wants the smaller area (Michelson, 1967, 195).

many of these people never achieve that goal.

Households in different stages of the life and family cycles thus require different dwelling types, mainly because of differing space demands. For this to produce residential separation, however, there must be reasons for areal clustering of the various dwelling types. Such reasons are spatial, depending not only on distance factors but also on actual location within the city, and so their consideration is postponed to the next chapter. Nevertheless, Jones (1969, 93) has provided evidence that the amount of segregation of some measures of family status in Melbourne in 1961 was as great as that for socio-economic status groups, though not as that for minority groups. (Table II.2: Jones' Gini coefficients of concentration, which vary from

TABLE II.2

RESIDENTIAL CONCENTRATION: MELBOURNE, 1961[1]

FAMILY STATUS MEASURES

Private Houses	0·59	Aged 15–24	0·11	Pensioners	0·28
Shared Private		Aged 25–44	0·13	Women in Home	
Houses	0·40	Aged 45–64	0·21	Duties	0·21
Flats	0·68	Aged 65+	0·33	Male	0·05
Rooms and		Males at Work	0·14	Never-Married	
Apartments	0·79	Females at Work	0·21	Adults	0·21
Non-Private		Divorced	0·39	Permanently	
Dwellings	0·67			Separated	0·34
Aged 0–14	0·23			Widowed	0·27

SOCIO-ECONOMIC STATUS MEASURES

Male Employers	0·35	Males Not at		Males in Finance	
		Work	0·32	and Property	0·37
Males in		Males in Com-		Education Ratio	0·46
Commerce	0·16	munity Services	0·33		
Females in		Owner-Occupied			
Manufacturing	0·33	Homes	0·53		

MINORITY GROUPS

Catholic	0·27	Orthodox	0·62	Lutheran	0·37
Presbyterian	0·25	Hebrew	0·77	Italian Born	0·64
Dutch Born	0·60	Alien Nationals	0·48		

[1] The measure is the Gini coefficient of concentration which, if multiplied by 100, can be interpreted in a similar way as Duncan and Duncan's index of residential segregation.

Source: Jones, 1969, 34, 54, 72.

o to 1·0, can be interpreted in the same way as the Duncan and Duncan indices, which vary from o to 100.) In particular, among the family status measures the various dwelling types were strongly separated, the various marital status groups less so, and the age groups were fairly evenly distributed except for the older persons.

THE CLUSTERING OF MIGRANT & MINORITY GROUPS

Urbanisation in the societies considered here has been largely caused by massive migrations of people to the cities, both from the rapidly depopulating rural areas and, in Australia, Canada, New Zealand, and the United States, by large injections of international immigrants. Even when rapid urbanisation ceased this migration continued, so that the burgeoning cities became the melting pots of their heterogeneous societies, in which the mixture of many minority groups often led to friction.

Residential separation of these groups has occurred for a number of reasons, not all of which need be present in a single city. The first, perhaps also the simplest, concerns their economic position. Many of the migrants, in particular those from rural areas and from abroad, have been unskilled and have had little or no capital. Thus they have been restricted to areas of low socio-economic status only by income level. In addition, migration has always been an age- and sex-selective process, and many of the young unmarried persons, a large majority of them males among the international immigrants, were drawn towards the typical living areas of the non-familism life style choice (Freedman, 1967).

An important difference between rural and urban societies, identified by Wirth and others, was that the former were characterised by strong kinship ties and community bonds, while anonymity was the norm in urban areas. Lewis (1965) and others have disputed this view, showing that the rural patterns often continue to exist after the move to the city. Thus while many segments of urban society are characterised by an unimportant role for the extended family, more impersonal contacts for individuals and overlapping friendship groups, some tight village-like communities can still be found within

47

cities. It was suggested in the previous section that these were particularly characteristic of the lowest classes in urban areas, to which so many of the new immigrants belong.

Residential clustering has been partly through economic and partly through community factors, therefore; heightened for many minority migrant groups by the nature of their movement to the cities. Were individuals to move at random to cities in their own or other countries, the development of migrant communities would be unlikely since few would know each other, although they may join migrant associations like those operated in West African cities (Little, 1965), or those groupings of Commonwealth migrants found in the Earls Court Road in London. Much migration is in the form of a chain process, however, in which there is a concentration of origins as well as destinations. Thus, for example, Maori communities in Auckland have been formed by villagers who moved there from rural Northland (Metge, 1952, 1964); most of the Yugoslavs in New Zealand are from Dalmatia (Trlin, 1968). Of Italian migrants to Australia during 1900–1919, 46 percent came from Lombardy; during 1950–1962 only 2·3 percent came from there but 21 percent were from Calabria (Price, 1963).

Chain migrations usually develop from the success of a few pioneers, who send back information (and often money) concerning their new home and its benefits. Their families and acquaintances decide to join them, and the pioneers help them to find accommodation and employment. Spatial clustering of residences is a natural consequence of this, and leads to the growth not only of a migrant quarter within the lower socioeconomic status suburbs but also separate 'villages' of the different groups within that quarter. Thus, for example, the index of residential dissimilarity between Italian- and Lithuanian-born persons in Chicago in 1950 was 84·7; each also had a high index of residential segregation (Table II.3), so groups are as much separated from each other as they are from the host society.

If this process were to continue over a long period of time, much of the modern city would become a congeries of villages, interdependent economically but independent socially. But in fact, the villages tend to break down as migrants and their children desert their local community and enter the general urban society. Their structural, identificational and behavioural assimilation—accompanied by declines in prejudice and discrimination towards them—allow them to spread through the city, and this is assisted by intermarriage between groups which destroys the original communities. Indeed, spatial distribution has been viewed not only as an indicator but also a determinant of the amount of assimilation. In ten American cities

> Highly segregated groups are less apt to become citizens or speak English; and these associations hold after differences between groups in their length of residence are taken into account. In addition, the degree of intermarriage is influenced by an immigrant group's residential segregation . . . Finally . . . it was found that highly segregated first generation groups were more apt to have second generation members deviate from the general pattern of intergenerational occupational choice (Lieberson, 1961, 57).

To some extent, therefore, segregation seems to be self-fulfilling.

Residential separation is partly forced upon most migrants therefore, in that they can only live where their socio-economic status allows, and it is partly the result of a choice to live together. In some cases, however, there is no choice, assimilation is not allowed, and residential segregation is forced on the minority group. Bergel (1953) has suggested six reasons which may contribute to this:

1. The number in the group, as segregation is usual only when it forms a sizeable minority. A few families of alien culture, behaviour or appearance do not intrude on the host society and threaten its values.

2. The group's economic situation, with segregation more likely when average incomes are low.

3. The degree to which the group deviates from the general culture. Groups very like the host society are much less likely to be discriminated against than are those which are very different, and Hoyt has reported the following 'ranking of races and nationalities with respect to their beneficial effect

upon land values' (Hoyt, 1933, 314) which presumably indicates their desirability as neighbours:

1. English, Germans, Scottish, Irish, Scandinavians. 2. North
Italians. 3. Bohemians or Czechoslovakians. 4. Poles.
5. Lithuanians. 6. Greeks. 7. Russian Jews of the Louvre
Class. 8. South Italians. 9. Negroes. 10. Mexicans.

A similar ranking was reported for Melbourne by Hammond
(1954).

4. The degree of traditional, institutionalised rejection of
the group. Adherents of the Jewish faith are in this category
in most societies, and similar attitudes have developed against
Negroes in American cities.

5. The group's position in the class structure, which is
closely related to its economic status.

6. The degree of conservatism in the host society.

In any urban society, therefore, the most recent arrivals
are most likely to be discriminated against and forced to live
in relatively segregated conditions, whether or not they desire
it. Thus Taeuber has shown that the segregation of Negroes in
Cleveland has not been produced merely by their low economic
status; 'If income were the only factor at work in determining
where white and Negro families live, there would be very little
racial residential segregation' (Taeuber, 1968, 10). Comparing
the actual distribution of low-income Negroes to an expected
distribution, which had the residential pattern of these persons
as the same as that for the low-income whites, he found an index
of dissimilarity of 77. For high-income Negroes the similar
index was 89.

Where groups are spatially assimilated, evidence suggests
that the amount of assimilation is related to the group's length
of residence in a city. Thus Duncan and Lieberson (1959)
found that in Chicago:

1. 'New' groups (the more recent arrivals) were most
segregated, except for Austrians. (The groups were those listed
in Table II.3; the 'old' groups were the first four in the list
there.)

TABLE II.3

RESIDENTIAL SEPARATION OF MIGRANT GROUPS: CHICAGO, 1930–1950

(Indices of Dissimilarity)[1]

	COUNTRY OF ORIGIN OR GROUP										
	1	2	3	4	5	6	7	8	9	10	11
1. England and Wales		24·7	30·7	35·0	64·6	60·0	34·3	50·1	62·5	53·4	83·6
2. Eire	28·5		42·4	44·1	68·3	63·7	43·9	59·5	62·2	56·6	84·3
3. Sweden	29·7	40·2		35·1	73·5	68·8	45·3	65·5	72·8	66·9	90·1
4. Germany	29·5	43·9	32·3		57·7	58·6	22·3	56·4	65·5	57·4	88·6
5. Poland	58·4	66·7	67·8	55·9		47·2	49·4	56·7	51·2	58·8	93·2
6. Czechoslovakia	55·9	63·2	66·0	47·2	43·5		49·1	62·5	49·9	63·6	92·7
7. Austria	26·3	38·3	38·8	21·3	47·3	47·8		48·2	57·1	52·2	88·4
8. USSR	38·3	54·2	54·0	47·2	58·3	61·4	45·6		68·6	56·7	89·8
9. Lithuania	56·8	59·8	66·2	54·3	50·8	50·5	53·8	67·5		66·4	90·9
10. Italy	45·7	52·0	60·9	54·3	52·6	55·9	45·6	57·5	61·6		79·2
11. Negroes	77·8	81·4	85·5	85·4	90·8	89·2	82·5	87·1	84·7	69·6	

[1] Above diagonal, 1930; Below diagonal, 1950.

Source: Duncan and Lieberson, 1959, 367–368.

2. Second-generation settlers were less segregated than their foreign-born parents.

3. Second-generation settlers from old countries were less segregated than those from new.

4. Between 1930 and 1960 there was much more 'desegregation' of the new than of the old groups.

5. Negroes were most highly segregated.

6. Dissimilarity was much less among the settlers from the four 'old' countries than among those from the six 'new' (Table II.3).

7. 'Although ethnic colonies were becoming less distinct during the period 1930–50, they still remained quite visible at the end of the period, especially those of the "new" immigrants' (Duncan and Lieberson, 1959, 368).

Lieberson (1963b), working partly on Zubrzycki's (1960) data, has demonstrated similar patterns among 'old' and 'new' immigrant groups in Australian cities.

In attempting to account for the variations in segregation levels, Duncan and Lieberson found strong correlations which indicated that segregation was inversely related to the amount of structural assimilation, but occupational patterns did not account for the residential separation among the migrant groups (similar findings were reported in Lieberson's (1963a) later detailed study of ten cities). For Melbourne, Jones (1967) also found a relationship between degree of segregation and length of a group's residence there, with occupational concentration and the amount of intra-group marriage adding further to the statistical explanation.

Residential separation of minority groups is therefore a measure of their degree of assimilation, on all of the dimensions of this process, with their host society. (Though with higher average standards of living, and greater personal mobility, communities *could* exist without propinquity: Goldstein and Goldscheider, 1968; Webber, 1964.) It applies equally well to persons of foreign birth, alien culture, alien religion or alien colour and is typical of most societies, even the supposedly multi-racial society of New Zealand.

THE TOTAL RESIDENTIAL STRUCTURE

So far, the three major dimensions of urban society (socio-economic status, family status, and minority groups) identified in the first chapter have been discussed separately, for ease of presentation. As pointed out earlier, the three are often assumed to be independent, so that each urban society can be divided into its majority and minority groups, each of whose residential areas can then be split along the two axes of socio-economic and family status. Thus, for example, each city's majority group should have its high socio-economic, high family status neighbourhoods, its low socio-economic, average family status districts, and so on. This raises two questions: first, do these independent dimensions exist, and secondly, are they the only dimensions of residential separation in cities?

Social Area Analysis

The earliest attempts to study the dimensions of urban society and the consequent residential patterns were by a group of sociologists in Los Angeles. Their first work involved identification of the social areas of that city and integration of the observed residential differentiation with a theory of social change (which formed the basis for much of the discussion in Chapter I here: Shevky and Williams, 1949). Subsequently the approach was applied to San Francisco (Bell, 1953), and was then published in a monograph 'to demonstrate the use of the typology as an analytic framework for the comparative study of certain aspects of the social structure of American cities' (Shevky and Bell, 1955, 2).

To apply their theoretical construct of societal structure to areal differentiation, Shevky and Bell selected indices of its various dimensions from the US Census. Thus, social rank (this was Shevky's term, Bell preferred economic status) was represented by the proportion of craftsmen, operatives and labourers among the employed males, and by the number of people aged over 25 whose education included no more than grade school; a composite index was formed from these two. Urbanisation (Bell's term was family status) was measured by an index combining a fertility ratio (children aged 0–4 per

53

females aged 15–44), the proportion of adult females in the labour force, and the proportion of detached single-family dwelling units. The index of segregation (ethnic status) was the proportion of the population who were Negro or born in

TABLE II.4

POPULATION DISTRIBUTION BY SOCIAL AREAS:
SAN FRANCISCO, 1940

(Percent of Population)

A. Total Population

URBANISATION	A. Low	B.	C.	D. HIGH
D. HIGH		3·2	10·4	6·5
C.	1·0	15·1	17·6	5·1
B.	3·7	17·0	13·8	5·8
A. Low		0·2	0·6	

B. Areas with Low Segregation Indices

URBANISATION	A. Low	B.	C.	D. HIGH
D. HIGH		0·8	5·2	5·8
C.		6·6	15·3	5·1
B.	0·4	11·4	13·5	5·8
A. Low		0·2	0·6	

C. Areas with High Segregation Indices

URBANISATION	A. Low	B.	C.	D. HIGH
D. HIGH		2·4	5·2	0·7
C.	1·0	8·5	2·3	
B.	3·3	5·6	0·3	
A. Low				

Source: Shevky and Bell, 1955, 32.

one of a number of foreign countries. The scores were then used to form a two-dimensional social space whose axes were the social rank and urbanisation dimensions. These were divided into four equal parts, giving sixteen social area types (Table II.4), and in addition each cell was subdivided into two according to whether it had a high or low index of segregation.

Diagrams such as that in Table II.4 suggest that the three

dimensions were not independent, and therefore that all three may not be necessary for the definition of social areas. However, in a separate study Bell (1955) tested hypotheses that:

1. The three separate dimensions existed.
2. Each of the variables loads onto the relevant index.

His tests used the techniques of factor analysis (see below, p. 59) in which the correlations between the six component variables of the three constructs were found to collapse to three dimensions, representing social rank, urbanisation, and segregation as hypothesised. However, he did find some correlation between the three dimensions, in particular a negative correlation between social rank and segregation, which indicated that minority groups tended to live in low socio-economic status areas. There was also a negative correlation between social rank and urbanisation, reflecting mainly a strong negative correlation between socio-economic status and fertility.

The Shevky-Bell schema has been widely used in the United States, particularly as a basis for sampling social areas (see a summary in Bell, 1958a), but has been applied little outside. McElrath (1962) used it in his study of Rome, and Herbert (1967) applied it to Newcastle-under-Lyme in England. The latter application proved mainly unsuccessful because:

1. The urbanisation construct was irrelevant, there being no correlation between fertility and women in the labour force.
2. Fifty-one of the 101 census tracts fell in the low social rank category, and 66 were in four of the 16 cells which indicated below-average social rank and average family status.

The segregation construct was not relevant in that town.

Considerable testing of the schema has been carried out by three University of Washington researchers, who applied it to a sample of ten cities. They concluded from their tests that the system 'has high generality for the cities included' (van Arsdol, Camilleri and Schmid, 1958b, 284), although they were careful to point out that they were only testing the empirical validity of the indices and not the theory itself. Their results were not wholly consistent with the schema, however. For four of the cities, all in the southern States, fertility was as much negatively related to social rank as it was positively associated with family status, and in Providence the proportion of single-family dwelling units was positively related to social rank and not associated with urbanisation. Some areal variations, probably related to the characteristics of the sampled cities, were thus suggested, although no further study has been made of them (see, however, Rees, 1969).

In later studies, van Arsdol, Camilleri and Schmid (1961) have proved not to be the ardent supporters of the Shevky-Bell schema that was perhaps suggested by their first work (at least to Bell; see Bell and Greer, 1962). The three University of Washington researchers argued that:

1. If the Shevky-Bell constructs represent the major dimensions of urban structure, they should correlate strongly with other variables, such as measures of stability and the proportion of older persons.

2. If the Shevky-Bell indices and the social area typology are valid, they should predict the values for certain criterion variables better than the combined individual measures which make up their indices.

On their evidence, both hypotheses were rejected.

Bell and Greer, in reply, questioned van Arsdol *et al*'s interpretation of their own results, and also the validity of their arguments:

> Shevky argues that there are three broad controlling variables in urban differentiation. They arise from increase in societal scale and have further consequences for differentiated behavior in various arenas. Specific prediction of one thing or another is a different matter; it does not reflect negatively on Shevky's schema to find that a particular low-order variable predicts some specific item better than social rank, urbanization, and segregation (Bell and Greer, 1962, 7).

van Arsdol *et al* (1962) replied, but introduced little that was new. Although the social area indices represented census tract differentiation in many places, no acceptable model accounting for areal patterns had been provided (for a recent summary see Bell, 1969).

In 1961, Anderson and Bean asked whether, although the six variables used by Shevky and Bell and van Arsdol *et al* generally confirmed the former workers' hypotheses, the inclusion of other variables would still result in the same three dimensions. They therefore studied the relationships among 13 variables for Toledo, Ohio, and, using factor analysis, found not three but four dimensions. One of these was clearly the social rank

TABLE II.5

FACTORIAL ECOLOGY: TOLEDO, 1950

VARIABLE	ROTATED FACTOR LOADINGS[1]			
	A	B	C	D
Low Occupational Status	−073	093	−932	−015
Poorly Educated	207	017	−979	−100
Fertility Ratio	−458	735	025	105
Females at Work	732	−444	−037	246
Multi-Family Dwellings	971	−017	041	073
Negro	297	−366	−206	−698
Residential Stability	−703	−105	−316	124
Married Percentage	−710	259	−031	−270
Median Family Income	−776	−019	482	286
Ratio Families/Unrelated Persons	−765	−188	−101	200
Owner-Occupancy	−986	−089	026	046
Double Occupancy	369	−510	−489	−449
Crowding	526	−040	−535	−587

[1] Decimal points omitted.

Source: Anderson and Bean, 1961, 121.

dimension (Factor C in Table II.5) since it had high correlations with occupation, education and income, as well as stability and crowding; another was identified as segregation, having its highest correlation with percent Negro. The other two dimensions, however, represented separate parts of what Shevky and Bell had presented as the single urbanisation construct.

1. The first had high positive correlations with crowding, apartment dwelling, and working females and high negative correlations with owner-occupancy, the proportion of families and of married people, and with both income and residential stability. Anderson and Bean suggested that this was equivalent

to Shevky and Bell's urbanisation construct since it separated the characteristic apartment and single-family dwelling-unit-type areas.

2. The highest correlation with the second factor (B in Table II.5) was fertility, plus negative correlations with working females and double occupancy. Anderson and Bean suggested average family status as a loose designation for this, and further investigation may have shown that it differentiated areas according to the various stages of the life cycle.

Although it provided a fairly full description of the main dimensions of spatial aspects of social structure in American cities, the Shevky-Bell scheme did not give a complete summary (see also Tryon, 1955). Major criticisms of the scheme, however, have concentrated not only on the measurement problems and the representativeness of the dimensions (which several critics have suggested were *ex post facto* rationalisations of empirical findings: Bell and Moskos (1964) virtually admitted this), but also on how a theory of social change can be translated to one of residential differentiation within urban areas (Hawley and Duncan 1957; Udry, 1954). Jones has suggested that the constructs of social area analysis could logically be applied to relatively inclusive systems or communities which

> differ in terms of scale (the range of interdependence) from village communities to towns, cities, regions, countries, and ultimately the world community . . . [but] census tracts are not communities in this sense but only partial segments of the urban community. They do not themselves vary in scale (Jones, 1969, 20).

Hawley and Duncan suggested four ways in which the link between the social theory and empirical results might be forged, but concluded that all Shevky and Bell had done was 'to signify the existence of a problem of scientific explanation rather than to point the way to its solution' (Hawley and Duncan, 1957, 345).

Yet the schema did differentiate basic dimensions of residential differentiation in cities. Jones suggested that Shevky and Bell had provided a set of sensitising concepts directing attention to basic forms of social differentiation in modern industrial society ... Granted that this analytic scheme in fact identifies basic dimensions of social differentiation, it is perfectly reasonable to anticipate that they may have consequences for the study of residential areas (Jones, 1969, 21)

and his attempts to link the two, based in particular upon the works of Beshers (1962) and Greer (1962)—see Jones, 1968— follow similar arguments to those presented earlier in this chapter (see also Orleans, 1966).

Factorial Ecologies

The study by Anderson and Bean (1961) initiated a research methodology using the factor analysis technique which produces what Sweetster (1965) has termed a factorial ecology. Berry and Rees (1969) have shown that this differs from both social area analysis *sensu stricto*, as defined by Shevky and Bell, and the subsequent factor analyses by Bell and by van Arsdol *et al*, which used the same set of variables, in that it is primarily an inductive approach. Instead of predetermining the variables which represent deductively obtained constructs, and then testing that these are true representations of the constructs, factorial ecologies analyse the associations between a whole battery of socio-economic, demographic and other characteristics, to see what dimensions result.

Common to all of these works is the use of factor analysis, or the relatively similar principal components analysis. This usually works on a correlation matrix (generally of product moment correlations) which represents the similarities between pairs of areal distributions. Thus, for example, a high positive correlation indicates two very similar distributions over a set of areas—where one value is big so is the other and vice versa; a nil correlation indicates no association, and a negative correlation indicates that where the value for one variable is high the other is low (see Gregory, 1963). Basically, factor analysis seeks for groups of variables with similar correlation patterns within this matrix, and does this by creating hybrid variables so as to maximise the correlations between these and the original variables. One of the constraints employed is that

59

the hybrid variables (usually termed factors or components) must themselves be uncorrelated. Initial determination of the factors is arbitrary, following only mathematical rules, and to aid interpretation they are usually rotated (often via the varimax criterion) to more comprehensible positions. The main outputs of such analyses are the *eigen* values, which show the relative importance of each factor in terms of the strength of the correlations between it and the original variables; the factor or component loadings, which are the correlations between the original variables and the factors; and the factor or component scores which are values for each of the original observations for the factors, derived from the original values for each variable and the factor loadings. (Rummel, 1967, is an excellent non-mathematical introduction to this technique.)

An early example of this methodology was Schmid and Tagashira's (1965) factorial ecology of Seattle, which used 42 variables drawn from 1960 census tract data. Eight factors were extracted, of which six were interpreted as representing:

1. Family organisation.
2. High socio-economic status.
3. Male residential areas (the Skid Row areas of down-and-out males; Bogue, 1963).
4. Population stability, basically recent migration *to* Seattle.
5. Ethnic status and minority groups.
6. Population mobility, basically recent migration *within* Seattle.

Further analyses with smaller selections of variables produced basically the same results, and the authors concluded that their 'interpretation of the structure of the measures and dimensions is basically consistent with the dimensions of city structure described by Shevky' (Schmid and Tagashira, 1965, 211).

Jones used this same technique to analyse the social areas of Melbourne. Instead of employing a single data matrix to inductively arrive at the main dimensions of the city's ecology, he argued that while 'There is no suggestion that social reality is uniquely and exhaustively explained by these three (Shevky) dimensions alone, . . . I have made an initial assumption that they will be more important than any others' (Jones, 1969, 25).

Thus, he first took 24 socio-economic measures, from which he identified three dimensions, named socio-economic status, zone in transition, and urban fringe. Secondly, he analysed 24 household and demographic characteristics, and again identified three components—one called household composition, one sex composition and the other unnamed but which seemed to represent age differentials. Finally, 22 ethnic and religious characteristics were reduced to the three dimensions of general ethnic composition, Northwestern European settlers, and Jewish areas.

At first sight, these nine components seem very different from the Shevky constructs and later findings. However, the three for family status conform to Anderson and Bean's breakdown of the urbanisation construct into two parts plus a Skid Row dimension, and the three minority dimensions were not unexpected in so diverse a city as Melbourne (Lieberson, 1963b; Jones, 1967). The main problem was with the socio-economic dimensions; however, the one termed the urban fringe clearly represents the inclusion of atypical areas, and the zone in transition correlated mainly with variables for which an urbanisation interpretation might have been more appropriate. Thus Jones seems to have been justified in selecting eight variables from each list for a final analysis whose three components were identified as socio-economic status (plus minority groups), familism, and Northwestern European settlers, thereby vindicating the Shevky-Bell scheme.

A number of factorial ecologies have been conducted recently in Britain, and in reviewing them Herbert (1968) has shown considerable congruence between the results of the five main studies. In each case the same two main components were identified. The first loaded highly on room densities and housing tenure, and served to isolate the public housing areas, and the second was consistently a measure of poor housing conditions. Others suggested family status (see also Robson, 1969), and economic status was closely tied to housing conditions.

Many of the factorial ecologies have used virtually the same sets of variables, so that it is not surprising that the same dimensions have so often been identified. However, the fact that the general dimensions of socio-economic status, life style and family status, and minority groups have so frequently emerged—as indicated in the reviews of factorial ecologies by Abu-Lughod (1969) and Rees (1970b, 1971, forthcoming)—validates the approach used in this book. (It has been suggested recently that the social area model requires greater elaboration; Johnston, 1971a.)

SUMMARY

Arguments have been presented in this chapter to suggest that differentiation within urban societies results in the spatial separation of the various groups, and evidence has been presented that the groups are residentially differentiated as suggested. No direct relationship has been shown between the two, however, but the inference is very strong.

Further studies have been cited which suggest that the three main dimensions of urban society outlined in Chapter I are the major elements in the spatial pattern of neighbourhoods, and that all three are relevant. The earliest studies to do this experienced severe criticism for their methodology, but later inductive research efforts, termed factorial ecologies, have generally confirmed the validity of the earlier approach. Several of them have indicated the existence of other dimensions, but investigation indicated that they were sub-dimensions of the main three (Johnston, 1971b). The method of analysis suggested that these dimensions were independent, but this supposition that non-correlation is the same as independence may not be valid (Coleman, 1964; Janson, 1969). Thus, while they are not statistically associated, socio-economic status, family status, and minority group residential patterns may not be independent; this topic is discussed in the later chapters.

It should be noted here that although there is considerable evidence of residential separation, this is not complete. Duncan and Duncan's 1955 study, for example, showed that there was separation but that the spatial overlap between the distributions of professionals and labourers—the polar occupational groups—was still 46 percent (some of which probably resulted from the location of census tract boundaries). Census tracts are not homogeneous, therefore, and the residential patterns are general but not universal.

Finally, two pieces of evidence indicate further problems of analysing census data. In criticising Shevky and Bell's scheme, Hawley and Duncan (1965) showed considerable differences between the white and non-white populations of 'mixed' residential areas, and correlations between the two groups on various measures were not high. Secondly, a small study of Toledo presented separate factorial ecologies for the white and non-white populations (Johnston, forthcoming). The dimensions for the former group were as expected but for the non-whites (almost all of them Negroes) socio-economic and family status measures were closely related and did not form separate components. Sub-societies within urban societies may have their own unique patterns of residential separation, therefore.

Despite these caveats, it has been concluded that for most purposes the three main dimensions of urban society have been validated as the bases of residential separation in the societies studied here. They are used, therefore, as the referrents for the ensuing discussions of spatial patterns of the segregated groups.

CHAPTER III

Models of Residential Patterns

THE PREVIOUS chapters have indicated the bases for residential separation of various groups within an urban society. Individuals have been allocated to various types of neighbourhood, but the essential geographic component of this pattern—location of the neighbourhood types within the spatial coordinates of the city—has been ignored so far. In this and the remaining chapters, therefore, the emphasis shifts to neighbourhood patterns in physical space, with emphasis on the main regularities which occur.

There is a growing interest in deductive model building in geography, but most generalisations are still reached by amalgamating the findings of a large number of case studies. Such an inductive procedure would have been necessary here if the task had not already been performed, albeit by non-geographers. In particular three models of the socio-economic mosaic of the city have been formulated and discussion of these forms the basis of the first section of the present chapter. Considerable space is given to two of these because they are relatively old and many of the details of the originals are rarely discussed in more recent works. Also, since these models form the background for the rest of the book, it seems essential to present them as completely as possible.

The spatial patterning of the city on the basis of family cycle and of minority group patterns has received much less overall attention in the literature. Much of the chapter thus refers to the socio-economic pattern of the city, to the three main models of this component of the total mosaic, and to some of their most important critics.

THE SOCIO-ECONOMIC MOSAIC

E. W. Burgess & the Concentric Zone Model

The first of these models, and the datum for later developments, was formulated in the early 1920s by E. W. Burgess, a Chicago sociologist. By then he had been collaborating for almost a decade with R. E. Park on the development of a scientific sociology (as indicated in their *Introduction to the Science of Society*, first published in 1921). In particular they were concerned with the sub-discipline now known as Human Ecology, an attempt, particularly by Park (1936a), to apply biological findings on plant and animal communities to their incipient science of human communities (see Orleans, 1966). Plants, animals and humans were all competing for space, and ecological concepts such as dominance and succession were applied to the study of human land use patterns. (Other workers, such as McKenzie (1924, 1926), interpreted the ecological concepts in more economic terms and many aspects were also foreseen by Hurd, 1924.) The city was the main product of the competition and interdependence, and was characterised by the mobility (social and geographical) of its population.

Burgess was interested in the city not for it own sake but for its role as a determinant of human behaviour, which role was explicitly stated by Wirth (1938). Burgess's courses in the 1920s were on Social Pathology, Crime and Its Social Treatment, the Theory of Personal Disorganisation, and The Family, and he constructed his model of the city from research associated with this teaching. The aim was to understand and then improve the city's social and moral order, and field studies of social pathology, which included a complete census, were conducted in Chicago. In his own words

> We were very impressed with the great differences between the various neighborhoods of the city, and one of our earliest goals was to try and find a pattern to this patchwork of differences, and to 'make sense of it'. Mapping was the method which seemed most appropriate for such a problem. (Burgess and Bogue, 1967, 6).

E   65

The large number of maps produced ('The students made maps of any data we could find in the city that could be plotted'; Burgess and Bogue, 1967, 6) allowed identification of the city's natural areas and from this Burgess produced his famous inductive conceptualisation of the city as a series of concentric zones. These were elements of a dynamic model, whose whole emphasis was on change and its effects on social disorganisation. Thus the zones were introduced by the statement that 'the typical process of the expansion of the city can best be illustrated, perhaps, by a series of concentric circles . . . an ideal construction of the tendency of any town or city to expand radially from its central business district' (Burgess, 1924, 86).

The zones were only briefly discussed in the original paper, and a later, full description (Burgess, 1929, 114–123) is repeated here:

ZONE I: The Central Business District . . . The heart of this district is the downtown retail district with its department stores, its smart shops, its office buildings, its clubs, its banks, its hotels, its theaters, its museums, and its head-quarters of economic, social, civic, and political life. Encircling this area of work and play is the less well-known Wholesale Business District with its 'market', its warehouses, and storage buildings.

ZONE II: The Zone in Transition . . . areas of residential deterioration caused by the encroaching of business and industry from Zone I . . . a Zone in Transition, with a factory district for its inner belt and an outer ring of retrogressing neighborhoods, of first-settlement immigrant colonies, of rooming-house districts, of homeless-men areas, of resorts of gambling, bootlegging, sexual vice, and of breeding-places of crime . . . As families and individuals prosper, they escape from this area into Zone III beyond, leaving behind as marooned a residium of the defeated, leaderless and helpless.

ZONE III: The Zone of Independent Workingmen's Homes . . . largely constituted by neighborhoods of second immigrant settlement. Its residents are those who desire to live near but not too close to their work . . . While the father

66

works in the factory, the son and daughter typically have jobs in the . . . [CBD], attend dance halls and motion pictures in the bright-light areas, and plan upon marriage to set up homes in Zone IV.

ZONE IV: The Zone of Better Residences . . . in which the great middle-class of native-born Americans live, small business men, professional people, clerks and salesmen . . . In this zone men are outnumbered by women, independence in voting is frequent, newspapers and books have wide circulation, and women are elected to the state legislature.

ZONE V: The Commuters' Zone . . . a ring of encircling small cities, towns and hamlets which . . . are also, in the main, dormitory suburbs . . . Thus the mother and the wife become the center of family life . . . The communities in this Commuters' Zone are probably the most highly segregated of any in the entire metropolitan area.

Most subsequent workers have interpreted these five zones as indicating a continual increase of socio-economic status away from the city centre. This is almost certainly true for the first four zones, accepting Burgess's assumption that immigrant groups rate lowly on socio-economic status, but the meaning of the fifth zone is not clear. Its name suggests a broad spectrum of the population who can afford to be commuters, and it is perhaps for this reason that researchers, such as Abu-Lughod (1969), have associated the zonal model with family status rather than social rank. Nevertheless, in the 1920s commuting over any great distance would have been confined to a much smaller proportion of Chicago's society than now, and in another paper Burgess (1927, 178) suggested that beyond the zone of workingmen's homes 'the professional and clerical groups employed in the downtown offices live still farther out, while those who can afford it and who prize suburban life escape to the commuters' zone'. This suggests a zonal correlation of wealth with space preferences, but Zone V was also described as the domain of the matricentric family, which has few socio-economic connotations. Similarly, Zone III residents were those who desire to live near but not too close to their work, who could be of any status level.

Clearly there is some confusion over whether Burgess meant

his model to apply to the socio-economic or the family status dimension of urban society. One interpretation is that it applies to both in its contemporary setting. The discussion in Chapter I indicated that these two dimensions only slowly became distinct and independent with continuing economic development, and it could be that they were still highly correlated in Chicago in the 1920s.

In his 1927 paper, Burgess renamed the zones:

Central Business District.
Zone in Transition (area of first immigrant settlement).
Zone of Second-generation Immigrant Settlement.
Middle-class Residential District.
Higher-class Residential District.

This nomination is generally used, and is adopted here; it suggests that the socio-economic status interpretation is valid.

Although the zonal model was presented as one of expansion outwards from the city centre, the original formulation gave little indication on how this proceeded, or on why the more wealthy residents chose to live at considerable distances from the city centre. The mechanism was outlined later as the now famous process of invasion and succession, in which one group succeeds another in the use of an area through the ecological process of competition (Burgess, 1928). (This process is a direct analogy from biology, and although Park only formalised it in a later paper (Park, 1936b), workers such as McKenzie (1924) had already been using it.) Burgess pointed out that 'every community as it grows expands outwards from its center. This . . . is due partly to business and industrial pressure and partly to residential pull' (Burgess, 1928, 105–106). Presumably the pulls were the attractions of suburbia for family living, but Burgess ignored these and focused his paper (on the Urban Negro) on the lower status groups and the inner parts of the city.

In stressing the role of central pressure on city growth. Burgess assumed that city populations increased mainly through in-migration, especially of low-status alien groups. (He was at pains in his 1928 paper to point out that Negro patterns parallel those of earlier, foreign migrants to Chicago, a statement which has proven to be false—see Chapter VI.) On arrival, these people concentrate in the zone of transition because

> for all new groups with one or more of the following characteristics—an alien culture, a low economic status and a different race—this point of arrival naturally tends to be in or near the central business district. A commercial district, a business street or a rooming-house area puts up notoriously slight resistance to the intrusion of a new group (Burgess, 1928, 109).

The alien group pushes outwards into other residential areas from the zone of transition as pressure builds up there through continued in-migration and the conversion of land and buildings to non-residential uses.

This process formed the basis of Burgess's statement of the invasion and succession mechanism, one which has been too readily accepted as a general urban growth process. He wrote:

> The population movements, from the center towards the periphery of the city or the resultant of outward pressure and local community, take the form, therefore, of successive waves of invasion. Succession as a process has been studied and its main course charted as (1) *invasion*, beginning often as an unnoticed or gradual penetration, followed by (2) *reaction*, or the resistance mild or violent of the inhabitants of the community, ultimately resulting in (3) the *influx* of newcomers and the rapid abandonment of the area by its old-time residents, and (4) *climax* or the achievement of a new equilibrium of communal stability (Burgess, 1928, 112).

An accompanying map (Figure III.1) charted the progress of a number of groups through Chicago.

Davie's Criticism

The zonal model was adopted by a number of Burgess's students as the basis for their detailed field studies (see, for example, Shaw, 1929), but only in 1938 did Davie report on what he considered the first attempt to verify the Burgess hypothesis. He criticised both the concept and its users. Re-examination of some of their data, notably Shaw's on delinquency areas, suggested to him that 'the more salient facts . . .

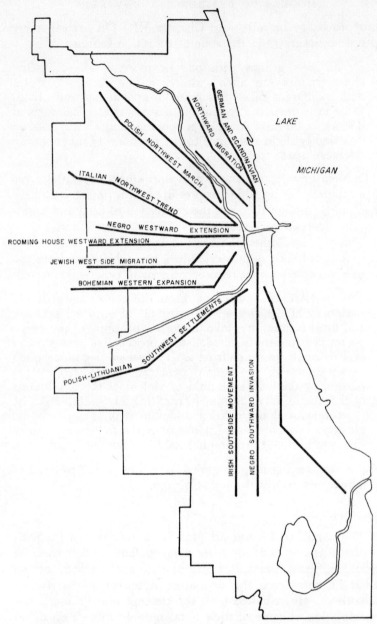

III.1 The movement of Migrant Groups within the city of Chicago, showing outward expansion along sectoral lines. *Source:* Burgess, 1928.

are obscured, and the data distorted, by considering the rates by zones', and he attributed the continued use of this spatial framework to an attitude that 'the hypothesis must be maintained whatever the facts may show' (Davie, 1938, 136). In particular he stressed Shaw's finding that highest delinquency rates occurred adjacent both to the CBD and to large industrial areas, and claimed that the spatial distribution of the latter in no way fitted the zonal model.

Davie's criticisms were backed by a detailed study of land use patterns in New Haven, Connecticut, and supplemented by less intensive observations of other cities. New Haven was divided into 22 natural areas, whose distribution in no way fitted the concentric zonal model. Low socio-economic status areas were generally adjacent to industrial and railroad properties (including those in the CBD), and were fairly evenly distributed through the city. This distribution of industry and low-income housing Davie considered to be the main downfall of Burgess's model, and he produced the following alternative five principles of urban structure:

(1) A central business district, irregular in size but more square or rectangular than circular.

(2) Commercial landuse extending along the main radial streets and concentrating at certain strategically placed points to form sub-centres.

(3) Industry located near rail and water transportation, wherever in the city this may be.

(4) Low-grade housing near the industrial and transport areas.

(5) Second- and first-grade housing anywhere else.

These, he claimed, 'seem to be the general principles governing the distribution of utilities. There is no universal pattern, not even of an "ideal" type' (Davie, 1938, 161).

Quinn's Response

Davie's—and other, less hostile, criticism, such as Leiffer, 1933—was not answered by Burgess, who published no further works on the city between 1930 and 1953. Instead, a spirited rebuttal and extensive development of the zonal model were presented by Quinn (1940a), a Chicago graduate who had been working in Cincinnatti for almost twenty years.

In his defence of the zonal model, Quinn recognised two types of criticism:

(1) A flat denial that the model has any validity in research or description.

(2) A contention that the number of real world distortions is so great as to destroy the model's value, even though the general tendency is as predicted.

His paper concentrated on the latter, for he claimed that if the general tendency exists, however slightly, then the model is valid. The defence then developed the zonal model to a more sophisticated form by relaxing some of the assumptions implicit in Burgess's enunciations.

Quinn presented two arguments. Firstly, he indicated that the zonal pattern as a series of *concentric* rings results only when there is a complete correspondence between straight-line and ecological (or time-cost) distance. Distance in miles as the crow flies is not the determinant of neighbourhood type; it is time distance (which can be equated with cost distance, although over long distances travel costs tend to increase less rapidly than time). Thus the outer edge of the zone of transition may be ten minutes' walking-time from the centre in all directions, but may be a quarter of a mile in one direction and only 200 yards in another, because of variations in transport time. Zones would probably extend further along major routeways, therefore, as shown in Figure III.2, so that accessibility surfaces distort the simple structure of the Burgess model and 'a *rectangular spatial* structure may be entirely consistent with a *circular ecological* (time-cost) structure' (Quinn, 1940a, 213).

In most urban areas the major routeways radiate outwards from the city centre like the spokes of a wheel, so that a time-cost zonal pattern takes the form of a number of projections of inner zones along these arteries, with re-entrants of outer zone, less accessible suburbs in the interstices. Quinn presented a detailed example of how the network of routeways and accessibility can shape a city (Figure III.3), producing a pattern which bears no resemblance to the simple structure of Burgess's model (Figure III.4), yet follows its theorems.

Quinn's second argument was an answer to Davie concerning the location of industry, particularly heavy industry, and its effects on the residential pattern. He conceded that this factor

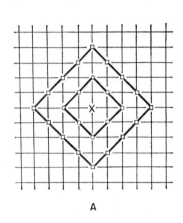

A

Rectangular spatial zones surrounding point X, computed in terms of checkerboard street system.

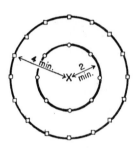

B

Theoretical ecological zones of equal time distances; no allowance made for checkerboard street system.

III.2 Different Zonal Patterns based on Time and Cost (A), or Ecological and Equal Transportation in All Directions (B). *Source:* Quinn, 1940a.

should be introduced as an extra ecological dominant (Park, 1936a) within the city, rather than merely treated as one of the distorting influences mentioned by Burgess. No real reply to the criticism was presented, however. Quinn admitted that where the city was poly-nucleated 'a simple concentric circular pattern no longer represents the ideal organization. Therefore, the Burgess hypothesis will require some reformulation' (Quinn, 1940a, 216) but, unfortunately, he did not essay any such reformulation.

Finally, Quinn himself criticised the model, claiming that

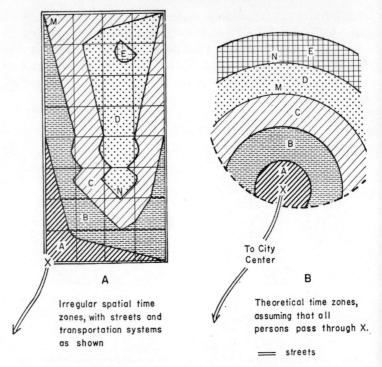

To City
Center

A

B

Irregular spatial time
zones, with streets and
transportation systems
as shown

Theoretical time zones,
assuming that all
persons pass through X.

===== streets

III.3 Application of the Time and Cost Distance Concepts to a zonal
pattern around point X. Diagram B shows the pattern that would
emerge with equal accessibility in all directions from X: diagram A
shows the result when movement is quickest along the peripheral
streets. *Source:* Quinn, 1940a.

Burgess ignored the factor of inertia. Immobility is considerable
within cities, for buildings, streets, railroads, and occasionally
even some cultural groups, are not easily transferred to other
locations. Accessibility surfaces also change over time, and not
uniformly, so that developing structural patterns are imposed
upon a generally conservative existing mosaic. The degree to
which a city re-orders itself to the new influences depends on
the mobility of people and capital, the readiness with which
people will move and write off earlier capital investments, and
the importance to them of marginal benefits in, for example,
accessibility.

74

If the inertia factor is to be included within the model, there-fore, a detailed history of a city is necessary for its proper comparison with the model, and Quinn ended his defence of Burgess with the statement that, to that date, a proper test had

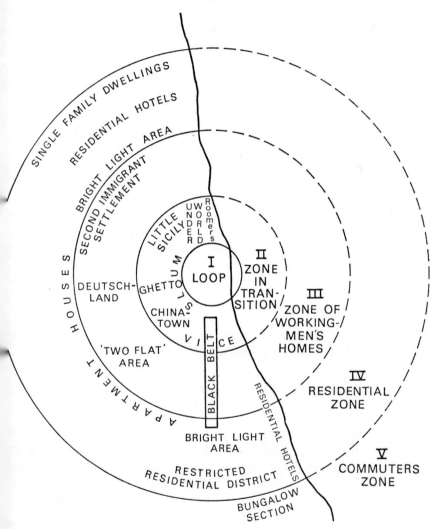

III.4 The Concentric Zonal Pattern of Urban Residential Areas, as applied to Chicago. *Source:* Burgess, 1924.

never been conducted. Given his criteria, such a study probably never will. He stated (Quinn, 1940a, 218):

An adequate research program for testing the Burgess zonal hypothesis in any given city involves at least the following items:

1. Thorough knowledge of existing topography and of those historical modifications of topography that have affected the growth of the city;

2. An adequate series of isochronal maps drawn in terms of changes in the street and transportation systems of the city; these maps should show the time-cost zones of the city at various periods of its historical growth;

3. The development and precision of adequate sets of ecological criteria for characterizing zones;

4. Adequate knowledge of the composition and distribution of local population;

5. Adequate knowledge of existing spatial distributions of all significant social and personal data;

6. Knowledge of important cultural items (1) which influence standards of living of different classes of the population, (2) which lead to concentrations of persons of distinctive cultural types, and (3) which give areas their traditional reputations thereby lessening mobility and increasing historical inertia;

7. The formulation of alternative hypotheses—possibly including non-circular zone patterns, patterns which involve either more or less than five zones, or various non-zonal patterns of ecological structure.

Only when these items have been taken into account can an adequate test of the Burgess hypothesis or any other ecological hypotheses of urban structure be made.

Other Criticisms

Another criticism, by Alihan (1938), was that Burgess included two contradictory spatial features in the various editions of his model, zones and gradients. This is not a wholly correct criticism, for while one of the later papers (Burgess, 1927) did indeed present data as gradients, these were made up of series of census tracts arranged by distance zones from the CBD and so were not truly continuous distributions. Nevertheless, Burgess did aggregate them into zones and Alihan's reworking of the figures showed that 'the standard zonal boundaries do not serve as demarcations in respect of the ecological or social phenomena they circumscribe, but are arbitrary divisions' (Alihan, 1938, 225). If regular gradients exist, any zonal division of them could appear apposite, but Alihan claimed that 'Burgess's description of the five zones clearly indicates that ecologists envisage these zones as distinct units, differentiated in terms of numerous factors' (Alihan, 1938, 225).

Such an argument against the zonal pattern is valid on statistical grounds. Burgess's conception of invasion and succession as the causes of city growth clearly suggested that the whole city was always in transition (see Bourne, 1968). Nevertheless, if cultural groups are slowly moving outwards from the city centre along these gradients, at any one point in time they will be concentrated in a certain area and if this extends right around the city then it forms a zone. To some extent the occupants of the zone are not synonymous with the behavioural variables of the gradients, so the two spatial configurations are not entirely contradictory and it is possible to identify the former superimposed onto the latter.

During the four decades since Burgess's first enunciation of his model, it has been used and criticised many times (for an early bibliography see Quinn, 1940b). Apart from Davie, only Hoyt has suggested any positive alternatives (see below). Recently, Gittus claimed that 'It seems that the theories of Burgess and Park may no longer be related to modern conditions and that a new framework is needed for the systematic study of the complexity of urban life. Some would even say that the situation is now so complex that it is impossible to devise an overall framework of any kind' (Gittus, 1964, 7). This quasi-defeatist attitude follows Davie in suggesting that each case is unique in its spatial pattern; the framework by Gittus therefore refers only to overall patterns of residential differentiation. Within Britain, this view is not supported in the work of Mann (1965), and Loewenstein wrote for the United States in 1965 that 'the viability of Burgess's descriptions today is testimony to his perception and insight' (Loewenstein, 1965, 102).

Debate on the value of the zonal model continues, therefore, and evidence for and against it is evaluated in Chapter IV.

Schnore's Exegesis

In summary, Burgess's zonal hypothesis, as developed by Quinn, is a simple model of a complex reality in that it makes the important assumptions of a mono-nucleated city with equal accessibility in all directions; it also ignores the role of inertia. All cities contain unique features of topography, micro-climate, street plan, and railroad lineaments which produce distortions from the idealised concentric circular zones, but Burgess nevertheless claimed 'so universal and powerful is the force of expansion outwards from the center that in every city the zones can be more or less clearly delimited' (Burgess, 1928, 108), although his evidence all referred to Chicago.

Burgess did not clearly specify the postulates on which his model was built, but this has been done recently by Schnore (1965a) who, building on Quinn's statement, summarised the main preconditions as:

1. A growing city.
2. Heterogeneity within its population, including some or all of (a) large foreign groups with different degrees of assimilation, (b) members of different races and (c) 'men and women who pursue different occupations, who enjoy different standards of living and who control different volumes of purchasing power [for] . . . social class gradations must actually exist if the residential population is to be sorted into bands occupied by different socio-economic strata' (Quinn, 1950, 120–121).
3. A mixed commercial-industrial base, necessary for the land use assemblage of the CBD and the zone of transition.
4. Certain economic and cultural factors within the society, such as private ownership of property, economic competition, and an efficient transport system.
5. Certain aspects of the geometry of urban space, including a single centre, with land in shortest supply close to that centre, this being economically the most desirable land because of both its short supply and its high accessibility to the whole urban area.

6. Certain occupancy patterns among the various socio-economic groups. The Burgess hypothesis

seems to assume that the more favored classes will ordinarily pre-empt the newer and more desirable housing areas [the criteria for desirability are not discussed]; with radial expansion, these areas typically have been located at the periphery in American cities. At the very least, the Burgess hypothesis assumes a high degree of locational freedom on the part of the wealthy, who may occupy practically any area, as compared with the lower classes, who are much more severely restricted with respect to residential choices (Schnore, 1965a, 354).

A number of economists have proposed deductive models of the same pattern. Notable among them is Alonso (1964; see also Beckmann, 1969), who pointed out that the ecologist's explanation for the peripheral location of the wealthy assumes a growing city. He showed that a similar pattern will emerge in a static situation, *given certain tastes*. Developing on the general notions of accessibility, Alonso indicated that lower-income groups are more location conscious than the wealthy because they cannot afford both high land costs and high transport costs to the central city workplaces, especially as their limited land holdings do not allow them to easily absorb increased transport costs. This the richer groups can do, *given that they have a strong appetite for land*. If these residents desire space they will live further from the city centre than lower-income people who cannot afford the commuting costs of such distances. Although an economic model, therefore, Alonso's formulation was dependent on the value systems of the society, and his interpretation of these was only one of several which could be applied to the same pattern (Harris, 1968; see page 226 below).

Homer Hoyt's Sector Model

Hoyt's model is generally treated as an alternative to Burgess's but it is in fact only a development of it and retains many of the concentric model's features. It was first presented in 1939, and, like Burgess, Hoyt developed his model inductively, though not on the basis of a single city. (Note, however, that the origins of the model can be traced to Hoyt's earlier (1933), monumental study of Chicago's real-estate market over a hundred years.) Instead, the sector concept was distilled from a large amount of material produced during the 1930s for some 204 urban places by the Real Property Inventories of the Civil Works Administration. A further similarity with Burgess's work was that the model was not produced as an end in itself; Hoyt's study was commissioned to provide basic data to 'guide the development of housing and the creation of a sound mortgage market' (preface by Fisher in Hoyt, 1939, iii). Finally, like Burgess, Hoyt produced a model of *city growth*, although he too focused strongly on the static patterns.

In his first chapter, Hoyt set out his criticisms of the concentric zone model, among them that:

1. The CBD is not the only major commercial centre in many large cities, and its boundaries are not always clearly defined as ribbons of commercial development extend along many of the main streets leading out of the CBD. (This criticism was answered in Quinn's substitution of time-cost for straight-line distance in ecological analyses.)

2. The wholesale and light manufacturing districts are adjacent to the CBD, but generally do not completely encircle it. (More recent discussion on this point is given in Griffin and Preston, 1966.)

3. 'The present pattern of industrial land use is frequently so different from [the] original concentric zone pattern that it is doubtful whether it can be asserted that there is any general tendency for a concentric zone of heavy industry to surround the central business district' (Hoyt, 1939, 20; to some extent this was a criticism of a non-existent part of the original theory). Hoyt suggested three reasons 'why heavy industries now follow railroad lines along river valleys or lake or ocean fronts in long bands of growth' (1939, 20):

   (a) Transportation facilities are better on the urban periphery.
   (b) Sites are cheaper and taxes lower on the periphery, allowing greater use of space.
   (c) The automobile has severed the close ties between workplace and worker's residence.

80

4. 'As factories do not form a concentric circle around the central business district, so neither do the workingmen's homes encircle the central core' (Hoyt, 1939, 23).

5. Rents do not always increase with distance from the city centre, and the social elite pay the highest rents for apartments very close to the CBD in some cities.

6. In the commuters' zone 'some of these settlements are occupied by fine homes, but other towns may be middle class in character and others may consist of shacks. It is not true that one progresses from dilapidated dwellings at the center to an encircling belt of mansions on all points of the periphery of the city' (Hoyt, 1939, 23).

Before presenting an alternative version of the Burgess model which would meet these criticisms, Hoyt devoted a considerable portion of his monograph to a discussion of techniques for analysing residential quality. He concluded that average block rental was the best measure of housing quality, an indicator more relevant in the 1930s than the 1960s. (In the 1968 reprint of his work, Hoyt added a number of maps showing where the rich and poor people lived in American cities in 1960. This time he used family income rather than rent as his index of housing quality.)

The static aspects of Hoyt's model were developed from study of schematic diagrams of rental patterns (using five categories) in 142 cities (some of these are reproduced in Figure III.5). The main elements of these maps were determined as:

1. The highest rental area is in every case located in one or more sectors on the side of the city . . .

2. High rent areas take the form of wedges extending in certain sectors along radial lines from the center to the periphery . . .

3. Intermediate rental areas, or areas falling just below the highest rental areas, tend to surround the highest rental areas or to adjoin such areas on one side . . .

4. Intermediate rental areas on the periphery of other sectors of the city besides the ones in which the highest rentals are located are found in certain cities . . .

5. Low rent areas extending from the center to the edge of settlement on one side or in certain sectors of the city are

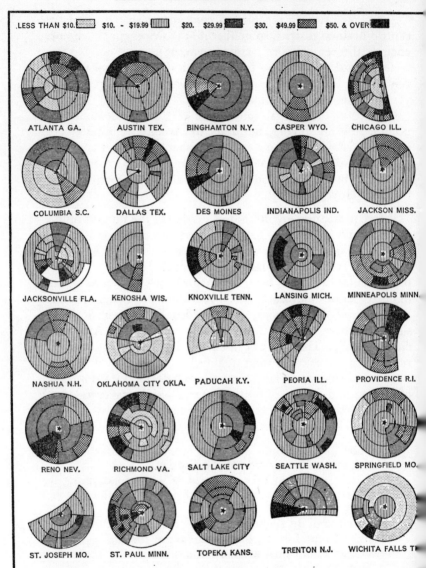

LESS THAN $10. $10. - $19.99 $20. $29.99 $30. $49.99 $50. & OVER

ATLANTA GA.   AUSTIN TEX.   BINGHAMTON N.Y.   CASPER WYO.   CHICAGO ILL.

COLUMBIA S.C.   DALLAS TEX.   DES MOINES   INDIANAPOLIS IND.   JACKSON MISS.

JACKSONVILLE FLA.   KENOSHA WIS.   KNOXVILLE TENN.   LANSING MICH.   MINNEAPOLIS MINN.

NASHUA N.H.   OKLAHOMA CITY OKLA.   PADUCAH K.Y.   PEORIA ILL.   PROVIDENCE R.I.

RENO NEV.   RICHMOND VA.   SALT LAKE CITY   SEATTLE WASH.   SPRINGFIELD MO.

ST. JOSEPH MO.   ST. PAUL MINN.   TOPEKA KANS.   TRENTON N.J.   WICHITA FALLS T

III.5   Schematic diagrams of the Sectoral and Zonal Distribution of Dwelling Rents in American cities during the 1930s. *Source:* Hoyt, 1939.

found in practically every city. There may be a low rent
wedge extending entirely through the center of the city . . .,
or from the center to the periphery on one side or sector . . .
Or a low rent area near the center of the city with an
intervening higher rent area may be matched by an area
with equally low rent on the periphery of the same sector . . .
One or more sections of a city thus acquire a low rent
character, and in these sectors there is no tendency towards
an upwards gradation of rents from the center to the
periphery (Hoyt, 1939, 75–76).

Hoyt concluded that the concentric zone theory was clearly
defective, although reading his fifth point might suggest that
an alternative generalisation was unlikely. The pattern of
increasing rents away from the centre which he observed in
some sectors could, if all sectors were amalgamated, produce
a gross zonal pattern which apparently confirmed the zonal
model. Hoyt's detailed maps, however, and his greater attention to suburban patterns (Burgess concentrated on the inner
zones), allowed him to make the important point that in few
cities did the highest rental areas occupy more than 25 percent
of the periphery. He proposed a

> sector theory of the location of rent areas in American cities
> [in which] rent areas . . . tend to conform to a pattern of
> sectors rather than of concentric circles. The highest rent
> areas of a city tend to be located in one or more sectors of the
> city. There is a gradient of rentals downwards from these
> high rental areas in all directions. Intermediate rental areas
> . . . adjoin the high rent areas on one or more sides, and tend
> to be located in the same sectors as the high rental areas.
> Low rent areas occupy other entire sectors of the city from
> the center to the periphery. On the outer edge of some high
> rent areas are intermediate rental areas. In small cities, or
> cities of slow growth, the highest rental areas may occupy
> parts of sectors directly adjacent to the business center. As
> in the large cities, the low rent sectors extend from the center
> to the periphery on one side of the city (Hoyt, 1939, 76).

No schematic diagram was presented as a visual illustration of
the model, but one was later drawn by Harris and Ullman
(1945), and is reproduced as Figure III.6.

This formulation was much more flexible than Burgess's, although it depended on many of the same assumptions. Socio-economic strata were allocated to various sectors, and the location of these was dealt with in discussions of city growth and changes in residential area characteristics. Because of lack of data, Hoyt studied only the changing distribution of high rental areas, basing his generalisations on cartograms (Figure III.7). He concluded from these that the fashionable

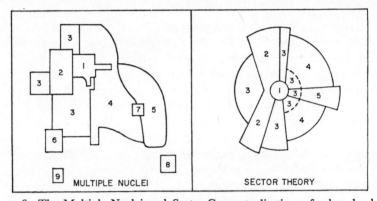

III.6 The Multiple Nuclei and Sector Conceptualisations of urban land use patterns.
KEY: 1, CBD; 2, Wholesale and Light Manufacturing; 3, Low-class Residential; 4, Middle-class Residential; 5, High-class Residential; 6, Heavy Manufacturing; 7, Outlying Business District; 8, Dormitory Suburb; 9, Industrial Suburb. *Source:* Harris and Ullman, 1945.

areas follow a definite ordered path during city growth, allowing development of the sector theory of residential structure into one of neighbourhood change. This is the most widely-known part of Hoyt's work, through its reproduction in a book edited by Mayer and Kohn (1959, 499–510).

The theory showed that the high-status residential sector initially develops alongside the retail and office centre, and in each city the direction and pattern of its future growth then tends to be governed by some combination of the following considerations:

(1) High grade residential growth tends to proceed from the given point of origin, along established lines of travel or

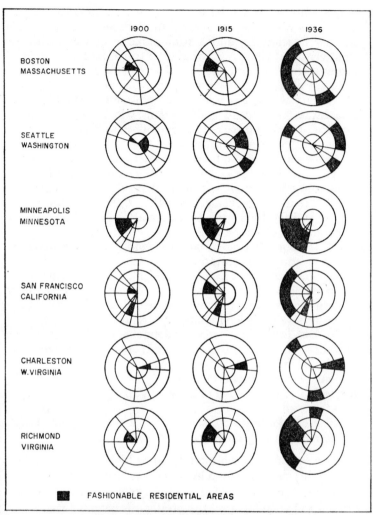

III.7 The changing distribution of Fashionable Residential Areas in six American cities. *Source:* Hoyt, 1939.

toward another existing nucleus of buildings or trading centers . . .

(2) the zone (*sic*) of high rent areas tends to progress toward high ground which is free from the risk of floods and to spread along lake, bay, river and ocean fronts, where such

85

waterfronts are not used for industry . . . where such . . . exist and offer the attractions of bathing, yachting, cool breezes in summer, and a wide expanse of water with its uninterrupted view, rent areas tend to follow the contour of the waterfront in long, narrow lines of growth.

(3) High rent districts tend to grow toward the section of the city which has free, open country beyond the edges and away from 'dead end' sections which are limited by natural or artificial barriers to expansion.—The lure of open fields, golf courses, country clubs, and country estates acts as a magnet to pull high grade residential areas . . .

(4) The higher priced residential neighborhood tends to grow towards the homes of the leaders of the community . . .

(5) Trends of movement of office buildings, banks and stores, pull the high priced residential neighborhoods in the same general direction . . .

(6) High grade residential areas tend to develop along the fastest existing transportation lines . . .

(7) The growth of high rent neighborhoods continues in the same direction for a long period of time . . . Except under the unusual conditions now to be described, there have been no reversals of this long continued trend.

(8) De Luxe high rent apartment areas tend to be established near the business center in old residential areas . . . When the high-rent single-family home areas have moved far out on the periphery of the city, some wealthy families desire to live in a colony of luxurious apartments close to the business center . . .

(9) Real estate promoters may bend the direction of high grade residential growth (Hoyt, 1939, 116–119).

Once a sector has been established as high grade, therefore, it retains this character for a long period of time, so the wealthy only have the greatest freedom of choice of residences if they are prepared to live away from the prestigious neighbourhoods: so Hoyt's model incorporates some of the factor of inertia suggested by Quinn. Growth of the high-status sector must be outwards when it occurs. Areas to either side and closer to the city centre are of lower status and only rarely will higher status individuals or groups move back into areas of lower prestige, pioneering their social rejuvenation (the exception to this is usually the redevelopment of areas with apartments, but there are a few cases—Georgetown, Washington; Chelsea, London; and Paddington, Sydney—of rejuvenation via renovation of older property).

Although much more explicit than Burgess on the dynamics of city growth, Hoyt did not include a full statement on the mechanism and his discussion was partly contradictory. Both centrifugal push forces and peripheral pull factors were discussed, but the former were only referred to in the chapter on changes in land use. The expansion of non-residential uses around the CBD meant that 'persons occupying residences near the heart of the city go farther out to live' (Hoyt, 1939, 107), a process accentuated by population influx to the city centre, particularly of alien groups, which 'causes a shifting, a filtering process that profoundly affects every neighborhood in the city' (Hoyt, 1939, 122). Nevertheless, Hoyt wrote that even in 1939 the invasion of residential areas by commercial users was being checked by (1) a reduction in the areal expansion of the CBD caused by skyscraper development and suburban business-centre growth, (2) the declining role of wholesaling in the transfer of goods from manufacturer to retailer, and (3) the relative, and often absolute, decline of industry in the inner city. Because of this, he believed that the zone in transition could become one of semi-permanent blight (see Griffin and Preston, 1966).

When referring particularly to residential uses, Hoyt paid most attention to endogenous characteristics of home and neighbourhood. The mechanism he suggested is now generally known as filtering, by which the higher-income groups periodically demand new housing and their former homes are bought by lower-income groups, for whom they represent an improvement in living standards. Thus homes slowly filter down the social scale and individuals filter up the housing scale. Clearly such a process will operate only in a growing city with an established demand for used property, and where the purchase of new dwellings is restricted to upper-income groups. (The same model can be applied to other large consumer items, such as motor-cars.)

The main reason suggested for the initiation of filtering was deterioration of the housing stock of an area. A neighbourhood

of 'new houses in the latest modern style . . . has the vitality to
fight off the disease of blight', which is caused by the invasion
of lower-status groups, especially aliens and Negroes. Neighbourhood desirability is correlated with age because

> Houses with increasing age are faced with higher repair bills.
> This steady process of deterioration is hastened by
> obsolescence; a new and more modern type of structure
> relegates these structures to the second rank. The older
> residents do not fight so strenuously to keep out inhar-
> monious forces. A lower income class succeeds the original
> occupants. Owner occupancy declines as the first owners sell
> out or move away or lose their homes by foreclosure. There
> is often a sudden decline in value due to a sharp transition
> in the character of the neighborhood (Hoyt, 1939, 121).

In fact, as the last sentence points out, filtering is unlikely to
produce a steady decline in neighbourhood status. Middle-class
groups can generally afford new housing of their own, rather
than following their immediate social 'superiors' faithfully as
they abandon areas, so that it is probably only groups immediately below the lowest income strata able to purchase new
homes who will initiate changes in neighbourhood status.

Both Burgess and Hoyt provided inductive descriptions of the
spatial structure of cities, therefore, accompanied by a number
of hypotheses on the mechanisms that produced the observed
patterns. Burgess was mainly interested in the city as a laboratory for studies of social disorganisation. Hoyt was more
directly concerned with housing quality and socio-economic
status, and so was more precise in his discussion of the location of
neighbourhood types, especially the more prestigious, although
he retained many of the salient elements of Burgess's model.
While Hoyt introduced the important modification with the
sectoral arrangement of housing quality, he nevertheless included
a *zonal pattern within most of the sectors*, and although suggesting
an alternative mechanism of filtering he acknowledged that
invasion and succession may play a significant role (even
though his suggestion was that invasion was not possible unless
neighbourhood resistance was low).

Firey & Rodwin on Hoyt

Firey's criticism of the sectoral model was part of a much broader attack on human ecology. He categorised its studies as either idealised descriptive, empirically rationalistic, or methodologically rationalistic, with the zonal and sectoral models both being placed in the first category. In particular, the former model was criticised because 'nowhere in the theory is there a definite statement of the modus operandi by which people and groups are propelled to their appointed niches in space' (Firey, 1947, 7).

The ecological studies reviewed by Firey were attacked for assuming that:

1. Physical space possesses qualities which are wholly devoid of cultural values.
2. Social systems passively comply to spatial distance.

Most of his book contains examples from Boston of the error of such assumptions, with Hoyt's model as the theorem based on them. Firey's final criticism was much like Davie's, that

> Though vague concentric and sector patterns are apparent in certain types of land use, the more important fact is the variation of land use within these zones . . . There are, to be sure, some rough cartographic patterns to be found now and then in land uses, which are just tangible enough to make the concentric-sector theories plausible. Indeed, if there were not, it would be something of a mystery how such theories had come to be formulated (Firey, 1947, 86).

Firey's whole thesis was that city land use patterns are not based on purely deterministic, economic mechanisms, but are the product of man's cultural and emotional evaluation of places. Sentiment and symbolism were cited as two crucial variables determining the pattern of activities (Firey, 1945), and he presented detailed case studies from Boston to show their effects. To a large extent paralleling the scheme proposed by Quinn, through his attention to the city's history, Firey pointed out, for example, the importance of cultural and historical symbolism in the retention of Boston Common and a number of churches in areas of very high land values close to the city centre; the importance of sentiment for an area in the retention of high prestige by the Beacon Hill residential suburb close to the Common; and the role of strong community ties in preserving an Italian neighbourhood in Boston's North End. All of these were at variance with the zonal and sectoral models and provided evidence for Firey's argument that maximum financial gain is not the only force, and perhaps not even the major one, which shapes the city's morphology.

Firey's basic criticism of Hoyt's and other studies was that they were attempting to produce generalisations about contemporary patterns and past tendencies (although predictions were implicit, none were presented), and he did not believe that any such statements could possibly be made. His alternative theory of cultural ecology is in effect only a methodology for the study of individual cities as unique phenomena.

That the main difference between Hoyt and Firey was philosophical was claimed by Rodwin who, while not specifically defending the former, pointed out that although Firey had shed considerable light on the historically contingent character of land use patterns and the role of values in their shaping, nevertheless he had not really questioned Hoyt's generalisations. (James (1948, 230) claimed that 'the most revealing finding of Firey's study was the remarkable way in which it tended to confirm, rather than refute, Hoyt's theory'.) Indeed, Rodwin showed that Firey was very selective in his attacks, raising many points which Hoyt had already covered, and that Firey concentrated too much on minutiae (the latter criticism could also be levelled at Jones (1960), who favoured Firey's findings). A simple example of this was Firey's claim that Hoyt's model was entirely mechanistic and based on economic factors alone, when one of the main influences on high-status neighbourhood movement listed by Hoyt was the location of the 'leaders of society'.

Rodwin's note on the Hoyt-Firey differences was an appendix to his main work on the housing experience of Boston's middle-income families. Most of this latter work concentrated on relationships between incomes and housing costs (and is discussed in Chapter IV), but one part was a study of spatial patterns and included Rodwin's own critique of the Hoyt model. (Some parts of this were published in a paper in 1950, but although the dissertation was completed in 1949 the book was not published until 1961.) In his criticism Rodwin was more circumspect than Firey, and tended to be constructive rather than destructive, pointing out that an individual city deviating from the general tendency need not invalidate the whole generalisation. Instead, study of such a place might provide evidence of weaknesses in the original and lead to their possible correction.

The main criticism was based on a scrutiny of three of Hoyt's terms and two of his assumptions. The terminological problems discussed were:

1. What was the precise meaning of sector, how should these be defined, and what were the constraints on their size? Within the framework of a generalisation some exceptions must be anticipated and, for example, the presence of a slum pocket within a high-class neighbourhood does not invalidate the whole model (despite Firey's claims that it would). Sectors are intended to be relatively homogeneous, however, but the wider they are (or the larger the angles they subtend) the greater the probability of heterogeneity. Testing of Hoyt's model thus requires a pragmatic approach to sector definition, which can be attacked as making the facts fit the theory—a criticism also made by Duncan and Duncan (1960). This does not seem too important, however: given the nature of the forces suggested by Hoyt it is clear that neighbourhood types cannot be allocated to certain locational positions without some prior knowledge of the relevant city. Rodwin recognised the complex interplay of economic, social and historical factors and concluded that, on his evidence, sectors existed. Presumably, then, any case study testing this model should first see whether any sectoral patterns can be discerned, and, secondly, enquire whether they have evolved as Hoyt hypothesised.

2. Leaders of society were suggested as major catalysts of the social topography of the city by Hoyt, but this represents a very simple view of the structure of society, which Hoyt had divided into only three income classes in some parts of his work.

In fact, most urban societies are amalgams of several parallel, partly interlocked stratigraphies (see Chapter II), some of them more isolated than others. Rodwin suggested that each of these strands would have its own leaders towards whose homes the residential patterns were oriented. The result would be a more complex pattern than the model, although built on the same lines. In effect, however, Hoyt anticipated this criticism because not all of his intermediate (middle) class clustered around the homes of the nabobs; some were content with the best locations (the peripheral) within other sectors.

3. Finally Hoyt paid almost all of his attention to the upper-income group, with some slight mention of those at the other extreme. His intermediate class (the subject of Rodwin's dissertation) was clearly very large and Rodwin pointed out that only those at its upper end could aspire to residential contiguity with the upper class. The rest would presumably be content with a wide range of neighbourhoods. Again, however, Hoyt appeared to have covered this in his fourth point (see page 81), that there were intermediate rental areas on the periphery of sectors other than those adjacent to the high-status one, so that the criticism can only be that he did not specify whom among this large 'class'.

Rodwin did not offer any fuller statement of a theory of urban structure, or even a solution to these problems. Also he merely pointed out that there were two limiting assumptions to the model. The first was a lack of concern by the FHA (Hoyt's sponsoring agency) for general housing conditions, so an overall view was not attempted; like so many academic works, it looked at its subject mainly from the middle-class (or above) position of the researcher. Secondly, Hoyt did not consider the role of government activity in producing city morphologies. Rodwin merely concluded by indicating the need for more information on the residential location decision, noting that

> Among the diverse conditions sought today are adequate access to employment centers for the principal and secondary wage earners; convenient location to schools and shopping centers; and physical settings providing adequate and

attractive housing, open space, traffic safety and recreation areas (Rodwin, 1961, 119–120).

Re-evaluations

Since 1930, Burgess's only published comment regarding his model was a short statement that his critics had misunderstood its conception as an idealised representation of the real world (Burgess, 1953). Hoyt, however, has twice written about his theory. The first time was a reply to Rodwin's (1950) critique. Five of the latter's points were answered; the only one involving new material referred to the government's role in determining urban residential patterns. Hoyt accepted that his sectoral model did not admit public housing on the urban periphery, but pointed out that his was a *laissez faire* model which had no room for a welfare state one. He clearly did not agree with increasing government participation in the housing market (he termed it 'the complete socialization of the United States' —Hoyt, 1950, 450—partly, it would seem, because it would affect the employment of appraisers). He also doubted the likelihood of producing a 'mongrel' theory incorporating both 'economic' and 'welfare' approaches. Rodwin's discussion was acknowledged as 'precise and logical . . . dismissing Firey's attack as merely grazing the writer's theory and not landing a really effective punch' (Hoyt, 1950, 450). Note that Firey also replied to Rodwin, simply reiterating his conclusion as answers to the question 'How many exceptions can a carto-graphic theory of land use . . . admit and still claim to be rigorous theory' (Firey, 1950, 451).

Hoyt's second paper (1964) presented a short but full discussion of the present relevance of both his and Burgess's models in the light of rapid urban growth, rises in car owner-ship, and increases in real income. Much of it was a discussion of changes within the CBD and its collar of non-residential uses, as a continuation of his 1939 presentation on these points. Regarding the residential areas, and with reference to the zonal model, Hoyt indicated the great development of expensive central city apartments, the rehabilitation of fashionable inner suburbs such as Georgetown, and the infilling of the interstices of the outer, commuter zone by large tracts of middle-class housing.

On his own model, Hoyt pointed out that much of the development of high-income areas was still markedly sectoral but that there was some scattering of small, expensive clusters. He concluded that

> The automobile and the resultant belt highways encircling American cities have opened up large regions beyond existing settled areas, and future high grade residential growth will probably not be confined entirely to rigidly defined sectors. As a result of the greater flexibility . . . some higher income communities are being developed beyond lower income sectors but these . . . usually do not enjoy as high a social rating as new neighborhoods located in the high income sector (Hoyt, 1964, 209).

Rodwin's points were never answered, however, let alone Firey's, and there are still several parts of Hoyt's work which are not entirely explained. His lack of much evidence on the dynamics of residential areas obviously led to a subjective analysis, but in a recent discussion of these, Morris (1968, 110) was 'not sure how generally applicable this sketch is. Hoyt's own maps show conformity to his sector theory only for Minneapolis; but since they do not reveal the location of industry, warehouses, waterfronts, high ground and open country, they are inconclusive' (see Figures III.5 and III.7). Similarly, it is not clear whether Hoyt was discussing the whole built-up area of a city, or only the administrative central city; most of the maps in his supplement refer to the latter only.

Harris & Ullman on Multiple Nuclei

Just as Rodwin recognised that urban society was not structured as simply as Burgess and Hoyt suggested, so, at about the same time, Harris and Ullman (1945) proposed that the spatial variables operating in the urban context were also more complex. (Their work seems to lead on from Davie's 1938 work, but they make no reference to it.) After reviewing the two models, the authors (both geographers and, again, working in Chicago) concluded:

> Both the concentric zone, as a general pattern, and the sector aspect, as applied primarily to residential patterns, assume

(although not explicitly) that there is but a single urban core around which land use is arranged symmetrically in either concentric or radial patterns. In broad theoretical terms such an assumption may be valid, inasmuch as the handicap of distance alone would favor as much concentration as possible in a small central core. Because of the actual physical impossibility of such concentration and the existence of separating factors, however, separate nuclei arise (Harris and Ullman, 1945, 17).

Four reasons were put forward for the development of separate space-organising dominant nuclei within a city:

1. Some uses need special facilities; for retailers these include accessibility, which has traditionally been greatest in the CBD, but ports and industries require waterfronts which may be eccentrically located within the city.

2. Like activities often cluster for external scale economies, as in office districts (Goddard, 1968) and industrial complexes (Rimmer, 1967).

3. Certain activities are detrimental to each other, such as noxious industries and high status residential areas.

4. Certain activities cannot afford the high rents of the most accessible locations and form their own subsidiary clusters. This happens, for example, within CBDs where the space-consuming furniture stores and car salesrooms are usually on the fringe (Scott, 1959).

Acting in conjunction over time, these four factors often lead to a multi-nucleated city, especially if this develops around a number of formerly independent settlements. In recognising this, Harris and Ullman did not provide any important modification of the existing models. They merely continued the process of bringing the original zonal model closer to the reality of large cities, a role which Hoyt also performed—though more importantly. Harris and Ullman suggested no changes in the modus operandi—in fact they spent only nine lines on residential districts—and the diagrammatic representation of their ideas is much more difficult to compare with maps of sample cities than for the previous two models (Figure III.6). Their main contribution was to suggest the role of unique factors in each city, over and above the general, and the need for a pragmatic approach in applying the high-order zonal and sectoral generalisations to reality.

The Mechanism of Neighbourhood Change: A Restatement

The zonal and sectoral conceptions of residential structure include intra-urban migration as a basic component of the process of neighbourhood change. As pointed out, however, neither Burgess nor Hoyt was very explicit on the nature of this mechanism, although the former emphasised external influences and the latter stressed those endogenous to the neighbourhood. More recently, however, a fuller statement has been provided which integrates the two.

In this, the external process of invasion and succession is a special case of the more general filtering mechanism by which housing is passed down the social scale. Filtering has several meanings within the literature on housing, however (Grigsby, 1963), so the definition adopted here is

> A change in occupancy down the income (or social) scale, of which the converse is the movement of individuals up the quality scale. This process depends on the creation of new supply.

Why do the upper-income groups regularly choose to leave their homes and build new ones? Lowry (1960) suggested three reasons:

1. Technological obsolescence, by which the internal structure and facilities of a house become outmoded and make it undesirable for those who can afford more modern offerings. Examples of such obsolescence would be plumbing, electrical wiring, heating and air-conditioning systems, the provision of servants' quarters, and very large gardens.

2. Style obsolescence, the process by which the architectural features of a home, often including construction materials, become outmoded and the dwelling loses its status-symbol value relative to newer developments.

3. Depreciation, or the decline in the quality and state of repair of a home which demands the expenditure of money and effort on its maintenance.

The first two of these are most likely to initiate the dissatisfaction which high-income people develop concerning a home. Of the two, style obsolescence is the most likely cause of a decision to seek another home since it should occur more rapidly than the other two. Except in periods of rapid change, technological obsolescence is not likely for several years after a house is built—unless that occurs just before a major development—and Grigsby suggested that depreciation does not generally even commence until a dwelling is about twelve years old.

In addition to Lowry's three suggested causes of filtering, Grigsby has proposed:

4. Site obsolescence, in which a local, external feature affects the desirability of a single dwelling. This could be caused by a road widening or by the introduction of an undesirable adjacent user, such as a non-residential land use or a low-income household (see the later section on migrants in cities): such obsolescence would only rarely occur in high-status areas.

5. Locational obsolescence, or the declining desirability of an area. Such obsolescence, and the consequent out-migration, could be triggered by a number of cases of site obsolescence in the same area. Invasion and succession clearly is in this category, and can be considered a special case of the more general filtering process.

The hypothesised pattern of neighbourhood change is thus one in which a number of moves at the periphery of a sector initiate a migration process which reacts back towards the city centre. It may be initiated by a few individual decisions to move to newer, better housing (which decision may be caused by dissatisfaction with present standards or by the actions of real-estate agents and developers of new building projects). A number of such moves then generate a more wholesale neighbourhood move, either because they cause those still in their former homes to become more dissatisfied with them relative to newer ones, or because the type of occupants moving into the initially vacated dwellings make the whole area less desirable. The result is a chain reaction of vacancies created by short-distance outward moves, and these are filled by other local residents who see in them an opportunity to improve their

THE FILTERING PROCESS

I. C.B.D.

Old housing
occupied by
lower status
groups.

Better housing
occupied by
lower middle
classes.

Best housing
occupied by
upper middle
classes.

II.

New ho⟨
built by
middle c⟨

III.

Lower classes move up the housing scale.

IV.

Low class migrants move into vacated, worst housin⟨

III.8 Simplified cross-section through a city, from CBD to periphery, to
show the working of the Filtering Process.

housing standards (Figure III.8). Such a process is supposed to
be initiated by factors endogenous to the dwelling rather than
the external influence of invasion and succession, Hoyt suggesting that the latter cannot take place unless filtering has already
begun for other reasons.

LIFE STYLE, THE FAMILY CYCLE,
& LOCATION

It was pointed out in the earlier chapters, that the life style
dimension consists of two related components. The life style

choice is between familism, consumerism and careerism; within the familism choice there are a number of sub-choices which are strongly, though not wholly, correlated with the age of the family members, and in some parts of the family cycle the life style can be similar to that in the other major choices. In the present discussion, attention is centred first on residential patterns for the three major life styles, and is followed by elucidation of probable patterns within the familism choice.

The broad choice of dwellings for households is between a single-family unit and one in a block of multi-family homes, although within each category there is a wide range also—from back-to-back terraced house to a mansion in the former choice, and a single-storey house divided into two flats to a multi-storey apartment building in the other. Within each of these markets the consumer makes another choice, again basically between two alternatives—whether to rent or whether to purchase (with or without the assistance of a mortgage). It was suggested in Chapter II that family-centred households would prefer single-family units, partly because of the available space external to the dwelling, and also, all other things being equal, would opt for home ownership, considering this an essential element of family security (see Turner, 1968). Career- and consumerism-oriented households, on the other hand, would more likely choose living in rented apartments. (Such values are culture-bound, of course, and vary to some extent between the societies discussed here, particularly in the importance of ownership where government provision of housing is considerable.)

This separation of the life style groups into two independent housing markets is clearly an over-simplification which will be amended in later paragraphs. Nevertheless, it allows for a useful first discussion of possible spatial patterns. If households can be differentiated into separate housing markets, then a residential structure will evolve if factors produce a spatial segregation of the various types of dwellings. Such factors include:

1. The Pattern of Land Values

Investigations have indicated a simple pattern of intra-urban land values decreasing away from a peak value somewhere

99

within the CBD, the decline being very rapid at first and then levelling off to a gentle slope over much of the city (Knos, 1962, is a good example of such studies). This pattern is explained in terms of the importance of accessibility to the city centre, land being a free-market commodity whose value depends on the price offered by the highest bidder. The latter are presumed to pay what they do because of the investment potential.

The main determinants of land prices are the bids made for non-residential land uses. Entrepreneurs, it is presumed, desire to locate their shops, offices, and factories at points where they minimise the costs of assembling their inputs (including customers) and maximise profits on their outputs. Because the accessibility pattern in most cities is based on communications networks and public transport systems, land at the city centre is thus the most valuable (this theory, from which there are many deviations due to inertia and non-rational behaviour, is elaborated in Alonso, 1964, and Wingo, 1961).

Residential uses are excluded from the most valuable land because their marginal gains from increased accessibility are much less than those for businessmen, who may lose substantially from their potential revenue at locations far from the most accessible point to possible customers. Beyond the non-residential areas, however, the continued, though less steep, decline in value is still attributed to the factor of accessibility. Employment is concentrated at the city centre, and since the journey-to-work is usually the principal trip originating from a household each day, then people will locate their homes to be as close to their workplace as possible, in order to minimise travel costs. Residential land is thus in greater demand close to the centre, with consequent effects on land values.

Such a model of residential land values assumes a great deal about the role of accessibility in household location decisions. It is based on a mono-nucleated city, but removal of this assumption does no more than bring it closer to reality with several superimposed zonal patterns (as Harris and Ullman did for the socio-economic status models). From the model's postulates, however, it can be suggested that housing markets will be segregated because:

(a) The greater the cost of a piece of land, the greater is the likelihood of its intensive use. This involves multi-family dwelling-unit structures, which spread the high land cost over a large number of purchasers or renters, so that the more expensive the land the higher its density of occupance. Close to the centre, therefore, one would expect high-rise apartment buildings, succeeded by low-rise apartments, row or terrace housing and single-storey apartment blocks (termed ownership units in several countries) and then single-family units with increasing distance from the CBD (though of course not all of these types might be found in some cities).

(b) In many cities, local taxes are raised in part or completely on the value of land. Even where the property is vacant, therefore, such costs are often high, especially on very valuable land, and this encourages its maximum usage in order to spread this cost. Single-family dwelling units are thus expensive to service on central city land, again suggesting their banishment to more distant locations.

The pattern of land values should therefore create a two-zonal structure with apartments close to the city centre and single-family units beyond. This does not allow for the factor of inertia, of course, for what is now an inner city district will once have been an outer suburb, and its houses have not been removed to make way for blocks of flats (because of unwillingness to move by owners, the lack of demand for flats, the unsuitability of the site, or the successful competition of relatively rich, family-oriented persons who can afford central city locations for their houses). Nevertheless, a general zonal pattern should occur, which would be reflected in the pattern of population densities.

(It should be pointed out here that Alonso's model of urban land values, when referring to residential areas, correlated distance from the city centre with densities of occupance and *socio-economic* status rather than *family status*. This was based on the assumption that only the higher-income households could afford to substitute space preferences for proximity to workplace, an assumption which may have been valid two or three decades ago in the countries studied here, but has very little relevance now.)

2. Differences in Environmental Requirements

The above model of urban structure based on land values is based on a desire to minimise commuting costs. This may be true for career-oriented households (for a discussion of variations between certain careers see Richards, 1963) but in family-centred units many other trips—to shops, to schools, to recreation areas—may be much more important. Minimisation of *total* travel costs could involve a long journey-to-work, especially if the costs are measured in non-financial terms such as effort (comparing driving a car to work with pushing a pram to shops). The greater the commitment to familism, especially compared to consumerism, the less important the city centre should be in the total activities of the household.

Families are not likely to place such a premium on access to the city centre as either people who build their lives around a career which is organised there or those devoted to consumerism, many of whose elements are mainly purchased downtown. Instead, they will prefer the environmental qualities of lower density, more peripheral suburbs. Away from main traffic routes in such areas, streets should be quieter and safer, and at a distance from the centre the air should be less polluted. For the raising of children, therefore, both single-family dwelling units and suburban locations should be preferred.

3. The Age of Housing

Cities grow outwards so that, apart from the usually small pockets of urban renewal, there is a strong negative correlation between distance from the city centre and housing age. The models of socio-economic status patterns discussed earlier suggested that housing is passed down the social scale as it ages. But many units, even when old, cannot be afforded by a single household because of their size. They are subdivided into flats, apartments, or rooms, therefore, in order to spread the total cost, and this type of housing is preferred by non-family-oriented households. (An alternative model might suggest that single households could afford to buy or rent such dwellings, but entrepreneurs see a greater return from subdivision.) Thus, older homes are found closest to the city centre; they are most likely to be subdivided; and such housing units are most attractive to career- and consumerism-oriented households: yet again, this suggests a zonal structure.

A major desire of most family-oriented households is home ownership, which can usually be attained only with large-scale financial aid. Loan agencies often advance money, at least in part, on the security of the dwelling itself and thus favour new or fairly new properties. For most families, therefore, the purchase of older dwellings is not possible, though perhaps desirable because of their price and size. Older, inner city housing could thus be left to older residents who have not felt the need to join in the filtering process (see below on the family cycle); to those with money—who generally would not want depreciated property 50–100 years old in any case; and to entrepreneurs who invest in housing and who prefer dwellings that can be subdivided in order to spread the risk of income loss through vacancy. Once more, therefore, a zonal pattern is suggested, with a dichotomy between central city rental areas and suburban home ownership.

The Family Cycle & Residential Choice

The three factors discussed above all suggest that the desirable qualities for family living—an owner-occupied house in a pleasant low-density environment on relatively cheap land —are best found in suburban areas. Alternatively, career- or consumer-oriented households, whose main preferences are for rented apartments requiring little effort or upkeep, and for accessibility to the external centres of their life-stage, find their needs best in a city's inner zones. A simple two-zonal structure is suggested by these preferences, distorted in part by the inertia factor of many single-family dwelling units remaining in the inner zones until they have completed their economically useful life, and disturbed much less by the construction of apartments in suburbia.

Within the familism choice, however, there are sub-choices which relate to the stage in the family cycle which a household has reached. The various stages of the cycle have been outlined in Chapter II, and the present discussion builds on these with a presentation of Abu-Lughod and Foley's model of locational requirements (in Foote *et al* 1960).

1. THE PRE-CHILD STAGE. In this, housing demands are broadly comparable to those for households who have chosen one of the other two life styles. Both members of the family are likely to be absent from the dwelling at work for much of the day, so demand for space will be low relative to that in later stages in the cycle. Accessibility to the centre is probably important. Other aspects of the family's behaviour could be very similar to that of consumer-oriented households, both types spending much of their leisure time away from the home. Finally, at early stages in the male's career his income is likely to be fairly low and his accumulated savings small. Home purchase is unlikely, therefore, and because of expectations of future housing demands of a different type with family growth, there will be fewer pressures on pre-child families to purchase an apartment than on adherents to the other two life styles. Families in this stage should live, therefore, in relatively cheap, central city rental apartments.

2. CHILD-BEARING. Following the normally short pre-child stage, the family should enter its period of most rapid growth and greatest mobility. Space demands increase as the wife now usually remains at home to raise her young children, and the demands continue to expand as the family grows in numbers and the offspring in years. Accessibility to the city centre or some other major nucleus becomes less important to the family while the quality of the local environment becomes more crucial, especially, in the societies under review, with regard to the provision of private open space. The husband will still be relatively little advanced along his career cycle, however, which in many occupations will mean a continued inability to buy his own home, perhaps coupled with a reluctance to because of anticipated inter-city moves as a result of job advancement. For such people, the solution is to rent a single-family dwelling unit, and these are usually most available in the adjacent zone to the apartment area comprising relatively old homes which have filtered a long way down the social

scale but which are as yet too far from the city centre to form attractive propositions for subdivision into flats.

3. CHILD-REARING. The family generally stops expanding during this period, but as the children grow and the husband reaches the apex of his career, home ownership, security and stability become important features of family life (many families, for example, will be reluctant to move far during this stage for fear of disrupting their children's education with changes of school). A relatively new suburban home, whose actual location may be determined by such accessibility factors as the quality of neighbourhood schools, will be purchased. Accessibility to the city centre becomes a very inferior good, and long-distance commuting is a usual part of the breadwinner's day.

4. CHILD-LAUNCHING. As children progress through their 'teens space demands build up again, but the family is usually more able to meet them now than in the second stage. Real income for the head is often at a maximum, the wife may have returned to work, and the equity held in the home may permit purchase of a newer, larger house. Neighbourhood ties are likely to induce the family to stay in the same general area, however, but Abu-Lughod and Foley (Foote *et al*, 1960, 110) suggested that the family might choose a higher socio-economic status area because 'when the children reach marriageable age a few years hence, they should perhaps have a more impressive home as a background'; this attitude is unlikely to be common over a wide portion of the class spectrum.

5. POST-CHILD. Soon after the move to more spacious quarters, family size declines as children leave home, and Abu-Lughod and Foley noted that 'during the period when space is most necessary it is often unobtainable; once it has been achieved, it is soon unnecessary' (Foote *et al*, 1960, 113). Nevertheless, many of the reduced families may not move into smaller accommodation, preferring to enjoy their space and retain it for visits by their children and grandchildren. Smaller homes and gardens might be more desirable for many, but these would probably only be available in (1) older stock, which would involve filtering down the neighbourhood scale, (2) new suburbs populated largely by young families, or (3) central city

apartments, built on expensive land and costing as much as a suburban home in many cases. Thus this stage should be marked by residential stability, though movement may be both desirable (in terms of total use of the housing stock) and desired.

6. LATER LIFE. The average family is dissolved by the male's death, but whether husband or wife dies first, a large number of the survivors no longer lead an independent existence, however much this might be desired (Abu-Lughod and Foley quoted 63 percent of all widows and 43 percent of all widowers moving to live with their children).

In the same volume, Foote derived a residential cycle, described by him as follows (Foote *et al*, 1960, 362):

From the time of its formation by a marriage, until shortly after its dissolution by death of one of the mates, a family tends to go through this typical sequence of changes of residential status:

1. Rental of small furnished apartment, perhaps briefly prefaced by living with parents of one mate.
2. Rental of larger unfurnished apartments, connected with changes of husband's jobs.
3. Purchase of small second-hand house, building of small equity.
4. Purchase of larger new house, often coincident with further changes of husband's jobs or income; further increase of equity.
5. Expansion of house by some remodelling; completion of payments; 'settling down' often while children are in high school.
6. For a few, custom-building of a house.
7. Children leave home, neighborhood begins to deteriorate.
8. Sale of house longest occupied; purchase of smaller house or rental of apartment near center of city.
9. Death of one mate; brief retention of separate home by survivor.
10. Sale of house, surviving mate moving in with a child or into an institution.

Although Foote suggested (Foote *et al*, 1960, 362) that 'there is widespread professional acceptance and use of such a generalized scheme', his outline differed in several respects from Abu Lughod and Foley's, not only in the greater detail and number of steps (the latter suggested that Foote's step 8 was atypical) but also in the omission of some, such as the rental of a house between Foote's steps 2 and 3. Nevertheless, the broad outlines are very similar and suggest that a family slowly moves out from the city centre to the periphery, as in Figure III.9, eventually slowing its rate of mobility and becoming engulfed in the suburban mass as the city continues to grow.

Like the models of residential structure based on socio-economic status, this family cycle and residential location construct is an inductive development for the United States only. Abu-Lughod and Foley based their model on the median family, from 1950 cross-sectional rather than longitudinal data, for all nonfarm U.S. residents, together with Glick's (1957) work on the family cycle. There are clearly many deviations from such a median pattern in terms of housing tenure, location, and mobility, the authors noting in particular unmarried adults, couples without children (25 percent of all households), smaller-than-average families, broken marriages, and low-income families.

Deviations from the model involve either the omission of certain of its steps or failure to complete the total sequence. The first two stages of Abu-Lughod and Foley's (and Foote's) scheme are most likely to be missed; by higher-income families who can afford house purchase immediately after marriage, by families which have very short pre-child stages, by families who live at a parental home until child-bearing and house rental or purchase, or by older couples with sufficient equity for immediate purchase. On the other hand, many families, especially in the lower-income groups, will never proceed beyond house rental whatever their stage in the family cycle, and thus will not live in the suburbs unless a house is provided by public agencies. A final, common deviation among households choosing familism is that 'after accomplishing the major objective of home ownership . . . half of America's families today never do buy a second home' (Foote et al, 1960, 109). Residential stability is usual, therefore, from middle-age onward.

THE FAMILY CYCLE AND LOCATION

A. ZONAL STRUCTURE

CBD   Periphery

1. Small Town

2. Growth: New houses in suburbs for young families leaving home.

3. Subdivision of old homes. More new suburban homes.

4. Flat Construction: Expansion of apartment area. Movement to new outer sub. Ageing of inner suburbs: less mobility.

B. INDIVIDUAL FAMILIES

1. New Apartment— New suburban home.

2. Subdivided house – Rente house – Suburban house.

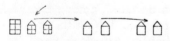

III.9   Simplified cross-section through a city, from CBD to periphery, to show the working of the Family Cycle Location Process.

108

Households which follow non-familism life styles are outside this model, although they share many of the characteristic housing and locational characteristics of the pre-child families. Accessibility to work and recreation is a more important good for single adults and childless couples, and home ownership has a low priority for most of them, compared to households with children. Abu-Lughod and Foley (Foote *et al*, 1960, 119) suggested that, among single adults, 'if they do buy, the urge overtakes them at a later stage when the expectation of marriage has more or less disappeared', and even if they do purchase a house rather than a flat their space demands will not change, so that they are unlikely to follow the 'suburban trail'. Thus, non-familism households are usually apartment renters living close to the city centre, less mobile than the expanding families during their twenties, but probably more so in their thirties and forties.

Through the operation of the land-value mechanism, the different preferences for accessibility, space and seclusion, plus the spatial patterns in the housing stock, a zonal pattern of life style choices should emerge within the city. The inner zone will contain high-density, often multi-family dwelling units which are generally rented—either by those who have chosen careerism or consumerism as their dominant life style or by young couples just commencing the family cycle. The outer zone will comprise new, low-density single-family dwelling units, housing completed but relatively young families. Between them is a more heterogeneous band, containing young families still saving for their aspired suburban home, older couples who have attained their goal and retain little incentive or ability to move, and finally other families at all stages in the cycle who are prevented by income constraints from moving any further.

This zonal pattern clearly should be reflected in the age structure of the population, with a succession of youth—old age—middle age—late youth/early middle age from city centre to periphery. It would be produced by a mobility pattern which essentially involves an outward progression from city centre to periphery, followed by stability while the periphery expands. In many respects the movement mechanism is similar to that of filtering, the migrations being caused by dissatisfaction with present housing and neighbourhood. Whole districts should experience population turnover as their occupants reach the next stage of the family cycle; this is theoretically less likely than in the filtering situation because of variations between families and the relationship between the technological obsolescence of homes (especially with regard to space) and variables such as family size.

MIGRANT & MINORITY GROUPS IN THE CITY

Elements of the spatial patterns and processes of recent migration to cities have already been mentioned. For example, in Chapter II it was suggested that recent arrivals are often poor, unskilled, and unused to city life so that, even if they are not discriminated against in the housing market, they tend to cluster in their own 'urban villages' for social and economic security. At this stage they live a social existence apart from the city, journeying from their 'village' each morning to work in the wider urban environment but returning to the community (often kinship) bonds each evening. In time, however, individuals become assimilated into the wider society, usually through a process of upward social mobility. Whatever the actual cause, the result is that the migrant group parallels the wider society in its occupational, income and family-type distributions so that the whole range of residential choices is opened to its members, who become gradually dispersed through the city's neighbourhoods.

Initial low incomes, incapacity for home ownership, and the need to be close to employment centres—often because of dependence on casual employment and inability to pay high transport costs—all suggest that recent migrants to a city will congregate where relatively cheap, high-density housing is available. The previous section has suggested that areas close to the city centre meet such requirements in their subdivided, obsolescent rental dwellings whose owners, because of the uncertainty of the timing of non-residential expansion or urban renewal in the area, do very little maintenance on dwellings.

The future of such inner city 'urban villages' depends largely on the future of the group and of migration to the city itself. Where the group retains a strong sense of community—as perhaps with Jewish migrants—other residents may be excluded from the 'village', producing a migrant ghetto. Such a spatial form is more likely to emerge because of discriminatory tendencies among the general population, however, which either prevent economic mobility among the migrants or, where this occurs, inhibit the successful from exercising the wide choice of residential locations which is allowed non-group members of similar incomes.

From the initial development of a ghetto (to which group members are limited), the ensuing spatial pattern may take a number of forms. These are:

1. If the group's population continues to grow, then some expansion of the ghetto must result. Some growth may be absorbed by increasing living densities but eventually the area must expand, initiating the invasion and succession process which is basic to Burgess's model. (Note that Burgess assumed that such movement would be outwards rather than sidewards, presumably because the whole zone of transition would be occupied by such migrant groups. Hoyt suggested that invasion was only likely where neighbourhood resistance was already low; see p. 88 above. Rose (1970) suggested that retreat may be a better descriptive term than invasion. If an expanding ghetto was entirely surrounded by resistant areas, presumably a second ghetto would develop in another part of the zone of transition.) From the initial cluster, therefore, a sectoral ghetto would develop outwards and, over time, may become very elongated within the city, although probably not reaching the periphery (Figure III.10A). Such a large, culturally-distinct community would probably develop its own system of social stratification, with the consequent residential separation, presumably of zones within a sector since the 'best' residences would be in its outer part.

2. If the group fails to grow, or expands only slowly by its own natural increase, which may not involve a rapid expansion of housing demand, it might:

(a) Remain in the same place within the city (Figure III.10B).

(b) Move outwards en masse as its economic condition improved (Figure III.10C).

(c) Move outwards en masse because of the expansion of another ghetto community 'behind' it (Figure III.10D). The group might prove resistant to such a process, of course, so that the new group had to outflank it (Figure III.10E).

Where no ghetto developed, but instead the migrant group was slowly assimilated into the larger society, then the urban village might slowly disappear as its members spread themselves through the city (Figure III.10F). As individuals progressed from the lowest paid occupations into higher echelons of urban society, their rewards would be the ability to rent a better home, perhaps a single-family dwelling unit of their own, and later to buy their own. At the same time they would become able to participate more widely in the general society. Thus ties with the 'urban village' community would be slowly relaxed and proximity to kin and community become much less important in the residential location decision (propinquity in any case is not necessary for the maintenance of family relationships among middle classes; Litwak, 1960a, 1960b).

Portions of some groups could continue the 'urban village' pattern, however. While the second- and later-generation settlers (the children and grandchildren of the original in-migrants) may aspire to assimilation within the host society, the first generation, especially if mainly of peasant stock, would probably be more conservative and want to retain the community and kinship ties. The 'village' may eventually disappear as this generation dies, but its existence could be continued by a small proportion of later 'conservatives'. If further members of the group migrated to the city such a village could provide a useful reference point for entry to the city, and a staging-post offering economic security to a recent arrival until he becomes adjusted to his new environment. In such a situation the 'urban village' may be a continuing feature though it may undergo considerable frequent population turnover (Figure III.10G).

MODELS OF RESIDENTIAL PATTERNS

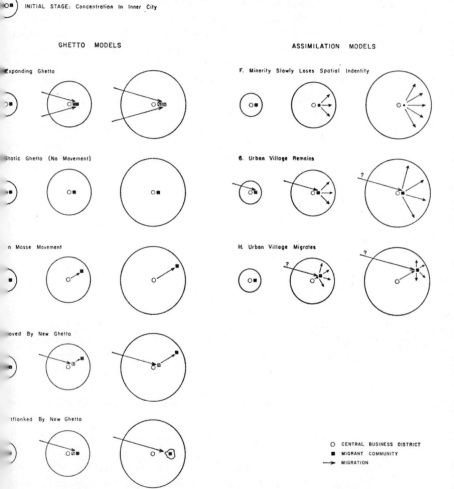

III.10 Schematic diagrams of a growing city, showing the various hypothesised distribution of migrant groups.

Like the ghetto, it might be moved outwards by the in-migration of other groups (Figure III.10H).

A variety of possible residential patterns is suggested for migrant groups within the city, therefore, with the relevant one for any group depending on its social and economic structure in relation to that in the rest of the city. In the general terms in which it is phrased, the present discussion clearly refers to groups of migrants very different from their hosts, particularly international migrants though there is no reason why the patterns deduced should not refer to intra-national groups to whom city life is alien, whether or not they are discriminated against. (This migrant model is not based on any particular source, since no full such construct has yet been reported. It clearly draws on Burgess, and also on Ward (1968), Handlin (1951, 1959), Glazer and Moynihan (1963), Firey (1945), Rose (1969, 1970) and Jakle and Wheeler (1969a, 1969b), among others, and is an inductive statement of what appear to be the implicit generalisations within the relevant literature.)

THE MINOR SOCIETAL DIMENSIONS

Studies by Anderson and Bean (1961), Jones (1969), and Schmid and Tagashira (1965), discussed in Chapter II, suggested other dimensions within urban society besides those of socio-economic status, life style and migrant groups covered in this chapter. Several authors have identified two separate components of the life style dimension; one, termed 'career women' by Sweester (1969), seems to cover the broad life style differentials, while the other covers family cycle differences. These have already been discussed separately.

A more important further factor, which has emerged in several recent factorial ecologies (see Rees, 1971, forthcoming) is that of intra-urban population mobility. Analyses have shown that the proportion of persons or households who have lived in their present home for a specified period (often five year because of the format of US census data) was but slightl correlated either with any other variables or with th other main dimensions. Several reasons can be suggested fo this:

1. All of the models presented so far in this chapter incorporate intra-urban migration within their theorems, and all suggest a constant stream of moves away from the city centre. Thus each part of the city might display the same mobility rate (20 percent moving per year, for example, and everybody moving once every five years), so that there would be no correlation between mobility and any other population or housing variable. The separate dimension would then emerge, given that it was represented in the initial selection of variables. This explanation is unlikely, on theoretical grounds, since the family cycle model suggested that after about the age of 35 movement becomes much less frequent. Mobility would then be correlated with age, though only partly so, and a dimension could still emerge which was separate from socio-economic status and life style. Empirically, other variables were associated with intra-urban migration (Schmid and Tagashira, 1965), so it was not independent of all other spatial patterns.

2. Each neighbourhood type categorised according to the other dimensions could be patterned according to mobility experience (as Shevky and Bell (1955) did with migrant status in their enunciation of social area analysis). Thus, for example, one could get high socio-economic status, high family status tracts which were very mobile (representing the child-bearing and launching stages) and others which were stable (representing the child-rearing). Similarly, high socio-economic status, low family status areas might be divided into mobile areas of single young persons moving from flat to flat and stable areas characterised by more permanent apartment dwellers who have definitely opted against familism. Mobility would then not be associated with any particular age group, and would appear as a separate dimension although no coherent spatial pattern can be suggested.

3. The other models, especially those of socio-economic status and migrant groups, do not specify the rate of neighbourhood change. Presumably it depends on the city's growth rate and, especially for invasion and succession, the nature and rate of migration to the city, but it is unlikely that the various types of filtering occur so rapidly as to involve frequent moves. For any one inter-censal period, therefore, rapid neighbourhood change

is likely to be confined to certain parts of the city. These parts could represent a wide spectrum of residential types, so that again a separate mobility dimension would emerge, again without any particular spatial pattern.

4. In any growing city there is a certain amount of new housing constructed during a time period, and its occupants will be represented as mobile by a succeeding census. If the large cities include new peripheral housing for the majority of social groups (especially where there is public housing for the lower-income segments) and urban renewal and apartment construction provide new homes for both lower-income and non-family-oriented households, then a separate mobility dimension would be identified because no one specific segment of society was excluded from new construction.

Of these four hypothesised situations, the last would be most plausible in situations where there is considerable new housing built for all groups. But if it caters only for the middle classes and above (as the filtering process suggests) then mobility could emerge as a separate dimension because of a triangular relationship between it and socio-economic status: all areas of high mobility are also of relatively high socio-economic status, but the reverse is not true (Johnston, 1971a). New, middle-class housing areas would not be the only districts with high rates of in-movement, since all of the models discussed in this chapter suggest that mobility is common throughout the city, but their newness ensures that they are well above average.

Similar arguments could be forwarded regarding Schmid and Tagashira's population stability dimension, which emphasised high rates of movement to the city. This separate component could indicate similar proportions of migrants to the city in all of its districts. But it is more likely to suggest another triangular relationship: the migrants are dominantly of certain age and socio-economic characteristics and so congregate in the typical areas for such people, but not all of these latter areas have attracted large numbers of migrants (see Johnston 1971a). The relevance of these arguments is assessed in later chapters.

Finally, an extra dimension in several studies has identified areas with very high proportions of males in their populations. Male life expectancy is lower than that for females, so some variation in the sex ratio may be anticipated among neighbourhoods according to their resident's position in the family cycle. The existence of a separate male dimension related strongly to no other variables except poor housing conditions suggested the 'Skid Row' area of Seattle to Schmid and Tagashira (1965); the area inhabited by down-and-out, largely unemployed males, who move frequently between cheap lodgings and institutions. Many of them are either alcoholics or criminals (Bogue, 1963). Their residential requirements are for cheap, low-quality rental accommodation, and Skid Rows are usually in the poorest housing adjacent to the CBD. The dimension is separate because all Skid Row areas have low socio-economic status and low family status, but all of the areas with these last two characteristics are not on Skid Row (Johnston, 1971a, 1971b).

CONCLUSIONS

The present chapter has reviewed a number of models which form the basis for most contemporary discussion of residential patterns and processes in the cities studied here, for each of the main societal dimensions. These form the framework for the more empirical discussions in the next three chapters which relate reality in the various countries to these constructs. As they stand, however, the models are independent representations of parts of the same whole, although the socio-economic status structures incorporate some of the migrant group hypotheses. Thus the pattern is incomplete, and this situation is further confused because:

1. Each group of models—of socio-economic status, of family status, and of migrant group assimilation—suggests some zonal pattern of population characteristics.
2. Each model suggests that neighbourhood change takes place because of a slow process of migration away from the city centre by most individuals and groups.

Clearly, therefore, there is a need for some attempt to synthesise the various models into a single paradigm of the city.

At this stage of the book this would prove extremely difficult, however, if not impossible, because evidence of the validity of the somewhat contradictory hypotheses has yet to be presented. Such an attempted synthesis will be inductively done on the basis of the next discussion, rather than through a deductive effort to produce any such structure from what has been written so far.

CHAPTER IV

The Changing Social Topography

THE PREVIOUS chapter has outlined the main models of
urban residential structure and the remainder of the book is
concerned with a discussion of their relevance. No attempt is
made at a total affirmation of rejection or any one model, or a
hypothesis which could be derived from it. Rather, a number of
studies have been chosen as generally indicative of recent
research, from which some idea of the present state of knowledge on urban residential patterns can be obtained. In this
and the next two chapters each of the three main dimensions
of urban society and residential structure is treated separately
and the final chapter then attempts an overall synthesis of the
urban residential mosaic.

THE GENERAL HYPOTHESIS

Burgess and Hoyt's models of the spatial pattern of socio-
economic status both place the highest status groups on the
city's periphery. Thus:

*I. The socio-economic status of areas increases as one moves away
from the city centre towards the periphery.*

But Hoyt suggested considerable variability within each
concentric zone because status areas are principally organised
in sectors. Thus, the hypothesis should read:

*Ia. Socio-economic status groups tend to concentrate within certain
sectors of the city. Within each of these sectors there is a zonal
pattern, with increasing status away from the city centre, but each
sector need not contain the full spectrum of social groups*

Over time, the city grows outwards by expansion at its fringe, and the new housing there should be occupied by the highest status elements within the relevant sector. These people move to such housing because of dissatisfaction with their present home or address as an indicator of their societal position, and the properties they vacate are occupied in turn by lower-status families also moving to improve their housing standards. Thus:

II. All areas decline in their socio-economic status over time, as a result of residential mobility and the outward migration of groups into better and newer housing further from the city centre.

SOME BROAD PATTERNS

The first hypothesis was tested by Burgess and his students at Chicago. Burgess's gradients, reproduced in Table IV.1, covered a number of population and dwelling characteristics, but most of the others, such as Shaw's (1929) on delinquency areas and Faris and Dunham's (1939) on mental disorders, concentrated only on a range of disorganisation phenomena.

TABLE IV.1

GRADIENTS IN THE GROWTH OF THE CITY: CHICAGO *c.* 1920

Zone[1]		Male[2]	Aged Over 20[2]	Foreign-Born[2]	Poverty[3]	Divorce[3]	Boy Delinquency[3]
I	1	85·5	88·2	39·0	2·0	2·0	443
II	2	66·3	81·2	33·0	3·2	2·9	58
	3	54·1	74·6	20·0	2·1	4·3	27
III	4	49·0	67·6	19·8	1·3	3·4	15
	5	46·1	74·8	18·3	0·1	2·0	4
IV	6	47·8	68·5	18·8	0·1	1·3	0
	7	49·8	67·1	19·0	0·1	1·0	
V	8	48·4	66·7	16·5	n.d.	n.d.	n.d.
	9	47·0	66·4	14·0	n.d.	n.d.	n.d.

[1] The Roman numerals refer to Burgess's zonal scheme, the Arabic to the concentric one-mile zones.
[2] Percent of the total population.
[3] Cases per 1,000.
n.d. No data

Source: Burgess, 1927, 182–183.

These were the works strongly criticised by Davie (1938) for not taking account of within-zone variability.

The same format was used by Blumenfeld in an analysis of Philadelphia in 1940. The city was divided into ten concentric bands, despite the irregular nature of the boundaries and the eccentric location of the CBD, and the gradients for twelve population and dwelling series were plotted. Given the problems of zonal definition, Blumenfeld (1949, 209) noted that 'all the more remarkable is the extreme consistency shown for all twelve series in zone 2 to 8'. Only four of his variables were directly related to socio-economic status, and all showed increasing values only for the first eight zones, followed by a decline. Thus, as indicated by property values, home ownership, and the proportion of the population in the labour force, what Blumenfeld (1949, 212) termed the 'economically privileged area of the city' was intermediate between the CBD and the 'not fully urbanized fringe' of the outer zones of the city. This suggested that the filtering mechanism was not working, since according to hypothesis II the furthermost zones of the city should be occupied by the highest-status residents.

Residential Centralisation in Chicago & Cleveland

Development of the gradient idea came with Duncan and Duncan's (1955) index of centralisation, for which a negative value indicated a tendency for the group under consideration to be concentrated in the outer zones of the city, and a positive value indicated a tendency towards centralisation. Unfortunately, a result close to zero could indicate either an even distribution of the group throughout the set of zones, or else its concentration within the intermediate zones between the city centre and the urban fringe. As the Duncans used more than twenty zones the latter result is possible, but since their results compare favourably with the anticipated pattern they are of value to the present discussion.

Following from the zonal model, one would expect that the amount of group decentralisation would be positively correlated with its socio-economic status, and the Chicago findings verified this (Table IV.2). Two exceptions occurred to the general rule. First, sales and clerical workers were more centralised than the lower-status craftsmen, foremen and kindred workers. Duncan and Duncan pointed out that this resulted from the discrepancies between ascribed status and purchasing power (see also Chapter II, p. 44). Clerical workers are more status-conscious and allot a larger proportion of their income to housing than do 'blue-collar' craftsmen (Duncan and Duncan, 1955, 499). Because of this, they can afford less for transport costs (see Alonso, 1964, and the discussion on pp. 78–79 above on this topic), and so tend to live much closer to their workplace than the other white-collar groups (in Chicago in 1950 white clerical workers travelled an average 5·1 miles to work, compared to 6·4 miles for the group immediately above them in the status scale—sales workers—and 4·6 miles for the craftsmen group; Duncan, 1956, 50). Clerical workers apparently seek out the 'best' areas they can afford which are close to their workplaces, therefore: on the other hand the craftsmen are less status-conscious and many live further out in cheaper areas (and, of course, fewer of them have central city jobs, manufacturing in Chicago being considerably decentralised).

As well as the zonal pattern over the whole metropolitan district, Duncan and Duncan reported indices of centralisation for five separate sectors of Chicago (Table IV.2). In three, the city-wide pattern was reproduced (including the clerical-craftsmen reversal) but for the two sectors following the Lake Michigan shoreline there were considerable variations from the anticipated structure. In both cases the lower-status labourer groups were not very centralised (the figures could indicate an even distribution or an intermediate zonal concentration; the interpretations favour the former). Duncan and Duncan equated this with the existence of industrial concentrations at the outer edges of these sectors at Gary and Milwaukee, and the strong centralisation of service workers in the southern sector which also had a concentration of Negroes in its inner zones. Thus they concluded that 'expectations based on the zonal hypothesis must be qualified by recognizing distortions of the zonal pattern produced by peripheral industrial concentrations . . . where these are absent, the zonal hypothesis leads to a realistic expectation concerning the

TABLE IV.2

CENTRALISATION OF OCCUPATION GROUPS: CHICAGO AND CLEVELAND
INDEX OF CENTRALISATION[1]

| OCCUPATION GROUP | CHICAGO 1950 | | | | | | CLEVELAND | |
	TOTAL	NORTH[2]	NORTH-WEST[2]	WEST[2]	SOUTH-WEST[2]	SOUTH[2]	1950 TOTAL	1960 TOTAL
Professional	−14	−15	−20	−29	−20	5	−22	−24
Managerial	−12	−20	−16	−19	−15	1	−21	−25
Sales	−5	−15	−12	−12	−9	8	−15	−19
Clerical	5	7	2	1	5	9	1	3
Craftsmen	−8	6	−6	−7	−5	−26	−2	−3
Operatives	10	21	16	18	8	−4	14	20
Service Workers	21	16	18	20	16	36	17	15
Labourers	7	9	21	30	16	−1	25	33

[1] For description of Index, see text p. 43
[2] Sector of Chicago.

Source: Duncan and Duncan, 1955, 499; Uyeki, 1964, 495.

pattern of residential centralization by socio-economic status' (Duncan and Duncan, 1955, 500).

The Duncans' study was replicated for Cleveland in 1950 and 1960 by Uyeki (1964), whose published data referred only to the whole city although he mentioned sectoral patterns. His 1950 results agreed entirely with those for Chicago in the rank ordering of the groups (Table IV.2), but by 1960

> The greatest change is the greater centralization of laborers. In addition, managerial workers have become more decentralized than professional workers, and clerical workers more centralized (Uyeki, 1964, 497).

In general, his longitudinal findings suggested a spatial polarisation of the white- and blue-collar classes, therefore, except that the clerical workers had not joined in the suburban drift of the former group.

These two American studies did not provide full investigation of the hypothesis of zones within sectors, for there was no indication of the degree of sectoral concentration of groups. Although there was a zonal pattern of increasing status with greater distance in each sector, were all the outer zones occupied by people of similar socio-economic levels? Uyeki suggested perhaps not:

> The pattern for the total area is reproduced in three of five sectors . . . The southwest sector still shows the professional workers as the most decentralized . . . the outlying areas in the southwest sector are not the high prestige suburban areas, and it is probable that managerial workers have not moved there in such proportions as elsewhere (Uyeki, 1964, 497).

But this did not go very far towards a test of the second hypothesis (p. 120).

Pretoria & Johannesburg

A similar study by Davies (1964) included indices of centralisation, sector concentration, and sector centralisation. Perhaps unfortunately, the study was of Johannesburg and Pretoria, where the nature of the caste society may affect the patterns. However, the general pattern of residential segregation in the two cities approximated the U-shaped curve observed for Chicago, with the greatest segregation at the two extremes of the class spectrum, so there is no reason to believe that distortions were so great as to preclude application of the model.

Davies's study of zonal and sectoral concentration showed that the latter was the more important element in the spatial configuration of residential areas. On the zonal pattern there was little evidence of the correlation between degree of decentralisation and socio-economic status displayed in Chicago; in Johannesburg mine workers were strongly centralised, but both there and in Pretoria the craftsmen and transport workers were decentralised, more so than any other groups except administrative workers in the former city. 'It is interesting to note also that the professional category previously established as the residentially most exclusive category in Pretoria, is not the most highly decentralized' (Davies, 1964, 35). Patterns of sector concentration, on the other hand, were clearly U-shaped, especially in Johannesburg, illustrating the tendency for the upper and lower status groups to be fairly strongly concentrated within certain sectors while the middle-class groups were more evenly distributed through the city (Table IV.3. There is no ambiguity in the interpretation of the sectoral statistic, for, unlike the zonal, it has no implicit order). This is in line with Hoyt's model, for one might expect higher status groups on the fringe of certain sectors, lower status groups in the inner parts of others, and intermediate groups in the inner parts of the former and the outer zones of the latter.

For Johannesburg only, Davies calculated centralisation indices separately for all but two of the sectors. In his interpretation he suggested 'a much closer resemblance in detail to the expected outward graduation in the concentration of occupational categories ranked according to status level . . . with the white collar workers relatively decentralized and the blue collar workers relatively centralized' (Davies, 1964, 37). Nevertheless, the tendencies were not particularly strong, as indeed they were not in Chicago and Cleveland, and in one of the main high-status sectors (5) the values in fact indicated that the white collar workers were evenly distributed through the five zones (maps accompanying Davies's paper indicated that the

TABLE IV.3

ZONAL AND SECTORAL PATTERNS OF OCCUPATION GROUPS: JOHANNESBURG AND PRETORIA, 1960

OCCUPATION GROUP

INDEX OF SECTOR CONCENTRATION[1]	Administrative	Professional	Sales	Clerical	Craftsmen	Transport	Miners
Johannesburg	0·35	0·34	0·17	0·09	0·35	0·42	0·50
Pretoria	0·29	0·36	0·24	0·17	0·27	0·34	—
INDEX OF CENTRALISATION[2]							
Pretoria	−0·04	0·03	0·03	0·14	−0·15	−0·14	—
Johannesburg	−0·13	−0·02	0·00	0·04	−0·04	−0·05	0·12
SECTORS OF JOHANNESBURG							
1	−0·03	−0·10	−0·02	−0·03	−0·05	0·11	0·09
2	−0·26	−0·10	−0·08	−0·03	0·20	0·35	−0·22
3	−0·12	−0·22	−0·07	−0·03	0·14	0·12	0·33
4	−0·33	−0·08	−0·02	0·12	0·18	0·21	0·41
5	−0·05	−0·08	−0·08	0·04	0·06	0·19	0·64
6	−0·03	−0·02	0·23	−0·04	−0·08	−0·11	0·03
8	0·00	−0·12	−0·05	0·01	0·01	−0·13	0·12

[1] An index of 0 shows complete dispersal of the group, one of 1·0 complete concentration of the group in one sector.
[2] An index of +1 shows complete centralisation, of −1 shows complete decentralisation, and of 0 an even distribution.

Source: Davies, 1964, 27 and 37.

alternative interpretation of these near-zero indices would not be valid). In the lower-status sectors there was much less evidence of centralisation of the blue-collar groups (Table IV.3).

L. F. SCHNORE & THE ECOLOGICAL TRANSITION

During the last decade one of the most productive investigators of the residential structure of American cities has been Leo F. Schnore. His initial research under Hawley at the University of Michigan (where O. D. Duncan also received his training) was on patterns of decentralisation in America, and he has published a number of essays on the causes and timing of this decentralisation—or sprawl—(Schnore, 1957a, 1957b, 1957c), paying close attention at the same time to the concomitant territorial annexation by the major cities (Schnore, 1962a; for a general discussion see Hawley's (1956) book on changes in metropolitan America).

From this initial work Schnore turned to the characteristics of suburbs, and more recently he has presented several tests of the zonal model. None would meet Quinn's (1940a) criteria for a full test; indeed while Burgess suggested a four-zone division of the residential area outside the CBD, Schnore has always used only a city-suburb dichotomy based on the administrative divides between the main city of an American census standard metropolitan statistical area (SMSA) and its peripheral communities. (To the non-American such a division seems amazingly arbitrary, but in the United States local government areas are much more than administrative units for the basic suburban services such as water, electricity, and garbage collection. They are the basic areal unit for education and are used extensively as social status devices. Thus city-suburb and suburb-suburb boundaries are often distinct social divides. The city-suburb dichotomy has some validity, therefore, although it is still a very simple device for testing the zonal model.)

As well as only a two-zone division, Schnore has ignored the sectoral model in his analyses, although his earlier work on types of suburbs (Schnore 1957a, 1957b, 1963a, 1963b) suggested intra-zonal variations. These were not discussed in relation to their location within the urban complex, however, and no test was presented of either the sector or the multi-nuclear model. A final, general criticism of Schnore's work is that he has dealt only with the largest SMSAs and urbanised Areas (UAs) in the United States. His defence of his approach has been that his work has 'primarily been directed towards an overview' (Schnore, 1968, 210), which is the best usage of the available census data and preferable to the detailed and tedious investigations of individual cases. The validity of this methodology may be doubted in the light of comments made in the rest of this chapter—and because Schnore himself is now using case studies (Schnore, 1968; Schnore and Evenson, 1966)

—but the work has formed a basis for more detailed thinking on the residential structure of cities.

City-Suburban Status Differences

The first of the papers relevant here, 'The Socioeconomic Status of Cities and Suburbs' (Schnore, 1963b), followed an earlier, brief note on the same topic (Schnore, 1962b), and presented city-suburban comparisons on percent of white-collar workers, median family income, and percent completing high school, for 200 UAs. From simple tabulations of the proportion of these places with higher values for suburbs than central cities, he concluded that 'the popular view of city-suburban differentials in socioeconomic status is derived mainly from the experience of the larger areas' (Schnore 1963b, 78). In an average presentation, values for the larger places bias the result so that 'the popular generalizations regarding city-suburban differences are accurate as descriptions of *individuals according to place of residence*, but they are misleading statements about *areas of habitation*' (Schnore, 1963b, 78). This was because the 38 largest—populations over 500,000—contained 70 percent of the total population of the 200 UAs, so that although the majority of suburban residents were of higher status than those of the central cities, in the smaller places 'the city itself is more likely to contain populations that are—on average—higher in status than those found in the suburban fringe' (Schnore, 1963b, 78).

An investigation of which of the 200 UAs had higher-status suburbs than central cities suggested that not only their size but also their age was closely related to the apparent relevance of the Burgess model (age was measured as the decade in which the central city first attained a population of 50,000). Higher suburban status was usually recorded for UAs with more than 500,000 residents in 1960, and also for those which first contained 50,000 in their central cities before 1880; the smaller and younger areas were more likely to exhibit the reverse of the expected pattern, with higher status in the central cities than in the suburbs. In a multivariate analysis using size, age, and percent of UA population living in the central city as independent variables (the third was included to standardise for varying amounts of annexation of suburban territory), age proved to be the best predictor of the direction of city-suburban differentials. The highest multiple correlation coefficient reported was only 0·5734, however, accounting for less than 35 percent of the variation in the dependent variable.

In his introduction to this paper, Schnore pointed out that suburbs lacking the characteristics ascribed to them by the Burgess model were common throughout the United States, and he concluded by asking whether the structures of the younger and older cities suggested a predictable 'evolutionary model'. He ascribed differences between the two types to the nature of the housing stock. The central cities of the older UAs comprise obsolescent dwellings not desirable for the upper status groups; this is not so in the younger centres, where decentralisation of functions from the CBD is also limiting the development of a zone of transition (as suggested by Hoyt in 1939). His evolutionary model proposed that 'with growth and expansion of the center, and with radical improvements in transportation and communication technology, the upper strata have shifted from central to peripheral residence, and the lower classes have increasingly taken up occupancy in the central areas abandoned by the elite' (Schnore, 1963b, 84). Nevertheless, Schnore pointed out (1963b, 85) that he had only thin evidence for this, and he suggested, but has not as yet published, more detailed analyses based on the finer grain of census tracts.

Intra-Metropolitan Distribution of Educational Status

A second paper (Schnore, 1964) contained a more detailed analysis of the degree of suburbanisation of status groups (with status defined as the completed years of education of persons aged 25 and over). Rather than a simple index, median school years completed, the city-suburban distributions of eight grades of education used in the census were tabulated (see Table IV.4), again for each of 200 UAs. Location quotients were constructed to indicate the degree of suburbanisation, values greater than 100 indicating that the group was over-represented in the central city and those of less than 100 indicating above average proportions in the suburbs. On the basis of the rank order of the eight indices for each place, a classification of the following six types of urban residential structure was developed:

A. The 'Tucson' type, whose 14 members exhibited a complete reversal of the Burgess pattern, with highly educated people concentrated in the central city and the less well educated living mainly in the suburbs.

B. The 'Albuquerque' type, whose ten members had a pattern similar to type A except that the groups with minimal education were less suburbanised (Table IV.4).

C. The 'Los Angeles' type, which was the modal category. In it, persons at the upper and lower ends of the educational scale were concentrated in the central city with the intermediate ranks over-represented in the suburbs.

D. The 'Baltimore' type (23 UAs), which deviated from the expected pattern of the Burgess zonal model only in the (slightly) relatively low level of suburbanisation of the college-educated population.

E. The 'New York' type, whose 67 members conformed to the zonal hypothesis for '(1) the city is characterized by an over-concentration of persons with minimal education, and (2) the suburbs are populated by a larger than expected proportion of persons with higher educational standing' (Schnore, 1964, 170).

F. The 'Miami' type whose four members displayed only one non-Burgess characteristic, the suburbanisation of the lowest educational group.

Finally, there were twelve areas—forming the 'Memphis' type—which could not be classified; they had each group similarly divided between city and suburb (Table IV.4).

This analysis implies that cities which conform to Burgess's zonal model were in a minority among the 200 UAs studied especially as the 'Baltimore' type could be viewed as a tendency away from the 'New York' towards the 'Los Angeles'. Schnore viewed the tendency in the other direction, however, and grouped types D and E together to give cities conforming to the zonal hypothesis a slight majority (types A and B were also amalgamated). In investigating reasons for the variation be

TABLE IV.4

RESIDENTIAL DISTRIBUTION OF EDUCATIONAL CLASSES: UNITED STATES, 1960[1]

TYPE	A	B	C	D	E	F	X
TYPE CITY	TUCSON	ALBUQUERQUE	LOS ANGELES	BALTIMORE	NEW YORK	MIAMI	MEMPHIS
SCHOOL YEARS COMPLETED							
None	90[2]	85	131	128	129	83	98
Grade: 1–4	93	81	113	124	119	137	101
Grade: 5–6	96	88	110	117	111	136	101
Grade: 7–8	99	93	99	104	107	115	101
High: 1–3	100	97	94	98	100	100	100
High: 4	101	103	97	86	91	89	99
College: 1–3	102	106	102	86	87	84	100
College: 4+	103	110	106	87	84	81	100
NUMBER OF AREAS	14	10	70	23	67	4	12

[1] The data refer to Urbanised Areas.
[2] The figures are location quotients; greater than 100 indicates that the group is over-represented in the central city, less than 100 that it is over-represented in the suburbs.

Source: Schnore, 1965b, 228.

tween UAs, he again pointed out the relevance of size, age, and amount of annexation; the larger and older places where the central cities had been least active in annexation were most likely to show the 'expected' Burgess pattern. Another important independent variable was also discovered; the most rapidly growing UAs were found less likely to have the expected pattern than the slower growing urban districts.

In concluding the discussion, Schnore again pointed out the possibility of an evolutionary pattern of zonal structures as cities grew and aged. He also pointed out that his findings related only to the white population, non-whites having very different patterns of city-suburban educational differentials, since 81 of the 180 UAs for which data were available were unclassifiable on the above scheme. Similar variations were also shown in a replication of Schnore's 1963 study by Schnore and Palen (1965), in which white and non-white patterns were separately discussed.

Income Groups

The above format was used again in an investigation of city-suburban differentials for 13 income categories (Schnore, 1966). Indices of centralisation (the same as the indices of suburbanisation in the earlier study) were produced, and the places grouped into four categories:

1. The 'Milwaukee' type, whose 74 members displayed the Burgess pattern with suburbanisation of high income groups and central city concentration of low income.
2. The 'New Orleans' type, with 83 members. In this, as in the 'Los Angeles' educational type, the extreme income groups were concentrated in the central city with those in the middle-income range over-represented in the suburbs (Table IV.5).
3. The 'Fort Smith' type, whose 19 members showed the same reversal of the Burgess pattern as the 'Tucson' type above in the education differentials study.
4. The 'Des Moines' type of 8 members with no recognisable pattern.

The evidence for the education study was equivocal on the modality of the concentric zonal pattern, therefore, but this investigation of income patterns showed the pattern with the highest and lowest socio-economic status groups concentrated in the central city as clearly the norm.

Schnore's major finding was of the irrelevance of Burgess's zonal model to a majority of United States UAs (and because it

TABLE IV.5

RESIDENTIAL DISTRIBUTION OF INCOME GROUPS:
UNITED STATES, 1960[1]

TYPE	A	B	C	X
TYPE CITY	MILWAUKEE	NEW ORLEANS	FORT SMITH	DES MOINES
FAMILY INCOME, 1959($)				
1,000	119[2]	115	82	103
1–1,999	119	114	88	102
2–2,999	118	114	89	104
3–3,999	117	108	94	102
4–4,999	114	103	99	101
5–5,999	107	94	108	98
6–6,999	102	89	112	101
7–7,999	98	85	113	99
8–8,999	96	87	113	99
9–9,999	96	88	117	100
10–14,999	89	92	119	99
15–24,999	67	102	122	97
25,000+	34	111	122	103
NUMBER OF AREAS	74	83	19	8

[1] Data refer to SMSAs.
[2] The figures are location quotients: a quotient greater than 100 indicates that the group is over-represented in the central city, less than 100 that it is over-represented in the suburbs.

Source: Schnore, 1966, 104.

appeared valid only for the largest and oldest of these it can be deduced that the model applies to only a small proportion of all cities in that country). For both income and education (no study of occupational patterns has been reported but Schnore and Jones (1969) indicated that one had been completed) a concentration of the highest and lowest status groups in the central city was more frequent than either the Burgess pattern or its converse, though it should be noted that for only

121 of the 184 areas included in both studies was the classification the same in both (indicating, among other things, the approximate nature of income and education as indices of socio-economic status). Schnore has inferred from this, and the relationships of the patterns with age, size, growth and annexation, that the middle classes move to the urban periphery before the upper classes, who move to the outer edges of the city only when it reaches a large size. Evidence presented later in this chapter suggests that this might not be the only interpretation, however.

Changing Status Distributions

As well as his major investigations of the 1960 residential structure of UAs, Schnore has also participated in studies of the changing structure over the previous decades (and later research in progress is covering an even longer time span, as discussed in his 1968 paper; some early results were given in Schnore and Evenson, 1966). In the first, as part of the 1964 paper, the question 'are the various educational classes becoming more or less like each other with respect to residence?' was answered by a study of educational patterns in 1940, 1950 and 1960 for the ten largest SMSAs. Of these, only Detroit (Table IV.6) and Washington provided unequivocal evidence of polarisation, with greater concentration of the better educated in the suburbs and the poorly educated in the central city, although Boston, Chicago, New York, Philadelphia, Pittsburgh, St. Louis and San Francisco did not deviate markedly from this. Los Angeles was exceptional; 'the city itself has gained persons of both high and low educational standing, but with a greater relative gain registered at the bottom of the educational ladder' (Schnore, 1964, 168).

This work was extended to cover 363 metropolitan areas for the 1950–1960 decade, using three rather than eight educational categories and producing six types of change (Schnore and Pinkerton, 1966). Increasing polarisation, as noted above for Detroit, was reported for 216 of the areas (Table IV. 7) and the 'Los Angeles' pattern of concentration of the two extreme groups in the central city occurred in a further 100. Tabulation of the results against a number of variables suggested the

Table IV.6

CHANGING EDUCATIONAL CLASS DISTRIBUTION: DETROIT, 1940–1960

SCHOOL YEARS COMPLETED[1]	PERCENT IN CITY			INDEX OF SUBURBANISATION			CHANGE OF INDEX		
	1940	1950	1960	1940	1950	1960	1940–1950	1950–1960	1940–1960
None	76·5	73·7	69·3	109·9	116·2	147·7	6·3	31·5	37·8
Grade: 1–4	72·1	71·3	64·6	103·6	112·4	138·3	6·8	25·9	34·7
Grade: 5–6	71·5	69·3	59·3	102·7	109·3	126·4	6·6	17·1	23·7
Grade: 7–8	69·1	62·8	51·4	99·3	98·8	109·5	−0·5	10·7	10·2
High: 1–3	69·0	62·2	45·9	99·1	98·1	97·8	−1·0	−0·3	−1·3
High: 4	70·4	61·2	40·5	101·2	96·5	86·3	−4·7	−10·2	−14·9
College: 1–3	69·9	63·3	40·1	100·4	99·8	85·5	−0·6	−14·3	−14·9
College: 4+	69·0	59·2	34·9	99·4	93·3	74·4	−5·8	−18·9	−24·7
TOTAL	69·6	63·4	46·9	100·0	100·0	100·0			

[1] For males aged 25 and over.

Source: Schnore, 1965b, 225.

TABLE IV.7

REDISTRIBUTION OF EDUCATIONAL CLASSES:
METROPOLITAN AREAS, 1950–1960

	PATTERN					
EDUCATIONAL CLASS	1	2	3	4	5	6
GRADE SCHOOL ONLY	D	D	D	I	I	I
SOME HIGH SCHOOL	I	I	D	I	D	D
SOME COLLEGE EDUCATION	I	D	I	D	I	D
NUMBER OF AREAS	216	100	12	16	9	10
Percent	59·5	27·5	3·3	4·4	2·5	2·8

D represents a disproportionate decline in the suburban population.
I represents a disproportionate increase in the suburban population.

Source: Schnore and Pinkerton, 1966, 495.

relevance of age and size; in accounting for differences in patterns of change smaller and younger metropolitan areas were most likely to be in the 'Los Angeles' type, suggesting that in the oldest cities (with the most deteriorated housing) the elite eventually leave their inner city neighbourhoods for the urban fringe.

In summarising the work to date, Schnore and Jones wrote in 1969 that

(1) smaller and younger central cities in the United States tend to be occupied by the local elite, while their peripheral, suburban areas contain the lower strata. With growth and the passage of time, however, this work implied that (2) the central city comes to be the main residential area for both the highest and the lowest strata, at least temporarily while the broad middle classes are overrepresented in the suburbs. (3) A subsequent stage in this evolutionary process is achieved when the suburbs have become the semi-private preserve of both the upper and middle strata, while the central city is largely given over to the lowest stratum. In a very rough fashion, of course, this last stage corresponds to the way in which the various social classes are arrayed in space according to the Burgess (1926) zonal hypothesis. (Schnore and Jones, 1969, 421–422).

In their own study, Schnore and Jones expanded the longitudinal analysis, using educational groups (they also noted two unpublished works which confirmed Schnore and Pinkerton's analysis (a) for smaller places and (b) for occupational groups). This involved replicating the 1960 study (Schnore, 1964) with 1950 data to enquire whether the evolutionary inferences were correct.

In general, Schnore and Jones felt their results disappointing, although there were many technical difficulties and the later discussion states that seminar audiences believed that 'the evolutionary hypothesis is given a large measure of support' (Schnore and Jones, 1969, 438). The 1950 cross-section again showed the age and size pattern and when the 1950 and 1960 typologies were compared it was shown that 64 percent of the places were in the same classes and a further 19 percent changed in the predicted direction (Table IV.8). Nevertheless, they

TABLE IV.8

CHANGES IN ZONAL PATTERNS: URBANISED
AREAS, 1950–1960

1950 TYPE	1960 TYPE				
	I	2	3	4	5
1. Highest educational classes over-represented in city	9	8	3	0	4
2. Highest and lowest over-represented in city	2	30	16	0	2
3. Lowest educational classes over-represented in city	0	3	49	0	0
4. Highest and lowest over-represented in suburbs	0	0	1	1	1
5. No systematic variation	0	3	9	0	1

Source: Schnore and Jones, 1969, 436.

concluded that 'based on the (1950–1960) change data in this analysis, however, we feel that the evidence for any evolutionary tendency is far from convincing, to say the least . . . the results of this study have not added very impressive weight to the work already completed' (Schnore and Jones, 1969, 437–438).

The Evolutionary Model: A General Statement

The series of papers by Schnore and his associates discussed so far has been very empirical in nature, aimed mainly at presenting the basic findings and making limited inferences from them (a reviewer of Schnore's work once described him as (Gutman, 1966, 282) 'an ecologist who obviously loves his data and believes in giving them an opportunity to speak for themselves'). The basic theoretical statement appeared in 1965, although Schnore and Jones (1969, 422) pointed out that it was prepared in 1962, before most of the empirical studies were conducted. The notion of an evolutionary process of city residential structure, from one in which socio-economic status of neighbourhoods declined with distance from the city centre to one in which it increased, was developed from a study of the literature on ecological patterns in Latin American cities (Schnore, 1965a). In particular, seven works were reviewed and the generalisations drawn from them were:

(1) All of the authors comment on the existence of the 'traditional' or 'colonial' pattern, in which higher-status groups tend to be found near the center. (2) In every case, however, this pattern is reported to be in one or another stage of 'breakdown'. (3) There is an apparent tendency for all of the cities (in Bolivia, Mexico and Guatemala) to shift in the general direction of the 'North American' pattern. (Schnore, 1965a, 358).

At least fifty other works were cited as supporting this conclusion, and a similar statement was made by Hoyt (1963) at about the same time.

The importance of these findings was that Schnore correlated the 'colonial' pattern with preindustrial cities generally, a view which was bolstered by quotations from Sjoberg's (1960) work on the preindustrial city, from Comhaire and Cahman's (1959) on the historical sociology of cities, and from work by Heberle (1948), Hoyt (1933, 1939) and others on the social topography of nineteenth-century US cities. The changing pattern in Latin American cities could be ascribed to the onset of modernisation, and so was relevant to the United States also at an earlier period, Schnore suggested it may be possible

that (a) the Burgess concentric zonal scheme, wrongly regarded as indigenous to the United States, and (b) the preindustrial pattern, erroneously identified as unique to

Latin America, are *both special cases more adequately subsumed under a more general theory of residential land uses in urban areas.* (Schnore, 1965a, 374).

His further research efforts have been aimed at formulating this theory, although when it was later pointed out that

> the law of urban development, at least in industrially-advanced countries, that the centre was declining in social status, and the suburbs were growing with high-income people, better educated and so on . . . was not true in cities as different as Paris, Milan, Warsaw, Barcelona, Amsterdam and Vienna, where the suburbs are left to the working class and seen as the worst part of the city (Bedarida, 1968, 212–213).

Schnore replied that he 'would be quite satisfied to be able to make a generalisation about the Anglo-Saxon world, and looked for no universal law' (Schnore, 1968, 213).

In elucidating his theory of Anglo-Saxon urban social topography, and in particular how the 'Latin American' zonal pattern became reversed and corresponded with that described by Burgess, Schnore suggested that importance of four independent variables (which Duncan and he (1959) have elsewhere defined as the ecological complex):

1. Environment, in particular the local topography, to which the spatial structure is adapted. (Although this may be an important factor in determining the exact urban form, as suggested by Amato (1969) in a study of Bogota, and by Forrest (1970) in work on Oamaru, New Zealand, it is doubtful whether a homogeneous physical environment would result in a structureless city, which seems to be Schnore's suggestion.)

2. Technology, notably technological change and the development of transport and communication facilities, which at first only the highest income groups can afford, and which allow the areal separation of functionally linked units, such as residence and workplace.

3. Three aspects of population:

(a) The city's size, which must reach a certain threshold before there is any significant development of socio-economic segregation.

(b) The city's rate of growth, as Burgess's model was one of urban growth, requiring central city expansion.

(c) The city's ethnic and racial composition. (Quinn (1940a) pointed out that the Burgess model assumed ethnic and racial heterogeneity, although socio-economic segregation would probably develop in its absence.)

4. Three aspects of the city's organisation:

(a) Its economic base, for the nature and distribution of non-residential uses will influence both social and spatial structure of the city.

(b) Its ecological organisation, particularly the contrast between the interdependent overlapping communities of industrial cities (Schnore terms the Latin American pattern as one of *cities composed of many communities*, and the United States as *communities composed of many cities*).

(c) Its social class composition, particularly the size and importance of a middle class.

Thus, the Burgess pattern is to be associated with large, rapidly-growing cities with mixed economies and populations, in which ease of movement is considerable and social classes are well developed.

There seems, however, to be some contradiction between the model as formulated for the United States on the basis of recent Latin American experience, and Schnore's discussion of his empirical studies in the former country. From the Latin American literature Schnore suggested that the *upper classes* left the central city first and moved to the periphery, setting up the concentric pattern first propounded by Burgess, and that this would have happened in the United States with the impact of the industrial revolution. (Hoyt, (1939, 82) presented evidence that in cities which have grown very little over the last century, the upper class still live close to the city centre.) But in the evolutionary sequence developed on the basis of the income and education patterns in UAs, Schnore suggested that the *middle class* first move to the suburbs, with a transition from 'Tucson' and 'Albuquerque' patterns (complete Burgess reversal), through 'Los Angeles' (centralisation of highest- and lowest-status groups) to 'New York' and 'Baltimore' (the

Burgess pattern). Much of the discussion in the rest of this chapter is oriented towards a possible reconciliation of these two views, for Schnore's model clearly offers a good working hypothesis for studying urban social topography.

Schnore's model has been considered in some detail because it probably represents the most significant development in the field since Burgess and Hoyt. Nevertheless it should be noted that it does not cover all of the hypotheses presented at the beginning of this chapter. The sectoral hypothesis is virtually ignored (although both Amato (1970) and Penalosa (1967) have successfully tested it recently in Latin American cities), and Schnore's use of the city-suburb dichotomy has not allowed full tests of the simpler zonal hypotheses; he has for example, provided no evidence that the highest-status groups actually live on the edge of the built-up area.

Testing of the hypotheses has been more difficult in other countries because of the relative paucity of data. The equivalents of the US census tract data were first made generally available in Britain for the 1961 Census, although special tabulations had been made for earlier studies (see Jones, 1960), and for Australia at the same date. Only in 1971 will they be made available in New Zealand for the first time. Researchers have thus made ingenious attempts to measure the status of areas, using such indices as possession of telephones (Williams and Herbert, 1962), pawnshop distributions (Robson, 1966), rating valuations (Herbert, 1967; Robson, 1969), entries in *Who's Who* (Johnston, 1966a, 1969c), settlement morphology (Whitehand, 1967), and even attendance at child-welfare clinics (Williams and Herbert, 1962). The following sections review such studies, in an attempt to expand on Schnore's findings.

AUSTRALASIAN STUDIES OF ELITE RESIDENTIAL AREAS

1. Melbourne Australia,

A cross-sectional test of the zonal and sectoral hypotheses for this city used the 1961 Census collectors' district data (Johnston, 1966c). There were more than 2,100 of these districts for the whole metropolitan area, with an average population of about 900 (see Jones, 1969), so the tests employed a 5 percent sample based on a geometric frame. The area was first divided into three sectors of various levels of socio-economic status (high, intermediate and low; the intermediate sector formed

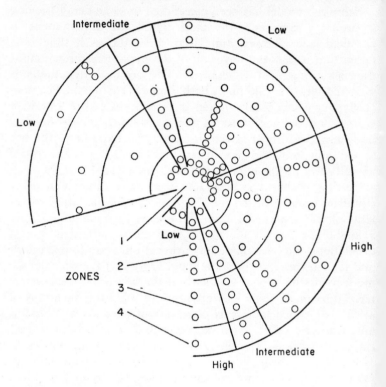

O Sample collector's district

IV.I   Schematic diagram showing the Zonal and Sectoral Distribution of Sample Collectors' Districts used in the study of the 1961 Census data for the Melbourne metropolitan area. *Source:* Johnston, 1969a.

two parts, giving six areas in all—Figure IV.1) on the basis of the educational level of the population. (This procedure was defended on the grounds that Hoyt did not suggest that sectors followed any geometric pattern but should be delimited pragmatically for each case.) Four zones were then defined to fit the number in Burgess's model, excluding the CBD. Each cell, zone within sector, was then represented by 5 percent of its constituent districts.

Unfortunately, no income or occupation information was provided, and only a surrogate for education (the proportion of the population aged over 15—the minimum school-leaving age—still in full-time education) could be obtained which paralleled the American data. Thirteen other measures were also selected, however (Table IV.9), and their spatial patterning tested by analyses of variance (see also Johnston, 1969d).

Of the 14 tests, only one did not produce a statistically significant pattern on the sectoral dimension (the exception was the proportion of males who were self-employed, Australia —like New Zealand (Franklin, 1969)—having a large self-employed element in most sectors of its society). This confirmed Hoyt's model, not surprisingly given the method of sectoral delimitation, but only five of the measures showed significant differences between the four zonal means; most of them were among the better indicators of socio-economic status (males with independent means, employers, males engaged in manufacturing, males in commerce, and males in public authority or professional jobs; Table IV.9).

The Hoyt model suggested zonal within the sectoral patterns, and the means for each variable indicated a fairly clear, though statistically insignificant, pattern, with the values for highest socio-economic status mainly in the second and third zones (Table IV.9). Only the proportion of self-employed males increased into the fourth zone, probably because of the large number of small horticultural holdings there. With males of independent means, for example, the value for zone 2 was twice that of 3 or 4. Thus, not only was there no significant zonal pattern, but that which appeared did not conform to the Hoyt model; the highest-status neighbourhoods were not on the urban fringe. Lack of statistically significant differences between zones was the result of variability within zones, suggesting that the geometrically-defined concentric system of zones was irrelevant.

Rodwin's critique of Hoyt's model suggested that different class groups might have different residential aspirations (Rodwin, 1961, 77), while Hoyt's own representation indicated

TABLE IV.9

ZONAL AND SECTORAL PATTERNS IN URBAN RESIDENTIAL STRUCTURE: MELBOURNE, 1961

	ZONAL MEANS[1]				SECTORAL MEANS[2]		
	1	2	3	4	HIGH	INTERMEDIATE	LOW
1. Education[3]	40·4	44·9	61·8	43·7	57·3	44·0	31·5
2. Independent Means[4]	1·5	2·3	1·1	0·4	2·0	1·9	0·9
3. Employers[4]	4·9	7·4	6·7	3·5	8·6	6·7	3·0
4. Self-Employed[4]	4·8	5·5	5·5	5·6	6·2	6·6	4·3
5. Manufacturing[4]	36·4	39·4	28·2	42·3	33·6	34·5	43·2
6. Transport and Utilities[4]	23·5	22·2	23·9	24·7	20·3	23·7	26·0
7. Commerce[4]	14·5	16·0	17·1	13·9	18·0	16·7	12·7
8. Finance and Property[4]	4·1	3·5	5·1	3·5	5·2	5·6	2·2
9. Public Authority and Professional[4]	2·7	4·1	5·6	3·7	5·0	4·6	3·1
10. Community and Business Services[4]	5·1	8·4	6·6	4·7	10·1	6·3	4·3
11. Women in Manufacturing[5]	37·8	35·4	31·1	40·5	28·2	31·0	44·7

1 Zone 1 is the inner zone, zone 4 the outer.
2 Sectors defined according to socio-economic status.
3 Percent those aged 15–20 in full-time education.
4 Percent employed males.
5 Percent employed females.

Source: Johnston, 1966c, 179–180.

little zonal differentiation in the lowest-status sector. Separate
statistical testing for the high- and low-status sectors of Melbourne
produced no better results, however, with only four significant
differences between zones in the high-status sector (the intermediate was not studied because of the small number of
districts). Whether this indicated a true representation of
reality or was the result of the imposition of a rigid, arbitrary
zonal framework and the poor data was not clear, however,

TABLE IV.10

ZONAL PATTERNS WITHIN SECTORS:
MELBOURNE, 1961

VARI-ABLE[1]	SECTOR ZONE	HIGH			LOW			
	1	2	3	4	1	2	3	4
1	44·6	62·2	61·8	43·7	35·0	31·3	30·2	27·6
2	2·0	3·1	1·5	0·7	1·0	1·4	0·5	0·2
3	4·3	12·0	9·5	4·1	4·7	3·6	3·2	2·0
4	3·9	6·6	6·1	8·1	4·8	4·4	4·3	2·9
5	37·0	32·9	31·6	35·2	37·2	45·8	42·0	50·3
6	22·4	17·6	21·4	21·3	25·0	26·0	26·5	27·1
7	11·9	19·9	19·7	17·5	13·3	12·3	13·7	10·9
8	1·3	5·6	7·3	4·0	2·5	1·7	2·3	2·5
9	3·0	4·8	6·2	5·3	2·1	3·2	4·8	2·2
10	10·0	14·2	7·6	7·6	5·2	3·5	5·5	2·4
11	38·8	22·7	24·8	34·1	38·7	49·0	40·9	51·8

[1] For key to variables see Table IV.9.

Source: Johnston, 1966c, 180–181.

although later discussion of other cities (pp. 330–340) suggests
the latter view.

Despite the lack of statistically significant results, however,
inspection of the zonal means for the two sectors suggested
interesting differences (Table IV.10). In the low-status sector
there were few commonalities between the 14 patterns; the
differences between means were often minimal. Only the self-
employed variable did not show the general patterns in the
high-status sector of the 'best' neighbourhoods in the intermediate zones of 2 and 3, however. This latter finding clearly
conflicts with the Burgess and Hoyt models, but the pattern
for the low-status sector was much as Hoyt and Rodwin might
have predicted.

The above investigation was extended to Melbourne's rural-urban fringe (Johnston, 1966b). If the city growth models, in particular Hoyt's, were correct, then the highest-status residents in each sector should be pioneering these new tracts and there should be marked differences in the populations of the various sectors within this outer zone. However, although there was some evidence of higher socio-economic status in the fringe than in the outer suburbs (for example in the proportion of males employed in manufacturing), between the two sectors there were significant differences in status in the outer suburbs and their most recent extensions but very few within the areas further out. This suggested a sharp transition from urban to rural with no extension of the suburban sectoral differences into the fringe.

Having shown a major deviation between model and reality at one date, it seemed desirable to test the longitudinal aspects of the model. No worthwhile census data were available so, apart from the sifting of contemporary suburban descriptions, only an index for the most prestigious neighbourhoods could be developed. This consisted of mapping the home addresses of all Melburnians listed in various editions of *Who's Who in Australia* since 1913; a source undoubtedly biased by the judgments of the compiler, but accepted as a valid indication of a society's elite elsewhere (Baltzell, 1953). In Australia it may be better, for a class structure based on inheritance rather than merit has had less time to develop there than in Britain, and even in the United States. The contemporary spatial pattern is very similar to that shown by census data (Jones, 1967b).

Accepting the addresses in *Who's Who* as indicative of the districts inhabited by the higher echelons of urban society, the research methodology was to map these addresses for 1913, 1922, 1933-4, 1941, 1950 and 1962 (Johnston, 1966a). Over this period of years the number of entries for Melbourne increased from 157 to 1,869, while the metropolitan population tripled (from 593,237 in 1911 to 1,911,896, in 1961). The addresses were mapped into a square-mile grid. With the rapid urban sprawl of the present century, the distribution of the elite became less concentrated over time, but the number of squares with one or more entries increased only by 400 percent compared with the 1,100 percent for the number of individuals (see Figure IV.2).

The major conclusion drawn from these maps was that the same square mile of Melbourne was the most desirable residential area for the elite at each of the six dates, and that, despite the great increase of Melburnians in *Who's Who*, its percentage of the total only dropped from 11 in 1913 to 9 in 1962. Yet this area is located within four miles of Melbourne's CBD, and at least ten miles from the nearest point on the edge of the built-up area in 1962. Also, of the ten squares with more than 34 elite residents at the last date (representing 20 percent of the number in the modal square), only three did not contain a similar proportion in 1913. All of these squares are clustered around the most prestigious, and the 'new' ones represented a slight eastward expansion of the most fashionable residential districts (Figure IV.2).

A brief glance at these maps suggests the irrelevance of the concentric zone model in Melbourne. The vast majority of its elite lived in the southeast of the city over the study period, in a two-pronged sector extending out from the same base but divided by a less desirable area (which contains considerable industrial development in its outer parts). Of the two prongs, the eastern has always contained the majority of the elite, mainly within the same area just east of the CBD. In the minor, coastal prong the mapped pattern suggested zonal change of the type suggested by Hoyt, for there has been a southward movement of the most desirable blocks along the cliffed coast and then to the hill suburbs some 30 miles south of the CBD (with an intervening swamp and sandhills area being 'leap-frogged').

Of the possible reasons for this major deviation from Hoyt's model with the inner suburban location of most of Melbourne's elite, the most compelling was the operation of social processes similar to those reported for Beacon Hill, Boston by Firey (1945, 1947). There was some evidence for this, for much of the area's residential development has been controlled by restrictive covenants on landuse, many of which were imposed in the nineteenth century but whose legal validity is still being upheld.

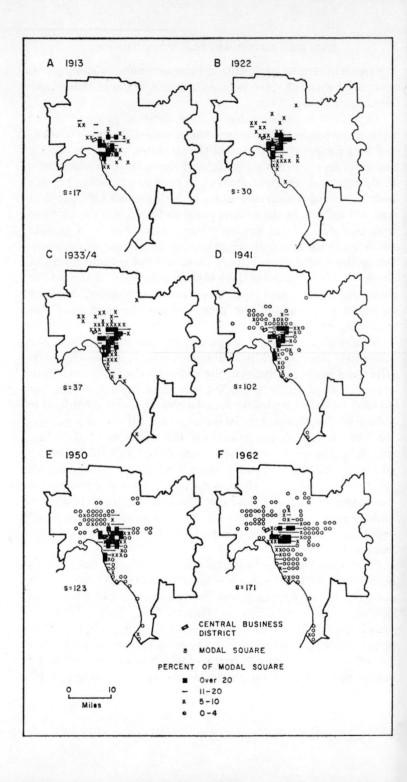

A 1913   B 1922

s=17   s=30

C 1933/4   D 1941

s=37   s=102

E 1950   F 1962

s=123   s=171

▰ CENTRAL BUSINESS
   DISTRICT

s MODAL SQUARE

PERCENT OF MODAL SQUARE
■ Over 20
— 11-20
x 5-10
o 0-4

0   10
Miles

Zoning restrictions helped retain the desirability, and this has been made possible also by the ability of the area to absorb the increase in elite population. Initial development of these high-class areas was in large, semi-rural estates of scores of acres in many cases, and these have been subdivided over the succeeding century to give greater densities of single-family homes (Johnston, 1968); at least sixteen new streets were constructed in the most fashionable square mile during a single year in the 1960s. In recent years, this ability to house greater numbers in the same area has been assisted by changes in tastes for types of dwelling. Despite the restrictive covenants, a large number of flats has been built in the area since World War II. The majority are expensive, but there has been some movement into the area of slightly lower-status residents, which may suggest that resistance in the area is weakening and invasion and succession may be commencing.

2. Christchurch, New Zealand

In the Melbourne study, the main emphasis was on the *pattern* of elite residences, although some *a posteriori* hypotheses were suggested concerning the *processes* related to the lack of change. But the Hoyt model suggested that:

1. The high status area should be continually moving outwards, to retain its position on the urban periphery (the *pattern hypothesis*).

2. Individual elite members should periodically move into new housing in more fashionable, developing suburbs (the *process* hypothesis).

As a test of both of these the basic methodology of the Melbourne study was used again in an investigation of high-status areas in the much smaller city of Christchurch, New Zealand (1966 population 247,248). The pattern hypothesis was tested by mapping the home addresses of the local residents listed in *Who's Who in New Zealand*, for 1951, 1956, 1961 and

---

IV.2 The Changing Distribution of High-status Residential Areas in metropolitan Melbourne. The data are the home addresses of Melburnians listed in *Who's Who in Australia* at the various dates, mapped into a square mile grid. *Source:* Johnston, 1966a.

1964, and the process hypothesis was investigated by studying the residential moves made by all these persons during the period of 13 years (Johnston, 1969c).

The resultant pattern was very similar to that noted for Melbourne (Figure IV.3), with the elite mainly living close to the city centre in the northwest sector (a second elite area occupied the lower slopes of the hills which fringe the city's southern boundaries). Over the thirteen years, however, some of the inner parts of the northwest sector lost status considerably, while outer parts apparently became more desirable, suggesting an outward migration of the elite areas.

According to Hoyt's model, the movement of the fashionable suburbs should result from elite out-migration from stylistically and technologically obsolescent dwellings to new ones in developing higher-class suburbs. But these people in Christchurch appear to have been fairly immobile, although there are no real yardsticks against which to judge this. Of the 59 persons listed in all four editions of *Who's Who*, 30 moved at least once between 1951 and 1964 (the median age of these persons in 1964 was 60–70, but the probability of movement did not vary with age); of the 52 listed in 1964 but not in 1951 but who were living in Christchurch at the earlier date (the median age of these was 50–60), 27 changed address at least once.

There appears to have been a high level of satisfaction with both dwelling and neighbourhood among the Christchurch elite as suggested for Melbourne, so the filtering mechanism is at least partially irrelevant. Even among those who changed address, the direction of their moves did not conform to the sector theory (Figure IV.4). During the 13 years there were only two moves from the established elite areas to the developing suburbs further out, as defined in Figure IV.4, and there were as many moves back from the outer areas to the older fashionable districts. The general impression given by the map of the moves is of a complex pattern of short-distance migration within the northwest sector, plus a slight net inflow into the southern hills suburbs.

Tabulations showed that the main component of the changing pattern of elite residences was the residential location of the

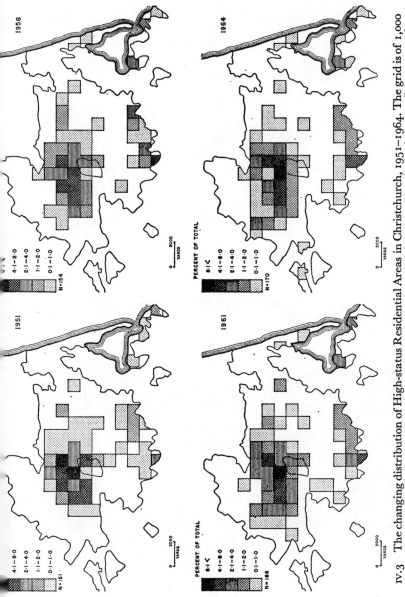

IV.3 The changing distribution of High-status Residential Areas in Christchurch, 1951–1964. The grid is of 1,000 yards square units, and the addresses were taken from *Who's Who in New Zealand. Source:* Johnston, 1969c.

MOVES BY PERSONS LISTED 1951-1964

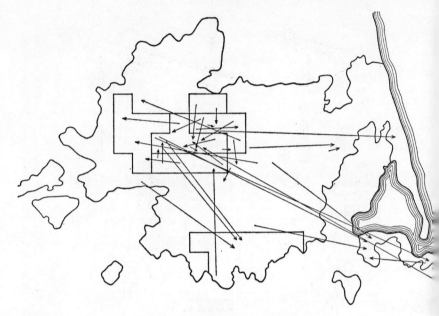

HIGH STATUS AREAS 1951-1964

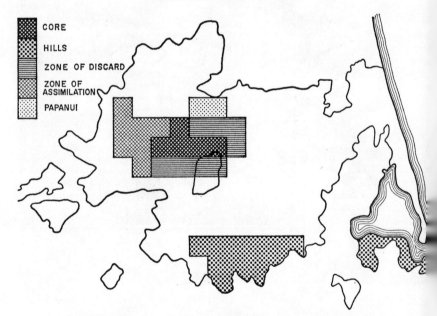

IV.4 A classification of High-status Residential Areas in Christchurch and the Moves among them, 1951–1964. *Source:* Johnston, 1969c.

new members of this group (Table IV.11). These persons presumably wanted a home and address which indicated their (perhaps potential at the time) elite membership, and probably

TABLE IV.11

PROCESSES OF CHANGE IN HIGH-STATUS
RESIDENTIAL AREAS: CHRISTCHURCH, 1951–1964[1]

Residents 1951	DISCARD	CORE	ASSIMILATION	HILLS	PAPANUI
	53	40	5	23	4
Omissions by 1956	18	10	1	8	1
Out-Migrants[2] 1951–1956	4	5	2	0	1
In-Migrants[3] 1951–1956	5	3	1	5	0
New Entries by 1956	4	11	12	9	6
Residents 1956	40	40	12	32	8
Omissions by 1961	11	12	1	3	2
Out-Migrants[2] 1956–1961	5	3	1	3	1
In-Migrants[3] 1956–1961	3	8	2	3	0
New Entries by 1961	10	16	7	15	5
Residents 1961	37	49	19	44	10
Omissions by 1964	13	11	7	7	3
Out-Migrants[2] 1961–1964	2	2	1	1	0
In-Migrants[3] 1961–1964	1	4	1	1	1
New Entries by 1964	0	13	4	5	1
Residents 1964	23	53	16	42	9

[1] Refers to individuals listed in *Who's Who in New Zealand*, 1951, 1956, 1961, 1964 editions.
[2] To other parts of Christchurch.
[3] From other parts of Christchurch.

Source: Johnston, 1969c, 9.

preferred new homes, which would have to be built in the developing suburbs. Elite members who died or left Christchurch mostly vacated older homes in the inner areas which would not have been desirable for new elite members, so that between 1951 and 1956 the zone of discard lost $4\frac{1}{2}$ times more elite residents than it gained, while the zone of assimilation gained nine but lost only one. In the 1961–1964 period, however, this latter zone lost more than it gained, suggesting a halt in the process of outward expansion.

Many of the homes in the core area of the northwest sector of Christchurch are as much as 50 years old, but this area has housed 40 of the new elite and was the destination for 15 of the intra-city moves (compared to 20 and 4 respectively for the zone of assimilation). Continued popularity of the core area seems related to the same factor as noted for Melbourne; its ability to absorb an increase through greater housing densities. The result was that the older members of the elite continued to live in their relatively large, often two-storey homes, while the younger element occupied new homes constructed in the former gardens of the older dwellings. Eventually the older homes were vacated; the younger elite did not take them over because of their relative obsolescence, and instead they have been split into flats, so that the area contains a mixture of two populations.

In Christchurch, therefore, because of the subdivision potential of the older elite suburbs, locational obsolescence of an area has not occurred concurrently with the stylistic and technological obsolescence of the original homes. The previously considered pattern-less migrations also fit this process, for many of the moves originating and terminating within the zone of discard were from the older homes into new dwellings on the recent subdivisions. Thus, filtering has taken place with movement into new homes, but there has been no attendant neighbourhood change as suggested by Hoyt.

While this process of neighbourhood repletion has been taking place within the lower-density core of the northwest sector (the zone of discard was developed at greater initial densities and so offered fewer opportunities for subdivision), suburbs of a lower status have been built further out, engulfing the elite areas by a general middle-class sprawl. And this is not peculiar to Christchurch, for McGee has recently pointed out for Auckland and Wellington that:

> there is no marked upward gradation in social grades towards the outer suburbs of these urban areas. Indeed . . . the upper-graded social areas abut directly on to the areas of the lower

social grades. Then there is a gradation outwards through upper-middle graded areas to middle graded areas on the fringes. The two exceptions to this pattern both . . . fall into the category of 'engulfed villages' swamped by the outward movement of the wealthier inhabitants of the city. They may be typical of the American pattern, but they are still largely anomalies in the New Zealand context (McGee 1969, 163–165).

From these observations, McGee suggested a major cause of the pattern to be the relative immobility of urban New Zealanders (for which there is little evidence for or against), suggesting that

> Once they have bought a house they tend to remain there for the rest of their lives; they are unmotivated by the prospects of residential status a shift in residence might obtain when they are wealthy enough . . . While information is scant, there are indications of increasing mobility among urban New Zealanders, and it is possible to suggest that in the future the American motivations may prevail, particularly as social stratification increases (McGee, 1969, 168).

McGee presented an alternative to the Burgess-Hoyt static model of the city for the New Zealand context (Figure IV.5) in which most of the high-grade areas were engulfed within the general middle-class suburbia which is spawned by the country's 'suburban peasantry' norms and its liberal house-purchase finance schemes. With this development of fashionable enclaves, once repletion is completed (assuming that it is possible) alternative locations must be sought for a growing elite. Simple outward expansion into lower-grade areas is socially undesirable (and financially impossible if redevelopment is to occur), unless building style declines in importance as a status symbol. New, fashionable districts must develop elsewhere; for a while, as McGee suggests, they may be on the urban fringe but, except in cases like the Christchurch hill suburbs, where little further outward development is possible, they will probably be outflanked by more general suburban development within a few years.

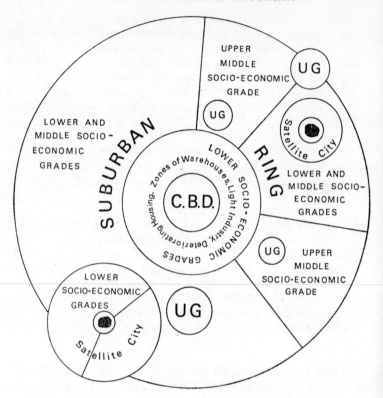

UG   Nodes of Upper Socio-Economic Groups

●   Retailing Centre

IV.5 A schematic diagram of the Major Elements in the Residential Pattern of New Zealand cities. *Source:* McGee, 1969.

NEIGHBOURHOOD PATTERNS IN THE UNITED KINGDOM

Few detailed studies have been made of the residential structure of British cities, undoubtedly reflecting the slow growth of sociology there, the lack of geographic interest in such matters, and the general paucity of data. Available information, however, suggests considerable similarities with patterns already discussed; for example, in Butlin's (1965) statement on the movement of Dublin's elite away from the city centre during the seventeenth century.

Manchester

Processes of high-status neighbourhood change have been studied in Manchester, where Rodgers (1962) traced the movement of the upper-middle classes away from the burgeoning industrial areas of the city centre and into rural areas which offered the desirable quality of fresh air. As the commercial metropolis grew, the merchant and industrial aristocracy separated themselves from the middle classes and moved into large villas set in exclusive parks (often protected by tollgates) alongside the roads following the higher ridges, especially to the south of the city. One such park, about three miles from the centre, covered 140 acres of land, but soon after it was developed in the 1830s railway expansion allowed a scattering of the elite to park developments 10–15 miles out. By the 1860s, according to Freeman (1962), the outlines of the present Manchester conurbation were set, and since then most expansion has merely filled in this framework.

The outer suburban parks on Manchester's fringe have remained as nuclei for better-class development, but those in the inner areas have been engulfed by inferior dwellings. For some time the latter were protected by their exclusiveness but in recent decades social and physical decay has been rapid; Rodgers has suggested a cycle of decay and change which starts with 'the occasional conversion of the most rambling houses into flats of a very pleasant type' (Rodgers, 1962, 11) and proceeds into either a dominance of flats and racial mixture or conversion to industrial uses.

Edinburgh

Manchester's pattern thus conforms closely to Hoyt's sectoral model, with the main deviation that the outer limits have remained stable for a long time, although they are now expanding rapidly in some parts. There was, of course, no complete high-class sector, just as Firey showed for Boston, but a series

157

of pockets of more fashionable homes within a general middle-class matrix (much as McGee showed for New Zealand). Gordon (1966) has recently mapped a similar pattern for Edinburgh—using property valuations as his index—but with other important exceptions. Apart from new fashionable suburban development in the south and west (on reasons for the choice of this part of the city see Smith, 1966) he noted the continued prestige of many inner suburbs. Thus for 1914 the upper-middle class areas were grouped into:

1. Those which were upper-middle class in 1855 and retained that status.
2. New areas developed since 1855 (the date of the previous mapping).
3. Those which were upper class in 1855 but had since declined in status.

and he noted that 'one interesting change in overall location was that the upper middle class areas were no longer the outer-most status areas' (Gordon, 1966, 23). Similarly, of the 1962 upper-class districts:

1. Some were remnants of the 1855 districts.
2. Most of the 1914 districts, except those close to the CBD invaded by commercial uses and a few subdivided into flats, retained their status.
3. Some were upgraded 1914 middle class areas.
4. Some were new areas developed on the urban margins.

While Rodgers's work tended to confirm the American models, therefore, Gordon's results were closer to those reported for Australasian cities. In reviewing his maps, the latter pointed out that in both 1914 and 1962 many more community leaders lived in central rather than peripheral residential areas. These would be in relatively old homes, for there is little room for repletion in Edinburgh, and it is interesting to note that these areas expanded by an upgrading of neighbouring middle-class areas. Collison and Mogey's (1959) study of Oxford also showed this phenomenon.

Sunderland

Recent study of Sunderland by Robson (1966, 1968, 1969) has provided a full description of the ecology of a British town in contrast to the concentration on higher-status areas in Manchester and Edinburgh. He first used rating values to pick out different status areas, and their changes between 1850 and 1963, along with data on the amount of subdivision of houses (Robson, 1966). He found validity for both the sectoral and the zonal model, within the private housing areas. South of the CBD, four sectors were recognised (Figure IV.6), three

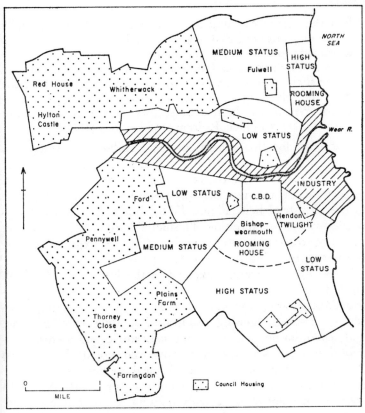

iv.6   The general pattern of Social Areas in Sunderland. *Source:* Robson, 1969.

of which were zonally structured in that the inner, older areas contained high proportions of subdivided homes. North of the River Wear and its associated industrial belt the structure was zonal, terminating with middle-class housing areas except in the coastal belt where there was a high-status district whose inner portions had been converted into a rooming-house district.

Clearly much in these results fits the hypotheses proposed earlier in this chapter, and the processes of neighbourhood change were also generally as expected, although Robson pointed out major differences between two types of subdivided housing areas:

> first the classic rooming house area to which the typically single or young married, transient and mobile population is attracted; and secondly the more residentially stable type of area which contains families of manual workers and is of lower social status . . . Both to the north and south of the river the (classic) rooming house areas are . . . at the townward apex of the high class sectors—again in accordance with the Hoyt model (Robson, 1966, 130–131).

To account for this general pattern, Robson suggested two factors: attraction to the CBD and repulsion from industrial areas. To the south of the city, a high-class sector developed because access to the CBD was possible without living close to the industrial belt (Figure IV.6), but to the north, access would involve juxtaposition of fashionable residential areas and industry, so a zonal pattern developed instead, with the highest status groups living on the urban periphery.

These findings were confirmed in the later study (Robson 1968) based on a factorial ecology of census enumeration district data. Four components were extracted, representing socio-economic status, housing conditions, subdivision of housing, and urbanisation, and the same concentric and sectoral distribution patterns as discussed above were noted. Nevertheless Robson pointed out that the classical models were mainly relevant to Sunderland's nineteenth-century pattern, for in 1961 40 percent of the town's housing was publicly owned, and a map in the 1968 paper showed how the distribution of these distorted the general pattern. Indeed, Robson had

earlier concluded that 'the game of hunt the Chicago model
seems to be exhausted as far as modern developments in
[British] urban areas are concerned' (Robson, 1966, 138),
although he quoted the blurring of social differentials as another
reason for this. Whether government activity in the housing
market should completely invalidate models developed for the
private sector is doubtful. It could be taken as a distorting
factor, or it may be an extension of the general patterns discussed here. Certainly the effect of council housing is considerable, as shown by Jones (1962), Forrest (1970) and Mabry
(1968).

In the most detailed discussion of his researches, Robson
(1969) mainly repeated the earlier findings. One extra set of
information, however, referred to the effects of the public
housing sector on the ecological pattern in Sunderland.
Correlation analyses were run separately on 30 (mainly
census) variables for the whole town and for the private sector
only. Within the latter the pattern of associations seemed to
correspond closely to the structures discussed in Chapter II,
but when the public sector was also included in the ecological
pattern it was more obscure. The private housing areas were
characterised by variations in their social and family status and
housing conditions, but the main differences between council
housing areas were age structure and household composition
and size (so that, for example, housing conditions varied
considerably between persons of similar status according to
whether or not they had a council house). A principal components analysis was only conducted on the total matrix,
however, so little information is available on spatial patterns of
council housing areas. Nevertheless, some of the components
at least partly reflected such differences (for example, one
contrasted the age structure of council areas), and a typology
of districts based on them separated estates of various ages
from each other and from areas of council flats. Thomas
(1966) and others have shown movement between estates,
some of which are generally accorded more prestige than others,
but as yet little detail has been provided on this topic.

Belfast

Very similar broad spatial patterns to those in Sunderland were noted in Belfast by Jones (1960). (Robson (1966, 137) claimed that Davie's (1938) maps of New Haven also displayed the same pattern.) Following very detailed discussions of the residential structure of Belfast as shown by the 1951 Census, Jones suggested that 'east of the Lagan . . . concentric zones are clearly differentiated' while 'Belfast west of the Lagan . . . lends itself to Hoyt's scheme' (Jones, 1960, 273). Like Firey, however, Jones claimed that fits between model and reality in terms of spatial pattern did not give causal accounts for the actual distributions. He suggested that the sectoral pattern of high-status residences (Figure IV.7) developed as the result

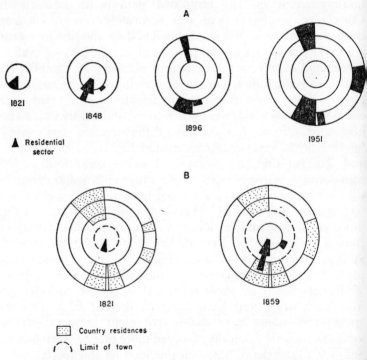

IV.7 Schematic representations of the location of Fashionable Neighbourhoods (residential sectors in the diagrams) in Belfast. *Source:* Jones 1960.

of social values, in particular the type of country into which they expanded, which was mainly composed of country estates (see also Smith, 1966). He claimed that although Hoyt suggested the role of community leaders and the location of their homes 'he does not make out a specific case—as seems necessary here—for the investing of land beyond an expanding town by social values which will become of paramount importance in deciding the future use of that land' (Jones, 1960, 279), and that it was not the physical structure of higher land that made it desirable, but the social valuation of altitude. But he asked too much of the model; Hoyt recognised the role of social values in determining the direction of sectors in a city, and presumably he stressed the role of certain physical features such as altitude and water frontages because of the social valuation given them.

The role of social valuations of environment was stressed in a recent adaptation of the Burgess-Hoyt models to industrial towns in northern England. From observations in Huddersfield, Nottingham and Sheffield, Mann (1965) suggested that higher-status neighbourhoods are found to the west of the city because the prevailing wind is from that direction and upwind locations avoid the pollution produced by industrial areas. His discussion was mainly based on Burgess's model, but he noted sectoral differences, such as: 'the examples of transition are best seen on the sides of the city which lead to the more middle class residential areas' (Mann 1965, 81); the outer zones contained planned council housing estates, haphazard private building development, and engulfed former villages (see Pahl, 1965). He presented an overview of this pattern (Figure IV.8), assuming a prevailing westerly wind, stating

> It is not claimed in any way that the above diagram depicts any town or city in this country. But if, by applying it to a city a better understanding of the ecological problems is gained, then the outline is justified (Mann, 1965, 96).

This is the rationale of most of the present book, also.

London

No one study of Britain's metropolis completely describes its residential structure, but important aspects can be gleaned

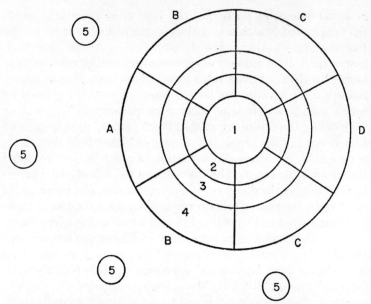

iv.8   Schematic representations of the Location of Residential Areas in industrial cities of Northern England.

KEY: 1, City Centre; 2, Transitional Zone; 3, Small Terrace Houses in Sectors C and D, Larger Bye-Law Houses in Sector B, Large Old Houses in Sector A; 4, Post-1918 Residential Areas, post-1945 on the periphery; 5, Commuting distance villages—A. Middle-class Sector; B. Lower-middle-class Sector; C. Working-class and main Municipal Housing Sector; D. Industry and Lowest Working-class areas. *Source:* Mann, 1965.

from a number of works. The first, and in many ways major, study was Booth's massive survey in the 1890s, although it is not generally recognised as an ecological work. It was a study of poverty and its causes, but Booth's seventeen volumes provided much information on the residential pattern of London (much of it in map form). Even more, as Pfautz (1967) has recently observed, many of Burgess's observations on Chicago in the 1920s parallel those made by Booth about London 30 years earlier ('residential London tends to be arranged by class in rings with the most uniform poverty at the centre'; Booth, 1889–1902, Final Volume, 205), and the latter's general law of successive migration (Booth, 1889–1902,

Religious Series, Volume V, 194) has much in common with the filtering and invasion and succession hypotheses.

Apart from the Atlas of London (Jones and Sinclair, 1968) based mainly on the 1961 Census but with no detailed commentary, the only recent London-wide survey has been Westergaard's (1964) analysis of 1951 census data. He defined six suburban types for the conurbation, whose distribution (Figure IV.9) followed a zone-within-sector pattern. Most inner suburbs were of low quality, with areal status increasing to north and south (more rapidly in the former), but to east and west working-class areas extended along the Thames to the urban periphery, except in the northeast where the middle-class area of Wanstead was situated (see Willmott and Young, 1960). The exception to the Hoyt model was in the mixed area of London's West End, containing both slums and some of the most desirable residences (the latter, according to Hauser (1951, 128) owe their stability to 'an ideal connection with places of work, recreation and civic activities'). A similar pattern was adopted by Smailes (1964) in his discussion of London's townscape.

Like Edinburgh, therefore, London has some of its best residential areas very close to the heart of the city, near to the political centre at Westminster which forms the apex for the whole northwest sector that ends with the 'cocktail belt' of the Chilterns (Reeder, 1968; Whitehand, 1967). Inner parts, such as Chelsea, declined in status but have been rejuvenated in recent years. Interesting accounts of how the other sectors obtained their residential characteristics are given in Pollins's study of relationships between social divisions and transport lines:

> The great working class concentration in north-east London, between the Lea and the Thames, is to some extent due to the enormous number of workmen's trains which the G.E.R. ran in the last quarter of the nineteenth century (Pollins, 1964, 43)

and the stability of status in the working-class areas has been described by Ashworth:

> The house ... vacated was most likely to be taken by a family of a social rank similar to that of the previous occupier. As

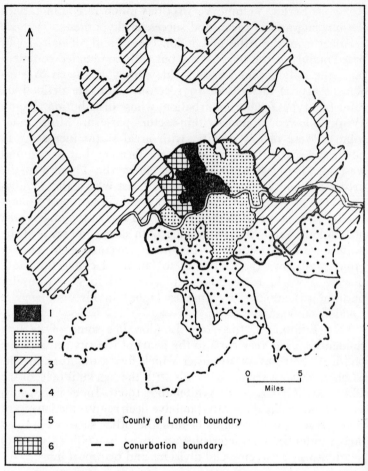

iv.9   Social Areas in Greater London, 1951.
       KEY: 1, Centre; 2, Inner Working Class; 3, Middle and Outer Zones
       of relatively Low Status; 4, Southern Intermediate Zone; 5, Outer
       Zones of Relatively High Status; 6, West End and Hampstead.
       Source: Westergaard, 1964.

houses deteriorated with age and as acceptable minimum
standards of residential accommodation were raised, the
social character of older districts might . . . be expected
gradually to fall . . . But it was very gradual and slight
(Ashworth, 1964, 80).

RESIDENTIAL PATTERNS OUTSIDE
THE US: A SUMMARY

These and other studies in Britain, Australia and New Zealand have all confirmed the hypothesis of sectoral patterns of socio-economic status. On zonal patterns within sectors, especially the high-status sectors, however, evidence is equivocal. In Melbourne, Christchurch and other Australasian cities, suburbs relatively close to the CBD have retained their prestige for long periods and have been outflanked by middle-class neighbourhoods. High-status areas close in were also noted for London and Edinburgh but not for Belfast and the industrial cities of northern England. In the British examples, the centrally-located elites occupied old dwellings, but in the Australasian cities many were living in new homes in older suburbs.

No clear reasons for these findings have emerged, but the following might be suggested:

1. Address has remained an important status symbol, but the style of the dwelling has not. Large opulent homes are financially impossible to run, and developments in architecture are now no longer the general status symbols that they were. Many of the upper class are now content with older homes in 'good' areas now that high-standard housing is available to a wide portion of the class spectrum, and so they choose to display their status in other ways.

2. In very large cities, peripheral homes involve long-distance commuting to the CBD, where most of the elite work. Such a residential location would only be preferred by those with strong demands for space not attainable with central city land values, so that others would accept higher density living (still in single-family dwellings) in inner suburbs.

3. In Australia and New Zealand, owner-occupation of a house in its quarter-acre plot is strongly entrenched in society norms (Donald Horne (1965) called this suburban peasantry), and great efforts are made to help the mass of the population achieve this goal. In New Zealand, for example, low-interest loans are provided for almost all the lower-income groups,

social security payments for children can be capitalised to provide a deposit, and insurance companies run schemes to allow land acquisition by hire purchase (it is estimated that 20 percent of all new homes are bought without the occupier requiring any capital for a down-payment). In addition, some 10 percent of the annual construction rate is of State housing. Such policies, which are particularly directed at the purchase of new homes, encourage sprawl, so that unless the elite are prepared to move frequently or, like the hill suburb residents in Christchurch, are protected from lower-class outflanking, peripheral location of the highest-status areas is unlikely.

In Britain, many of the households obtain their 'castles' by renting houses from local authorities. Large-scale development of council estates also produces outflanking.

4. In rapidly-growing cities, either the elite will have to move frequently to remain on the periphery or they must resist invasion of their neighbourhoods by lower-status groups, and become outflanked. Infilling and interstitial filling are alternatives to outward expansion, as Hoyt (1939, 96) pointed out. In Manchester, and the industrial cities studied by Mann and Jones, population growth has been relatively slow in the present century and the peripheral high-status areas established before then may have come under very little pressure since. Thus Hoyt's model seems more appropriate to such places than to others, such as London, Edinburgh, and Melbourne, where the elite would wish to remain in contact with the CBD and where the inner city environment would not be as repulsive as, say, in Sheffield.

THE UNITED STATES REVISITED

The first studies reviewed in this chapter, by the Duncans, Blumenfeld, and Davies, gave some hints that zonal patterns were not always as hypothesised, and the sections prior to this have given strong support to such a conclusion. Schnore's work in the United States suggested that the Burgess model was widely applicable, especially in older cities, but in view of the later discussion it seems necessary to re-open the topic for that country, in an attempt to develop a general process model.

1. The Central City Location of Elite Areas

Schnore suggested that his findings indicated an evolutionary trend by which the highest-status groups moved to the periphery of the city, but investigation of his data sources suggests that he was really discussing a much larger group. With education, for example, half a million people in New York (12 percent of those aged over 24) had four or more years of college education in 1960, and 45 percent of them lived in the central city. These represent much of the middle class, as do the white-collar workers whose distributions formed indices of areal status in other studies. Only Schnore's third measure of socio-economic status, median family income above $25,000 in several studies, refers clearly to the upper class, but in Detroit, for example, these form 2 percent of the families and 30 percent of them lived in the central city in 1960.

Schnore's studies might be reinterpreted, therefore, as showing that in the largest, oldest centres the upper-middle classes tend to live in the suburban municipalities, and there is no explicit evidence that the most fashionable areas are on the periphery. Indeed, Schnore has noted this several times, remarking on 'the persistence of elite areas near the centers of many cities' (Schnore, 1963b, 84); in a later statement he claimed:

> I'm sure there's one of these in every city. There's a tendency for one or two little enclaves of great wealth, despite the fact that on the average city inhabitants are much less well-educated, much poorer, and have much lower status occupations (Schnore, 1968, 213).

But this statement suggests that such elite areas are small deviations from a general pattern, although they are common.

Other studies have suggested that patterns in United States cities are similar to those described for Australian, British and New Zealand centres, although home purchase is not as easy for younger people in the United States (for the 1950 Census, Abu-Lughod and Foley (in Foote *et al*, 1960) quoted an average age of 35 at the time of first home purchase). Dobriner, for example, has attempted to explode the myth of homogeneous, middle-class suburbia consisting of 'warrens of young executives on the way up' (Dobriner, 1963, 38), by showing that suburbs are very variable in character, including many of the lower middle class whose lives are 'secure, unexciting and comfortable': in addition 'the working classes are also outward bound on the suburban trail'. Detailed study of one working-class suburb by Berger (1960) showed that Whyte's description of Chicago's Park Forest as full of organisation men intent on upward social mobility (Whyte, 1960) was not typical of American suburbia. As in Australasia, suburbs in the United States now house a wide, if not complete, range of social groups, a fact noted by Schnore in his earlier works (Schnore, 1957c, 1963a).

New York, according to Schnore (1964), has a zonal pattern in accord with the Burgess model, but Hoover and Vernon's (1962) chapter on 'Who Lives Where and Why?' in that metropolitan area provides evidence in support of the alternative view being formulated here. They divide the New York region into (1) Manhattan, (2) the Core outside Manhattan, (3) the Inner Ring, and (4) the Outer Ring, and showed that both of the highest status occupation groups (professional/technical and administrative/managerial) were under-represented in the Core outside Manhattan and over-represented in the Inner Ring. Fewer managers than expected on the basis of total population distribution were also noted for the Core and the Outer Ring; professionals were over-represented in both of these zones, but only slightly so in the latter. Similarly, the two highest average per capita personal incomes were recorded for Inner Ring counties, followed by Manhattan, one Outer Ring county, and two other Inner Ring counties; Hoover and Vernon concluded that the top income group inhabited three different types of neighbourhood:

1. The apartment areas of central Manhattan.
2. The older exclusive suburbs of the Inner Ring which are well protected by zoning.
3. 'The deliberately inaccessible—hence, naturally exclusive —exurb' (Hoover and Vernon, 1962, 165).

On the other hand, the lower-income population had little choice and predominated in the old, former middle-class suburbs where they could rent apartments and homes, while the middle classes shifted away from such obsolescent property and into the suburbs because of 'the rising trend of living standards. A middle-income household today wants and can afford a somewhat better house than did a household in a corresponding middle position in the income scale a generation ago' (Hoover and Vernon, 1962, 303–304; see also Clark 1966, on the role of suburban political structure).

Similar findings have been reported by Goldsmith and his associates, whose research methodology has been similar to Schnore's except that instead of the city-suburban dichotomy they have divided metropolitan areas into:

1. Their central cities.
2. Their suburbs; the contiguous parts of the UA outside the central cities which met certain density and land use requirements.
3. Their fringe areas, within the SMSA but not within the UA (Murphy, 1966, contains a good discussion of these census concepts).

Where possible, the populations of these outer suburban zones were split into their urban, rural non-farm and rural farm population components.

The first paper using this approach dealt with the SMSAs which in 1960 had 1 million inhabitants and whose central cities contained at least 50,000 by 1870. It showed a consistent pattern in which 'white residents of suburbs had a higher socio-economic status than the white residents of either city or fringe areas' (Goldsmith and Lee, 1966, 212). Generally the magnitude of the differences was small, except between city and suburb, but the findings contradicted Schnore's conclusion that these were the UAs that showed the Burgess pattern.

The second study, by Goldsmith and Stockwell (1969a), dealt with 76 SMSAs that had populations greater than 300,000 in 1960: it investigated patterns of occupational selectivity, in a similar way to Schnore's later research method. Four groups of central cities were identified, with two of them—containing 39 of the 76—characterised by an over-representation of at least three of the four white-collar occupations. In 47 cases the

suburbs had over-representation of white and under-representation of blue-collar workers, and the most common pattern
in the fringe areas (for 36 of the 67 for which data were available) was 'under-representation of the white collar occupations
and service workers and . . . over-representation of craftsmen,
operatives and laborers' (Goldsmith and Stockwell, 1969a,
200); six others differed from this only through an over-representation of service workers.

A general pattern deducible from these researches is of a
low-status central-city, high-status suburban ring and inter-
mediate-status fringe area. Goldsmith and Stockwell noted,
however, that almost as many fringe areas of SMSAs with the
above central city and suburban patterns had over- rather than
under-representation of white-collar workers, and interpreted
this as 'suggesting that the Burgess hypothesis . . . does have
some validity' (Goldsmith and Stockwell, 1969a, 202). Like
Schnore, they found that 'the older, larger, northern, industrial
SMSAs are more likely to have internal selectivity patterns
consistent with the Burgess hypothesis than are the newer,
smaller, predominantly southern SMSAs' and they agreed with
Schnore that 'residential distributions in the larger metropolitan
areas evolve in a predictable pattern' (Goldsmith and Stockwell, 1969a, 203).

In a third paper, Goldsmith and Stockwell investigated
whether certain occupational selectivity patterns were features
of certain types of urban areas, by correlating the occupational
selectivity 'profile order' of the 14 sub-sets against 29 independent variables. (The 14 sub-sets were divisions of the 4 main
types discussed in the preceding paragraph. The 'profile order'
ranked these from 1 to 14, from that with all four white-collar
occupations over-represented in the central city to that with
most of the white-collar groups under-represented. Most of the
independent variables were averages for the metropolitan areas
in the various subsets.) Statistically significant correlations were
recorded in 19 of the cases, suggesting to the authors that 'the
older, larger, primarily northern water-based industrial centers
have different occupational selectivity patterns than do the
newer and smaller, predominantly southern metropolitan areas'
(Goldsmith and Stockwell 1969b, 389).

THE CHANGING SOCIAL TOPOGRAPHY

Such findings again generally agree with Schnore's evolutionary model, but Goldsmith and Stockwell (1969b, 394) cautioned that:

> although the data are consistent with the position that large cities grow in a predictable pattern, it is dangerous to draw conclusions regarding social and economic change from cross-sectional data. It might be more appropriate to view the observed patterns of the older and larger cities and of the newer and smaller ones as representing responses to the new faster, more flexible modes of transportation and communication that have developed in the past 20 or 30 years. In the older and larger cities, the original need for intensive use of land at the center of the city can give way to a more horizontal and less intensive use of land at the periphery ... The newer cities can develop initially with dispersed but accessible patterns of activities, since there is less need for intensive use of land at the center of the city.

Despite its slightly more detailed zonal framework, Goldsmith's work has also concealed much of the possible pattern. Because there is little doubt that most cities contain major sectoral patterns of socio-economic status, then the great variety of neighbourhood characteristics within each zone could produce the relative similarity between central city, suburb and fringe which was noted by Goldsmith and Lee (1966). Laserwitz once noted that although the general city-suburban differences of the Burgess hypothesis still exist, 'another suburban trend is a growth in occupational heterogeneity' (Laserwitz, 1960, 252). Powers (1964a, 1964b) made the same point more forcefully after an investigation of the amount of heterogeneity in the predominantly white central cities and suburbs of 13 New England SMSAs. Although the suburban areas registered the highest socio-economic levels, with income her main finding was '*not* that the income level of families in both locations is the same, but that the similarity is greater than the difference' (Powers, 1964b, 132). Much of the central city-suburban difference could, in fact, be accounted for by the difference in the ages of the two populations and in their housing stock; for example 'persons 65 years old and over are disproportionately represented among the lowest educat-

173

ional categories' (Powers, 1964b, 136) and these persons are concentrated within the central city (as the family-cycle models suggest; see the next chapter).

A suggestion that United States urban residential structure has the zonal pattern noted in the Australasian cities is implicit in a recent investigation of Anderson's (1966), which set out four questions.

1. Is the city centre the best reference point for pattern description?

2. What form does the relationship between distance from the city centre and housing take?

3. Do relationships between housing variables depend on distance from the city centre?

4. Is housing cost related to distance from the city centre or only to the different types of housing, which themselves are related to the distance measure?

To answer these, samples of approximately 100 census tracts were taken from each of ten SMSAs. Ten characteristics were chosen as the dependent variables, and twelve positional measures were chosen as the independent variables (Table IV.12).

TABLE IV.12

VARIABLES USED IN ANDERSON'S ANALYSIS

DEPENDENT VARIABLES	INDEPENDENT VARIABLES
Housing Age	Political (Central City, Large
Percent built pre 1939	Suburb, Small Suburb, Fringe)
Percent built post 1950	Closest Major Highway
Housing Cost	Distance from city centre
Median contract rent (rental	Distance to nearest railroad
units)	Distance to nearest large
Median value (owner-	residential area
occupied units)	Distance to nearest large park
Housing Quality	Direction from the city centre
Median Rooms per unit	Altitude
Percent units no or shared bath	Distance from three nearest
Percent units 2 or more baths	large bodies of water
Percent units unsound	
Housing Density	
Percent multi-unit structure	
Percent owner-occupied	

From correlation of the two sets of variables, Anderson concluded that 'For each and every one of the ten housing characteristics, that measure of position which accounted for the largest proportion of the variance was distance from the center of the city' (Anderson, 1966, 10). This positional variable in fact accounted for 60 percent of the variation in tract density (not necessarily a socio-economic status index for areas), 54 percent of the variation in housing age, 40 percent in housing quality, and about 30 percent in housing cost. Thus, while the zonal gradient around a single nucleus proved more apt than any of the other concepts tested, it did not give a very full account of the total pattern.

The lack of congruence between model and reality was accounted for in the form of the relationships. Aggregating the ten SMSAs into one, Anderson found a curvilinear relationship in which 'rents rise rather sharply for a few miles as one leaves the center . . . [and] thereafter steadily decline until, at the actual periphery they approximate levels found in or near the center itself' (Anderson 1966, 13). He concluded that the relationships were continuous rather than stepped, indicating the absence of any 'natural' zones. His four main findings were:

1. The centre of the city was the most important point around which the housing pattern is organised.

2. The relationship of housing cost and quality to distance was curvilinear (as also was the relationship between the last variable and housing age, which could simply be the result of rapid post-1950 growth over wide suburban areas).

3. The relationship between housing quality, age and density varied with distance from the city centre.

4. There was a direct relationship between distance from the centre and housing cost, which was independent of quality, age or density.

All of these researches, and particularly Anderson's, have suggested that the zonal pattern in many United States cities is not that which Burgess presented in his model. The outer zone is only of middle-class status in many cities, while in others the fringe has only similar status to the city centre. The highest-status suburbs, on the other hand, are somewhere intermediate between the centre and the periphery, as in Australasia and some British cities, which suggests the need to develop a more detailed model of the city incorporating this general pattern.

2. The Stability of Elite Residential Areas

The Burgess and Hoyt models both suggested that neighbourhood change would be continuous with city growth (although there was no indication of the possible pace of change), but the Melbourne, Christchurch, Edinburgh and London studies discussed here have indicated stability which was probably much greater than any envisaged by the pioneer theoreticians. Similar evidence can be found for American cities. In reviewing the role of filtering in providing a worthwhile housing stock for lower-income groups, Winnick noted that:

> The main reason for the shortcomings of the filtering program is the failure of the relatively well-to-do to place good quality existing housing on the market in such volume as to produce a significant reduction in its relative price (in Foote *et al*, 1960, 18).

He concluded that the wealthier segments of American society no longer chose to spend large portions of their growing incomes on housing; they were satisfactorily housed and reluctant to build again, perhaps because:

> The affluent apparently no longer feel a need for 'grand houses'. Income taxes and the high cost of domestic service play a part, but it also appears to be true that the rich, grown more sensitive to egalitarian influences, are no longer house-proud or concerned with the ostentatious glitter their grandfathers found necessary (in Foote *et al*, 1960, 16–17).

Detailed investigation of the elite and the aristocracy in Philadelphia has shown a longevity for certain fashionable districts, especially in recent decades, which parallels this longevity in status for homes. Suburbs along the Main Line and in Germantown have retained their status for more than a generation, though Baltzell pointed out, following Sorokin, 'that communities distinguished by rapid success and accumulation

176

of great wealth have less staying power than communities with more moderate rates of social mobility' (Baltzell, 1966, 213). (A similar conclusion has been reached for some New Zealand cities. In Christchurch, for example, it is mainly the business elite—the most stable elite group and perhaps the closest to an aristocracy in that country—who occupy the oldest, high-status neighbourhoods, while the newer elite groups, such as university professors and artists—the 'meritocracy'—more often reside outside the 'core' in areas whose prestige is more ephemeral.) In Philadelphia, Baltzell has indicated a quite considerable separation of elite and upper class, with corresponding variations in neighbourhood stability.

A geographical study with considerable relevance to this topic was J. Tait Davis's investigation of middle-class housing patterns in 10 United States central cities. He showed that the amount of such housing in the central cities declined considerably over the decade 1950–1960, while lower-class areas expanded. Many middle-class areas in 1950 were occupied by lower-income groups ten years later, but the middle classes did not in turn move into the former upper-income districts—as the filtering or invasion and succession models suggest. Instead, these prestigious areas have remained remarkably stable, so Davis concluded that while the lower classes have been taking over the former middle-income areas:

the boundary between the middle class housing and the higher class housing experienced little change ... The higher value housing areas seem able to preserve themselves from invasions of lower income groups and to constitute a relatively stable part of the central city residential structure (Davis, 1965, 250).

Thus, the middle classes are being squeezed out of the central city by the expansion of lower-income residential areas forcing them against the impenetrable housing value barriers around the elite districts. They must move to suburbia, leaving the central city as an area populated by the lowest and highest income groups in the urban society.

Davis's work has put Winnick's findings into a spatial framework and provided considerable evidence to support the argument that the best residential districts in American cities (even in the older northeast) are not on the periphery of the built-up area (although there may be exclusive settlements within the exurban belt). High-income residents who are satisfied with their homes and neighbourhoods do not allow middle-class people to move in—by keeping it too expensive for them—thus supporting Hoyt's hypothesis that either filtering or invasion of a neighbourhood only takes place when resistance to it is low. Davis's analysis dealt only with central city areas, but there seems no reason why his findings should not be extended to fashionable areas on the other side of the political boundary, which also could become engulfed in a sea of middle-class suburbia.

Davis's findings directly contradict Schnore and Jones' (1969), if they can be expanded from his sample to the wider population of SMSAs in the USA. The latter's analyses of 1950 and 1960 data suggested that a number of cities have changed from having both lowest and highest educational groups concentrated in the central city to having only the lowest groups so concentrated; this was the major trend which they showed (Table IV.8), and fits Schnore's evolutionary model (Schnore, 1965). But Davis's findings suggested stability for the high-status areas within the central city. Further, albeit slight, analysis indicates that both may be right and that Davis's findings were more relevant to a study of evolutionary trends in urban residential structure.

During the decade 1950–1960 the American population became a much better educated one; in 1950 the median number of school years completed for persons aged 25 and over was 9·3, in 1960 it was 10·6. The greatest growth has been in the numbers with a college education (Table IV.13), and these form the group who are supposed to have changed their residential locations in 16 cities according to Schnore and Jones, or have remained stable according to Davis—unfortunately the latter used income data and housing values so this statement is only a broad inference. Davis showed that the lower-status groups were taking over much of the central city, so there was no room there for the new educational elite, who must have joined the 'suburban trek'. In effect, the changes reported by Schnore and Jones could have occurred without any decline in higher (educational) status numbers in the central city, but merely as a result of the 'upper-middle class explosion'. And Schnore's earlier finding (p. 132) that the amount of annexation affected the city-suburban differential could suggest that the highest-status group straddle the boundary between these two areas: Schnore suggested that the

TABLE IV.13

THE CHANGING EDUCATIONAL STATUS OF
THE US POPULATION

	Persons 25 and over having completed (in thousands)		per cent change
ELEMENTARY SCHOOL	*1950*	*1960*	
Less than 5 years	9,446	8,303	−12·1
5–7 years	13,911	13,754	−0·1
8 years	17,706	17,433	−0·1
HIGH SCHOOL			
1–3 years	14,801	19,116	+19·1
4 years	17,663	24,455	+38·4
COLLEGE			
1–3 years	6,259	8,742	+39·7
4 years	5,285	7,625	+44·3
TOTAL	87,483	99,438	+13·7

Source: Computed from various editions of the Statistical Abstract of the United States.

greater the amount of annexation, the more likely that the upper classes would be over-represented in the central city.

3. The Process

Few studies have dealt with the process of neighbourhood change, except for particular cases referring to the invasion of areas by distinct racial groups (see Chapter VI). Movement has generally been inferred from information on neighbourhood changes, and recent studies have concentrated on the characteristics of the migrants themselves, rather than on the areas they have vacated and moved to (see Chapter VII). Details about the people moving into and out of an area are generally insufficient to allow for proper tests of the filtering hypotheses. (There are exceptions, of course; 1961 Census data for London were used to show that in-migrants lived at higher room densities and were less likely to be buying or renting unfurnished property than were the persons they were replacing (Johnston, 1969b), and a detailed study of a Christchurch suburb gave some evidence of filtering-down, but overall suggested stability (Fairbairn, 1963).)

Keystones of the Burgess and Hoyt models are that city growth is initiated at the centre and that most recent in-migrants concentrate into the inner zones of the city. It is not clear whether the latter has ever been true; it seems to have suggested itself, to Burgess (1928) in particular, because the lower-income international and Negro migrants who did converge on the zone of transition were so apparent, both in the city itself and in the available data. But is this so now? Recent investigations by the Taeubers (1965a, discussed in Chapter VI) suggested that it is not for Negro movers, while the flow of international immigrants to American cities, who once thronged into the zone of transition, is very small now.

That the original models might be wrong in this aspect was suggested by Freedman's analysis of 1940 Census data for Chicago. In general, migrants to the city were of higher socio-economic rank, and indeed 'only the male rural farm migrants were found to have characteristics indicative of low social and economic status' (Freedman, 1967, 100). Within the city there was a 'migrant zone' (following most of the Lake Michigan shoreline), within which there was a clear-cut segregation of the recent arrivals according to their socio-economic characteristics. High correlations between the migrant and non-migrant populations indicated similarities on most of these characteristics; concentration in a (largely but not entirely) inner city migrant zone was the result not of socio-economic but of family status characteristics, for

> the migrants tended to be relatively well-educated young adults on the threshold of their productive years, ready and willing to work, and able to find employment (Freedman, 1967, 114).

Nevertheless, there was still much central city concentration, although probably less than Burgess and Hoyt envisaged, so Freedman concluded:

> that theories of the growth and changes of the structure of American cities based on the migrant settlement pattern of the great period of foreign immigration may need to be modified . . . the settlement pattern of recent migrants, whether internal or foreign, is essentially different from that of the great mass of foreign immigrants of earlier periods . . . Both the characteristics of the migrants and their 'port of entry' within the city appear to have changed (Freedman, 1967, 114).

This trend has continued, as shown by a recent examination of white migration to the 12 largest SMSAs (Taeuber and Taeuber, 1964). In most of these, substantially more people from an origin outside the SMSA migrated straight to the suburban ring than to the central city; in two cases (Boston and Pittsburgh) the suburbs got a greater percentage of their migrants from other SMSAs than did the central city, and in Los Angeles, San Francisco, Boston and Washington the suburbs gained a greater proportion of their migrants from other metropolitan areas than from the central cities of their own. Migrants fron non-metropolitan areas formed less than 20 percent of the total to all but the four smallest central cities, and the authors concluded that 'As we ascend the metropolitan hierarchy, inter-metropolitan migrants should become of greater relative importance' Taeuber (and Taeuber, 1964, 721).

Within individual metropolitan areas, movement from city to suburb far exceeded flows in the reverse direction, but in socio-economic characteristics there were few differences between the two streams. A polarisation of status differences was not being produced by such movements, therefore, as others have suggested (Goldstein and Mayer, 1964c). Similarly there were few differences between the streams of in-migrants to the suburbs and to the city from elsewhere, although the latter area appeared to receive slightly lower status persons on average. What has happened is that:

> Since non-migrants in the city are of lower status than non-migrants in the ring (suburbs), the addition of similar

relative volumes of in-migrants to city and ring would raise the average status level of the city relative to that of the ring. Out-migration, on the other hand, tends to remove from the cities persons of distinctly higher status than those remaining behind, while the rings lose migrants whose status is only slightly higher. Out-migration, by itself, tends to widen the status gap between cities and rings (Taeuber and Taeuber, 1964, 728).

Taeuber and Taeuber have characterised contemporary in-migration patterns within the United States as the inter-metropolitan circulation of elites (persons such as the organisation men in Whyte's (1960) analysis). Thus, although 72·7 percent of in-migrants to New York were high school graduates, only 40·5 percent of the non-migrants were; standardised for age and sex, the respective percentages were 57 and 39 for the central city and 52 and 50 for the suburbs (see also Miller, 1967). An interesting consequence of this is shown in Goldstein and Mayer's (1965a) analysis of migration to various areas of Providence-Pawtucket, which were defined according to their socio-economic status. In both the central cities and the immediate suburbs, the higher the status of an area the greater its proportion of in-migrants from outside Rhode Island (Table IV.14; note also that 40 percent of the class I area inhabitants lived in the central cities and not the immediate suburbs). If this finding applies to other cities (experimentation with the cities studied by Davis suggested that it does) then the higher the status of a district, the greater its stability in terms of its characteristics, and the greater its interaction with the wider urban system.

SYNTHESIS

With regard to the two hypotheses formulated at the beginning of this chapter, the evidence discussed here has suggested:

1. That in most cities there is a clear sectoral patterning of socio-economic status attributes of the population. The sectors, especially those which are generally of greater prestige, are not homogeneous in their characteristics, but the

TABLE IV.14

NEIGHBOURHOOD STATUS AND MIGRATION: PROVIDENCE, 1955–1960
(PERCENT)[1]

1960 RESIDENCE	NON-MOVER	CENTRAL CITY	ELSEWHERE IN PROVIDENCE	OUTSIDE PROVIDENCE
CENTRAL CITY				
Status of Tract[2]				
I	56·4	22·9	5·5	12·8
II	60·4	28·0	3·7	5·6
III	59·7	29·1	4·8	4·1
IV	56·9	32·1	4·6	4·1
V	42·3	32·7	10·5	5·0
IMMEDIATE SUBURBS				
Status of Tract[2]				
I	51·2	11·5	24·1	12·5
II	58·7	14·0	18·7	7·1
III	60·7	9·5	23·3	5·2
IV	64·2	9·9	21·0	3·1
V	71·6	0·4	25·7	1·6
SATELLITE CITIES[3]				
Status of Tract[2]				
III	63·1	0·9	31·7	4·0
IV	56·8	3·8	34·5	3·8
V	57·7	2·2	36·2	2·9

[1] Percentages do not add to a 100·0 because of those giving no 1955 address.
[2] Type I have the highest socio-economic status, type V the lowest.
[3] There were no type I or II tracts in these areas.

Source: Goldstein and Mayer, 1965a.

similarities within them are much greater than those between sectors.

2. Zonal patterns are generally not as suggested. The bulk of the evidence agrees with the models of urban residential structure in placing the majority of the lower-class residents in central zones, but beyond that the findings are both contradictory and incomplete. Some studies have suggested that the socio-economic status of neighbourhoods increases with distance from the city centre, but others (often at a finer scale of analysis) have indicated that such an increase generally ceases before the edge of the built-up area is reached and that the outer zones are more homogeneously middle class, with occasional working-class suburbs.

3. The amount of evidence on neighbourhood change is small, but there is a suggestion of considerable stability in an area's socio-economic position, despite high levels of residential mobility. This is particularly true for the highest status areas in many cities.

4. There is some suggestion of an evolutionary sequence in the development of an urban residential structure. This begins with a negative relationship between socio-economic status and distance from the city centre in small, young cities which is reversed when the upper-status groups move from the city centre to the periphery. Intermediate to this, however, is a stage when the middle classes have left the central area for suburbia so that the highest and lowest status groups remain in the former area.

This sequence has been argued persuasively by Schnore with a lot of evidence for the 1950–1960 decade from large American cities. His data support it (Table IV.8), for the majority of places which recorded a change in their structure over the decade moved in the expected direction. But other evidence contradicts this, and suggests that the sequence is instead:

1. Highest classes concentrated in the inner zone.
2. Highest classes move to the outer zone.
3. Middle classes move beyond the highest-class areas.

This sequence is drawn from Davis (1965) and others (as well as Schnore's (1965a) Latin American paper), and has led to the following evolutionary model which draws on both view-points.

1. The Preindustrial Stage

In this period the city is small and grows only slowly, if at all. The elite occupy neighbourhoods immediately adjacent to the central business area—which is also expanding very little—and the lower classes are organised in small neighbourhoods elsewhere; they may or may not surround the elite areas to give a complete low-status, outer zone.

2. The Industrial Take-Off

During this short period the city's growth rate suddenly accelerates, and there is increasing pressure on the central residential areas, both from the burgeoning expansion of non-residential uses and from the great influx of under-privileged migrants who contribute so much to the total urban growth. One of the prime causes of urbanisation is usually an improvement in transport technology. As with most innovations, early forms of passenger transport are generally expensive and can only be afforded by the upper-income groups, who can escape from the expanding city centre and its uncongenial environment to suburban areas, where pressure on land is slight and low-density living encouraged.

This marked change in the residential structure may represent a complete reversal of the former pattern, as Schnore suggested, with the upper-income groups now occupying the outer zone and the lower groups the inner; between them are pinched the middle classes. However, such a leapfrogging of a former lower-status ring does not seem to have occurred in most places, either in the developed world (such as London and Melbourne) or in the under-developed (Amato, 1970). The pattern instead seems to have been the simple one of sectoral expansion as propounded by Hoyt in 1939.

3. The Industrial Stage

Continued urban growth and central expansion puts further pressure on the inhabitants of outer zones, which they must repel, or else accede to by moving further out and building again. The latter alternative is often encouraged by continued technological developments and the growth of commercial enterprises which:

a. Lead to the creation of new elites, based on industrial wealth. Expansion of elite numbers requires more elite living space. The existing high-status areas may be able to absorb such an expansion, but if not, the development of new suburban areas by the nouveaux-riches will produce new status-rich addresses to which other elite groups will be attracted. (The amount of movement which such a process will generate is likely to vary between societies. Where there is antipathy between an aristocracy and the elite the former are unlikely to be drawn to the latter's areas so that a bi-polar high-status residential pattern may develop. Such a development would be less likely in cities and societies which lack a traditional aristocracy.)

b. Result in frequent innovations in living styles and arrangements making existing homes obsolete and creating demands for new dwellings (which must be built in outer zones). Such innovations would only be available to the highest income groups, and their purchase of them would initiate a filtering process with a zonal pattern, within the high-status sector, of decreasing status towards the city centre.

This industrial period and its concomitant expansion of market economies and tertiary occupations will also see the rise in numerical importance of the middle classes. Their financial status will make many of the transport innovations available to them, and small shopkeepers, managers and the like will be freed from workplace-residence ties (Warner, 1962). Some may aspire to higher things and join in the filtering process by occupying the hand-downs of the upper and upper-middle classes. Others will have more limited social aims and be content with home ownership in a relatively pleasant environment. For them a new (or fairly new) semi-detached or detached home on the periphery of the lower-status sectors would be sufficient, perhaps creating a zonal pattern for the first time in such sectors; one which Ashworth (1964) has shown to be very stable over time.

4. The Post-Industrial Stage

Once the great initial boom of industrialisation is over, society tends to settle down again, with consequent effects on urban residential structure. Vertical mobility is still considerable but the making of great fortunes is not as common as in the earlier period. The elite, particularly the business elite, may become more stable in its membership; there is then less competition to display one's position in society, and, coupled with high living standards, this leads to satisfaction with housing and a stability of elite residential areas. A common feature at this stage is a growing equity of income distribution, and in many societies outer suburban home-ownership becomes available at least as far down the status scale as the upper-lower classes. Indeed this period might be categorised as the era of the middle classes, and many of the new elites (the 'meritocracy') are in fact members of these groups in terms of the usual indices of socio-economic status.

It is suggested, therefore, that this final stage is reflected in the residential structure of cities by a rapid growth of middle-class suburbia which encloses the former peripheral high-status areas on the outer edge of their sectors (see Figure IV.5). The key to this development is the size of the segment of society which can move to suburban housing, and requires further discussion.

The Middle Class Housing Experience & the Suburban Pattern

The upper and upper-middle classes form but a small part of most urban societies, and if filtering-down of their former dwellings were the only way of housing the lower-status groups very rapid migration rates would be necessary in most growing cities. But in fact, some middle-class people have been able to afford new housing for many decades, as Warner (1962) has shown, and entrepreneurs have built housing especially for the working classes in many cities (Vance, 1966, 1967).

New housing is almost always provided on the urban periphery, usually alongside main transport routes, and much of the initial development of suburbia seems to have been through small-scale speculation by entrepreneurs. Warner's

(1962) investigation of one sector in Boston showed that it was common for a middle-class person with some capital to build his own home and develop adjacent sites via a multiplicity of mortgages and loans (see also Saunders, 1967). This produced suburban homogeneity, although most of the dwellings were rented rather than bought in the nineteenth century because of the structure of the mortgage market. Rodwin's data showed that 18 percent of Boston families owned their own homes in 1890 compared with 25 percent in 1950, but of these only 39 percent held mortgages at the former date as against 67 percent at the latter (Rodwin, 1961, 29–30).

Although a good number of people could afford to buy or rent new suburban homes in the United States, nevertheless the structure of the housing market restricted this opportunity to certain income groups, which would lead to the general zonal pattern suggested by the Burgess model. Rodwin's analysis of housing availability in Boston was based on assumptions that:

1. One-sixth of gross income is the optimum outlay on shelter rent (the cost of the house alone.)
2. 23 percent of gross income is the accepted proportion to be spent on gross rent (shelter plus utilities).

Using these he was able to compute median rent-paying ability at various dates to compare with median asking rents for new and used properties (Table IV.15). Over the 110 years the costs of new housing increased much more than paying capacity, so that unless they were prepared to commit increasing proportions of their income to housing, the lower middle-class persons were progressively debarred from new housing.

As rental of new homes became financially impossible the Boston middle classes could have turned towards ownership. But costs have risen rapidly in this sector too; despite the great increase in the number of mortgages granted, the market has not been opened very wide. The average value of homes on which advances have been made has increased more rapidly than middle-class incomes: in 1875–1884 average home value was only 185 percent of average income, but in 1930–1939 it was 303 percent.

TABLE IV.15

MIDDLE-INCOME HOUSING COSTS: BOSTON

	1846	1875–84	1885–99	1900–14	1920–29	1930–39	1946–47	1956–59
				DATE				
FAMILY INCOME ($)								
Midpoint	759	950	901	1,248	2,122	1,700	3,250	5,000
% of 1846	100	125	119	164	280	224	428	659
RENT PAYING CAPACITY ($)								
Midpoint	127	159	151	208	354	284	542	834
RENT FOR EXISTING, MINIMUM-STANDARD HOUSING ($)								
Midpoint	124	158	168	258	462	348	396	846
% of 1846	100	127	135	208	372	281	319	682
% of Income	16	17	19	21	22	20	12	17
RENT FOR NEW, MINIMUM-STANDARD HOUSING ($)								
Midpoint	133	202	222	294	600	480	1,050	1,500
% of 1846	100	152	167	221	451	361	790	1,128
% of Income	18	21	25	24	28	28	32	30

Source: Rodwin, 1961, 17.

Similar findings were reported for Los Angeles during the 1950–1959 decade. There 'home values have increased at more than twice the rate of consumer prices . . . [because] rising land values account for the greater part of the home value enhancements . . . market prices expanded about two and one-half times and residential construction costs rose by about one-third' (Mittelbach, 1963, 15). In Los Angeles, therefore, new housing is provided mainly for the upper income groups, as a careful analysis by Smith (1966) has shown (Table IV.16); it might be noted, however, that it was not concentrated at the highest income levels, where larger proportions of the population remained in the existing stock. Instead, new housing was more the prerogative of the upper-middle classes. Restriction to these groups was the result of the operation of the mortgage market; the median loan held in 1960 was for $10,000 payable over 18 years at 6 percent, which, with real estate tax as well, involved an outlay of 19 percent of annual income. And the costs were increasing: in 1950, 4·3 percent of all conventional first-mortgages cost more than 6 percent per annum; in 1960 such rates applied to 25·2 percent of such loans (Mittelbach, 1963).

In the United States new home ownership has been very much restricted to the higher income echelons of the urban society, therefore, and lower-income groups, except where specific suburban developments have been made for them, have had to depend on the filtering process or the actions of entrepreneurs. This has produced a zonal pattern somewhat akin to Burgess's suggestion, but, because of the high costs of moving perhaps (Grigsby (1963) estimated them as 10 percent of the value of the dwelling being purchased), the filtering process does not seem to be working: instead purchase of new housing has been 'forced' on the middle class. Crowding and high rents also have resulted in the inner zones of growing cities, which may be countered by large-scale speculative developments—such as Levittowns (Gans, 1967) and the three-decker suburbs of Boston (Rodwin, 1961).

A similar pattern would probably occur in the United Kingdom but for the much greater amount of government participation in the housing market. Purchase of a new house

TABLE IV.16

ASSIGNMENT OF 1960 HOUSING STOCK: LOS ANGELES

	1960 INCOME ($)							
	2,000–	2–2,999	3–3,999	4–4,999	5–5,999	6–6,999	7–9,999	10,000+
OLD HOUSES BY INCOME OF 1950 OCCUPANTS ($)								
2,000–	62							
2–2,999	29	41						
3–3,999			27					
4–4,999			14	48				
5–5,999					61	29		14
6–6,999						35	82	48
7–9,999							66	56
10,000+								44
1960 HOUSEHOLDS IN 1950 STOCK	91	41	41	48	61	64	148	162
HOUSEHOLDS IN HOUSES BUILT 1950–1960	28	14	19	30	52	70	186	190
TOTAL HOUSEHOLDS IN 1960	119	55	60	78	113	134	334	352

Source: Smith, 1966, 153.

costs much more per week than does renting a dwelling from a local authority, and requires an initial deposit as well, so only the better-paid groups can afford owner-occupation. For 1951 Wendt (1962, 44) showed that average weekly payments for council housing were 10/- to 15/-, whereas weekly outlays on mortgages averaged between 27/6 and 42/8. From 1951 to 1958 average interest rates for mortgages rose from 4 to 6 percent. In total, annual outlays for a mortgaged home would have been about £82, compared to less than £40 on a council house.

Council housing is not available to all persons, most local authorities having (often long) waiting lists as well as imposing residential and financial qualifications. Nevertheless, 2·3 million publicly-owned homes were erected between 1945 and 1959, compared with only 850,000 by the private sector (Wendt, 1962, 55). Any zonal pattern produced by the restriction of the latter type to high-income groups is thus considerably distorted by the erection of large council housing estates, as Robson's (1969) work has shown. Sectoral patterns sometimes have emerged, but the siting of council estates is not usually decided on the location of high-status sectors (for some examples see Ward, 1962), and many of the latter have been truncated in recent years by such developments. In fact a random pattern may emerge, for Jones (1962) has noted that higher-status groups often object to living next to a council estate and move elsewhere.

As a final example, housing demand has not been met in New Zealand by large-scale provision of State housing (although this comprises about 10 percent of the annual increment to the housing stock) but by providing the means for a large proportion of the society to purchase their own home. Whereas in the United States 'Home ownership was . . . the socially compulsive ideal, highly favored by the tax system and by families with children, rising income and middle-class aspirations' (Rodwin, 1961, 39), legislation in New Zealand in recent decades has translated such an ideal into reality. The government-financed State Advances Corporation provides loans of up to two-thirds of the cost of a new home (or a fixed sum, whichever is smaller), at 3 percent interest for persons below a certain income and $5\frac{1}{2}$ percent for others (these restraints were liberalised prior to the 1969 general election) and allows families to capitalise in advance the 14 years of social security benefits which they would receive for their children, in order to pay the deposit. Households with incomes above a certain level can obtain government-backed loans from insurance companies for costs of the land, and it has been estimated that 20 percent of all new homes in the country are acquired without any capital deposit by the buyer. Such schemes clearly influence the social topography of the country's cities, for suburbia and a new home are within the reach of a majority of the population. Class-like clustering still occurs within the outer zones because of segregative tendencies and land market operations, producing a clear sectoral pattern in some cases, but the general zonal model is inapplicable.

It can be claimed, on the basis of the three societies discussed in this section, that the evolutionary model set forth here as an alternative to Schnore's must incorporate the important variable of societal attitudes and governmental participation in the housing market. In particular, the kind of provision for the middle classes seems to be a key influence on the spatial pattern, and the whole sequence can be re-written in these terms, as follows:

1. In the preindustrial city, upper-status groups have a strong residence-workplace tie with the CBD. Other groups, mainly artisan, work either in their homes or in small workshops and have little contact outside; a small middle class of traders live on their business premises. Thus, the upper classes occupy residential areas in the centre of the city, and most of the remainder live in small neighbourhoods elsewhere.

2. With improvements in transportation the upper classes are freed from their workplace ties and move to the urban periphery (where some might already own land and country homes) to build large homes in very large tracts of land.

3. One or a small number of dominant clusters of high-status 'rural retreats' tend to develop, perhaps around the homes of community leaders, or around an existing settlement served by one of the new transport routes—whose fares and timetable

may make it exclusive to the wealthy (Dickinson, 1962; Pollins, 1964).

4. Increasing real incomes and changes in societal structure create an upper-middle class who move into suburbia. They may be attracted to districts around the homes of the nabobs, or they may develop their own neighbourhoods elsewhere.

5. Changes in dwelling become desirable for status retention, so that the upper-income groups build new homes on the periphery of their sector(s), initiating a filtering process.

6. More members of the middle class can afford a suburban move, though perhaps to its inner rather than its outer parts. Because of this, many portions of the outer zone become less desirable for the higher-income groups who will move towards the dominant clusters and produce a clearer sectoral pattern of status districts. Their earlier, more dispersed pattern will still be visible in many townscapes in the occasional large house and grounds (both perhaps now subdivided), relics of the period when only the wealthy could afford urban fringe living before the development of large, middle-class tracts.

7. The majority of the middle class are now freed from workplace ties and move away from the central areas, perhaps being forced by lower-class expansion. Most cannot afford new personal homes but are dependent on mass developments of large estates which usually offer a limited choice. These could be in the interstices of the earlier pattern, filling up the inner suburban zone, but where rapid transport is available the outer edges of the city may be similarly developed.

8. Much of the population is satisfactorily housed, especially in the upper- and middle-income groups, for whom dwelling style—but less so address—becomes a much less important status symbol. Their movement then slows down, with consequent effects on the amount of filtering. In a growing city this results in pressure on the existing stock, which can be met by:

a. No public or private action, so that occupance densities and rents increase and general living standards deteriorate, as the amount added to the housing stock is insufficient to meet the demands at earlier standards.

b. The availability of house purchase, particularly of new

housing, is widened so that large segments of the society can afford suburban homes. A middle- to upper-lower class outer zone of housing is the usual result.

c. Large areas of public housing are provided, both in suburban estates and central city apartment blocks. The spatial pattern of these may preserve a pre-existing sectoral structure, or it may produce a scattered, almost random pattern of residential areas.

None of the societies discussed here has followed one of these latter alternatives to the exclusion of all others. Obviously Britain has concentrated mainly on the third plus some development of the second, with the result that—except where council estates distort the private market situation—its cities, especially the many slowly growing ones, still have an increase of status with distance from the centre in the various sectors. In New Zealand most attention has been given to the second choice with the resultant engulfing of high-status sectors and nodes by suburban sprawl; social policy has not been quite as broad in Australia but its rapidly growing cities and middle class have produced sufficient sprawl to give a similar spatial pattern. Finally, in the United States the first choice has been more closely followed, although the second is clearly also true because of rising real incomes. The Hoyt and Burgess models are thus more relevant there, although again there has been enough middle-class sprawl to produce an outer zone which is not highest in status (especially in the rapidly growing cities, which, in terms of Schnore's model, are often the youngest also).

CONCLUSION

This chapter has attempted to evaluate the models of the socio-economic spatial structure of cities in several societies. Criticisms of the models have often stressed their deterministic natures and their ignorance of cultural values, and in understanding individual cities such influences must clearly be investigated. On the broader scale, however, it has been shown that the models still have much merit in providing a benchmark for discussion of this topic, although cultural attitudes have been suggested as possible explanations for variations between countries in the way these patterns have evolved. It has proved possible to tie these together into a general evolutionary model, however, which does not allow the easy visual depiction of the earlier formulations but draws heavily on these for its basic format.

CHAPTER V

Life Styles, the Family Cycle & Residential Location

DISCUSSION IN Chapter I of the transformations wrought in society by industrialisation suggested that, for the first time, individuals and family groups could choose from various methods of organising their lives. In particular, adults could not only decide whether or not to marry, but also, if they married, whether or not raising a family should be their prime concern. Those who chose not to marry were offered alternative styles of living, for the household was no longer the basic economic as well as social unit. Industrialisation offered ways of making a living other than by tilling the land or working in home-based craft industries; individuals could exist outside nuclear families; nuclear families could exist away from extended families. At first, as with so many innovations, the choices were only available to certain groups, usually those with wealth. Gradually, however, the opportunities became available to the population at large and, as shown in Chapter II, life style and socio-economic status are now apparently independent aspects of urban population structures in 'developed' societies.

The three life styles of familism, careerism and consumerism are available to all persons, therefore, and in Chapter III it was suggested that individuals and households would be spatially separated within cities according to their choice among these. Because of land values, different environmental demands, and variations in housing age, persons having chosen familism as their dominant life style would occupy low-density, suburban areas; those choosing the other two would be found in central

197

city areas, living at high densities in multi-family dwelling units. Thus it can be hypothesised that:

I. There will be a zonal dichotomy between family-oriented suburbs and career- and consumerism-oriented central city residential areas, and this will be reflected in population densities.

II. Since life style choice is open to all groups, these zonal patterns will be independent of any patterning of socio-economic status which might exist.

For households which choose familism as their major life-style, this represents a commitment for at least two decades in most cases. Thus, in any city which is more than reproducing itself (either by natural increase or in-migration) and in which the proportionate choice of familism shows no marked decline, the housing supply will not meet the suburban demand and new rings of low-density housing will be needed on the urban periphery. Such new housing will presumably be provided mainly for new families, characterised by their relative youth, so that:

III. Within the zone in which familism is the major life style there will be a further zonal pattern differentiating this segment of society according to age and stage in the family cycle.

(It was shown in Chapter III that the average young family cannot immediately afford home purchase. Some, particularly if they are childless, will live in similar style and areas to those who have opted against familism, the only difference between the two groups being their aims and probably future commitments. Others, especially those with children, will rent houses in their inner suburbs characterised by older families; such homes will have become available through family dissolution and out-migration. Thus the zonal pattern may not show the youngest families in the outer ring; rather these will be dispersed through all rings—see Figure III.9.)

As a city grows, there will be greater demands not only for new suburban housing but also for more apartments to accommodate those who prefer such homes in a central city location. Thus the inner ring should expand into the ageing family suburbs so that, not only:

IV. The population structure of family-oriented suburbs should age over time.

but also

V. The non-familism zone of mainly apartment dwellings will expand concentrically outwards, producing subdivision of single-family homes into rooms and flats and redevelopment of such areas with apartment building.

THE BROAD ZONAL PATTERN:
MELBOURNE, AUSTRALIA

Not only has there been less theoretical work on this aspect of urban residential structure, compared to that on socio-economic patterns, but the number of empirical studies against which to test the hypothesised patterns is also small. Consequently, this section deals with the zonal aspects of the first three hypotheses in but a single city. This offers little foundation for any firm statements (for the Melbourne study was one of the main sources for the above hypotheses), but there is plenty of implicit evidence in other work to suggest that the patterns described here are in fact typical of cities in the societies covered in this book.

Investigation of family status patterns in Melbourne's residential structure was part of the study quoted earlier (pp. 141–146) on that city's social topography (Johnston, 1966c). The same sample of census collectors' districts was employed, and eighteen variables were studied, six each representing family status, demographic structure and housing characteristics. All eighteen displayed statistically significant differences between the means for the four zones, and only four of the gradients from city centre to periphery differed from the hypothesised patterns (Table V.1).

Among the six familism measures, fertility increased away from the city centre, especially over the last two zones, as would be expected with the move towards younger suburbs. The proportion of the population of marriageable age, the proportion of males and adult females in the work force, and the percentage of married persons listed as either divorced or legally separated (a measure of family disorganisation), all

TABLE V.1

ZONAL PATTERNS OF LIFE STYLE AND
FAMILY STATUS: MELBOURNE, 1961

	ZONE			
	1	2	3	4
A. FAMILY STATUS				
Women in the Work Force (%)	47·7	40·1	31·0	31·0
Males in the Work Force (%)	70·4	66·9	60·4	58·8
Fertility (°/₀₀)	352	358	465	645
Not Married Over 14 (%)	35·9	30·1	22·6	16·9
Divorced and Separated (%)	5·1	3·5	1·7	1·2
Married Females in Home Duties (%)	47·8	56·7	66·2	64·7
B. DEMOGRAPHIC STRUCTURE				
Aged 0–14 (%)	18·7	20·7	29·8	37·9
Aged 15–44 (%)	44·5	42·1	42·6	46·4
Aged 45–64 (%)	25·1	24·8	19·2	13·5
Aged Over 64 (%)	11·5	12·4	7·9	3·3
Males Per Females (°/₀₀)	1,119	957	973	1,025
Dependents (%)	45·1	51·2	59·3	60·2
C. HOUSING CHARACTERISTICS				
Owner-occupied (%)	30·2	49·1	41·3	32·4
Being Purchased (%)	11·9	15·8	27·0	54·0
Tenanted (%)	55·1	35·0	15·2	9·2
Flats (%)	21·0	13·6	5·4	1·1
Share of Private House (%)	6·5	6·2	3·9	2·1
Apartments and Rooms (%)	8·6	5·6	0·6	0·1

Source: Johnston, 1966c, 180–184.

decreased with increasing distance from the CBD. The only exception to the anticipated pattern was in the percentage of married women who gave their occupation as home duties; here there was a slight fall from zone 3 to zone 4, which was unexpected because the latter contains the youngest population, with most children and with highest fertility, thus comprising families where the mother would perhaps be most needed at home. This deviation could indicate a number of as yet childless families who already resided in the outer zone or, as suggested in the caveat to hypothesis III, that some families in this zone would have all their children at school because a new, outer suburban home could not be bought in the early years of child-raising. For some time families would rent homes in older suburbs. When they could afford a new home, the children would all be at school, so the mother could go to work. Further investigation of the data suggested the latter, for the deviant zonal gradient in fact only occurred in the low socio-economic-status sector, where such slow family progress to an owner-occupied home in the outer zone might be most frequent.

Departures from the regular zonal gradient occurred with three of the six indices of demographic structure (Table V.1). As expected, the percentage of children increased away from the centre, doubling from zone 1 to zone 4, and was presumably the main reason for the percentage of dependants showing the same trend. Among the other three groups, the proportion aged 45–64 declined towards the newer suburbs, as anticipated, but the relative number of younger adults first dropped from zone 1 to zone 2 before beginning an increase with greater distance from the city centre, and the proportion aged 65 and over displayed the converse pattern (increase from zone 1 to zone 2 and then decrease). Finally, the ratio of males to females followed the same gradient as the 15–44 age group.

All three of these apparent deviations in fact fit the hypotheses, and a smooth zonal gradient should not be anticipated. The central city should be dominated by young adults, as yet not far advanced in their family cycles (if at all), and those of them not in this area should be in the outer zone where the highest proportions of children are recorded; hence the bimodal gradient. Similarly, although some of the senior citizens might live in the inner apartment zone, the majority should be where they were observed, in the inner part of the broad family status zonal structure. (The zones were not constructed to exactly separate the two types of living area, of course, so some overlap was expected.) Finally, the sex ratios reflected the age structure, especially in zone 2 where females should predominate because of their greater longevity. Male dominance in the inner zone probably resulted from the concentration of international immigrants there, as well as a Skid Row area, and in the outer zone it would indicate the majority of males at birth and the first few years of life.

Five of the six housing characteristic gradients displayed

the expected form. Flats, apartments, shared private houses, and tenancies all declined, as proportions of all dwellings, away from the city centre. The gradients were steep, especially between the second and third zones, thereby suggesting a marked break between the two types of living area (Table V.1). The other gradient conforming to the hypothesis showed a rapid increase in the proportion of dwellings being purchased by their owners away from the centre, and the only deviation, not unexpectedly, was in the percentage of homes which were owner-occupied. For this, the highest percentage was recorded in zone 2, and value declined outwards from that inner-suburban peak; such a pattern fits the family-cycle model of the older suburbs housing older families who have not moved since buying their first homes.

Within Melbourne in 1961, therefore, the central residential areas contained a relatively large population of young adults and many unmarried persons; a large proportion of their households lived in rented flats or rooms. The majority of the inhabitants were members of the work force and, compared to the city at large, the area contained many males and divorced or separated persons. Outer suburbs, on the other hand, were characterised by a predominance of nuclear families in single-family dwelling units, and less than one-fifth of all persons aged over 14 were unmarried. Adults were mostly under 45, there were many children, most homes were mortgaged, and, relative to other areas, large proportions of the population were not earning an income. Between these two polar types, which closely approximate those of the model, were the older, inner suburbs with their middle-aged and old populations and high proportions of owner-occupied homes. Flats and renting were quite common here, however, suggesting both the expansion of inner-zone residential types and the provision of relatively temporary housing for lower-income families not yet able to purchase their own.

These findings all accord with the outline of family status patterns in the city which has already been presented, both in the form of the gradients and the statistical significance of between-zone differences. The hypothesis of no sectoral patterns was also verified in Melbourne, with only three of the eighteen tests producing statistically significant differences between the three sectors. These were in the percentage of adult women giving home duties as their occupation, with more women in the higher socio-economic status areas remaining at home; in the percentage of the population aged 65 and over, this being highest in the intermediate and high-status sectors; and in the ratio of males to females, the former being dominant in the low-status sector (where recent international immigrants to the city were concentrated). While these three suggest some slight interdependence between spatial patterns of social and family status, this broad survey has produced no strong evidence against the hypothesis of no sectoral patterns.

THE DETAILED DEMOGRAPHIC PATTERN

The third hypothesis presented in this chapter suggests a zonal pattern of age structures within the suburban zones—the data and areal framework of the Melbourne study were too coarse to test this, although the general findings were affirmative. Most censuses provide more detail on the age and sex structure of city areas, however, and several studies have used this.

In an early investigation of intra-urban age structures, data were used for 36 areas of the City of Wellington from the 1956 Census (the city's population at that time was 138,300); these areas varied considerably in size, from 310 to 10,560 inhabitants, but were the only such available.

Although some use was made of five-year age groups, particularly in the presentation of typical age-sex pyramids (Figure V.1), the bulk of the discussion used an amalgamation of the groups to fit a triangular graph whose axes were the percentage of the population aged under 15, 15 to 64 and over 64 (for an example see Figure V.3). From this, the authors recognised five demographic areal types, and mapping indicated a concentric zonal pattern (Franklin, Gibson, and Treeby, 1963). These, and their main characteristics were:

I. THE SENILE CBD. Only one district was in this type, and it encompassed Wellington's business heart. There were almost no children, and though there was a fairly high percentage of old persons, the area was dominated by young adults, especially males, between the ages of 15 and 35 (15 and 30 for females, indicating the lower average age at marriage for women; Figure V.1). This district mainly comprised of old two-storey homes which had been converted into apartments.

II. THE OLD ZONE, containing, and characterised by, a high percentage of persons aged over 64.

III. THE MATURE ZONE, not completely encircling the other two, because of Wellington's accidented topography. It had the most evenly distributed age structure of all five zones, suggesting a mixture of households at all stages of the family cycle. This fitted the hypothesised pattern closely, suggesting an intermediate area of relatively immobile old and middle-aged families interspersed with younger families who were renting an old home as a waypost on their 'suburban trek'.

IV. THE EARLY MATURE ZONE, in which, for the first time, the characteristic broad base of the age-sex pyramid appeared and the modal age group was 0–4 (Figure V.1). The researchers also recognised a sub-category which was termed composite early mature: its age structure was bi-modal, peaking at 5–9, and 45–49, and presumably contained mainly older families beyond the child-bearing stage.

V. THE YOUNG ZONE, a discontinuous belt of outer suburbs, whose populations included very few old persons; as much as 40 percent of the residents were under 15. The characteristic adult ages were 30–40 indicating the youth of the families.

This study did not impose a zonal pattern on its data, as did that of Melbourne, but one emerged very clearly from its analyses. The pattern was a very close approximation of that hypothesised, despite the fairly coarse nature of the data and observation units, and the methodology has been repeated in a number of recent studies of Auckland (another New Zealand city whose topography is far from the homogeneous plain of the model structures). Here, perhaps because 65 rather than 36 areal units were used, eight demographic types were recognised, along with 'something of a concentric pattern of development

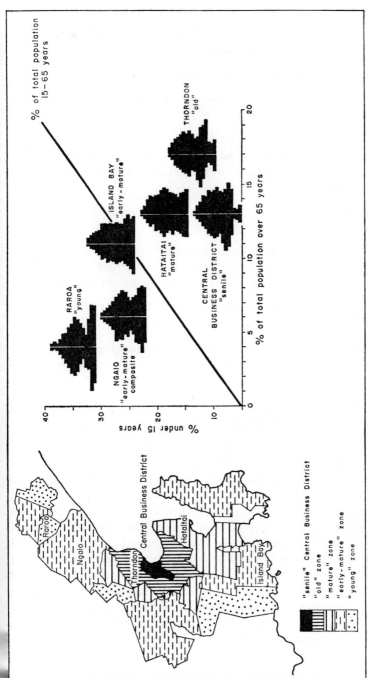

v.1 Demographic Areas of Wellington City, showing the zonal distribution of neighbourhood types and typical age-sex pyramids for each. *Source:* Franklin, Gibson and Treeby, 1963.

around the CBD' (Curson, 1967a, 29). The eight types, many very similar to Franklin's, were:

I. SENILE; dominated by the 15–24 and 45–59 age group.

II. OLD; with slightly older persons and children than the previous type.

III. LATE MATURE; a more balanced structure than I or II, but with a dominance still of young adults, suggesting outward extension of the old zone with increasing pressure on available housing space.

IV. MATURE; differing from the late mature only by its smaller proportion of old persons.

V. EARLY MATURE; a continuation of the traverse from oldest to newest suburbs, these being characterised by the child launching stage with 10–19 and 40–49 as the modal ages.

VI. TRANSITIONAL TO EARLY MATURE; a further small category with almost one-third of the population under 15.

VII. LATE YOUTH; outer suburbs dominated by children but with a small older element because the areas had developed around formerly separate settlements.

VIII. YOUTH; areas with very few people aged over 45 and a quarter of them under 10.

In justifying use of only three age groups to produce a typology of Auckland's demographic areas, Curson pointed out that although the age-sex pyramid is a valuable graphic tool, comparison of two or more pyramids is extremely difficult, since each has about 40 components. The loss of information by aggregation has recently been attacked by Coulson, however, who used more sophisticated tools to generalise an age structure by five-year groups (differences between sexes were ignored). He argued that age structures should display a negative linear relationship between age and numbers (Figure V.2) and fitted regression lines to Kansas City census tract data to confirm this contention for all but a small number of tracts whose populations were dominated by old persons (Coulson, 1968). In general, the older an area's population, the less steep the relationship (Figure V.2). When the slope parameters for each tract were graphed, no grouping of demographic types emerged; instead an almost unbroken continuum of age structures from the very old to the very young was suggested (and this same conclusion might be drawn from Curson's work).

A map of the slope parameters indicated a far from random distribution. As in Auckland and Wellington, there was a general zonal pattern, with the oldest populations clustered around the CBD, though also stretching away from it in the southern sector. From this area the indices increased in all directions towards the highest values on the urban periphery, but even in those areas dominated by young people there were some nodes of older individuals representing formerly independent towns now engulfed by Kansas City.

TEMPORAL CHANGE IN SPATIAL PATTERNS OF FAMILY STATUS

What is apparently almost overwhelming evidence in favour of hypotheses I–III has been presented so far, but this all refers to the situation at one date. The use of terms apparently drawn from the Davisian model of landform development in the New Zealand studies, however, suggested a process of ageing of areas in line with hypothesis IV.

Population Ageing: Auckland, New Zealand

Changes over time in two portions of the Auckland urban area have been studied by Curson (1967a, 1967b). He again used triangular graphs to separate children, adults and old persons, and his findings were clear-cut, indicating a trend from youth through maturity to old age (Figure V.3). In the earliest years of Auckland City (founded 1840), however, the data for 1864, 1867 and 1871 identified a period of increasing youthfulness in the age structure, following the adult-dominated early years of the colony.

For both of the study areas (Auckland City—the core of the urban area with a population of 143,583 in 1961—and Newmarket Borough—a very small independent unit, now forming an inner suburb, which has never exceeded a population of

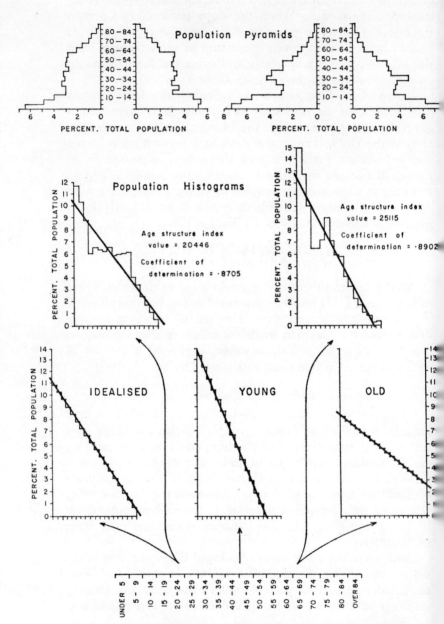

v.2 Population Age Structures—Kansas City, showing the method of fitting regression lines to the structures and hypothetical patterns for various structures. *Source:* Coulson, 1968.

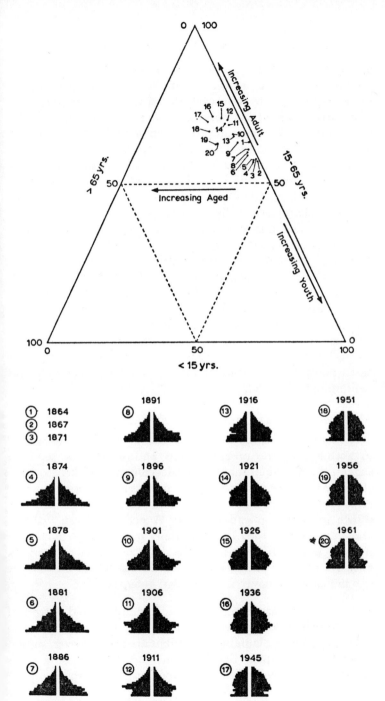

v.3 The changing Age Structure of Auckland city, 1864–1961. The tri-graph is scaled in percentages of the total population, and the numbers refer to the age-sex scales below. *Source:* Curson, 1967b.

3,000) Curson found the general trend to be an increasing proportion of adults, with a maximum of about 75 percent in the 15–64 age group. In its early decades as many as 40 percent of an area's inhabitants may be children, and throughout the period up to the maximum proportion of adults the percentage of old persons remains stable at 5–10 percent. Only after this does the relative number of the over-64s increase, and after that, some areas, especially those close to the CBD, may undergo a rejuvenation with expansion of the senile zone (see p. 206), characterised by its younger apartment dwellers.

In discussing this sequence, Curson (1967b, 183) noted 'it is important to remember that not all areas follow such a regular evolution and that this general pattern is often interrupted by specific social, economic, historical and political factors', which in Auckland included the stifling of immigration in some periods, an inter-war decline in the birth rate, war conditions, and the post-1945 baby boom. Full verification of this model, although it agrees with the hypothesis presented here, therefore awaits further case studies and will be assisted by more sophisticated analyses which can standardise for national trends and so illuminate the local.

Neighbourhood Changes in New York & Los Angeles

A more detailed model, 'which can be tested by its ability to account for the observed facts and which can serve to suggest the directions that further development is likely to take' (Hoover and Vernon, 1962, 198), has been developed out of a regional planning study of New York. (Its general validity was shown in later application to Los Angeles; Duncan, Sabagh and van Arsdol, 1962.) The authors outlined a sequence of five stages which 'describes what has happened in general terms, and there are plenty of variations when we look at specific cases' (Hoover and Vernon, 1962, 198).

I. NEW SINGLE-FAMILY SUBDIVISIONS. Usually a rapid process of rural-to-urban land conversion, this takes only a few years to complete. Where planning regulations are lax, however, spotty, sprawling, incomplete development may characterise a landscape for many years (Tunnard and Pushkarev, 1963).

II. THE TRANSITION TO APARTMENTS. Following the almost complete occupation of an area by single-family homes comes continued population growth, made possible through replacement of the former dwellings by apartment blocks. No time-lag is indicated before areas enter this transitional stage, but as Hoover and Vernon stated that dwellings are replaced this suggests that the single-family homes will have served an economic life of several decades, though in some locations the determinant could be land value rather than building deterioration. Also, the areas of New York placed in this category in the late 1950s were in its inner suburban ring, with the exception of some very accessible commuter settlements on Long Island.

III. DOWN-GRADING AND CONVERSION. There is little new construction in this period, but population growth continues through adaptation of single and multiple dwelling units for higher-density occupance (in some respects one might expect this to occur before Stage II). Slums often develop, and they are correlated with the entry of lower socio-economic status occupants, especially 'with the spread of districts occupied by more or less segregated ethnic and minority groups' (Hoover and Vernon, 1962, 188); nevertheless, this is not universal and several areas of New York showed no sign of moving from II to III.

IV. THINNING-OUT; the first period of population and density decline since initial development. There is almost no construction and 'most of the shrinkage comes about through a decline in household size' (Hoover and Vernon, 1962, 191), which is a feature of the later stages of the family cycle. In the down-grading period a lot of young families seeking the security of home ownership move into an area; many may take in lodgers to ease the burden of loan repayment. With time the latter leave, and then children desert their parental home. The married couple remain into this next period, so thinning-out correlates with population ageing.

V. RENEWAL. The final stage, in which the obsolete original housing is replaced by new multi-family units, usually by a public agency.

This five-stage progression was presented as a descriptive model of New York; a sequence not necessarily followed by all areas. Some neighbourhoods may remain in a stage almost indefinitely, although the authors claimed that the increasing suburban dispersal of employment, the increasing freedom for persons in choice of living area (generated by car ownership), and the relaxing of many of the barriers operating against

TABLE V.2

HYPOTHESISED PATTERNS IN THE
HOOVER–VERNON MODEL OF URBAN AREA
DIFFERENTION

VARIABLE	*STAGE*			
	Initial Building Up	*Transition*	*Downgrading*	*Thinning Out*
POPULATION				
Aged 0–4 (%)	I	D	I	D
Aged 64 and over (%)	D	I	I	I
White-collar Males (%)	I	D	D	D
Negro (%)	D	I	I	I
HOUSING				
Median Value	I	D	D	D
Median Contract Rent	I	D	D	D
Single-family Units (%)	I	D	D	D
Owner-occupied (%)	I	D	D	D

I–Increase Hypothesised   D–Decrease Hypothesised

Source: Butler and Barclay, 1967, 5.

minority groups, were all leading to 'a quickening progression of stages in neighborhood evolution, at all major points in the sequence' (Hoover and Vernon, 1962, 227).

A relatively precise test of this model was an examination of population characteristics in the component parts of Los Angeles (Butler and Barclay, 1967). Eight population and housing characteristics were chosen to represent the expected features of the process (Table V.2), and trends were hypothesised for each. Thus in the first stage (termed initial-building-up by Butler and Barclay) the percentages of children and of white-collar workers were expected to increase, along with the value of the housing, and as areas proceeded downwards through the scale the proportion of white-collar workers and owner-occupied, single-family homes would decrease (along with rents), while the relative numbers of old persons and of Negroes increased.

To test these hypotheses each of the census tracts in Los Angeles had to be classified according to its position in the sequence at the starting date for the study (1940). The following assumptions were made:

1. Areas built-up by 1940 were in the transition stage during the 1940–1950 decade and the downgrading stage during 1950–1960 (the criterion for a tract being built-up was a housing density of two or more per acre).

2. Areas built-up during 1940–1950 were in the subdivision stage during that decade and the transitional during 1950–1960.

3. Tracts built-up during the decade 1950–1960 were in the subdivision stage over the full twenty years.

No predictions were made for tracts still below the threshold density in 1960, but for the others hypotheses were presented, both for each separate decade and for the whole twenty years.

Seventy-three percent of the hypotheses (Table V.2) were verified: in general, the older the area the better the prediction. For areas built-up before 1940, 22 of the 24 projected trends were confirmed (Table V.3), the only failure being with the percentage of the population aged under 5. (This variable was most prone to failure in all of the tests, probably because of post World War II changes in the birth rate. More detailed analysis could have standardised for this, perhaps by comparing tract data with those for the city as a whole.) The common pattern was thus one of socio-economic decline and an ageing population.

There was a much poorer fit between model and reality for tracts built up between 1940 and 1950; it was not clear whether this was due to faulty hypotheses or a wrong identification of the location of areas in the sequence. Tracts appeared to enter a stage of socio-economic decline almost immediately after they were built over, and rents, house values, the percentage of single-family and of owner-occupied units, and the proportion

TABLE V.3
TESTS OF HOOVER–VERNON MODEL: LOS ANGELES 1940–1960

VARIABLE[1]

	1.	2.	3.	4.	5.	6.	7.	8.
A. AREAS BUILT UP PRIOR TO 1940								
1940–1950	*D*	I	D	I	D	D	D	D
1950–1960	*I*	I	D	I	D	D	D	D
1940–1960	*I*	I	D	I	D	D	D	D
B. AREAS BUILT UP 1940–1950								
1940–1950	D	D	I	*I*	I	I	*D*	*D*
1950–1960	D	I	*I*	*D*	*I*	*I*	D	D
1940–1960[2]	D	I	I	I	I	I	D	D
C. AREAS BUILT UP 1950–1960								
1940–1950[2]	I	D	I	D	I	D	D	I
1950–1960	*D*	D	I	D	I	I	*D*	I
1940–1960[2]	I	D	I	D	I	I	D	I
D. AREAS NOT BUILT UP BY 1960								
1940–1950[2]	I	D	I	D	D	D	D	I
1950–1960[2]	D	D	I	D	I	I	I	I
1940–1960[2]	I	D	I	D	I	I	I	I

I—Increase Reported D—Decrease Reported

Where the letter is italicised this indicates a trend in the opposite direction to the hypothesis.

[1] The order of the variables is as in Table V.2.

[2] No predictions were made for this time-period.

Source: Butler and Barclay, 1967, 15–18.

of white-collar workers all declined between 1950 and 1960, while the proportion of Negroes increased. In the Los Angeles context in particular this might suggest that the threshold density of two houses per acre (this was apparently a gross density measure) was too high; the subdivision stage may have been virtually completed much earlier and Butler and Barclay were identifying the transitional rather than the building up stage. However, most hypotheses were validated for areas not built over until 1950–1960 (Table V.3), and similar patterns were observed for the tracts still below the critical density at the latter date.

Apartment Development in Toronto

The study of Los Angeles confirmed the descriptive validity of Hoover and Vernon's model in another city, but more recent work has suggested important modifications to it (much as Hoyt suggested changes to Burgess's model). Bourne's first (1967) study of redevelopment in the city of Toronto, where apartment buildings formed 33 percent of the additions to the housing stock during 1952–1962, indicated that the spatial pattern of this process was in no way zonal. Instead redevelopment areas were clustered, to some extent in sectors, with a tendency towards location in higher-income areas. However, there were no strong correlations between the amount of apartment building and areal population characteristics; indeed the strongest relationships merely indicated that the pattern of redevelopment 'has a strong basis in growth in preceding decades' (Bourne, 1967, 143). This suggested a clustered pattern resulting from a type of chain reaction produced by the operation of factors at two levels. At the macro-scale there was a general areal demand for apartments related to the physical and socio-economic environment and to accessibility within the urban area; at the micro-level specific site factors allocated redevelopment among the areas of existing demand according not only to land availability (vacant or otherwise) but also the ability to overcome zoning regulations and community resistance (see the discussion on Hoyt's formulation of the filtering model on p. 88). Once redevelopment has commenced in an area, other new building follows until land values rise such that the area loses its comparative advantage.

From this initial statement, Bourne (1969) has developed a more detailed outline of the processes involved in the spatial patterns of both redevelopment and new construction, involving the operation of spatial constraints at three scales on intra-urban location decisions. He proposed three sets of independent variables affecting the redevelopment and residential construction pattern:

1. Those acting at the regional level, including the existing spatial structure of land uses and buildings, the persistence of

earlier growth patterns, and the accessibility of all points to the city centre, to mass transit routes and to the population generally.

2. Those acting at the area level, including the structural condition of buildings and the socio-economic characteristics of populations.

3. Those operating at the level of specific sites, notably the cost and availability of land, especially the size of properties, and the amount of vacant land.

The hypothesised relationships between these variables and measures of the amount of residential construction of various types were tested by multiple regression techniques, with relatively poor results. For example, only 36 percent of the areal variation in the amount of apartment construction could be accounted for by four variables (the only statistically significant ones in the regression equation), one of which was merely a measure of the size of the tract. In terms of the model, only the anticipated effects of the amount of existing apartment development, accessibility to the city population, and proximity to a subway were observed. Similarly with the amount of total residential construction, only 46 percent of the variation was accounted for by the proportion of apartments already existing, the percentage of dwellings constructed before 1920, the size of the lots, and proximity to the subway. (The importance of prior apartment development relates to the use of only the political City of Toronto as the observation unit and the large proportion of recent new construction there which has been in apartments.)

These findings suggested that redevelopment is not a necessary correlate of the age of a district's housing stock and its proximity to the city centre. Instead, apartment development was concentrated into a few areas (Figure V.4) which reflected 'the channeling effects of zoning on the location of urban land uses, as well as the tendency for new construction to follow existing land use concentrations and previous directions of growth' (Bourne, 1969, 187). Indeed, a sectoral pattern was so pronounced that separate regressions were run for the main high- and low-status sectors; in the former the percent explana-

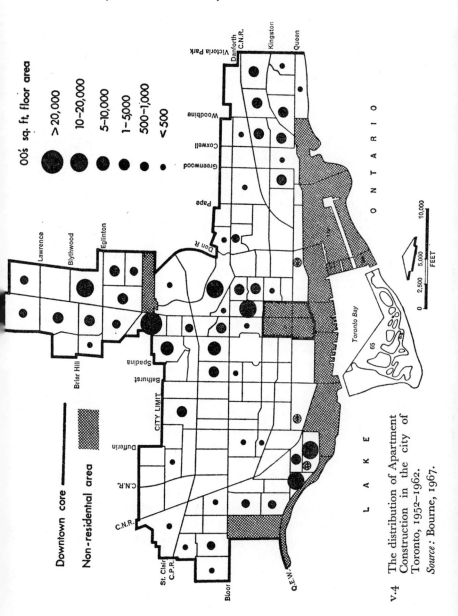

v.4 The distribution of Apartment Construction in the city of Toronto, 1952–1962.

Source: Bourne, 1967.

tion of variation in apartment development increased from 36 in the city as a whole to 49, but in the latter it fell to 13, no doubt reflecting the small amount of redevelopment there.

If such patterns exist in other cities, then important modifications to the Hoover-Vernon model are needed. Within higher socio-economic status sectors of the city the five-stage evolutionary sequence may be noted, depending on the size of areal unit used since the redevelopment process is very spotty. In lower socio-economic districts, however, it is likely that areas will pass directly from the building-up to the downgrading stages on some of the characteristics studied by Butler and Barclay, only to be eventually rejuvenated by massive injections of public money in the form of renewal programmes.

Bourne's analyses of the spatial pattern of single-family housing construction in the City of Toronto (that is, new subdivision) showed that the most important variables were distance from the city centre, employment density, and the amount of local industry. Apparently there was more development at greater distances from the CBD (not surprisingly in an already almost completely built-over city) and away from the main concentrations of employment. These findings broadly agree with the models of urban expansion; nevertheless only 54 percent of the spatial pattern could be accounted for, and there was no relationship with the amount of vacant land, Bourne noting that its presence 'clearly tends to influence the location of new construction within but not between broad neighborhood units' (Bourne, 1969, 190).

The Residential Development Process

A number of important studies of the location of new residential construction has been conducted at the University of North Carolina, using local cities as the testing laboratory. The earliest used multiple regression techniques to describe the spatial pattern of development, mainly in terms of the location of various areas and the availability of certain services. Typical of their findings were the following (Chapin and Weiss, 1962, 446).

1. Poor drainage characteristics tend to discourage land development in vacant areas.

218

2. Location of major routes of transportation tends to intensify land development.

3. Location of work areas with large employment potential tends to intensify land development.

4. The availability of community services and facilities (fire protection, sewer service, water service, and schools) tends to intensify land development.

5. Proximity to blighted areas and proximity to non-white areas tend to discourage urban development which might normally occur in the absence of these influences.

Later studies have developed on the predictive ability of this model, but more recently the team has concentrated on a detailed model of the development process. In this, 'the landowner, developer and household consumer are viewed as three key decision agents, with supporting roles provided by realtors, financiers and public officials' (Kaiser and Weiss, 1969b, 598). Patterns relating to the decisions of these three were as follows.

1. The predevelopment landowner. Non-resident owners, retired owners, joint owners and those who have owned land only a short period are most likely to sell their property for development, especially if that property is adjacent to already built-up urban land, and has a high value.

2. The developer. Ten variables were evaluated 'to distinguish the type of sites where subdivision occurs from the type of site where it does not' (Kaiser and Weiss, 1969b, 613; the variables were: proportion of marginal land, proportion of poor soil, socio-economic rank of the location, distance to nearest major street, distance to nearest elementary school, accessibility to employment, distance to CBD, amount of contiguous residential development, availability of utilities and services, and zoning protection). Of these, socio-economic rank proved to be the major discriminant and distance to the CBD of minor importance, but there were marked differences according to the size of the developer firm and the market it was serving.

3. The housing consumer. Again, socio-economic variables were the major determinants of whether a household, which had decided to move, chose a new dwelling. The role of accessibility was slight, there was 'no evidence that households

improve their accessibility as a result of the move' (Kaiser and Weiss, 1969a, 78).

Apartments in the Suburbs

Bourne's findings can be equated with the hypothesis of zonal expansion of apartment areas. As with most zonal patterns, there is no continuous transportation surface but the process may be as suggested with resulting patterns contorted by the time-cost configuration of the communications network (Quinn, 1940a). Thus, apartments could be expected to develop along major transit lines, which they did; the clustering noted in Toronto resulted from government intervention in the property market through zoning (see Hoyt, 1950).

But a recent study in the United States has not repeated Bourne's findings. During the last decade, apartment-building has been a large, if not major, part of the total construction in metropolitan areas (Neutze, 1968). Of the several reasons suggested for this, Neutze has preferred a combination of the changing demographic structure (an increasing proportion of households—old and young—without children) and rising real incomes which allow the relative freedom of renting rather than purchasing. Most important of his findings was that the larger proportion of apartment construction was occurring in the suburbs.

Neutze (1968, 168) attributed this new pattern of development to simply 'the latest phase in the general suburbanization of activities and the correspondingly slow rate of inner city redevelopment'. Apartments have followed houses, shops, factories and offices to the suburbs, to areas more conducive to the operations of speculators and developers (especially in obtaining re-zoning of areas). Apartment occupiers in the suburbs often lose little in accessibility to the city centre relative to their inner-city counterparts because of the benefits of freeways; low-density living is desired by them, Neutze claimed and 'The important feature of apartments is not density: it is that they are rented' (Neutze, 1968, 168). Within the suburbs, Neutze found some evidence of a decline in the number of apartments away from the city centre, but this accounted for only 16 percent of the spatial pattern. In addition, there was no evidence (a correlation of 0·066) of any clustering of apartments. If this is a general pattern and develops further then the model of spatial patterns—indeed any model suggesting spatial regularities—will be invalid.

BUT IS IT QUITE THAT SIMPLE?

So far almost all the evidence discussed in this chapter has suggested that the model of family status and life style patterns outlined in Chapter III, and represented by the hypotheses tested here, is a close representation of reality. The gradients in Melbourne pointed to a clear break between the familism- and non-familism-oriented areas of the city, and data on age structures in various places illustrated the anticipated zonal pattern within areas of family living. And the evolution of these patterns over time also fitted the hypotheses, except for some relatively localised sectoral development, and the patterns described by Neutze.

Despite all these findings, however, a number of the pieces of evidence suggested two areas of conflict between model and reality:

1. The presumed independence of family status and socio-economic status variables in the description of residential patterns. Hoover and Vernon's model of New York suggested that most areas are first subdivided at relatively high socio-economic levels, so that, although characterised by their youthfulness, new suburbs did not contain a representative cross-section of the urban society. Kaiser and Weiss also showed socio-economic status of adjacent built-over areas to be an important determinant of whether nearby land was also subdivided, again suggesting the role of socio-economic rather than family status characteristics in determining the populations of new developments. Similar relationships may be noted in the apartment areas; Bourne, for example, suggested that these were only constructed for the top 20–30 percent of the population along the income scale.

2. The absence of some of the expected spatial patterns, especially in analyses using detailed areal breakdowns of urban areas. Thus, although the Melbourne study gave broad verifi-

cation of the hypothesised zonal pattern, Bourne's detailed work on the inner zones indicated that apartment blocks were both sectorally segregated and areally clustered.

The remainder of this chapter attempts to reconcile the general model of the city with these apparent contradictions. In the first section, some aspects of the hypothesised determinants of the spatial structure of life styles are discussed, and this is followed by sections on the inhabitants of the various parts of the city.

Land Values & Population Densities

Economic models of the city, such as Alonso's (1964), assume that land values decline with distance from the city centre, although some workers have accepted that there may be more than one node in large urban areas, producing a more complex pattern (see Berry, 1963). There is evidence for the validity of this idea, both in studies as old as Hurd's (1924) classic work on values and in more recent investigations, such as that by Knos (1962).

Other works have suggested differently, however. Some, such as Daly's (1967), have mainly indicated the multi-nuclear structure of the cities in which they were working; but his investigation in Newcastle showed that in the main built-up area the major influence on land values was distance from the CBD. In a more detailed study of Chicago (unfortunately only for the central city of the metropolitan area), Yeates (1965) showed that the role of this area in determining the pattern of land values declined considerably during the period 1910–1960. His multiple regression analyses related land values at six dates to the following independent variables:

1. Distance from the CBD.
2. Distance from the nearest regional shopping centre (a test of the multiple-nuclei model).
3. Distance from Lake Michigan (a test of the role of values, particularly for environment, as suggested by Hoyt and Firey).
4. Distance from the nearest rapid transit system (an attempt to modify the distance effect according to the intra-urban accessibility surface, as suggested by Quinn).

5. Population density of the observation area (a test of the relationship between values and densities, although, as suggested in Chapter III, values should determine densities and not vice versa).

6. The proportion of nonwhites in the observation area (testing a hypothesis that the presence of such persons affects the desirability of areas and this is reflected in land values).

Over the fifty-year period the ability of these six variables to accurately predict the form of the land value surface in

TABLE V.4

LAND VALUES IN CHICAGO

Percentage of Variation in Values accounted for by Six Variables

	1910	1920	1930	1940	1950	1960
	77	65	37	34	24	18

Rank Order of Six Variables in Importance in Accounting for Values

	1910	1920	1930	1940	1950	1960
Distance from CBD	1	1	3	2	3	3
Distance from Regional Shopping Centre	6	4	5	5	6	5
Distance from Lake Michigan	2	2	1	1	2	2
Distance from Rapid Transit System	3	3	2	4	1	6
Population Density	4	6	6	6	5	4
Percent Nonwhite	5	5	4	3	4	1

Source: Yeates, 1966, 64–65.

Chicago declined from 77 to 18 percent of the variation being statistically explained. In particular, the declining power of the regression model resulted from a reduction of the influence of the CBD on land value patterns. In 1910 and 1920 this was the major determinant, but by 1960, while still statistically relevant, it had been superseded by both the distance to Lake Michigan and the proportion nonwhite variables (Table V.4). After an initial rise in its influence from third to second position, the measure of distance from transport systems fell to the last place by 1960, at which date it was not a statistically significant influence on the pattern. The other accessibility measure, distance from regional shopping centres, never exceeded fourth place and was statistically insignificant at two of the six dates.

From this analysis, Yeates concluded that accessibility to the various parts of the city has ceased to be an important determinant of land values. (Rees (1970a, 301) has disputed some of Yeates's findings but he quotes a similar decline in the role of accessibility.) Indeed, when he divided Chicago into six sectors he found that in three of them land values increased towards the urban periphery and only in an area around the CBD was the expected pattern clearly substantiated. Similar results were reported from a study of land values in Christchurch (Leslie, 1968). From 1914 to 1964 the proportion

Table V.5

LAND VALUES IN CHRISTCHURCH

Percentage of Variation in Values accounted for by Two Accessibility Measures[1]

	1914	*1921*	*1929*	*1937*	*1950*	*1955*	*1964*
Total City	94·7	50·0	62·4	58·5	61·6	54·7	47·8
CBD	67·1	70·9	74·0	75·0	62·3	76·8	68·9
Residential Areas	0	12·8	23·7	22·9	29·9	15·6	7·3

[1] The Measures were (i) Distance from the CBD peak land value.
(ii) Distance from a public transport route.

Source: Leslie, 1968.

of the variation in land values which could be accounted for by distance from the CBD and from public transport routes declined from 94·7 to 47·8 percent (Table V.5: in most cases the second variable was statistically significant in accounting for the pattern, but the amount of the variation which it accounted for was very small). When the CBD was separated from the rest of the city, however, two very different trends appeared. In the business heart the percentage of the variation explained remained almost constant, but in the residential areas, although statistically significant at each date from 1921 on, the accessibility measures accounted for very little of the pattern (Table V.5; no reasons could be found for the upward trend in the explanation in the residential areas up to 1950).

Both of these studies suggested that in modern cities where the population have high living standards and levels of personal

mobility, the main determinants of land values are the environmental qualities of areas (both physical and social). Thus,
Yeates found that in 1960 in Chicago the main influences on
values were the nonwhite proportion (illustrating the low
desirability of Negro areas for the rest of the population) and
distance from Lake Michigan (illustrating the attractivenesss
of its shoreline for high-status areas, especially to the north of
the CBD). In analyses of the residuals from his regression of the
accessibility measures on land values, Leslie found that land
was most highly prized in the fashionable residential areas,
in elevated areas, in those with sea and river frontages, and in
areas in which a water-borne sewerage system existed. Values
also declined away from regional shopping centres, but only
for short distances.

It has been assumed that population densities are a product
of variations in land values, but Yeates's analyses showed little
relationship between the two. This may be because densities
are still closely related (negatively) to distance from the CBD.
This relationship was first formalised by Clark (1951), and in
a recent book (Clark, 1967) he summarised the results of a large
number of works which demonstrated that:

1. Densities decline with distance from the city centre,
according to a negative exponential curve.

2. Over time steepness of the curve declines, and central
densities tend to become lower.

Further evidence has been presented by Muth (1961, 1969),
and by Berry, Simmons and Tennant (1963), who produced a
simple temporal model of the population density pattern
(Figure V.5). This developed on Clark's findings, except that
central densities were to follow a sine curve, first increasing
over time and then declining (see also Newling, 1969).

Most observers have accounted for the negative exponential
density decline in terms of social and economic factors rather
than by the demographic influences which were postulated for
testing here (see pp. 78–79). In particular, residential
location has been associated with the assumption that the
richer the household the more it will value spacious living above
access to the CBD and to workplaces, so that higher-income

P   225

A. CROSS-SECTIONAL

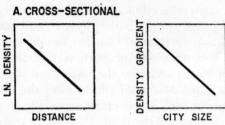

B. TEMPORAL (time periods 1,2,3,..........to n)

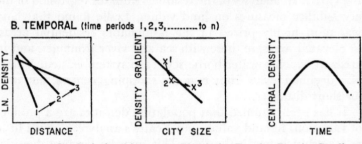

v.5 Generalised relationships among Population Density, Density Gradient, City Size, Central Density, Time and Distance from the city centre. *Source:* Berry, Simmons and Tennant, 1963.

groups purchase the cheaper land at the urban periphery where they can live at lower densities. Poorer groups, on the other hand, must crowd onto the dearer, more accessible land, so the density curve is a result of the social evaluation of spacious living by the rich and the economic evaluation of access by the poor.

Such reasoning has recently been criticised by Harris who claimed that 'these theories rest rather heavily upon speculations regarding consumer preferences for increased space versus the convenience of shortened travel. These speculations are almost wholly unsupported by careful empirical studies' (Harris, 1968, 393). He suggested that each of the following hypotheses could account for the observed density patterns:

1. There is a general preference for low densities which the well-to-do are always most able to afford.

2. Preferences in the United States are not so much for low density as for good housing, neighbourhood cleanliness and, perhaps, housing novelty (the effect of style obsolescence). Rapid city growth with changing transport technology has

resulted in the spatial coincidence of age of housing, deterioration, obsolescence and high densities, so that the presumed preferences for suburbia might be accidental. The main factor is housing quality, and spatial variations in this might account for 'differing location patterns in the slower-growing and better-maintained cities of Europe and Latin America' (Harris, 1968, 394).

3. High-income and status groups are anxious to be socially and geographically separated, and move into suburbia where land is cheaper in order to avoid the invasions of lower-status groups (Harris did not indicate why the lower-status groups do not also move to the cheap land; presumably hypothesis 3 must be taken together with hypothesis 1).

He concluded that each of these hypotheses was completely plausible, but that 'owing to the very high correlation between density, blight, obsolescence and social status in American metropolises, it is going to be difficult to distinguish by critical tests between these three' (Harris, 1968, 394).

Harris also contended that 'the density law is purely descriptive, since it is not derived from any detailed specification of cause and effect, while the detailed examination of the behavior of aggregates of households has yet to be integrated into a complete analysis of urban function and development' (Harris, 1968, 368). Nevertheless, a number of detailed analyses by Muth have illuminated some of the probable determinants of population densities via correlation analyses. For example, he attempted to account for density variations in South Chicago and found that 'even when other measures of accessibility, the age and condition of dwellings, and the income and race of their inhabitants are held constant, there is a strong tendency for the intensity of residential land use to decline with distance from the city center' (Muth, 1965, 182). Similarly, a study of six cities found a relationship between density and distance from the CBD which was independent of income and the age of dwellings in each of the four largest cities, so that 'among comparably located tracts, densities tend to be positively associated with age of dwellings, but... the association between [these two] is not as strong as between density and distance. Finally, the

227

partial association between density and income is quite weak, and the one significant negative relationship observed could easily result from sampling variability' (Muth, 1968, 321).

Each of the first two of Harris's hypotheses could be considered as partially verified by Muth's data, therefore, but one can also find evidence for another. As densities declined outwards irrespective of income, age of dwellings and other variables, the relationships between density and family status variables postulated here (pp. 197–199) might prove correct. Nevertheless, it can still be suggested that it is mainly the higher-income groups who can afford low-density living; there is a residual not accounted for by the income variable because not all high-income people are in the stages of the family cycle which demand spacious living.

The work on land values suggested little gradient from central city to periphery in residential land costs; instead, the main determinants were the economic reflections of social evaluations of neighbourhood desirability. Berry's model of urban population densities over time also showed a decline in the density gradient which may be correlated with the changing land value structure. Muth's investigation of density gradients in 46 US cities in 1950 confirmed this, for he found 'a significant tendency for density gradients to be smaller or cities more spread out where transport costs are low' (Muth, 1961, 219). My general conclusion to this section, therefore, is that two of the determinants of family status patterns (land values and population densities) are not now particularly relevant and alternative accounts must be sought for the patterns discussed earlier in this chapter. And if the patterns for the independent variables are not as hypothesised, are those for the dependents (the population characteristics)?

CENTRAL CITY POPULATION CHARACTERISTICS

The evidence cited in the preceding section suggested that the determinants of urban spatial structure according to family status may not be as expected. As a result, despite the broad findings of the Melbourne and other studies, the residential patterns of family types may also not be as anticipated. The present section deals with the inner zones.

The Apartment Dwellers

According to the life style model, the inner city should be the home of the most 'urbanised' sections of the city's society, those who have preferred either or both of promotion of their careers and pursuit of the 'good life' to the majority choice of family-centred living. These people are assumed to prefer a central city apartment to a suburban house, as are those who have chosen familism but are not in the family-cycle stages in which welfare of the children significantly affects the choice of residence.

The Shevky-Bell model of urban society and the later factorial ecologies all showed life style choice to be independent of socio-economic status, so the apartment dwellers should be of all income and occupational levels. Yet Shevky and Bell's own diagrams indicated that the two were not independent, especially in the white residential areas (Table V.6). Tracts in San Francisco characterised by high levels of urbanisation were also characterised by high social rank, so that, although correlation techniques applied to such a table would show non-correlation the independence of the two dimensions of society should not also be inferred. Indeed, much of Bell's Theory of Social Choice as related to residential location decisions may be strongly criticised. He cited data which showed that 'the suburbanites of the fifties were largely persons who had chosen familism as an important element in their life styles' (Bell, 1968, 159), and indeed the consumerism and career styles were apparently associated with central city living. His figures were stratified by high and low socio-economic status areas, however, and reworking gives the following results:

	Percent Choosing		
	Familism	Career	Consumership
High Socio-Economic Status	53	22	25
Low Socio-Economic Status	61	17	17

229

Thus households who would choose either of the alternatives to familism are generally of high socio-economic status (the questions related to ways in which 'the respondent did, or would like, to spend his time and money' (Bell, 1968, 158), so it is not possible to infer whether this means actual or desired

TABLE V.6

SAN FRANCISCO'S SOCIAL SPACE: 1950
(Percent of Population in Areas)

A. TOTAL POPULATION

	SOCIAL RANK	1. Low	2.	3.	4. HIGH
FAMILY STATUS	1. Low			7·0	9·0
	2.	0·1	9·7	15·1	9·0
	3.		14·0	21·0	12·6
	4. HIGH			1·1	1·4

B. POPULATION OF AREAS WITH FEW MINORITY-GROUP MEMBERS

	SOCIAL RANK	1. Low	2.	3.	4. HIGH
FAMILY STATUS	1. Low			3·9	7·8
	2.		2·0	11·7	8·2
	3.		2·9	19·5	12·6
	4. HIGH			1·1	1·4

C. POPULATION OF AREAS WITH MANY MINORITY-GROUP MEMBERS

	SOCIAL RANK	1. Low	2.	3.	4. HIGH
FAMILY STATUS	1. Low			3·1	1·2
	2.	0·1	7·7	3·4	0·8
	3.		11·1	1·5	
	4. HIGH				

Source: Shevky and Bell, 1955, 34.

life styles). To show that family-oriented households prefer suburban living is not sufficient to indicate separate residential patterns according to social choice which are irrespective of socio-economic status, therefore, and we have no information on why many of Bell's respondents did not live in the expected areas.

Certain life styles are apparently restricted to certain socio-economic status groups, therefore, and their desired dwelling types (apartments) are similarly restricted (except where the blocks of flats are built by public rather than private enterprise).

Bourne's comments on the income range for whom apartments were built in Toronto have already been mentioned; this was also shown in a recent study of apartment dwellers by Abu-Lughod (in Foote *et al*, 1960), who was concerned with discovering the characteristics of the people who choose city centre in preference to suburban living. Respondents thus had to be of sufficient income to afford suburbia and, because city centre was defined as an area within ten minutes rapid transportation time of the CBD, they had to be living very close in. She was also interested only in persons who had recently chosen to live in the area, which restricted her to newly-constructed de luxe apartment buildings and extremely modernised, converted older homes.

Abu-Lughod's profile of her respondents closely corresponds with the stereotype anticipated from Bell's theory of social choice. The main findings were:

1. Eighty percent of the households were not the typical American family of two parents plus children. Over 32 percent were unattached individuals and another 38 percent were couples without children.

2. One-eighth of the households had no persons employed (the proportion was 25 percent among the one-person households), but 28 percent of the two- or more person households had two or more people working.

3. The majority of the employed were downtown white-collar workers, and almost half had incomes exceeding $15,000 annually.

4. Higher-income people were concentrated in the apartment buildings; blue-collar workers mainly lived in the converted homes.

5. The great majority paid between $100–350 monthly in rent (the survey was conducted in the mid 'fifties), and 30 percent of all households spent more than a quarter of their gross income on rent.

6. Unattached individuals spent most on rent relative to their incomes and young couples spent proportionately little.

7. Young people were highly mobile, but respondents aged over 40 changed address but rarely and were very satisfied with their present housing. Abu-Lughod noted the differences between the majority who have 'reasonable expectations from a dwelling unit and do not move capriciously or without cause' and younger renters whose 'mobility is related to both their . . . ages and to the rapidly changing pace of family-cycle changes experienced before and after marriage and during the early era of child-raising' (Foote *et al*, 1960, 423).

8. Most people moved within the apartment district, the main in-migrants from other parts of the city being older couples who moved from suburbia.

9. 'Center-city residents seem to make extensive and varied use of their leisure, but many of the things they do (watching television, reading, entertaining friends etc.) hardly require a choice central location. Even their out-of-the-home activities . . . very seldom were necessarily tied to downtown, although many engaged in them in that location' (Abu-Lughod in Foote *et al*, 1960, 441–442). Almost a third of the respondents reported that they frequently ate in restaurants and 27 percent often visited cinemas or theatres, both proportions being undoubtedly higher than would be recorded for suburban family-oriented people. (See also Chapin and Hightower, 1966.)

All these features fit the expected pattern, but although they showed that central city apartments were occupied by the types of households expected, re-working of the same data for Philadelphia showed that only one-sixth of all households which were childless and with a head aged over 44, who worked downtown and earned over $10,000 a year, lived in the apartments: 'of the group that possesses the attributes that characterize downtown housing demands, 97 percent have chosen to live elsewhere' (Rapkin and Grigsby, 1960a, 49).

Others in the Inner Areas

If only a small proportion of an urban population qualify for the type of dwelling supposedly typical of the inner zones, and only a small proportion of these actually choose to live in that location, then the central residential areas are not as

homogeneous as the model suggests. This can be seen in the
Melbourne data; for example, although the fertility level was
only half as high in the inner as in the outer zone (Table V.1),
nevertheless there were still 350 children to every 1,000 women
of child-bearing age, which does not accord with the view of
the central city as an area of non-family living.

Writing on urbanism and suburbanism as ways of life, Gans
has shown that Wirth's stereotype of the urban resident is not
correct, and most Americans only conform to it for a short
period of their life; 'high density, heterogeneous surroundings
are for most people a temporary place of residence; other than
for the Park Avenue or Greenwich Village cosmopolites, they
are a result of necessity rather than choice. As soon as they
can afford to do so, most Americans head for the single-family
house and . . . the low-density neighborhood' (Gans, 1962a,
646). He characterised as cosmopolites the intellectuals and
professionals, who live in the city centre to be near its cultural
facilities. Many are unmarried or childless, and all but the
most affluent with children must move to the suburbs to rear
them.

In addition to this group, comparable to those described by
Abu-Lughod, Gans recognised four other types of inner area
residents:

1. The unmarried or childless, divided into the temporary
members of this group, who eventually move to suburbia to
raise children, and the permanents, who mostly remain in the
city centre.

2. The 'ethnic villagers', immigrant groups who live in their
own separate communities in the inner suburbs (they are
discussed on pages 279–284 below). The cosmopolites and the
unmarried or childless live in the central city by choice, but
these are there through a combination of necessity and tradition;
the next two groups are there of necessity.

3. The deprived, who are mostly the poor, the emotionally
disturbed, the broken families and the nonwhites. They must
live in the slums because they cannot, or are not allowed to,
afford better housing.

4. The trapped, who are also deprived and unable to move

out to better housing. Many are old persons on fixed incomes; others are moving down the social scale.

In addition to these groups there are those who are neither cosmopolite, unmarried, childless, nor ethnic villagers but who still prefer to live in the relatively poor housing conditions of the central neighbourhoods. In many ways they are very similar to the ethnic villagers so well described by Gans (1962b), for their ties with the inner areas are with the community there, whether or not it is of kin (see Fried, 1967, and Fried and Gleicher, 1961). Some of the best examples of such urban villagers are given in the description of the matricentric societies of Bethnal Green (Young and Willmott, 1962) and Crown St. (Vereker and Mays, 1961), which contrasted the strong family and social connections of these old areas with the anonymity and loneliness of outer suburbs. Hartman (1963) has described similar attitudes to living areas in the movement to public housing from renewal areas in Boston's West End. Of the households dislocated by the renewal program, half were not eligible for public housing, but only one-third of those eligible actually went (one-sixth in the case of whites), and these people were the less stable and more deviant elements. The majority of the 'respectable working class' refused to move to public housing, preferring instead to find their own homes within another inner city 'village' (to them, public housing projects implied a lack of privacy, high crime rates and an institutional form of existence).

SUBURBIA

Suburban areas are common recipients of attacks by social scientists and journalistic commentators for their appearance and their quality of life (termed by Riesman the suburban sadness). Clark has recently described this attack as part of a continuing process in American society of romantically yearning for former living areas and conditions. Until the last two or three decades this usually meant an attack on the city, which represented all that was 'evil, depraved, and corrupt in the American way of life' (Clark, 1966, 5) and the glorification of the rural environment and society. Today the student of American society has learned to love the city in the manner that he has long loved the country, and now it is suburbia, portrayed in terms of a slavish conformity, fetish of togetherness, and craze for organization, which is set over against a romantic image of the city . . . producing a way of life which seemingly brings out all that is best in man (Clark, 1966, 5).

Perhaps the best collection of the proposed suburban maladies is that presented by Bell, the suburban sadness being

characterized by refugees from the urban rat races; a negative reaction to man's daily labors; budgets that remain constantly beyond incomes; states of precarious equilibrium; terrible anxieties; isolated women; tremendously demanding schedules; women envious of the professional and social outlets available to their husbands in the city; bored and impatient women; women escaping by concentrating on children, extra-marital sexual activities, or drinking; the pervasive role of liquor in leisure activities; social life that is a means to career goals; relaxation at full speed; vicious party games; futile secret dreams; awareness of self betrayal that is avoided by manic hyperactivity, —cynicism or psychotherapy; an abundance of psychosomatic ills,—incuding sexual impotence and frigidity; disturbed family lives; upward mobile transients; standardized variation; dedication to social adjustment; forced participation in the neighborhood; togetherness; conformity and homogeneity; marginal differentiation instead of true individuality; superficial friendships; other-directedness; a surface facade of health and happiness covering despair and mental disturbances; confused parents; uncertainty; a plethora of different and often conflicting norms, especially the breakdown of child-rearing norms; strategically displayed property; punctuality and regularity; (overly) intense 'family life' weekends; fear of the future; preoccupation of the male with business success and of the female with housewife-community success; and the fragmentation of the life cycle (Bell, 1968, 144, after Stein, 1960).

Such negative attitudes represent an intellectual, upper-middle-class attitude, and one which has been attacked by Gans (1969) for attempting to impose one group's chosen style of life on the rest of society.

Other workers have shown, however, that the suburban stereotype presented above and so often criticised is, in fact, atypical. It is based on studies, such as those by Seeley, Sim and Loosley (1956), Spectorsky (1955) and Whyte (1960), which concentrated on areas inhabited by fairly wealthy people who were rising in the social scale and were highly conscious of this. In other suburban areas there is little evidence of such characteristics, and Gans (1969) has suggested that there is nothing in the physical environment of suburbs which causes behavioural changes. Bracey's (1964) study of life on representative suburban estates in Bristol, England and Columbus, Ohio provided many findings to contradict those mentioned earlier, and Berger's (1960) study of a working-class suburb indicated few changes in style of life as a result of the suburban move:

> They were still overwhelmingly Democrats, they attended church as infrequently as they ever did; like most working-class people, their informal contacts were largely limited to kin; they neither gave nor went to parties; on the whole they had no great hopes of getting ahead in their jobs; and instead of a transient psychology, most of them harbored a view of their new suburban homes as a paradise permanently gained (Berger, 1968, 435).

From this, and a review of other works, Berger concluded that 'the reported changes in the lives of suburbanites were not *caused* by the move to suburbia, but were reasons for moving there in the first place' (Berger, 1968, 436).

Who, then, are the residents of suburbia, and what general residential pattern can be discerned? Bell's several studies (1958b, 1968) have shown that the main reason for choosing a suburban residence was the desire for a spacious, clean environment in which to raise children, and most other studies, such as Bracey's (1964), have shown that families with children living at home are the predominant household form there. But, in one of the most detailed investigations of suburban society, Clark has shown that in Toronto the demand for spacious

236

family living is not a complete causal answer to the question of who moves to suburbia.

> There was thus in a negative fashion an ethnic and class selection of the suburban population. People highly dependent upon established social ties and associations, and this was very much the case with respect to the rich and the poor and the recent immigrant, were not prepared to risk the move to the suburbs except where a sheltered environment was offered. It was people of no strong ethnic or social class attachments who were the most likely to make the move. These were people with no position to protect, whose economic or social welfare was not dependent upon maintaining established ethnic or class ties. They had nothing to lose by the move (Clark, 1966, 98).

These findings fit those mentioned earlier in this book, notably the spatial stability of high-class residential areas, Hartman's and Young and Willmott's reports of respectable working-class families unwilling to move to suburban areas, and Bracey's indication of the loneliness of many estate dwellers, especially in the more aloof English society. Movers to suburbia in Toronto, and probably elsewhere, were the middle class; the rich may have moved beyond the city limits, but mainly only to inner suburban high-class developments which were a long way from the urban periphery and offered a 'good address'.

Most of the people going to outer suburban developments in Toronto did so because the city could not offer the required environment for raising children; those who moved met the only requirement—'the ability to pay'. Many could only just pay and were suffering financially because of this, and many other suburban deprivations were felt, such as the lack of utilities and facilities, and initial loneliness. Nevertheless, Bracey and others have indicated that the majority of suburban residents are satisfied with their neighbourhoods, and Clark suggested that this was because a community develops there (however distant it may be in English suburbs): see Mowrer's (1958) comments on the ephemeral nature of such contacts, however.

To a large extent, therefore, suburbia is the area occupied by middle-class households with few strong community or kinship ties to other parts of the city and with few social and economic aspirations (although 'organization man' suburbs of rapid vertical climbers such as Park Forest (Whyte, 1960) may

TABLE V.7

ATTITUDES OF MIDDLE CLASS SUBURBAN HOUSEWIVES IN ENGLAND

A. Percent Looking Forward To

Being a Grandmother	60
Freedom to Travel	77
Doing a Full-Time Job	20
Going Out More with Husband	85
More Local Activities	37
More Relaxation at Home	58
More Attention to Husband	55

B. Percent who Hoped Husband at 50 Would Be

Wealthy and Successful	60
Contented Family Man	100
Respected Local Community Member	60
With Power and Influence but no Great Wealth	10
Pleasant Companion to do Things with	100

C. Importance of Certain Items for Daughter (Number of Persons)

	Essential	Very Important	Important	Don't Mind	Not Important
Healthy, Happy Children	17	14	9	1	
Specialist Career Training	4	6	17	13	
Wealth	1	1	4	17	17
An Exciting and Adventurous Time		3	10	12	12
Someone Like a Doctor or MP as Husband			8	16	15
A Nice House with a Kind Husband and Steady Income	10	10	10	5	1
Freedom to be Herself	21	8	10	1	

Source: Pahl, 1968, 190–191.

exist as islands within this general area). Also, these people are strongly family-oriented, as shown in a survey of a Hertfordshire middle-class suburb, of 'nest-centred newcomers' (Pahl, 1968, 186). Most housewives in these areas valued the security of home and family and were completely home- and family-centred in their outlook and future aspirations. As Table V.7 shows, the majority of these middle-class women had few social and economic goals beyond their family, a very different set of attitudes from the more common view of suburban women discussed earlier. Apart from the tabulated results, the survey also showed that if the husband's income were doubled most of the wives would want a bigger house, a few wives would have liked their husband to get a job which took him away from home more or one which 'would stretch him to the limit of his capacity'. Nor did they wish to work themselves, and Pahl noted his 'strong impression that an ordinary, comfortable existence is the highest goal. These wives seem afraid of too-successful husbands' (Pahl, 1968, 193).

SYNTHESIS

The outer portions of a city, generally termed its suburban belt, are characterised by households who have chosen the familism life style. Most of those who have opted for career or consumerism life styles reside in central city neighbourhoods, however, because these offer them the type of dwelling which they prefer and the accessibility to workplace, friends, and leisure activites which they find desirable. This suggests a zonal division of the city into two distinct types of living area, which is entirely in line with the hypothesis presented at the beginning of this chapter. But this is an incomplete picture of life style patterns in the city.

The main reason for this last statement is that while the suburban areas of a city generally house few who have not chosen the familism life style, because their low-density environment has not been attractive (see Neutze, 1968) to those who do not base their regular activities on the child-centred family, many of those who fit the familism stereotype either do not, or are unable to, choose to live in the suburbs. Among the former group are both higher socio-economic class families who prefer established neighbourhoods and who no longer need the frequent display of status given by a new home, and members of lower-income groups who have strong community, and especially kinship, ties within high-density city neighbourhoods which they are loath to leave; in particular among the latter are members of minority groups, although native working-class inner-city communities often exist in large urban areas. Some of these people would also fall into the second category, those unable to afford a suburban home (unless, as with State housing, it is in some way subsidised), but in some societies this group also includes many who would aspire to a suburban residence on the urban fringe but cannot afford it. Of those who can move out, therefore, the suburban resident was categorised by Clark as one

> whose only distinguishing characteristic was his social standing. For such people, settlement in the suburbs, where their distinctive ways of urban living were built into the structure of the community, offered a means of preserving their identity . . . The struggle here was one for space . . . It was people who were just becoming a part of the urban society—characteristically young married couples with one or two children—who were pitched most fully into the struggle (Clark, 1966, 189–190).

Not only is the outer zone a residential area for households with certain structural characteristics, therefore, but it also contains only those with certain incomes and sets of values. There are differences between societies in the range of income groups who can afford a new or fairly new home in the outer suburbs, and most of these peripheral zones are divided into clusters of different socio-economic levels whose locations often continue the sectoral pattern of status areas in the central city. But such findings suggest that socio-economic status and family status are not independent spatial elements of the residential structure of cities, and, apart from the Shevky and Bell example already quoted, several data sets indicate the nature of the relationship. In Melbourne, the outer zone had more married women going out to work in its lower-status sector, and in Providence the lower-status suburbs had slightly older populations than their more fashionable counterparts (Goldstein and Mayer, 1965b).

The central residential areas are much more mixed in their population characteristics. The majority of the households who are not in the child-bearing to child-launching stages of the family cycle have tended to live there, but such people do not always dominate the population structure. Many other house-

holds, who qualify for suburbia by their structural characteristics, live in the city centre and the inner suburbs, either
through choice or financial necessity. And finally, the residential pattern of the non-familism elements within these central
areas is not uniform, again for socio-economic status reasons. The
highly-urbanised life styles are only available to higher socio-
economic status elements of an urban society, so that their
characteristic dwelling-types are found mainly in the high-
status sectors of cities (in Melbourne's second zone flats
formed 21·5 percent of all dwelling units in the high-status
sector but only 6·1 percent in the low). Within these sectors
clusters of apartment buildings are widely scattered as a result
of recent changes in land values and accessibility. All of this
suggests that, although the family-status patterns within a
city are as hypothesised, the main determinant of the residential structure is socio-economic status, from which the family-
status societal dimension is not entirely independent.

CHAPTER VI

Residential Patterns of
Minority Groups

THE THIRD component of urban residential structure has generally been termed ethnic status, because most of the relevant studies have been in the United States where the dominant minority group at present is characterised by its racial characteristics. Negroes are not the only minority in American cities, but many of the others are only distinguishable by 'less visible' characteristics such as language and birthplace. In other places, too, there are, and have been, other minorities, such as the religious groups in Ulster, for which the term ethnic is inapplicable. McElrath (1965) thus suggested two minority-group components; ethnic status and migrant status. In factorial ecologies the two might appear as independent but the models of residential patterns presented in Chapter III do not necessarily distinguish between them. Two basic spatial process models were suggested. The first referred to a ghetto (an area to which certain groups are restricted), which results from continuing segregation tendencies either within or outside the ghetto community. The other was a spatial assimilation process that parallels social and economic assimilation. The groups involved in these two may differ on racial grounds, but the aim here is to test the relevance of the models, irrespective of such overtones, to whichever groups they apply.

1. THE GHETTO MODELS

To some extent, these models are special cases of the assimilation models, the ghetto patterns resulting from impediments to the spatial assimilation process. Members of the majority group in the urban society are unwilling to live in the same areas as members of certain minorities, even when they are economic equals, so the latter are forced to live in separate areas, generally termed ghettoes (Taeuber, 1968). Two separate hypotheses on their spatial patterns are presented, depending on whether the population of the ghetto society is expanding or relatively stable.

I. Ghetto Expansion. As the ghetto population expands, its original community area cannot absorb all of the increase and so extends, via the invasion and succession process. Since the original clusters are almost always in the lowest socio-economic status areas of a city's inner zone, this expansion will most likely be sectoral.

The line of least resistance to invasion would often be sectoral in form, since sideways movement is usually precluded by growth in other sectors.

II. The Stable Ghetto Population. Where, after its initial development, a minority community ceases to grow by in-migration, areal expansion of the ghetto is unlikely. Instead it may (a) remain in the same place for long periods, or (b) move en masse, along sectoral lines, to better residential areas, either as a result of general economic advancement, or because of pressure from the expansion of other communities (residential or non-residential) close to the city centre.

(Note that no mention is made of declining ghettoes, whose characteristics should parallel that shown in Figure III.10G or H.)

In many, especially the large, ghetto communities, stratification systems should develop, presumably based on socio-economic and family status and paralleling those of their host society. Since it has already been hypothesised that the ghetto will be sectoral in form, such stratification systems should produce zonal patterns within the sectors. Thus

III. In large ghetto communities there will be residential differentiation of component groups, which should be zonally distributed.

2. THE ASSIMILATION MODELS

These apply to groups which are socially and economically segregated within a society for only relatively short periods (perhaps a few decades), with their structural and cultural assimilation accompanied by more general spatial dispersal within cities. For such groups, central city ghettoes are thus an ephemeral stage in their entry to and acceptance within the host society, so that:

IV. As minority groups become assimilated their residential distribution becomes dispersed and shows few differences from that of the total population. At early stages of their residence they will be concentrated in communities in the city's inner zones, but these will disappear over time and the group spread through the whole city.

This hypothesis assumes that, after its inception, the minority community ceases to grow, except by its own natural increase. While the parallel societal assimilation and spatial dispersal processes are operating among the first generation of in-migrants, however, further movement into the community could preserve a ghetto which houses the newcomers, so that

V. With a minority group that continues to grow via in-migration, the ghetto community might remain, and, as expansion should be sectoral, there will be a zonal pattern within the minority group reflecting the related characteristics of degree of socio-economic assimilation and length of residence.

Finally, it has been suggested several times during the book that minority groups within cities, especially of international migrants, often build up very strong kinship and community ties which they retain by living together in their own 'urban villages'. Where this occurs, the ghetto will remain, irrespective of the economic advancement of its individual members. The strong community ties will be most important to the original migrants, and later generations in the group (especially those born within the ghetto) might be more attracted to the host society and become spatially as well as economically assimilated. In this way:

VI. A ghetto community might continue to exist throughout the period of assimilation, for part of the minority group. If other ghettoes are developing in the same zone, this earlier node may be forced to move out, but while it exists it will probably form the first residential area for other members of the group migrating to that city.

Most of the testing of these hypotheses must refer to United States cities. As with the other dimensions of urban residential patterns, this is because of better data available there and a greater number of studies. More importantly, however, it is because, among the societies studied, only the United States has experienced considerable minority group presence for a long period. After the initial, predominantly British, settlement (within which there were minority group patterns, notably the Irish), by the end of the nineteenth century there had been considerable movement to many American cities of Scandinavian and North European minorities followed by Eastern Europeans (particularly of Jewish stock), and then by Southern Europeans, mainly Italians (Cressey, 1938, discussed these waves of migration in Chicago; Handlin, 1951, 1959, discussed them for New York and Boston). In the present century, there has been a mass movement of Negroes within the United States (Hart, 1960), and also of Puerto Ricans and Mexican Americans to certain cities. Thus, it should be that all of the hypotheses can be tested in the American context, for, as Chapter II showed, many of these groups have become socially and spatially assimilated while others have been virtually condemned to an almost indefinite ghetto existence.

Although Britain has received many waves of minority group in-migrants, some of which, like the Jews, have lived in ghetto circumstances since before the industrial revolution, and others, like the Irish (Jackson, 1964), have been slowly assimilated, charting of the spatial processes is not well advanced there. Only since the Second World War has there been any great immigration of minority groups to the country. Some of this was a post-war flow of refugees, and more was a movement of manual workers, particularly Italians (Sibley, 1962), but these people were usually widely dispersed through the country. More recently, there has been a large-scale movement of Commonwealth, mainly coloured, immigrants (Davison, 1963, 1966; Patterson, 1960; Peach, 1966, 1968); these have led to similar residential patterns and problems as experienced by Negroes in United States cities, though with less severity as yet.

Australia and New Zealand have both been dominated by

immigration of people of British stock. In Australia there was some early movement of North Europeans and Scandinavians, paralleling, but overshadowed by, their movement to the United States, and since 1945 there has been a great influx of immigrants from many countries, especially Italians, Greeks, Maltese and Dutch (Zubrzycki, 1960). Jones (1967a) and Lieberson (1963b) have indicated differences between the 'old' and 'new' groups of immigrants in their societal and spatial assimilation, and Jones (1964) has described the conversion of a former Jewish neighbourhood to an Italian residential area, but detailed studies of spatial patterns are as yet few. New Zealand contains Dutch (Thomson, 1967), Yugoslav (Trlin, 1968), Indian (McGee, 1962), and Italian, Polish and Greek communities, among others (Thomson and Trlin, 1970), but these are all small and the country is dominated by British stock—with interesting regional variations, now muted, result-ing from the various colonial origins; Dunedin, for example, was part of a Scottish settlement; the former gold fields of the South Island's West Coast retain their Irish background: both are reflected in the present religious distribution (Heenan, 1967). The rapidly growing Maori community is moving to New Zealand's cities, however, and is being joined there by migrants from the Polynesian islands (Pool, 1961; Curson, 1968, 1970; Rowland, 1971). Their patterns can be compared with the American, but the recency of this development, as in Britain and Australia, limits the extent to which the assimilation model can be tested.

GENERAL PATTERNS

The general processes of residential assimilation or ghetto formation in the United States were referred to in Chapter II (see Lieberson, 1963a). So far, however, their direct spatial expressions have not been discussed. This first empirical section presents material to indicate which groups have experi-enced which processes.

Among the best evidence for such a task are a number of studies of the zonal patterns of minority groups in Chicago. These follow the classic Burgess schema of presenting data as gradients over a number of zones, and the first, by Cressey

(1938), was a product of the main years of Burgess's work on the city. He assembled data from the 1910, 1920 and 1930 national censuses, plus an 1898 Chicago School Board census, arranging them in ten concentric one-mile zones. By the latest date, Chicago contained no less than seven immigrant groups with more than 100,000 members each, in addition to 250,000 Negroes, and Cressey concluded that 'The distribution of these various groups reflects a definite process of succession. Immigrant stocks follow a regular sequence of settlement in successive areas of increasing stability and status . . . [which] represents the ecological setting within which the assimilation of the foreign population takes place' (Cressey, 1938, 61).

One of the groups which had gone through the entire spatial assimilation process by 1930 was the German. This colony expanded rapidly in the decade prior to 1860, when it formed 20 percent of Chicago's population. Initial settlement was on the North Side and two remnants of this ghetto remained in 1930, though several miles from the original node (Zorbaugh, 1929, 18–20, 149–150). Over time, they had moved out through the northern residential districts (see Figure III.1) and by 1930 'The great majority of the group has ceased to live in specific German communities and is scattered through more or less cosmopolitan residential areas. This widespread dispersion is an index of the decline of social unity among the Germans and of their gradual absorption into the general life of the city' (Cressey, 1938, 65).

Cressey's work was updated in 1950 by Ford, who added data for 1930 and 1940 to the original information for the ten zones, although he noted that 17 were feasible so that the last one was very broad (Ford, 1950; he referred to Cressey's 1929 doctoral dissertation and not the 1938 paper). The data were plotted on graphs, some of which are reproduced in Figure VI.1, and were interpreted by Ford as indicating an orderly movement of each group outwards from the city centre (though with little change between 1930 and 1940 because of the depression, the low rate of home construction, and the small net growth of the City of Chicago—only 20,000 persons).

Finally, Kiang has updated the data to 1960, presenting the information in tabular form (Table VI.1) for four dates and

247

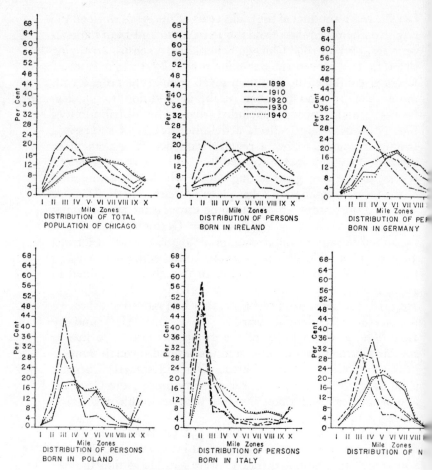

VI.I Transects showing the zonal distribution of Minority Groups in the city of Chicago. *Source:* Ford, 1950.

only three zones (Kiang, 1968). His conclusion followed those of the earlier studies: 'In 1960 the distribution of the leading ethnic groups in Chicago was partially due to a time factor in that those of the earliest group, such as the Irish and Swedish, were found farther from the Loop than the newcomers—the Mexicans and Puerto Ricans and the Negroes' (Kiang, 1968, 293). There has been much less change for the latter group, however, as shown both in Kiang's tables and Ford's graphs, and the following points have been drawn from Table VI.1:

1. In 1898, all of the minority groups were over-represented in the inner zone only. (Throughout this discussion over- and under-representation relates the percentage of the total population in a zone to the percentage of a group population.)

2. By 1920, the 'oldest' groups (Germans, Irish and Swedes) were under-represented in zone 1, and over-represented in

TABLE VI.1

THE DISTRIBUTION OF MINORITY GROUPS IN CHICAGO
(percent)

MILE ZONE	1898	1920	1940	1960	MILE ZONE	1898	1920	1940	1960
A. GERMANS					E. ITALIANS				
1–3	44	19	12	6	1–3	*85*	25	15	*13*
4–9	51	*74*	*80*	*69*	4–9	12	*73*	*83*	61
10+	5	7	*8*	*25*	10+	3	2	2	*26*
B. IRISH					F. RUSSIANS				
1–3	*46*	19	10	0	1–3	*72*	*30*	8	6
4–9	50	*76*	*81*	53	4–9	25	*66*	*88*	74
10+	4	5	*9*	*47*	10+	3	4	4	*20*
C. SWEDES					G. CZECHS				
1–3	*38*	10	*8*	1	1–3	*65*	27	*17*	0
4–9	52	*78*	*81*	*73*	4–9	33	70	*80*	87
10+	*10*	*12*	*11*	*26*	10+	2	3	3	13
D. POLES					H. NEGROES				
1–3	60	*38*	20	8	1–3	66	*24*	15	*13*
4–9	29	*48*	69	66	4–9	33	75	*84*	*78*
10+	*11*	*14*	11	*26*	10+	1	1	1	9

MILE ZONE	1898	1920	1940	1960
I. TOTAL POPULATION				
1–3	25	23	15	11
4–9	70	70	78	67
10+	5	7	7	22

Zones in which groups were over-represented are italicised.

Source: Kiang, 1968, 294.

zone 2. The latter were also slightly over-represented in zone 3, indicating their spatial diffusion.

3. At the same date, the 'newer' groups (Czechs, Italians, Poles, and Russians) were still over-represented in zone 1, though there had been some outward movement.

4. From 1898 to 1920, outward diffusion of Negroes was almost as rapid as for the other groups. Over the last forty years, however, they have remained concentrated in zone 2, while their numbers increased from 109,000 to 840,000.

5. By 1940, of the non-Negro groups only the Czechs and Poles were still slightly over-represented in the inner zone. The three oldest groups were relatively numerous in both of zones 2 and 3, while the younger were mainly concentrated in zone 2 (the Poles were the exception, having a bi-modal pattern of over-representation).

6. Of the seven groups originating in Europe, only the Italians were still over-represented in the inner zone by 1960, suggesting an urban village; there were no Czechs and Irish and few Swedes resident there. Five of the groups were over-represented in the outer zone, with almost half of the Irish there compared with less than a quarter of the total population. The Russians and Czechs, however, were still concentrated in the second zone, suggesting a continuity of the ghetto-form of settlement associated with the fact that many of them were members of the Jewish faith.

All three studies dealt only with the City of Chicago, and so no evidence is available to suggest the total spatial distribution of the minority groups. Nevertheless, considerable evidence has been presented on spatial patterns (and is confirmed in Duncan and Lieberson, 1959), which, in combination with the information on residential differentiation in Chapter II, suggests a ghetto expansion pattern for the Negroes, a stable ghetto population pattern for the East European Jews, and outward spatial assimilation of the other groups. For the latter, however, it should be noted that their 1960 distribution did not accord with the total population distribution. Instead, they were concentrated within the middle-class zones, avoiding the lower socio-economic status areas of the inner city.

THE EXPANDING GHETTO:
NEGROES IN AMERICAN CITIES

Negro residential patterns have been studied by sociologists since the early days of Park and Burgess's work at Chicago, one of the first detailed studies being Frazier's 1931 doctoral dissertation. More recently, two detailed monographs have been published by University of Chicago husband-and-wife research teams, both focussing strongly on the spatial aspects of Negro residence in large American cities.

The Negro Population of Chicago

The first of these monographs, by Duncan and Duncan (1957), dealt with the Negro population of Chicago up to and including 1950. During the first half of this century, Negro numbers increased sixteenfold within the city itself, to a total of 492,000. These people have always been highly segregated from the total population, and in 1950 over half of them lived in census tracts whose Negroes formed at least 97·5 percent of all residents. The ghetto's spatial form closely followed the anticipated: 'The general outlines of the Negro residential area had been established by 1920. In so far as expansion . . . has occurred, it has been in terms of adding areas contiguous to existing areas of Negro concentrations' (Duncan and Duncan 1957, 95). The main Negro quarter was a narrow wedge extending southwards from the CBD towards some early isolated Negro settlements near the city boundary (Figure VI.2), although a secondary, two-pronged 'black belt' had developed to the west of the city centre and a further core to the north had given Negroes almost exclusive occupance of the inner zone by 1950. Growth has been by Negro expansion into adjacent neighbourhoods, a process which has rarely been arrested or reversed by the white population regaining their former dominance of an area.

Invasion and succession has clearly been the mode of expansion for the ghetto in Chicago, therefore, and, using census tract data for the 1920–1950 period, Duncan and Duncan have suggested that its usual progression follows an S-shaped curve (Figure VI.3). Invasion is preceded by a long period of slow

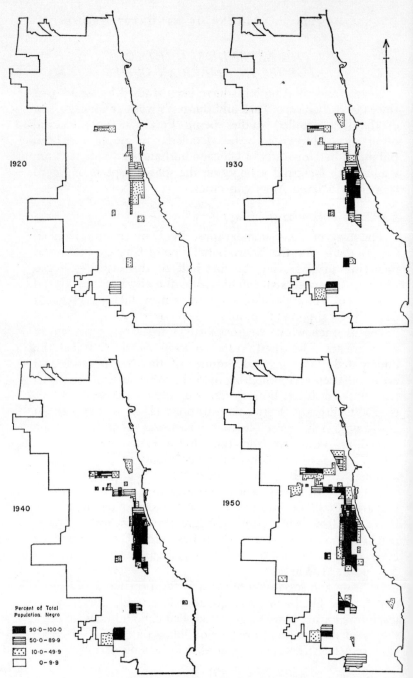

VI.2   Distribution of Negroes in the city of Chicago as a percentage of each census tract's population. *Source:* Duncan and Duncan, 1957.

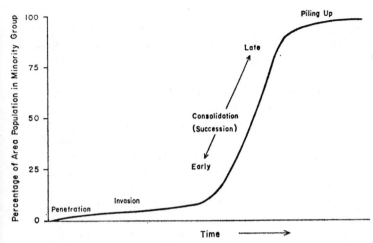

VI.3   The process of Invasion and Succession, showing the typical stages according to the percentage of an area's population who are of the invading group.

infiltration, and is followed by rapid in-movement of Negroes (succession), that continues until they become the sole inhabitants of the tract. More detailed study of the 1940s was based on a classification of the portions of this curve into the following four stages:

1. PENETRATION, during which a few Negro families enter a formerly all-white area.

2. INVASION, involving the in-movement of a substantial number of Negroes.

3. CONSOLIDATION, which shows a continuation of the number and proportion of Negroes.

4. PILING-UP, a final stage in which Negro numbers continue to increase after their proportion of the area's population has stabilised, usually at a very high level.

Full application of this schema depends on data availability, and in 1950 Census tract information on the nonwhite population was only given where their numbers exceeded 250. Thus nothing could be learned of the penetration tracts, but 154 tracts could be categorised as one of:

1. INVASION. Tracts with less than 2 percent Negroes in 1940, and also less than 250, but which by 1950 contained more than 250. The rapidity with which succession occasionally took place is illustrated by the fact that some tracts in this category were as much as 98 percent nonwhite by 1950.

2. EARLY CONSOLIDATION. These tracts had fewer than 250 nonwhites in 1940, but they formed more than 2 percent of the population. By 1950 there were more than 250 nonwhites, indicating that succession was proceeding during the decade but was not complete by 1950. (Such tracts were separated from those in the next category because of the absence of detailed data for them in the 1940 Census.)

3. CONSOLIDATION. There were more than 250 nonwhites in these tracts at both end years of the decade, but in 1940 they formed less than 80 percent of the population total. They thus represent the final stages of succession.

4. LATE CONSOLIDATION, whose tracts were similar to those in the preceding category except that nonwhites were more than 80 percent of the residents at both dates. By 1950, all were at least 92 percent Negro.

5. PILING-UP, the final stage in which nonwhites were at least 97·5 percent up the population at both dates. Generally the Negro numbers increased, with consequences on housing densities.

From the model of ghetto expansion in Figure III.10A a zonal pattern of these neighbourhoods within the Negro sectors was anticipated, with the invasion tracts furthest from the city centre and the piling-up closest. Only partial confirmation of this was given, however (Figure VI.4). One reason was that the ghetto expansion was not confined to sectors originating close to the CBD; outlying Negro concentrations existed in South Chicago by 1920 (Figure VI.2), whose core areas were 90 percent nonwhite by 1930. The main deviation between model and reality, however, was in the concentration of piling-up tracts in the centre of the main sector, with late consolidation areas closer in. This may not indicate a failure in the hypothesis but rather in the construction of the taxonomy. The piling-up stage involves increasing Negro densities;

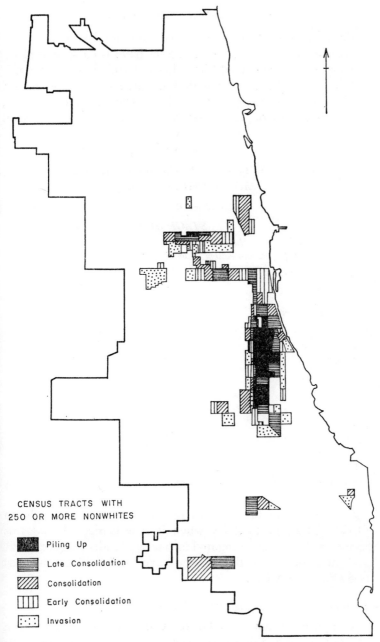

CENSUS TRACTS WITH
250 OR MORE NONWHITES

▓ Piling Up

≡ Late Consolidation

▨ Consolidation

Ⅲ Early Consolidation

∷ Invasion

VI.4 Classification of the Negro Residential Areas of Chicago, 1950.
  Source: Duncan and Duncan, 1957.

if the inner tracts are, as expected, the oldest sections of the ghetto, then they would presumably have been saturated by 1940 and such areas could have been classified as late consolidation. Nevertheless, although the pattern 'is by no means equivalent to a zonal classification' (Duncan and Duncan, 1957, 259), there is considerable concordance between

TABLE VI.2

ZONAL PATTERNS OF NEGRO RESIDENTIAL
AREAS: CHICAGO, 1950

(number of tracts)

STAGE OF SUCCESSION

Distance (Miles)	Piling Up	Late Consolidation	Consolidation	Early Consolidation	Invasion
A. NORTHERN SECTOR					
0–2			6	3	
B. WESTERN SECTOR					
1–2		1	4	2	3
2–3	1	3	7	7	3
3–5		2	3	2	11
C. SOUTHERN SECTOR					
1–3		4	3	2	
3–4	10	6	3	2	
4–5	12	2	1	3	3
5–6	5	4	1	1	4
6–8	4	3	4	4	7
9–15		3	3		2

Source: Duncan and Duncan, 1957, 260.

hypothesis and reality in the main, southern sector of the ghetto (Table VI.2), particularly when it is remembered that this sector has been very elongated for many decades (Figure VI.2) and much of its growth has been lateral rather than outwards (see also Table VI.1).

Invasion & Succession and Negro Migration

Evidence presented so far on Chicago has suggested the validity of the invasion and succession model to ghetto expansion. Complete verification of this, however, requires answers to the following:

What is the role of migration in the process?
How does invasion proceed?
What ecological patterns and processes exist within the ghetto?

The change of a neighbourhood's character from all-white to virtually all-Negro must involve migration, but the invasion and succession model has the change produced by pressure at the centre of the city, possibly from the expansion of non-residential uses but more likely from the growth of the ghetto community by migration to it from outside the city. Participants in the latter process are expected to settle in the inner zones of the sector, placing such demands on the housing supply there that older inhabitants are forced to move out, initiating a rippling migration pattern which ends with Negroes at the outer edge of the ghetto invading new neighbourhoods.

Recent evidence has generally discredited such a model (though perhaps Rose's (1964) report on the ghetto in Miami displayed the expected pattern). Duncan and Duncan showed that 72 percent of the Negro population growth in Chicago over the ten-year period ending in 1950 was the result of in-migration, but 'while the bulk of the Negro migrants enter areas of established Negro settlement, recent migrants are just as important an element in areas of recent or less concentrated Negro settlement as in areas in which Negroes constitute a very large proportion of the population' (Duncan and Duncan, 1957, 131). That statement was based on the following analysis of the 1950 Negro population. Four percent of all 1950 Chicago Negroes were resident outside that city in 1949. If these recent arrivals were evenly distributed through the city, they would form about 4 percent of each tract's nonwhite population, but the percentage of tracts with greater than this proportion of in-migrants was

Piling-Up 75
Late Consolidation 64 Consolidation 37 Early Consolidation 23
Invasion 21

The majority of the migrants entered the established parts of the ghetto, therefore (though whether these were the older, inner parts of the ghetto is not clear because of the previously discussed spatial pattern of the various neighbourhood types and the large 'migrant areas' used elsewhere in the Duncans' analysis). However, many recent arrivals were apparently living outside the established areas within a year of reaching Chicago.

Analysis of a 1959–1961 sample survey of Chicago residents has shown that the pattern noted by Duncan and Duncan for 1950 became even more apparent during the ensuing decade. Only 45 percent of long-term ghetto inhabitants moved to areas with fewer nonwhites than the areas which they left, compared to 70 percent of relatively recent members of the ghetto community (migrants to Chicago). This suggests that the actual invasion was not by the most established members of the community, and led to the conclusion that 'the "port-of-entry" model for Negro migration to cities is no longer adequate' (Straits, 1968, 5).

In 1899, DuBois wrote that 'The new [Negro] immigrants usually settle in pretty well-defined localities in or near the slums, and thus get the worst possible introduction to city life' (DuBois, 1899, 81), but analysis of 1960 Census data indicated a very different situation. Taeuber and Taeuber (1965b) classified each census tract in ten cities according to its position in the succession process during the 1950–1960 decade, as one of:

1. ESTABLISHED NEGRO AREAS, with more than 90 percent Negro residents at both dates.
2. CONSOLIDATION:
   a. Succession; containing 250 or more nonwhites at both dates, with the nonwhite proportion increasing and the white decreasing during the decade.
   b. Invasion; less than 250 nonwhites in 1950, more in 1960: nonwhite increase and white decrease in population.
   c. Growing; nonwhite increase greater than white.
   d. Declining; nonwhite decrease slower than white.
3. STABLE.
4. DISPLACEMENT.

(The last two categories are mainly irrelevant to the present discussion.)

The distribution of recent Negro migrants (1955–1960) to the cities showed that these people were more likely to move to invasion tracts than to the established Negro areas (Table VI.3). Of the ten cities, only in St. Louis, New Orleans and

TABLE VI.3

DISTRIBUTION OF NEGRO IN-MIGRANTS:
TEN CITIES, 1960

CITY	Percent Tracts with In-Migrants Over-represented[1]				
	Established Negro Areas	Succession	Invasion	Declining	Index of Dissimilarity[2]
DETROIT	17	42	49	30	17·6
CLEVELAND	8	68	50	30	18·2
PHILADELPHIA	67[3]	48	64	31	14·8
ST. LOUIS	50[3]	38	75	25[3]	13·6
WASHINGTON	0	57	80	20	13·7
BALTIMORE	33	35	55	33	18·1
NEW ORLEANS	71	44	67[3]	38	22·3
ATLANTA	0	40	100[3]	100[3]	21·3
BIRMINGHAM	33	42	—	67	10·4
MEMPHIS	27	55	—	40	15·1

[1] Relative to the total nonwhite population.
[2] Between total nonwhite and in-migrant populations.
[3] Percentage based on less than 5 tracts.

Source: Taeuber and Taeuber, 1965b, 148–149.

Birmingham did the established areas contain a greater percentage of the migrants than of the total Negro population (and in St. Louis the figures were 15·5 and 15·4 percent respectively). In Cleveland the established areas contained 23·9 percent of the 1960 Negro population, but received only 14·3 percent of the reported in-migrants. Far from moving into the main sections of the ghetto, therefore, the new arrivals tended to congregate in the newer Negro neighbourhoods (although the indices of dissimilarity in Table VI.3 suggest a fairly even distribution of them throughout the Negro community). But this finding *may not* completely invalidate the model portrayed

259

in Figure III.10A, for many of the in-migrants *could* have resided first in the established areas and then moved again before the census date, suggesting a pattern of rapid mobility via an 'urban village', akin to that suggested for the assimilation model in Figure III,10G.

This unanticipated finding has resulted from marked changes in the character of Negro migration in the United States over recent years (paralleling those for the white population discussed on pages 179–182). Until the 1950s 'Negro in-migrants to cities were of lower social and economic status than both the resident Negro and white populations' (Taeuber and Taeuber, 1965a, 429). Such migrations were dominated by the rural-to-urban, South-to-North drift of the Negro population (Hart, 1960), but during 1955–1960 there was a substantial inter-metropolitan flow of Negroes, especially in the northeast of the United States.

Along with this changing spatial pattern have occurred changes in the characteristics of the migrants. Over the 13 largest SMSAs, excluding Los Angeles and Newark, Taeuber and Taeuber found that:

1. Compared to already resident nonwhites, in-migrants were better educated and more held white-collar occupations.

2. When standardised for age differences, in-migrants from non-metropolitan origins had lower socio-economic status than those from metropolitan areas, but similar status to the nonwhites already resident at their destinations.

3. Compared to the in-migrant nonwhites, out-migrants had higher educational and occupational status.

In contrast with earlier decades, therefore, Negro migration patterns and characteristics have become similar to those of non-Negroes, with a now small rural-to-urban stream being overshadowed by an inter-metropolitan flow of high-status people: 'Once Negroes become metropolitan residents, the tendency is to remain in metropolitan areas and to move, if at all, within national streams of intermetropolitan migration' (Taeuber and Taeuber, 1965a, 437). Many of the Negro in-migrants do not go to the high-density slums, therefore, but to the more salubrious, outer portions of the ghetto.

The Process of Invasion & Succession

The model of ghetto expansion presented in Chapter III, termed the 'port-of-entry' model by Straits (1968), indicated that the invaders among the minority group would be its highest status group (in terms of the host society's norms this would mean best educated and paid). In general, this appears to be a valid representation of the process, and Duncan and Duncan, for example, showed for invasion tracts in Chicago that:

1. As nonwhites invaded a formerly white neighbourhood, they entered at higher levels of crowding than those of the persons they displaced, which is an indication of their need to spread the high housing costs.

2. Invasion was mainly accomplished by owner-occupier acquisition of property. In part, this was because of an apparent preference for single-family dwelling units (Duncan and Duncan (1957, 234) suggested that this may be due to a 'handicap in finding quarters in apartment buildings'), and also because of difficulties in securing adequate rental property.

3. In all but four of the 33 invasion tracts, the nonwhites paid much higher rents than the whites, so that 'non-whites invading an area must pay a premium rental, which they are able to finance only by using residential space very intensively, e.g. by doubling-up families in the household or by including relations or lodgers in the household' (Duncan and Duncan, 1957, 236). The same point was made recently in a study of the Negro population of Wilmington, Delaware: 'For the same rents as whites, Negroes were getting less space and worse housing. They were doing it on much lower incomes. The increase in the quality of their housing over the decade [1950–1960] was not nearly proportionate to the increase in its price. It must be that the average Negro family enormously increased the share of its income devoted to housing, and got a small improvement for that increased investment.' (Tilly, Jackson and Kay, 1965, 91).

A generally held view of invasion and succession is that as a few nonwhites move into an area, the whites rapidly panic, sell, and move out, often incurring heavy financial losses. Interesting case studies of this have been reported by Rapkin and Grigsby (1960b). On an all-white, middle-income block of suburban Philadelphia, a home owner was unable to sell her property, until an estate agent presented a Negro family prepared to pay an acceptable price. The vendor reasoned her choice as 'either to lose her friends or her money, and she was afraid it would have to be her friends' (Rapkin and Grigsby, 1960b, 140). She entered into a contract with the Negro family, therefore, and from then on:

> events moved rapidly. The following morning real estate salesmen were out contacting all homeowners in the block, and by mid-afternoon a number of the residents had decided to sell. A local real estate broker . . . who had not solicited any listings in the block was asked by four owners to list their homes . . . The extent to which panic was generated by the real estate salesmen and the extent to which it would have developed in any event cannot be determined. It could be reasoned that the undercurrents of panic had been in motion for years waiting to come to the surface. The purchase viewed as a violation of the sanctity of the block may have been the only event necessary to precipitate the ensuing hysteria (Rapkin and Grigsby, 1960b, 141).

The first sale was concluded on February 28; a week later two 'For Sale' signs had been erected: by December four more Negro families had moved in; and 'within a year transition was well under way' (Rapkin and Grigsby, 1960b, 142).

Although Duncan and Duncan's maps (Figure VI.2) suggest that many areas remain in the infiltration or invasion stages for a considerable time, there is evidence that in most cases infiltration is rapidly followed by succession. Rapkin and Grigsby (1960b, 67) suggested that where white discrimination levels were low and few Negroes were moving in, succession need not be inevitable. This is unlikely with the present burgeoning growth of Negro urban populations, however, so that while the succession process is not a natural law,

> In Philadelphia . . . white attitudes regarding mixed areas are apparently so widely held at this time that the presence of more than a few Negroes in an area outweighs all other

factors which influence the purchase of homes by white families (Rapkin and Grigsby, 1960b, 66).

This conclusion was drawn from detailed study of succession in parts of West Philadelphia, whose results are initially surprising as they indicated white households still purchasing homes in mixed areas (including households with children, generally expected to be most against mixed areas because of the consequent school problems). There was an attrition in white demand as the proportion of Negro occupance rose, however. The authors estimated that when the Negro percentage reached 30, white housing demand was 85–94 percent down on its former level, and even where there was only a Negro proportion of 5 percent, white housing demand was reduced by 50–60 percent.

Taeuber and Taeuber's analysis of the 1960 Census data throws further light on this question, for they reported that the white population in Negro residential areas were more mobile than those living elsewhere in the city. If, as some studies have shown, these persons are also renters, then they will have few ties to the area and could easily move on (see Taeuber and Taeuber, 1965b, 149 and 173). Such analyses (see also Straits, 1968) have also shown that the whites most likely to move from an invaded area are the higher-income residents. Lower-status groups can less afford to move; indeed, in the general housing situation of American cities, they may find obtaining alternative, comparable accommodation extremely difficult.

One area where succession did not follow invasion, although there was more than 60 percent attrition in white demand for housing by the time the Negro percentage was 5, was in the upper-class neighbourhood of West Mt. Airy in Germantown, Philadelphia. The first Negro purchase was in January, 1951, the second more than a year later and, by the end of 1955, 46 nonwhite families were in residence. Two factors made this invasion unusual:

1. The invaders were not moving from an adjacent Negro community.
2. The Negroes 'enjoyed satisfactory incomes and at least moderate wealth and social status . . . the new Negro arrivals

263

were persons of education and professional attainment and in this regard undoubtedly compared very favourably with the resident population' (Rapkin and Grigsby, 1960b, 130).

Thus Negro demand was not great and did not threaten to become so, and the neighbourhood's standing was not under heavy attack. In contrast to most invasions there was some decline in prices for property after the infiltration, but housing turnover was not great, due apparently to strong community action against discrimination.

In 1963, in response to an increase in the number of homes placed on the market, an active campaign was initiated by community leaders to discourage homeowners from making hasty and ill-considered sales and to urge them to reappraise their responses to their new Negro neighbors. These efforts together with the unattractive offers made by would-be buyers seem to have encouraged many to withdraw their properties from the market (Rapkin and Grigsby, 1960b, 135).

Such community organisations are very common in transition areas in American cities, and they are 'devoted to the goal of achieving biracial stability' (Molotch, 1969, 227); more, it would seem, in order to financially protect the remaining whites than through deeper moral concerns.

One aspect of the West Mt. Airy situation was very atypical, for prices paid by Negro invaders are usually higher than those paid by non-Negroes in the same area in preceding years. From controlled tests in San Francisco, Oakland and Philadelphia, and evidence from four other cities, Laurenti (1960) showed that property prices only rarely fell after Negro invasion (see also Schietinger, 1951). Indeed, there was a 4 to 1 chance that prices would stay firm or increase, whatever the relative size of the invasion, given a general real-estate market of rising prices. Laurenti suggested a continuum of possible consequences of invasion ranging from:

1. A glutted market, in which whites panic and offer more property to the market than there is demand for, so that prices fall.

to 2. A shortage market in which whites are reluctant to leave, but nonwhite demand is such that they will pay premium prices.

The present American situation is closer to the latter possibility, because of the general housing shortage. Relatively low-income families among a rapidly growing Negro urban population must pay very high prices for housing which they desperately need, and which they must occupy at very high densities.

Detailed studies of Negro succession by Wolf and others in Detroit have suggested that the sequence is a self-fulfilling prophecy. A few Negroes moved in; a few more whites moved out; Negroes take their place, and this generates 'Belief by the whites that a Negro invasion is imminent [which] leads them to move out of the neighborhood, the very action that makes the invasion possible' (Wolf, 1957, 9). Interview results indicated that people did not move out because of anti-Negro prejudice, but rather 'Clear-cut identification with reference groups which stress the importance of a conventional prestige-address, degree of concern with the local public schools as an influence upon their children, and previous experience in changing neighborhoods' (Wolf, 1957, 16).

The relevance of this finding was shown in a comparison of two middle-class, white neighbourhoods undergoing succession in Detroit and Cleveland. There were considerable variations between the two areas on several factors which should influence the rate of succession—including the status of the invaders, the desirability of the districts, the closeness of major Negro districts, and the amount of real-estate activity—but $2\frac{1}{2}$ years after the initial invasion, both areas were about 25 percent Negro (Caplan and Wolf, 1960). Indeed, Wolf has shown that middle-class residents often assess their residential areas as undesirable even before any infiltration by Negroes has taken place, apparently by extrapolating the trends in adjacent neighbourhoods (Wolf, 1963). She suggested that real-estate agents were important generators of such attitudes (see also Tilly, Jackson and Kay, 1965, 40–41), acting as experts advising the inhabitants, and these are assisted by the negative attitudes of lending agencies towards financing proposed home purchases by whites in threatened areas.

In a more recent study, Wolf (1965) has suggested that trends in a Detroit neighbourhood may indicate new patterns of succession. Some invasion had taken place, but it was proceeding rather slowly, despite the anticipated change-over by the resident population. One of the reasons for the slow rate was the inability of Negroes to purchase homes there at a time of considerable unemployment in Detroit, while the relatively old, white residents were not as prepared to move out as younger middle-class families (to whom the school problem would be more important) might be. This perhaps suggested more resistance, but Molotch has recently compared two middle-class communities in Chicago, of which one is being rapidly invaded, and shown that real property transfers indicated that the invaded neighbourhood was in fact the more stable. Racial transition was coming about because turnover was generally high in the city (over 50 percent moved in the five years prior to 1960), allowing Negroes to move in. He concluded 'It is likely that a similar number of persons would have moved no matter what racial conditions existed in the area' (Molotch, 1969, 236), so that rapid Negro succession *could* occur under normal circumstances of property turnover and would be more likely to if the area was adjacent to a Negro community —irrespective of white attitudes to succession. If this is so, then Rose's (1970) suggested terminology of retreat and succession would seem preferable to invasion.

Predicting Ghetto Expansion

Two geographers have attempted to simulate the pattern of ghetto expansion, using models which incorporate the processes discussed here. The first represented ghetto expansion 'as a spatial diffusion process, in which Negro migrants gradually penetrate the surrounding white area' (Morrill, 1965, 348). This model was founded on a premise that the role of proximity is crucial, and it was used to simulate Seattle's ghetto expansion, given the rate of Negro population growth. The basis of the procedure was a distance-biased migration process in which the space-searching procedure of finding a new home outside the ghetto was represented by the drawing of random numbers to indicate which block was selected. Comparison of actual and simulated expansion for two decades indicated close correspondence between the two in areal extent, in Negro density, and in Negro exclusiveness: the main variation between model and reality was that the former paid too little attention to the role of topography. Extension of the ghetto was along a valley floor, with the adjacent 'ridge and view' properties proving relatively resistant to invasion.

Rose criticised Morrill's use of a diffusion process, suggesting that ghetto expansion patterns also depended very much on white adjustment to a Negro threat. (Morrill did incorporate different resistance rates for neighbourhoods.) He thus constructed an alternative model, incorporating not only 'the residential search behavior of prospective home seekers' but also 'white propensity for residential desegregation' (Rose, 1970, 9). There were three components to the model:

1. Demographic, which generated housing demand estimates from age-specific birth and death rates plus migration rates.

2. Producer, which estimated the housing supply for Negroes through rates of white abandonment at given Negro proportions.

3. Consumer, which allocated Negro home seekers to these neighbourhoods, using rents there as weights for probable entries.

Evaluation of the model was through a simulation of ghetto expansion for Milwaukee, with the general result that it tended to scatter Negro residents rather more widely than in fact occurred.

Spatial Patterns within the Ghetto

The changing pattern of Negro migration in recent years, and the consequent intra-city distribution, suggest that the spatial structure of the ghetto might be similar to that for the total socio-economic status dimension, as discussed in Chapter IV. However, it was indicated in Chapter II that a factorial ecology for the Negro population of one American city produced very different results from a parallel one for the white population

TABLE VI.4

FACTORIAL ECOLOGY: TOLEDO, OHIO, 1960

ROTATED COMPONENT LOADINGS[1]

VARIABLE	Non-Negro Population					Negro Population				
COMPONENT	I	II	III	IV	V	I	II	III	IV	V
% Unemployed	68	49	06	19	03	62	36	05	45	10
% Professional/Technical	-14	-91	13	-17	-02	-88	05	05	17	-20
% Labourers	33	44	-04	59	09	38	32	-78	10	10
% College Education	-17	-91	20	-14	04	-91	03	21	-06	-16
% Low Income	80	35	06	23	06	37	-07	-38	20	77
% Owner-occupiers	-90	-11	-16	-08	25	-17	31	87	-20	-12
Persons per Unit	-73	06	04	-27	55	22	73	28	-30	20
Crowding	-07	54	14	00	69	10	31	02	-02	93
% Working Females	13	17	09	-04	-89	57	-05	-16	-13	-68
% Under 15	-64	12	20	-28	60	-08	88	-12	-27	30
Marital Status	-61	-08	58	18	12	-27	25	40	-57	-17
% Single	81	08	-04	28	-13	66	-54	-17	02	33
% Same House 1955-60	-17	22	-91	05	01	39	-10	76	40	18
% Male	10	27	17	85	00	08	-90	07	-28	04
% Negro	43	-06	-23	66	-19	-10	-02	02	90	04

[1] Decimal points omitted: Loadings greater than ·35 italicised.

Source: Johnston (forthcoming).

(Table VI.4). Thus a separate Negro residential structure exists.

Frazier's thesis on the Negro family in Chicago indicated a zonal pattern within the ghetto. Data were presented for seven zones within the Black Belt to test the hypothesis that 'family disorganization among Negroes was an aspect of the selective and segregative process of the urban community'

TABLE VI.5

ZONAL PATTERNS IN THE NEGRO
COMMUNITY: CHICAGO

	ZONE						
	I	II	III	IV	V	VI	VII
Percent Illiterate[1]	13·4	4·6	3·2	2·3	3·3	2·9	2·7
Percent Males Professional and White Collar	5·8	5·5	10·7	11·2	12·5	13·4	34·2
Percent Family Heads born in South	77·7	77·0	74·7	73·8	72·6	69·0	65·2
Percent Adult Males Single	38·6	38·1	35·9	32·0	30·7	27·3	24.7
Percent Families with Female Heads	22·0	23·1	20·8	20·4	20·5	15·2	11·9
Percent House Owners	0	1·2	6·2	7·2	8·3	11·4	29·8
Rate of Family Desertion[2]	2·5	2·6	2·1	1·5	1·1	0·4	0·2
Rate of Juvenile Delinquency[2]	42·8	31·4	30·0	28·8	15·7	9·6	1·4

[1] Of persons aged 10 and older.
[2] Per 100 base population.

Source: Frazier, 1967, 227–231.

(Frazier, 1967, 236). Almost all of his indices of family life, social disorganisation, and economic and family status indicated clear zonal trends; levels of disorganisation decreased away from the centre while both family and socio-economic status increased (Table VI.5).

The Chicago study was largely replicated in a later investigation of Harlem (New York), using a series of five concentric zones based on the point of original Negro settlement there. Again, levels of family status (measured by such items as fertility and proportion married) increased towards the outer zones, and levels of disorganisation similarly declined away from the centre, but there was no apparent pattern in the crime rates. Nevertheless, Frazier concluded that:

> where a racial or cultural group is strongly segregated and carries on a more or less independent community life, such local communities may develop the same pattern of zones as the larger urban community (Frazier, 1937, 88).

and he was basically correct, especially since, like Burgess, he was mainly interested in the disorganisation variables.

Recent work by Duncan and Duncan and by Schnore has reproduced Frazier's findings for later dates. The former authors found in 1950 Chicago that within the western and southern sectors 'the socio-economic status of the population increases and the quality of housing improves as distance from the center increases, whereas congestion and family disorganization decrease' (Duncan and Duncan, 1957, 292). One exception to this was in the outer parts of the southern sectors, which contained some relatively old, peripheral Negro settlements.

Schnore expanded this research methodology to cover 24 different large cities at 1960, using the three traditional measures of socio-economic status (completed education, family income, and white-collar occupations). With some deviations (some of them the result of data aggregation into one zonal set when, as in Chicago, there may have been more than one Negro sector) he concluded that zonal patterns of socio-economic status within the ghetto displayed the Burgess pattern. Thus, although over the last few decades the family and socio-economic status patterns have become, at least relatively, spatially independent among the white population, there have been few changes within the ghetto so that the two patterns are still related; the highest socio-economic status areas are also those of highest family status.

Given these zonal patterns and the outward expansion of the ghetto, a further characteristic should be a process of invasion and succession within Negro residential areas. The Negroes who invade white neighbourhoods are high in socio-economic and family status for their segment of society, but unfortunately few data are available for an enquiry into whether the status of areas within the ghetto declines over time.

Some information has been gleaned from Duncan and Duncan's study of Chicago, using their tract classification system. This is difficult to interpret, however, because of both the lack of nonwhite data for many tracts at the 1940 census and temporal changes in some of the measures (for example, there were great improvements in the overall standard of education of the nonwhite population during the decade). The process of succession was clearly associated with increases in density and crowding, however, especially in the early stages,

TABLE VI.6

THE CHANGING STRUCTURE OF THE NEGRO
GHETTO: CHICAGO, 1940–1950[1]

DENSITY (100s per square mile)			CROWDING (% Dwellings 1·5/Room+)		
Tracts	1940	1950	Tracts	1940	1950
Piling-Up	523	615	Piling-Up	25·3	31·1
Late Consolidation	287	374	Late Consolidation	14·4	24·8
Consolidation	301	378	Consolidation	9·5	25·6
Early Consolidation	252	336	Early Consolidation	12·0	33·6
Invasion	357	410	Invasion	8·9	15·7

OCCUPATION (% Males White-collar)			UNEMPLOYMENT (% of Males)		
Tracts	1940	1950	Tracts	1940	1950
Piling-Up	15·5	15·5	Piling-Up	40·0	12·5
Late Consolidation	17·9	15·6	Late Consolidation	39·3	12·3
Consolidation	24·9	19·2	Consolidation	24·4	7·8
Early Consolidation	27·4	13·4	Early Consolidation	27·9	11·4
Invasion	37·8	17·4	Invasion	20·0	10·2

HOME OWNERSHIP (% Dwellings)			EDUCATION (% 1 year High School)[2]		
Tracts	1940	1950	Tracts	1940	1950
Piling-Up	5·9	9·6	Piling-Up	26·6	37·4
Late Consolidation	13·8	14·0	Late Consolidation	26·6	36·3
Consolidation	7·9	14·8	Consolidation	21·6	31·7
Early Consolidation	7·6	15·4	Early Consolidation	27·5	36·9
Invasion	14·4	22·2	Invasion	37·2	38·2

[1] For Early Consolidation and Invasion Tracts: 1940 data, total population, 1950, nonwhite population.
[2] Standardised for age differentials.

Source: Duncan and Duncan, 1957, Chapter VII.

and also with declines in socio-economic status (the last point is not well-documented because the 1940 data for some tracts referred to the total population). For home ownership, the small increase for consolidation tracts relative to the total suggests the postulated status decline (Table VI.6), but the unemployment changes were not as clear-cut.

From a number of regression analyses of 1950 on 1940 tract values, Duncan and Duncan reported considerable stability, concluding that

> any changes in these characteristics associated with succession amount to somewhat minor variations on a pattern of areal differentiation with considerable inertia or resistance to change. The implication is that succession is a selective process, inasmuch as the incoming population is sorted into residential areas in much the same way as these areas differentiated the outgoing population (Duncan and Duncan, 1957, 267–268).

The Taeubers reached a similar conclusion, so that, since the pattern of zonal differentiation was the same at both dates and the ghetto had expanded greatly between the two, then it can be inferred that some process of invasion and succession (or filtering) was occurring within the segregated districts.

THE STABLE GHETTO POPULATION: JEWISH RESIDENTIAL DISTRICTS

The usually-quoted example of a minority group within an urban society who *choose* to live in ghetto situations, when indeed they need not, is the Jewish population. Two reasons are suggested for this: firstly, the Jews have for so long been excluded from general society that they have accepted such isolation and still live with it, even though they might now be fully acceptable to the wider population (see Wirth, 1956, 287), and secondly, the Jewish society believes in inbreeding so that 'fear of intermarriage is . . . one of the reasons that Jewish centers are so popular: they permit the teen-agers to get together' (Glazer and Moynihan, 1964, 164: see also Beshers, 1962).

The development and changing location of the Chicago

ghetto were described by Wirth, but with little detail on spatial patterns. This has been the case with most studies of American Jewry, because of the absence of data on Jewish residential patterns (the American Census authorities consider the Jews a religious rather than a racial group, and do not collect data on religious identification). Some of Wirth's points are of relevance, however: for example, he showed the separate development of low and high socio-economic status ghettoes and the significant class segregation within Chicago's Jewish community, both in line with hypothesis III presented here. In addition, he suggested that many Jews lived in the ghetto without knowing it: they took what accommodation they could when they reached Chicago and didn't realise there was anything odd in the large Jewish population around them, because this was what they were used to (Wirth, 1956, 241–243).

A major recent study showed that the Jewish population of the Providence urbanised area declined slightly between 1951 and 1963, so that if the stable ghetto hypothesis applied to this group, its spatial correlates should be apparent. Residential clustering was not as great as might have been anticipated, however. There was a central ghetto with a very strong concentration of Jews, but in addition a considerable number were scattered fairly widely through the suburban areas (in only one suburban tract did Jews form as much as 25 percent of the total population). A core ghetto area has persisted, and according to the survey data on mobility intentions will continue to do so, but an important trend in recent years has been 'a more general residential integration of the Jewish community into the larger population of the metropolitan area' (Goldstein and Goldscheider, 1968, 49).

The members of the Jewish community who moved to the suburbs were generally the younger families, the better educated and those in the higher-status occupations. In addition, the suburbanites generally had weaker ties to Judaism, although, as the authors noted, there was no evidence on whether the weaker ties were the cause or the result of moves away from the community's centre (Goldstein and Goldscheider, 1968, 60). From this, changes in the form of residential segregation within the ghetto were inferred:

The previous distinctions were drawn between the old ghetto area, with its high concentration of foreign born, and the newer urban and suburban centers with their disproportionate number of second- and third-generation Jews; the new distinctions may be . . . drawn not on the basis of generation status and its associated characteristics, but rather on the basis of socio-economic status and strength of ties with Jewish institutions and practices. The residential choice of the future may be between living in areas of Jewish concentration . . . and integrating more fully into the larger community by movement to the suburbs (Goldstein and Goldscheider, 1968, 91).

Goldstein and Goldscheider represented the ghetto community as breaking down, at least in part, as some of its members moved to the suburbs to become assimilated into American society (and the Jews moving to the suburbs shared many characteristics with the non-Jews making the same move). There was evidence that the ghetto itself had moved during its long years of persistence, in Providence, as well as in New York, in Chicago and elsewhere (the best empirical evidence, however, is in Lipman's (1964) small investigation of one synagogue in London). Its present breakdown, however, suggests that the self-imposed ghetto in the United States was ephemeral. In this way, the spatial patterns are more akin to those outlined for spatial assimilation in hypotheses IV and VI, and to the patterns discussed in the next section, although the timelag between ghetto development and decay may have been much greater in the Jewish case.

MIGRANT ASSIMILATION INTO AMERICAN URBAN SOCIETY: THE SPATIAL PATTERN

As suggested earlier, the ghetto patterns just described reflect either inability or unwillingness to spread themselves through the various residential districts of the city among minority groups, following their economic assimilation into its society. For groups to whom this doesn't apply, the ghetto is an ephemeral district.

The ghetto stage occurs during the early years of a group's residence in an urban area, according to the model, and the general view is that the ghettoes develop in the worst slum areas of the city. Recent work by Ward (1969) has suggested that this was not entirely true in late nineteenth-century New York. Using data from a special census taken for New York and Brooklyn in 1890, he identified four, apparently independent, components of the spatial pattern of immigrant residential districts there; high mortality, age structure, population densities, and established immigrant groups. In part, these represented the expected pattern in the inner parts of a city, with a transition from the high-population density areas of the most central portions (occupied mainly by the newer immigrants) to the lower-density, inner suburban areas to which longer-established groups had moved. But the independence of the population density and mortality factors was less expected; areas of high population density and mortality only occurred in the transitional districts between the Russian-Jewish and Italian ghettoes. In part this may have been the result of differences between the two groups, yet it points up the complexity of the phenomenon.

For other groups, also, the model does not provide a complete description of their urban residential patterns, because of some social, economic or demographic peculiarities. This is shown in a study of Dutch migrants in Kalamazoo, Michigan—one of the few attempts by geographers to chart the spatial characteristics of migrant acculturation and assimilation. The first Dutch families moved there in the mid-nineteenth century, but by 1870, when they numbered about 1,000, there was no visible ghetto development except for a small concentration in the celery-growing area south of the city (Figure VI.5). This was explained as:

> From no residential section of the city were the Dutch, for being Dutch, systematically excluded for presumably the community at large, faced with but a light in-migration of Netherlanders, had been able psychologically, socially and economically to absorb this particular foreign element without recourse to group segregation (Jakle and Wheeler, 1969a, 250–252)

which fits Bergel's (1953) model of segregation (see page 49).

By 1910, the Dutch population had quadrupled and there

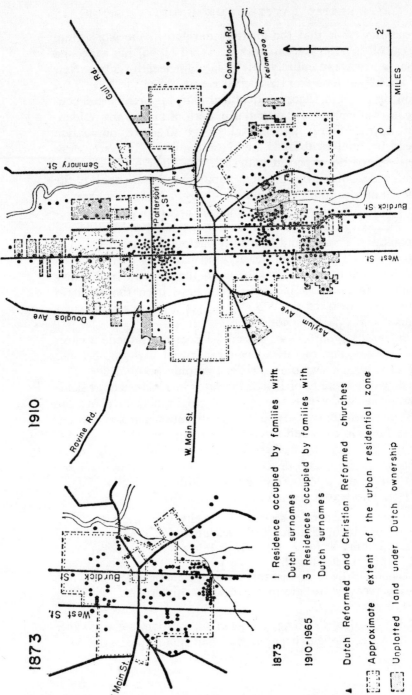

VI.5 The changing distribution of Dutch households in Kalamazoo, 1873 and 1910. *Source:* Jakle and Wheeler, 1969a.

1910

1873

Rovine Rd.

Comstock Rd.

Kalamazoo R.

Gull Rd.

Seminary St.

Patterson St.

Burdick St.

West St.

Douglas Ave.

Asylum Ave.

W. Main St.

West St.

Burdick St.

W. Main St.

1 Residence occupied by families with Dutch surnames

3 Residences occupied by families with Dutch surnames

Dutch Reformed and Christian Reformed churches

1873
1910-1965

Approximate extent of the urban residential zone

Unplotted land under Dutch ownership

MILES

0   1   2

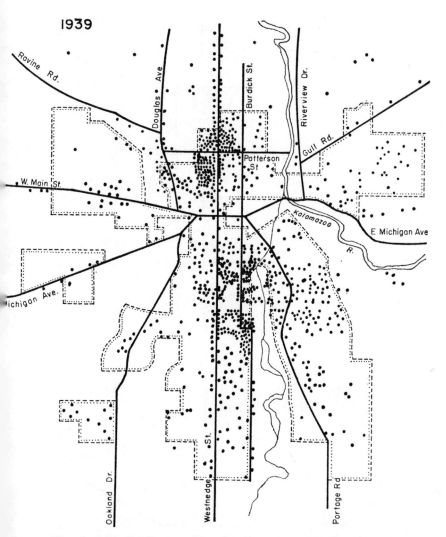

VI.5 The changing distribution of Dutch households in Kalamazoo, 1939.
Source: Jakle and Wheeler, 1969a.

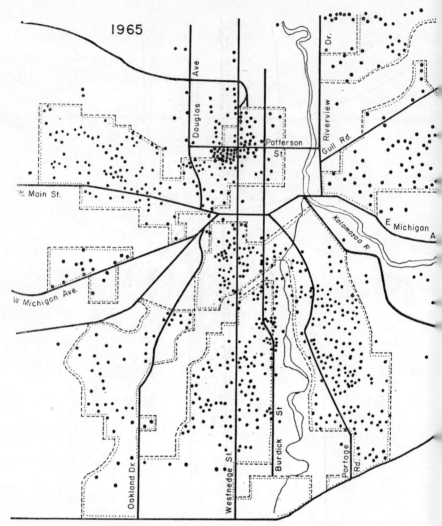

VI.5 The changing distribution of Dutch households in Kalamazoo, 1965.
Source: Jakle and Wheeler, 1969a.

was clear evidence of ghetto growth, not in the city centre but on the outskirts in the market-gardening areas, where most of the Dutch were employed (Figure VI.5). Continued migration led to the expansion of these ghetto areas, but was accompanied by a slow dispersal of households away from such areas as a result of a general 'Americanization' of the Dutch population (Jakle and Wheeler, 1969b, 453). The weakening of community bonds was assisted by increasing personal mobility, which allowed families to retain contact without the intense proximity of the ghetto, and this was reflected in the decline of the latter districts as shown in 1939 and 1965 maps (Figure VI.5). Only Kalamazoo's Negro district (north of the city centre) now shows an absence of Dutch.

In many respects this pattern reflects the model outlined in hypothesis IV and V, the main deviation being in the location of the ghettoes which grew on the city fringe because of the 'Dutchmen's rather unique perception of the local physical environment and his derived resource management schemes' (Jale and Wheeler, 1969b, 459). For other groups which lacked such important territorial attractants for their ghettoes, however, the pattern has generally fitted the hypothesis very closely. This was shown in Simirenko's investigation of the Minneapolis Russian community, whom he divided into three groups:

1. The Pilgrims; the old people within the Russian community who are anxious to preserve the established life of the community.

2. The Colonists, members of the second generation who find themselves torn between the incentives of membership in the majority community and a persistent loyalty to their parents' way of life.

3. The Frontiersmen, those in the second generation who have made the break with ethnic colleagues to seek their individual fortunes within the majority community (Simirenko, 1964, 20).

The original Russian settlement in Minneapolis was to the northeast of the city centre, around St. Mary's Church, and it was from this node that the ghetto grew and the migrant population was gradually dispersed, particularly northwards

(Table VI.7). Of the present Russian population, it has been the frontiersmen and, to a lesser extent, the colonists who have moved away from this ghetto community, and since there was a clear correlation between group membership and socio-economic status (the frontiersmen were by far the highest-status group and the pilgrims the lowest), these findings satisfy

TABLE VI.7

THE RUSSIAN COMMUNITY IN MINNEAPOLIS

RESIDENTIAL AREAS

	Northeast	North Minneapolis[1]	Other Cities and Suburban Districts
A. THE EVOLVING PATTERN[2]			
1890	11	0	0
1900	58	1	0
1910	131	1	7
1920	234	6	13
1930	399	18	49
1940	455	28	71
1950	405	50	92
1959	320	76	106
B. GROUP MEMBERSHIP AND LOCATION, 1959[3]			
Pilgrims	86·2	0	13·8
Colonists	57·1	26·2	16·7
Frontiersmen	20·6	23·5	55·9

[1] Mainly areas adjacent to the Northeastern core.
[2] All Russians listed in directories with certain surnames.
[3] Percent of sample groups.

Source: Simirenko, 1964, 88, 127.

both the population characteristics and locational patterns of the general model.

Despite the length of time which the Russian community had been resident in Minneapolis, there was still evidence of a ghetto in 1959 and a strong attachment to community values. This suggests the validity of the hypothesis (VI) of a continuing 'urban village' for this group, and other evidence indicates similar residential patterns among many migrant populations (irrespective of whether they continue to grow). Perhaps the best examples of this are in two studies of Italian communities in Boston. The first formed part of Firey's (1947) attack on the culture-less approach of human ecologists, and was a detailed study of the North End. This was physically one of the worst of Boston's slums, but Firey showed that it contained none of the expected correlates of social disorganisation. Instead it comprised a very strong community, who lived in the slum area at least partly through volition.

The Italian community in the North End developed after 1880, by displacing the area's former Irish residents, and its 1940s strength depended on three aspects of its social structure; the mutual aid societies, the *paesani* and the extended family, of which the last was most important. The *paesani* were groups of immigrants from the same villages or province of Italy, which often occupied their own small neighbourhoods within the community. The strength of their ties is shown in Firey's own words:

> At the core of the Italian value system are those sentiments which pertain to the family and the *paesani*. Both of these put a high premium upon maintenance of residence in the North End . . . it is in the North End that the *festes*, anniversaries, and other old-world occasions are held, and such is their frequency that residence in the district is almost indispensable to regular participation . . . Equally significant is the localistic character of the Italian family. So great is its solidarity that it is not uncommon to find a tenement entirely occupied by a single extended family . . . The ideal pattern is for the daughter to continue living in her mother's house . . . Over the course of time the young couple is expected to accumulate savings and buy their own home, preferably not far away (Firey, 1945, 147).

To move away from the North End was to repudiate the concepts of the Italian community and to replace them by those of the wider American society. The strength of the ties within the area was reflected in the low rates of property and population turnover there, and in the large proportion of Italians owning property. Those who broke away from such a situation were mainly the young, to whom North End residence was distasteful, 'partly because of the physical undesirability of the neighborhood but primarily because of its status connotations' (Firey, 1947, 209); those who aspired to acceptance within American society could not admit to residence in what was generally accepted as one of Boston's worst slums. Most moved to the suburbs, and those remaining were the ones who held most strongly to the concept of the Italian community, even though they may never have seen their motherland, and only occasionally—especially among the women—travelled a few blocks 'down to America'.

Such Italian communities (in Melbourne and Sydney as well as Boston and Chicago) are characterised still by use of the native language and its dialects, and of the simple peasant dress (mainly among the older women). Such villages still existed within Boston almost 20 years after Firey's work, as indicated by Gans' participant-observation of another slum area, the West End. The pattern he discussed was one of assimilation without acculturation; the residents were part of the American economic system, but not of its social structure. Instead they had a culture of their own, not based on any identification with Italy, but on kinship networks and friendship contacts which involved frequent visiting in each others' homes. Outward display was important to these people, not the impersonal show of house and neighbourhood, but more personal display of 'high expenditures of food, clothing, and other expenses of group life' (Gans, 1962b, 83) which was restricted to their peer groups.

As Myers has demonstrated for the Italian population of New Haven, Connecticut, 'Residential dispersion is part of the group's incorporation into the dominant social system' (Myers, 1950, 370), but it would seem that many Italians (and probably Russians, Slavs and members of other immigrants groups) do not choose to join the dominant social system, even when they are economically eligible. Indeed, Jonassen has reported on the residential patterns of a Norwegian community in New York that remained very clustered for a century, despite obvious economic advances. In the 1940s, after several moves, the community was closely segregated into 'a section of one-and two-family houses with small lawns, backyards and tree-planted streets . . . which . . . is, when compared with other areas of New York and Brooklyn, one of the best' (Jonassen, 1949, 34).

Why do such 'urban villages' continue to exist? Often their residents are the least successful of the immigrant group (apart from a few businessmen and local politicians whose success will be related to the village itself rather than to the wider society). Thus, Kosa's study of Hungarians in Toronto suggested that 'The pursuit of success did not permit the building up of strong and stable communities with localized social solidarity' (Kosa, 1956, 64), and Beynon's (1936) study of persons of the same nationality in Detroit showed that the potential leaders of the community were those who repudiated its concepts and left. The situation in Canada was compared by Kosa to that in the United States, where Hungarian immigrants found property acquisition much more difficult, with consequent stronger, more stable 'urban villages'. This, he found, was due to the cultural lag of the group; the Hungarians moving to the United States were predominantly illiterate, those going to Canada could almost all read and write. Cultural lag (and visibility, the other 'village' producing variable) were thought to be interrelated with class origins, and Kosa concluded that:

> stable ethnic islands were characteristic formations of the old immigration. New immigrants, unless they arrive with a 'visibility', have less inclination to form ethnic colonies. They do not tend to reside among their compatriots for a long time, but, soon after arrival, take over the general residential mobility (Kosa, 1956, 370).

Although the exact meaning of 'old' and 'new' in this context is not clear, Kosa was presumably suggesting that 'urban villages' will not be formed again in American cities, except by visible groups (such as the present Negro, Puerto Rican and Mexican arrivals). This is perhaps an unsatisfactory argument for a settlement form which is typical of the 'respectable working class' as well as of the foreign immigrants in many large cities. The urban villages would seem to result from groups requiring a much more personal social system, based largely on kinship, than is general within an urban environment. For this, they are prepared to forego some of the usual products of economic advancement, such as a more prestigious

283

address (or a council house in Britain), in order to expend their incomes on the characteristic forms of display in their own society. This society may be an alien one, and 'urban villages' may be more characteristic of immigrant groups, but such a statement may simply be the result of a biased research effort towards these more visible groups.

PATTERNS ELSEWHERE

Great Britain

As pointed out earlier, much less work has been done on the distributions of migrants in cities outside the United States. What evidence there is, however, suggests very similar patterns. In London, for example, Irish immigrants once concentrated in the central residential areas (Jackson, 1964, 301; Lees, 1969) but have since moved eastwards towards the dock areas (where many are employed) and, in greater numbers, to the west. More recently, however, the main migration streams to London from overseas have been from the West Indies, India, Pakistan and other Commonwealth countries, and recent Irish (and Scottish) movers to the city have been settling some distance from the central area, which is the main focus for the 'newer' immigrant groups (Johnston, 1969b, 75).

For the recent foreign in-migrants to London (excluding those from Ireland) the seven boroughs of Chelsea, Hampstead, Kensington, Paddington, St. Marylebone, St. Pancras and Westminster, ringed around the northwest of the city centre, absorbed 28 percent of arrivals during 1960–1961. It can be inferred that the migration to these areas has initiated an invasion and succession sequence, since the number of foreign-born proceeding there was probably far greater than the absolute numerical increase in foreign-born residents would suggest. For boroughs further from the centre of the city, the increase of foreign-born residents was much greater than the number of in-migrants housed there would suggest, and the integration of these two findings provides some evidence to support a hypothesis of ghetto-expansion (for the figures, see Johnston, 1969b, 76–80). Note, however, that the degree of segregation of the coloured communities in London (and elsewhere in the United Kingdom) is not as great as that of

Negroes in American cities: 'even in Paddington, the most densely populated "coloured" area in London, the number of coloured people is considerably less than one in ten' (Davison, 1966, 21). Davison's indices of concentration were based on the large metropolitan boroughs, and not census tracts, but he found that the most concentrated groups were the Italians, Germans, and Australians, followed by the Cypriots, Russians and West Indians (there was a correlation, however, between degree of concentration and size of group), and that different groups were concentrated into different parts of the inner zone (Davison, 1963).

Work in Birmingham dealt separately with coloured (West Indian and Indian) and Irish immigrants, and found both concentrated in the intermediate zone of the three into which that city was divided. There was also a sectoral pattern, with the Irish mainly occupying the southeastern quadrant and the coloureds (especially the West Indians) the northwestern. Absence of the Irish immigrants from the central residential areas of the city was not too surprising, since they have been a significant minority in Birmingham for many decades and, as P. N. Jones' (1967) evidence suggested, they have probably moved outwards over time: in addition, they are much less highly concentrated than the coloured immigrants. The relative absence of the newer migrant groups from the inner residential areas (Figure VI.6) was apparently due to the type of housing there, its tiny houses being both unsuited to high-density migrant occupants and generally unavailable, as they were owned by the city corporation and used to house families on its list. The most attractive housing, for all three groups, was the by-law terraces and villas, many of them constructed for a middle-class population, which were generally available on short leases only, and so not attractive to mortgage buyers. On the other hand, they could be bought for cash, perhaps at high interest rates, and then subdivided and let to migrants to produce a good income (Jones, 1967, 21–22).

There is evidence in the Birmingham example, therefore, of the one-group-succeeding-another model which has proven accurate in the American context. For the immigrant quarters of London, evidence has also been provided of segregation

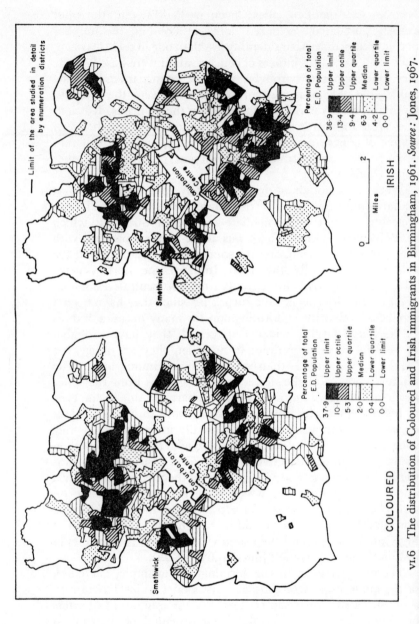

vi.6 The distribution of Coloured and Irish immigrants in Birmingham, 1961. *Source*: Jones, 1967.

patterns which parallel those discussed earlier for the Negro and Jewish ghettoes. One of the main West Indian concentrations has been south of the Thames, in Brixton, where 'there are now so many West Indian owned houses . . . that the more particular can even choose their place and district of residence' (Patterson, 1960, 35). Patterson suggested a three-zone division of the area; an inner zone housing the new arrivals and the older residents who haven't advanced economically; an intermediate zone containing the financially secure and settled; and lastly, an outer zone, with a few West Indians who have been the most successful economically, living in dominantly white areas (see Patterson, 1965, 259–260). Social contacts were mainly within the incipient ghetto, but Patterson reported little evidence of any real community development. With the lack of formal associations, however, the similarities between this group and the urban villages described earlier are considerable.

Australia and New Zealand

Ghetto-like inner suburban communities of Italians, Greeks, Maltese, and Yugoslavs, with their own shopping areas and newspapers, are common in Australian cities, although their spatial extent and growth have been poorly documented. By 1961, one of Melbourne's inner suburbs—Fitzroy—had 32 percent of its population born in Greece, Italy or Malta, plus a large number of their children. To the south of the city centre was a large Jewish area, again complete with its own shopping area, and other groups (excepting the Dutch and Germans because of their occupational patterns) were clustered in different parts of the inner zone and portions of the outer areas of the low-status sector (Johnston, 1966c; Jones, 1969; Stimson, 1968) (see figure vi.7).

In New Zealand, Curson has applied Taeuber and Taeuber's (1965b) tract classification scheme to the constituent census districts of the Auckland urban area, in a study of Polynesian residential patterns (Curson, 1970). His map (which referred to the decade 1956–1966) showed the Established Polynesian Area grouped around the city centre on the side of the low status sector, and its expansion progressing in a general sectoral manner away from these. Within the main Polynesian residen-

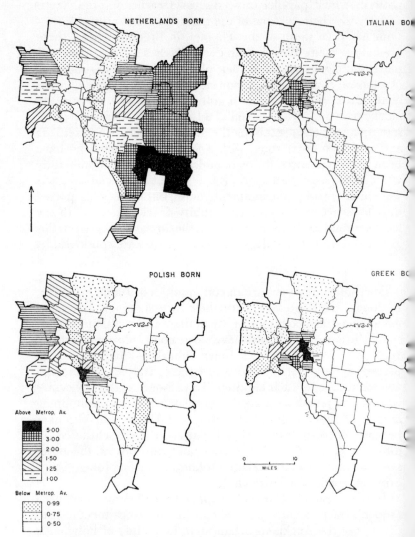

VI.7 The distribution of Migrant Groups in the Melbourne metropolitan area, 1961. (The data are location quotients, which divide the percentage of an area's population in that group by the percentage in the total population. Quotients greater than 1·0 thus show a concentration of that group in the area.) *Source:* Stimson, 1968.

tial areas there was not only concentration of the various Island groups (for example, over half of the 2,300 Niueans resident in 1966 lived in areas containing less than 7 percent of Auckland's total population) but also considerable residential dissimilarity among the groups (Table VI.8). Notable among the indices in this table are those of the degree of residential separation between the Polynesians and New Zealand's indigenous Maoris who have also been recent migrants to the city and are of similarly low socio-economic status. Another study by Curson (1968) has indeed indicated that one island community, the

TABLE VI.8

INDICES OF RESIDENTIAL DISSIMILARITY:
AUCKLAND, 1966

	Cook Islanders	Samoans	Niueans	Tongans	Other Polynesians	Maoris
Europeans	42·3	36·8	49·6	31·9	36·4	31·2
Cook Islanders		16·4	20·2	32·4	23·3	32·2
Samoans			25·4	29·5	20·4	32·0
Niueans				37·3	28·3	40·8
Tongans					28·3	35·7
Other Polynesians						38·7

Source: Curson, 1970, 172.

Cook Islanders, has been replacing the Maori in certain central areas of Auckland.

Recent Maori migration to Auckland has suggested the irrelevance of a port-of-entry model (Rowland, 1971). Some 40 percent of the new arrivals during 1961–1966 took up residence in the outer, southern suburbs, which are characterised by rapid industrial growth and large tracts of State and relatively cheap State-financed housing. Only 15 percent moved to inner city addresses, most of them young, single adults. (This latter percentage was undoubtedly underestimated because the study could only consider persons aged 21 and over.) Lack of a 'port-of-entry' situation results from the liberal housing programme for low-income households, and the fact that the migration stream is dominated by families with young children. It is not a dominantly inter-urban stream, as with the American Negro, however: most of the in-migrants came

T

URBAN RESIDENTIAL PATTERNS

from north of Auckland, only one-third of these from the main towns there.

Studies have been made recently of several of the smaller immigrant groups in New Zealand (Thomson and Trlin, 1970): their approximate numbers in the country were: Chinese 8,520, Indians 4,200, Yugoslavs 3,870, Greeks 2,650, Poles, 2,100, Dutch 10,300, Cook Islanders 8,660. The last four groups were of more recent origin, many of the Europeans being displaced persons after the Second World War. A common feature of all groups, however, has been the importance of chain migrations, with a concentration of origins in a few parts of the country of birth in several cases. With the exception of the Dutch, a common feature has also been the residential clustering of the migrants within the inner portions of the larger cities, especially Auckland and Wellington. Their relatively low economic status is in part the cause for this, as well as their cultural systems which are alien to those of New Zealand (except, of course, for the Dutch). But the chain migration system has been a strong factor influencing their concentration: new migrants to New Zealand must be sponsored (Cook Islanders are New Zealand citizens, however), and the sponsor must arrange or provide accommodation as well as employment. Once in the cities, members of the colonies have tended to move out to the suburbs over time, as Burnley's (Thomson and Trlin, 1970, 114) table of the first, second and latest residences of Greek migrants in Wellington shows.

In Australasia, then, recent migrations of ethnic groups to the large cities have been producing residential patterns and processes which fit many of the hypotheses developed and tested mainly in the United States. As in Britain, the clustering of migrants in the Antipodes has not been of the same magnitudes as has produced the American ghettoes. Nevertheless, there has been clustering and diffusion outwards from the original nodes of settlement. The length of time which many of the groups have spent in the cities has not usually been sufficient for the relative validity of the ghetto and assimilation models to be tested, nor indeed has there been any attempt to test the assumption made in most studies that spatial diffusion is a correlate of assimilation.

CONCLUSION

The six hypotheses presented at the beginning of this chapter fall basically along a continuum from complete ghettoisation over time because of exogenous controls, through complete endogenous ghettoisation, to the ephemeral ghetto followed by spatial assimilation. A further hypothesis suggested that if complete ghettoisation existed, then there would be spatial patterns within the 'city within a city'. This latter hypothesis has been generally supported.

Testing of the other propositions, mainly on American data, has not provided convincing evidence on the relevance of them all. Certainly, there is little doubt that discriminated groups live in ghettoes, which expand when they must via invasion and succession, though the importance of actual *invasion* seems in doubt. Similarly, there is plenty of evidence from all societies that over time the majority of the members of a minority group become spatially as well as socially and economically assimilated within the urban scene. But, the evidence also suggests that with such groups the ghetto-like residential clustering never completely disappears, and this clustering— as with the Irish in Britain—cannot simply be ascribed to factors such as low socio-economic status. Cultural bonds have often been strong enough to survive the urbanisation process, at least for the length of time covered in most of the studies discussed here, and the result has been the existence in the inner districts of many cities of 'urban villages' (which, it has been pointed out, are not solely a characteristic of alien migrant settlement patterns).

For many communities, therefore, there is evidence of continued residential clustering where community bonds exist, at any socio-economic level according to Jonassen's study of a Norwegian community in New York. On the other hand, no evidence has been presented here of the continued existence of a voluntary ghetto. This may simply be a feature of the evidence gathered, but the Jewish community seemed the best example for testing the second hypothesis. Certainly their ghettoes have existed for long periods, but it could be that the Italian 'urban villages' will voluntarily last just as long (though this is unlikely,

and in any case the degree of homogeneity within their neighbourhoods is much less than it has been in Jewish ghettoes).
Goldstein and Goldscheider's study indicated considerable
'leakage' from the ghetto in Providence; no evidence has been
found on how much of this there was in the past. Undoubtedly
there was less than in the present Italian or Maori communities,
but the resulting spatial patterns probably differ only in degree
rather than in kind.

In summary, then, there appear to be three main influences on
the settlement patterns of minority groups within urban areas:

1. The discriminatory attitude of the majority population
towards the group. Where this is very strong, a minority ghetto
is the probable result, as with Negroes in Chicago and Roman
Catholics in Londonderry, and if it is sustained, spatial patterns
will develop within the ghetto, although they may not fit Berry
and Rees' statement that 'the segregated area is a microcosm
of the whole, compressed spatially, reproducing a miniature the
metropolitan-wide pattern' (Berry and Rees, 1969, 459).

2. The community ties within the minority group and the
degree to which they wish to be spatially assimilated with their
host society. Such ties can refer to the whole group and lead
to continued ghettoisation long after discriminatory attitudes
have been removed, or they can characterise only a portion who
choose to remain in relatively separate neighbourhoods. Those
not so choosing will have their residential patterns determined
by the third influence only.

3. The socio-economic status of the group members. This
influence is always operative and will be a strong determinant
(at least in a negative manner) on the locations of ghettoes
and urban villages. Where individuals become spatially as well
as economically assimilated, it will probably be the prime
determinant. Kiang's Chicago data (Table VI.1) showed that
even the 'oldest' migrant groups were not evenly distributed
through that city, and in Boston a factorial ecology has produced
an Irish middle-class component (Sweetster, 1969). Some spatial
clustering will probably be evident, however: having started from
a node somewhere in the inner city, the group is likely to become
spatially assimilated through a sector subtended on that node.

CHAPTER VII

Residential Mobility and Residential Patterns

THE CRUCIAL role of migration in generating changes to urban residential patterns has been referred to many times in the preceding chapters. Each set of models for the main societal dimensions (socio-economic status, family status, and minority groups) included intra-urban migration as a basic process; to some extent their hypotheses on this process are in conflict (see pages 117–118). All of them suggest that most movement will be away from the city centre, but the socio-economic status models claim that this is the result of a desire to maintain social standing within the city, the family status models postulate movement as a result of changing space requirements of households, and those relating to minority groups associate movement with either the expansion of a ghetto or the spatial correlate of societal assimilation. All three processes could be operating concurrently; but are they? And if so, are they of equal importance in accounting for the volume of movement between various parts of the city?

A conceptual framework has recently been developed for the study of intra-urban migrations, incorporating both the traditional 'push-and-pull' forces model, referring to people and to places, and the constraints to movement (Lee, 1966). Household structural and compositional changes can be associated with four sets of forces (Sabagh, van Arsdol, and Butler, 1969), which are central to the decision to move

1. THE FAMILY LIFE CYCLE & FAMILISM. Decisions to move are related to characteristics such as family size and housing

293

requirements, the latter incorporating features of the local environment such as accessibility to family, friends, and facilities.

2. SOCIAL MOBILITY & SOCIAL MOBILITY ASPIRATIONS. Residential mobility is more likely to result when the present address is inconsistent with new or aspired socio-economic status.

3. THE RESIDENTIAL ENVIRONMENT. Apart from the above factors, people may move if they become dissatisfied with aspects of their present home because of deterioration in the neighborhood's housing fabric, or in the character of its area's residents.

4. SOCIAL & LOCALITY PARTICIPATION. 'In some situations, active social participation and informal interaction in one's neighborhood or local area is involved in the decision to move or stay' (Sabagh, van Arsdol, and Butler, 1969): in general, the greater a person is locally involved, the less will he want to leave his home area. There are, in addition, a number of factors which could impede or facilitate movement: the nature of the housing market, and the potential mover's available resources. It is the interaction of these forces which determines whether or not a move is made, after the decision to move has been taken (see also Brown and Moore 1968, 1970).

Of the four factors listed above as affecting the decision to move, the first, third and fourth have already been discussed in this book. The family status set clearly fits into the models set out in Chapter V; the residential environment set encompasses the filtering and invasion and succession concepts; and the social and locality participation set covers some of the aspects of sentiment and symbolism referred to in relation to areal status persistence (see pages 176–178). Social mobility has not been previously mentioned in this context, however. It was pointed out in Chapter I that inter- and intra-generational mobility are characteristic features of the societies under review, but the socio-economic residential pattern models discussed in Chapters III and IV appear to assume a caste-like society, with very little inter-class mobility.

Introduction of the social mobility dimension to the study of intra-urban movement introduces yet another conflicting hypothesis. People moving up through the socio-economic class ladder should also be moving up through the system of neighbourhoods, and hence away from the city centre (although this latter pattern could be complicated by the general finding of Chapter IV that the highest status areas are not on the urban periphery). Thus, unravelling the complex pattern of intra-urban migration into its component strands is a difficult problem.

Clearly, since the same spatial pattern of migrations could be produced by a number of processes, it is not possible to observe a pattern and infer back to its cause. Study of the spatial pattern of moves should parallel that of the process, therefore, although very few investigations have treated both aspects of the topic. In addition, a spatial component should be vital in the decision where to move, once the decision to move is made. The constricting role of distance in the distribution of information has been mentioned several times. Many people may, therefore, have little or no knowledge of certain parts of their home city, so that their moves will be constrained to those portions of the urban space of which they are aware (Brown and Moore, 1968, 1970).

MIGRATION RATES

High levels of geographical mobility are common within the societies discussed here, although fully comparative data are not available. In Greater London, for example, 3 percent of the 1961 population had moved there during the preceding year, about 3 percent of the 1960 number had left, and a further 8 percent moved within the conurbation during the year. In the United States, only 47·8 percent of the population aged 5 and over occupied the same dwelling in 1960 as in 1955. Of 30,000 households sampled in Melbourne in 1964, nearly 17 percent had moved to their current address during the preceding twelve months and another 29 percent in the four years previous to that. Finally, more than 4,800 residential shifts were recorded *within* Christchurch in 1965 (that is, started and ended within the urban area, which contained some 70,000 dwellings at that date).

If the models presented in Chapter III include all aspects of the intra-urban migration process, then those mobility rates could be extrapolated to suggest very rapid neighbourhood change. However, such high mobility levels can exist with neighbourhood stability. During the decade 1940–1950 there was almost no change in the relative position of the various census tracts in San Francisco on three dimensions representing economic, family and ethnic status. From their 1940 component scores, Tryon (1967, 1968) was able to predict the 1950 tract scores extremely accurately (with correlations of 0·98 between family status scores at the two dates, and 0·95 for each of the other two components).

These findings suggested that 'there is no change in each neighborhood's distinctive demographic characteristics from 1940 to 1950' (Tryon, 1967, 466). This was an important finding since, extrapolating from 1949–1950 migration data, 'even for those neighborhoods with the lowest rates of turnover of around, say, 10 percent, after ten years two out of every three persons would have been replaced . . . [so that] urban social areas are not only stable but they appear to persist in their biosocial characteristics unaffected by the *particular* persons who inhabit them' (Tryon, 1967, 467). As the regression equations were not reported, Tryon's conclusions need not be the only interpretation of such high correlations. Instead of stability they could indicate that all areas have changed by the same amount and remained in similar relative positions on an interval scale. Such a pattern could be feasible as the study dealt with only the central parts of San Francisco, encompassing little new residential development, but unlikely as patterns of change are rarely constant over such a large number of small areas (including redevelopment districts).

Although changes in the residential pattern of a city cannot occur independent of migrations, therefore, the latter may take place within a stable residential structure. There are several partially independent aspects of migration and neighbourhood change within a city, however, and these are treated in the following sections.

GENERAL FEATURES OF INTRA-URBAN MIGRATION

Figures indicating the amount of intra-urban movement have already been quoted, but in order to test the models discussed in Chapter III information is required not only on numbers but also on the characteristics of the movers, their dwellings, and the areas which they move to and from. Such data are difficult to acquire because of a general lack of interest in such micro-scale migrations by most statistical agencies.

Migration Matrices for Philadelphia

Grigsby (1963) has analysed the 1956 National Housing Inventory data for Philadelphia, which provided information on the origin and destination of movers during the year 1955–1956, according to dwelling tenure, value and location. He constructed matrices from this, some of which are reproduced in Figure VII.1, that indicate a very complex pattern of which intra-urban migration comprised only about two-thirds, the rest resulting from household dissolution, migration to and from the SMSA, and household formation. Of the new households and the in-migrants to Philadelphia, many did not conform to the general representations of the migration process. For example, of the 43,000 newly-formed households, 14,000 were living in an owner-occupier unit and 19,000 lived in the suburbs. Similarly, of the 29,000 in-migrants from outside Philadelphia, 23,000 went directly to the suburbs (or were living in the latter area within a year of moving to the SMSA). To a large degree, these findings agree with Taeuber and Taeuber's (1965a), discussed earlier, indicating the partial irrelevance of the 'port-of-entry' model for migrants to the city, at least as Burgess conceived it.

The housing inventory data did not allow full testing of all hypotheses that can be drawn from the filtering and family-cycle models, both of which involve outward movement from rental to ownership, and to better-quality homes. There was evidence of these processes, but only as part of a complex pattern. Thus, there was considerably more movement from the rental to the owner market than vice versa, but nevertheless 30 percent of owners who moved went to the rental market, yet only the latter stage of the family-cycle model suggests such moves. If filtering can be measured by the amount of movement into the more expensive homes, then it was clearly much more prevalent in the owner-occupier than in the renter market (Table VII.1), and was more important in the suburban than

TABLE VII.1

INTRA-AREA MOVES: PHILADELPHIA, 1955-1956

MOVE TO	FORMER TENURE STATUS	
	Owner	Renter
1. TOTAL SMSA		
No Tenure Change. No Value Change	5,000	20,000
More Expensive Unit	23,000	32,000
Less Expensive Unit	7,000	27,000
Other Tenure Status	15,000	64,000
2. CENTRAL CITY		
No Tenure Change. No Value Change	2,000	14,000
More Expensive Unit	8,000	21,000
Less Expensive Unit	4,000	16,000
Other Tenure Status	7,000	19,000
3. SUBURBS		
No Tenure Change. No Value Change	2,000	5,000
More Expensive Unit	9,000	10,000
Less Expensive Unit	2,000	10,000
Other Tenure Status	7,000	31,000

Source: Grigsby, 1963, 71-73.

in the central city owner-occupier market. In both areas there was considerable movement between units of the same value within the rental sector.

More detailed consideration of the owner-occupier market indicated complex movements also. According to the filtering model, there should be a progression from rental to used owner-occupied to new owner-occupied (and indeed, the family-cycle model suggests a similar progression). In fact, 40 percent of the former renters went direct to new homes, over 45 percent of the former owners moved into used properties, and a similar proportion of newly-formed households moved direct to a new home (Figure VII.1). If the data are looked at in another way, however, 35 percent of the new homes went to former owners, who made up less than 30 percent of all persons moving to an owner-occupied unit. This suggests some validity for the anticipated progression, especially in the central city, where only 11 percent of renters moving into the other market

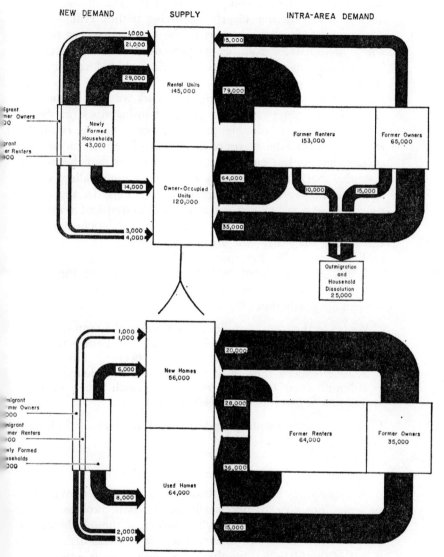

VII.1   Schematic representation of Household Migration into, within and
         from the Philadelphia metropolitan area, 1955–1956. *Source:* Grigsby,
         1963.

occupied new homes, compared to 75 percent of the former owners. Filtering was clearly occurring within Philadelphia, therefore, but it was only part of the total movement pattern which included, for example, 41 percent of the owner-occupier homes valued at more than $20,000 being sold to former renters (Grigsby, 1963, 58).

A final major finding of Grigsby's work was on the amount of downward movement through the housing stock, as shown by moves to less valuable property. Some of this could be expected in the later stages of the family cycle with moves into smaller homes, but 20 percent of all moves within the owner-occupier market (the majority of them in the smaller central city market) were to less expensive dwellings. In the rental market downward movement was almost as frequent as upward (Table VII.1). Models of changing urban socio-economic residential structure all implicitly assume upward social mobility and filtering (presumably extrapolating from net trends), but downward mobility was clearly an important aspect of the Philadelphia housing market. Indeed, Maisel has written elsewhere that:

> We know that some families move because they can no longer afford their houses. It would appear that in both percentage and absolute numbers those who move because of insufficient finances exceed those who move to upgrade their housing, although it is the latter reason to which much of their mobility is attributed (Maisel, 1966, 107).

Clearly a complementary spatial model of downward filtering is an important research need.

New Homes & Poor People: The Efficiency of Filtering

Another study has also illustrated the complexity of migration patterns, not all of it necessarily intra-urban, probing deeper into the topic than Grigsby's analysis, although based on only a small number of moves. The research was organised as a test of the filtering hypothesis, to consider such questions as

> What is the economic level of the people who move into new housing? If rich people move into new housing, do poor people benefit indirectly by moving into vacancies farther

along in the sequences? Or, do the sequences stop before they reach low income people? If low income whites benefit, do low income Negroes also benefit by moving into these vacancies? Are sequences which start with expensive housing longer than those which start with moderate priced housing? (Lansing, Clifton and Morgan, 1969, iii).

Answers to these were attempted by selection of a sample of new dwellings and study of their occupants, the persons who moved into their former homes, the persons who moved into these people's former homes, and so on until the chain of moves ended.

The average sequence contained 3·5 moves, so that the construction of most new dwellings initiated two moves subsequent to that of their first occupants. Most sequences ended, not because of the removal of a home from the existing stock through demolition or conversion—only 20 percent ended in this way—but because the whole household did not leave the point of origin. In 47 percent of all cases, the sequence ended with a vacant dwelling being occupied by persons whose parents remained at their former home: in another 14 percent other relatives stayed behind. And, to complicate the process, 13 percent of all movers inhabited temporary quarters during their move, most of them for more than a month, and 17 percent for more than six months.

The filtering hypothesis implies that people move into better-quality housing and the survey data indicated that this was so: for example, the median value of new owner-occupied units was $25,000, while for units fifth in a sequence it was only $18,000. But it also suggests that the socio-economic status of movers to a dwelling is lower than that of those moving from it, and in general this also proved true. Measuring status by income, the authors found that only 6 percent of families occupying new homes received less than $3,000 per annum, compared with 16 percent of those moving into the fifth house in a sequence of moves. Consideration of the income levels of individual in- and out-movers at the same dwelling, however, showed that while 55 percent of the former had lower incomes than those they were replacing, 25 percent earned more and the lower down the sequence of moves the greater the probability of movers-in having a higher income than the movers-out. Similarly, when completed education was inserted as the measure of socio-economic status, 40 percent of the in-movers were of lower status than the out-movers but 32 percent were ranked higher.

While not the complete representation of the migration process, therefore, it appeared that the filtering hypothesis accounted for a good proportion of the total (though no indication of a causal relationship was indicated). The remainder could have resulted from moves engendered by family-cycle requirements. The survey data indeed showed patterns anticipated in view of the family cycle, but little analysis was performed to see if this was complementary to or associated with the filtering patterns. Thus, 41 percent of out-moving families were in a later stage of the family cycle than the in-movers who succeeded them (the reverse occurred in 28 percent of the situations), the in-movers were generally younger than the out-movers and people mostly moved to larger homes (which suggest a positive association between filtering and family-cycle moves). The part of the family-cycle model most convincingly confirmed, however, was that the movers to new apartments rather than single-family units were most likely to be either young couples leaving the parental home (and thus not initiating a sequence of moves) or else older families late in the life cycle moving from a single-family home. And among the movers to new dwellings, the higher the income the greater the likelihood of choosing an apartment rather than a single-family unit, clearly suggesting a relationship between socio-economic status and life style.

None of the main models of intra-urban migration were properly validated in this study, therefore. Both the filtering and family-cycle models were shown as at least partially accurate, and the spatial correlates were as expected (the further along a sequence of moves, the closer one got to the CBD so that 'People who wish to better their housing situation in the city move further out in order to do so': Lansing, Clifton and Morgan, 1969, 20). But the evidence presented did not properly test either hypothesis, although the conclusions favoured the filtering model. This was shown by the finding that poor people (except Negroes to a large extent) do benefit indirectly from new construction, and that 'people of quite different state in the life cycle often succeed each other in the same housing unit . . . quarters which differ in number of rooms must be quite close substitutes' (Lansing, Clifton and Morgan, 1969, 66–67). Perhaps, then, family demands may be the catalysts for movement but socio-economic status is the determinant of to where and to what.

Central City Migration Rates: Movers & Stayers

Grigsby's data showed much more movement within the rental market than the owner-occupier (40 percent annual turnover compared to six), which agrees with the family-cycle model hypothesis of greater stability with home ownership. Since the rental market is concentrated within the central residential areas, this suggests a spatial pattern of mobility rates, one which has been shown in several studies (Johnston, 1969a). But do those people moving around in the central city later settle down in a suburban house? Clearly some do, but many are apparently part of a separate migration strand.

This strand was identified in a detailed study of residence histories in a Philadelphia satellite town between 1910 and 1950, where:

> in most decades, at least one-third of the population resident in Norristown at the beginning of the decade had moved out of the community before the end of that same decade; and, contrariwise, at least one-third of those resident there at the end of the decade had moved in during the course of the preceding ten years. In some decades, the rates indicated that as much as one-half of the adult male population was affected in this way (Goldstein, 1958, 196).

There was no complete turnover of the population every decade or so, however, for many of the in-migrants were later out-migrants and many of the latter were former in-migrants, so that

> there was no general turnover in the total population of Norristown, but only in a certain segment of that population —the migrant group. While migrants came and went, a

large segment of the population continued to remain in the community throughout . . . and thereby provided a high degree of stability to the population of the community (Goldstein, 1954, 539–540.)

A mover/stayer dichotomy was thus suggested, and has since been confirmed by studies which indicated that the probability of persons leaving a place was negatively related to their length of residence there (Knights, 1969; Morrison, 1967; Wilkinson and Merry, 1965). The movers were of all socio-economic

TABLE VII.2

NUMBER OF RESIDENCES PER TEN YEARS
OF RESIDENCE: NORRISTOWN

STATUS

	1910–1930	1920–1940	1930–1950
Continuous Resident Throughout	1·5	1·4	1·3
Resident in First Decade—Out-migrant in Second[1]	2·1	1·7	1·7
In-migrant in First Decade—Resident in Second	2·1	1·8	1·7
In-migrant in First Decade—Out-migrant in Second	4·0	3·3	3·1

[1] The term resident covers any person who lived continuously in Norristown during the stated time period.

Source: Goldstein, 1958, 211.

levels, ranging from transient labourers to the organisation men (Whyte, 1960).

Goldstein also found that while in a place, the movers changed address more frequently than the stayers. During an average period of ten years' residence in Norristown, the persons moving through the community lived at more addresses than the stayers (Table VII.2). The rank order of the mobility rates was the same in each time period, but the rates fell, probably, according to Goldstein, because of increasing rates of home ownership.

Norristown is a relatively small community within the outer portions of the Philadelphia SMSA, and it was not clear whether Goldstein's findings could be extrapolated to larger communities, to be used to account for high mobility levels in the central city renter market. However, a later sample survey in Los Angeles has produced similar results. Individuals who moved during 1960–1961 were much more likely to move in the following year than were those who remained at the same address during the previous 12 months (Table VII.3). Of those who moved within Los Angeles during 1960–1961, 58 percent moved during 1961–1962, almost half of them away from the metropolitan area; on the other hand, of those who did not move in the first year they were in the city, only 16 percent moved in the second, the vast majority of them within

TABLE VII.3

RETROSPECTIVE AND SUBSEQUENT MOBILITY:
LOS ANGELES

1961-1962 Mobility (percent)

1960–1961 Mobility	*Moved*	*Moved Away*	*Moved Within*	*Proportion Moved Away*
Moved	46·7	12·4	34·3	0·27
Moved Within	58·3	27·8	30·5	0·48
Moved Into	44·2	9·2	35·0	0·21
Did Not Move	16·4	2·0	14·4	0·12

Source: van Arsdol Jr, Sabagh and Butler, 1968, 256.

Los Angeles. As in other studies (for example Maisel, 1966 and Moore, 1969) age was an important determinant of mobility rates, but when associated with other variables, such as past mobility, mobility desires and anticipated mobility, it was possible to predict 80 percent of the 1961–1962 moves. One of the causes of this was that prior movers

> are more oriented toward future mobility than are persons who have not moved in the past and are better able to actualize a moving plan and choice. Past stayers, on the other hand, are oriented toward continued stability (van Arsdol Jr, Sabagh and Butler, 1968, 266–267).

According to these analyses, mobility levels are in part determined by past experience, and there is a segment within urban societies which is constantly moving within and between cities, particularly their inner area rental housing. Thus Moore (1969) found a strong negative correlation (-0.7) between the rate of population turnover and distance from the CBD in Brisbane. Simple location was not the determinant of the mobility rate, of course, though it was suggested that accessibility was 'a surrogate for a factor having an adverse effect on the stability of a given community—that of traffic flow and the dangers and disturbances associated with it' (Moore, 1969, 29); instead, the two were mainly linked because of the central city clustering of the more mobile young people and non-Australians (the 'port-of-entry' model) and the rental property which they preferred.

Suburban Migration: Family Cycle or Filtering?

Within the main body of an urban area, the determinants of population turnover rates will be only slightly affected by the distribution of inter-city movers. Instead there are the two hypotheses:

I. That people move to improve, or maintain, their social position.
II. That people move because of the pressures of family requirements.

Most evidence seems to support the latter, at least by inference, because of the characteristics of the movers; for example, Maisel's analyses showed that 'for a low income, young, single-person household the probabilities [of moving] are almost 100 percent . . . More single people move. More couples purchase. Older people are more stable. . . . A family already owning a home is less likely to move' (Maisel, 1966, 97–99). Some of the causes are indirect, however, being a feature of certain types of people only because they tend to congregate in certain dwelling types. For example, of a sample of 313 moves in Christchurch in 1965, 33 were due to evictions and 35 more were temporary moves while the individuals awaited another dwelling (Clark, 1968); Abu-Lughod and Foley have similarly estimated that about 20 percent of all moves are involuntary. Eviction is usually from rental property, which is concentrated in certain areas and more popular for certain groups within society.

In attempting to assess the relative importance of filtering and family-cycle pressures in producing moves, Simmons has estimated that

> within a moderately growing city more than 50 percent of the intra-urban mobility results from the changing needs generated by the life cycle . . . about 30 percent of intra-urban moves are involuntary, with 10 percent following the creation of new households and 20 percent resulting from demolition, destruction by fire, or eviction. Perhaps another 10 percent reflect changes outside the life cycle, such as social mobility, ethnic assimilation, and neighborhood invasion. The most meaningful aspects of the housing adjustments are the size and facilities of the dwelling unit, followed by the social environment of the neighborhood. The physical site and access to other parts of the city are relatively insignificant (Simmons, 1968, 636–637).

Much of this statement, and others like it, was based on a study of reasons for movement conducted in Philadelphia some two decades ago, which showed

> the major function of mobility to be the process by which families adjust their housing to the housing needs that are generated by the shifts in family composition that accompany life cycle changes (Rossi, 1955, 9).

Rossi's study of why families move selected four census tracts in Philadelphia city to give a cross section of areas according to socio-economic status and population turnover levels. His initial surveys classified the sample families according to their rating on two indices:

1. A mobility potential index which indicated the strength of the desire to move. Such families were characterised by their age, size and tenure preference.
2. A complaints index which represented the amount of dissatisfaction with present housing.

These two were independent (since one could have a high potential but no complaints immediately after a successful move), but clearly when put together they were closely related to mobility desires (Table VII.4).

TABLE VII.4

DESIRED AND ACTUAL MOBILITY:
PHILADELPHIA, 1955

A. PERCENT WISHING TO MOVE

Mobility Potential Index	COMPLAINTS INDEX			
	0	1–2	3–4	5+
0–1	11	34	56	47
2–3	21	40	67	80
4+	60	70	87	93

B. PERCENT WHO MOVED

Complaints Index	0	1–2	3–4	5+	
	8	10	16	26	
Mobility Potential Index	0	1	2	3	4–5
	5	8	10	13	31

Mobility Inclinations	Anxious to stay	4	Stay but not Anxious 9
	Move but not Anxious 11		Anxious to Move 33

Source: Rossi, 1955, 94, 108.

The sample families were contacted again ten months after the initial interviews, and the two indices proved very successful in predicting who had moved (Table VII.4), as did the reported intentions of the families during the original interviews. About a 90 percent success rate was claimed for intentions and 75 percent for the combined indices, and many of the deviants were easily accounted for; for example, most of those who failed to move in fact did not because they were unable to find an acceptable alternative, while many of the unexpected movers were:

> young, small, poor households, free from ties of owning, dissatisfied with their old abodes, but reconciled to remaining on. When opportunities presented themselves, their predispositions to move crystallised into immediate action (Rossi, 1955, 115).

These people Rossi termed windfall movers.

As one in every four of the moves Rossi noted were classified as involuntary (resulting from divorce, long-distance job change etc.) then the rest of the reported mobility was mainly due to family-cycle demands. Many of the complaints against the presently occupied housing were directed at its inappropri-

ate size or similar characteristics, rather than its status connotations, although where complaints were made about the
neighbourhood's social composition these were usually followed
by a move (Rossi, 1955, 146). Residents seemed to be generally
unconcerned about population turnover in their home districts,
especially where this was very rapid, and few expressed any
concern about the effects of such mobility on their neighbourhood's status.

Whereas Rossi found that position in the family cycle was
the major determinant of intra-urban mobility (at least of the
various mechanisms suggested here), this was contradicted in
a survey of a relatively new suburban area of Lafayette, Indiana.
In this, stated mobility intentions were regressed against the
following variables representing family-cycle stage and career
pattern:

1. Age of household head.
2. Household size.
3. House tenure.
4. Years of education for head.
5. Head's estimate of his social class relative to neighbours'.
6. Head's estimate of his upward social mobility prospects.
7. Attitudes to present dwelling.
8. Attitudes to present neighbourhood.

Together these eight variables accounted for over 50 percent
of the stated intentions, but more than 30 percent was statistically explained by variables 4, 5, 6 and 7. Movement was most
desired among well-educated people who disliked their present
dwelling, had good prospects of upward social mobility, and
thought themselves in a higher social class than their neighbours. Indeed, of the 47 respondents with social mobility
expectations, 44 indicated an intention to change their address,
compared with 20 of the 164 with no such prospects. They
also were more likely to achieve their goal, for the socially
mobile tended to underestimate the likelihood of a geographical
move while the 'non-upwardly mobile respondents overestimate
the opportunities for residential mobility' (Leslie and Richardson, 1961, 899).

From this, Leslie and Richardson suggested a much broader

paradigm of residential mobility than Rossi's, based on both social mobility and family life-cycle stages, with complaints about presently occupied dwellings as the intermediate variable. They did not suggest that Rossi's findings were atypical, therefore, but amalgamated the two sets of results in attempting to produce a better model. Such an approach was justified because of great differences between the two studies in the characteristics of the respondents; Rossi dealt with a broad spectrum but the Lafayette sample included few renters or household heads aged over 50, and no single-person households (the latter being a very mobile group, irrespective of socio-economic status). In addition, Rossi worked in a central city and Leslie and Richardson in a new suburb. Suburbia is the goal of many families and having attained it they may have no further housing aspirations, in which case the social mobility factor is likely to be more influential on migration intentions there than in an older area whose residents are still striving for their suburban home.

One other aspect of the Lafayette study was that the households classified as having significant mobility potential

came entirely from professional, business and upper white-collar ranks. The 154 household heads who were classified as non-socially mobile came from the lower white-collar, skilled, and semi-skilled ranks . . . persons presently in the lower ranks were never classified as potentially mobile, while some upper white-collar and business people were classified as non-mobile (Leslie and Richardson, 1961, 899).

Extrapolating from this, it can be suggested that the higher a suburb's status the greater the likelihood that social factors will be a prime influence on residential mobility, and thus of filtering as the spatial process. (This is because highly paid people can normally afford a large enough first home to meet all future family needs.) Thus, Whitney and Gregg (1958) found the quest for status to be very strong among a group of college student families and 90 percent of their respondents' moves were for status reasons, but in a Levittown study Wattell found that only 22 percent of the, apparently lower middle-class, residents 'entertained the idea of leaving the community for a higher status neighborhood' (Wattell, 1958, 304).

A later study which attempted to investigate the relative importance of the socio-economic and family status models of residential mobility basically confirmed Rossi's findings, using a wider sampling frame. Two middle-class, white residential areas in Los Angeles were sampled, one high on family status and the other low. When the two samples were considered together, age of the household head and degree of housing satisfaction proved the main discriminators between movers and non-movers. Age was not a significant independent variable in the central city district alone, however, suggesting that all age groups were equally mobile there. (This finding disagrees with the earlier discussion, which expected more family-cycle-influenced moves in the inner area.)

Further tests held some of the independent variables constant. The results were not compatible for the urban and suburban areas, and the main findings were:

1. Family type was not a major discriminant between movers and non-movers, but age of the household head was.

2. Housing satisfaction was almost as important.

3. 'The hypothesis that neighborhood satisfaction was related negatively to residential mobility was rejected except for respondents from full families and those with high social mobility commitment' (Butler, Sabagh and van Arsdol Jr, 1963, 151).

4. 'Social mobility commitment for the most part, did not differentiate movers from non-movers' (Butler, Sabagh, and van Arsdol, 1963, 151).

In general, therefore, it is the family-cycle model of residential mobility which has been verified in the reported empirical studies of suburban areas. There is very high mobility among single-person households and renters in the city centre; elsewhere, family requirements and housing satisfaction—which may be the same thing—are the major determinants of moving.

SPATIAL PATTERNS OF MOVEMENT

Given that most people move to meet their family requirements and their dissatisfactions with previous dwellings, the spatial correlates should be that:

1. Most moves will be made to a similar neighbourhood on a socio-economic status scale.

2. Since areas of similar socio-economic status tend to cluster together within a city, then such moves should be over relatively short distances.

3. Many moves are for only relatively small differences in dwellings, such as an extra room or more cupboard space (the main exception to this comes at the start of the family cycle). Since most neighbourhoods provide a variety of house sizes within a price range, most requirements should be met within a short distance of a dwelling, except perhaps when there is a strong demand for housing relative to supply and vacancies are few.

4. Short-distance moves should also be common when they are generated by socio-economic status changes. Most vertical mobility is in short steps along the occupational scale, so if there is a gradation of neighbourhood status, acceptable dwellings—better or poorer—should be available fairly close to the migration origin.

These propositions are considered in the next two sections: the first deals with movements among communities, irrespective of location, and the second with moves in physical space.

Moves in Community Space

'The majority of moves adjust housing within neighborhoods of similar characteristics' (Simmons, 1968, 632). This statement was based on Table VII.5, produced as part of Goldstein

TABLE VII.5

MOVES AMONG SOCIAL AREAS: RHODE ISLAND,
1955–1960
(percent from each origin)

SOCIAL CLASS OF ORIGIN TRACT	SOCIAL CLASS OF DESTINATION TRACT				
	I (High)	II	III	IV	V (Low)
I (High)	63·8	12·0	11·3	8·2	4·8
II	8·2	51·0	20·6	13·3	6·8
III	6·1	18·8	50·4	16·7	8·1
IV	5·1	13·0	21·0	52·7	8·1
V	4·1	13·2	17·3	17·4	48·1

Source: Goldstein and Mayer, 1961, 51.

and Mayer's (1961) detailed study of the changing ecology of Providence. It shows that:

1. The dominant movement from tracts of all socio-economic class groupings was to similar tracts.
2. The higher the class of a tract, the greater the probability of a move to a similar tract (except for class IV).
3. From the lowest class origins there was a fairly wide diffusion of migrants, but elsewhere more than three-quarters of movers went to similar or adjacent class areas.
4. There was more upward than downward mobility in the lower middle classes III and IV, especially in IV, but much more downward than upward movement from class II districts. This could indicate either:
   a. Greater social mobility among the lower classes.
or b. Increasing 'exclusiveness' of areas up the social hierarchy so that few can move into the highest status, class I areas.

A drawback of Goldstein and Mayer's study was that it classified tracts by socio-economic status only, so it was not possible to extract information on the causes of movement. A better approximation of the community space suggested in the above discussion has been provided in a number of studies of Cedar Rapids, Iowa, where neighbourhoods were defined on the basis of a factorial ecology of the city. This produced five factors, representing family status, housing differentials, income differentials, residential densities, and residential stability/ethnic groups. On the basis of their five component scores, the sixty-four districts of Cedar Rapids were classified into the following type areas:

I. Middle Life Cycle, Middle Class.
II. Late Life Cycle, Upper Middle Class.
III. Lower Economic Status, Young Families.
IV. Lower Economic Status, Unsound Dwellings, Retired Persons.
V. Downtown.
VI. Industrial Districts with no Residences.

Omitting the last two types, these areas form continua of both economic status (IV-III-I-II) and family status (IV-III-

I-II-IV). Migrants might be expected to move along this scale of areas with some exceptions; for example, upper-middle class, late life-cycle families are unlikely to retire to type IV areas.

The amount of movement between these various areas was obtained from telephone company records for 1966–1967, and was analysed in two ways. In the first, Brown and Long-brake (1968) correlated various aspects of the migration process with the component scores. One of these produced a correlation of 0·67 between the five scores and the level of population turnover—with correlations of 0·74, 0·69 and 0·80 for separate correlations on type I, II and IV areas respectively. Mobility rates were highest in low socio-economic status areas, especially those with many renters, and were also related in type II and IV areas to family-cycle stage. These findings generally agreed with Rossi's, and the high turnover rates in the low-quality multi-family dwelling-unit areas were ascribed to 'partly a function of neighborhood *mood*, as well as of the household type' (Brown and Longbrake, 1968, 14).

Further regressions between the component scores and the proportion of an area's 1967 residents not living there in 1966 (with separate investigations of intra-urban and inter-urban migrants) indicated strong negative relationships between housing quality and attractiveness, presumably because there were more vacancies in the poorer areas. In addition 'within the set of zones with vacancies, those with family characteristics are favored' (Brown and Longbrake, 1968, 16), and the 'port-of-entry' process seemed to operate, since within type IV areas:

1. In-migrants to the city—mostly young, single transients from mid-western rural areas—sought lower economic and family status areas.

2. Intra-urban migrants sought out the better housing of the higher-family status and economic status areas.

For those remaining in Cedar Rapids, therefore, entry into the family cycle was partially associated with filtering.

The second type of analysis concentrated on the matrix of migrations between the various areas (Table VII.6). The migration matrix was converted into probabilities of going to a certain destination from a given origin (so that 39 percent of movers from type II go to type I areas; Table VII.6B), and this was then converted into a Mean First Passage Time Matrix which indicated the average number of moves necessary

TABLE VII.6

INTER- AND INTRA-COMMUNITY MIGRATION:
CEDAR RAPIDS, 1966–1967

A. NUMBER OF MOVES

FROM	TO	I	II	III	IV	V
I		283	131	56	38	0
II		194	180	49	67	3
III		117	76	91	56	1
IV		120	104	86	175	3
V		6	10	9	12	1

B. MIGRATION PROBABILITIES

FROM	TO	I	II	III	IV	V
I		0·56	0·26	0·11	0·07	0·00
II		0·39	0·36	0·10	0·14	0·01
III		0·34	0·22	0·27	0·17	0·00
IV		0·24	0·21	0·18	0·36	0·01
V		0·16	0·26	9·24	0·31	0·03

C. MEAN FIRST PASSAGE TIMES

FROM	TO	I	II	III	IV	V
I		2·30	4·04	8·62	9·61	335·64
II		2·78	3·62	8·66	8·95	333·18
III		2·93	4·24	7·19	8·61	224·28
IV		3·34	4·31	7·81	6·83	332·79
V		3·59	4·11	7·30	7·10	325·94

D. MEAN FIRST PASSAGE TIMES: HARD CORE AREAS ONLY

FROM	TO	I	II	III	IV
I		1·65	5·26	25·02	11·46
II		2·07	4·61	24·80	10·67
III		2·44	5·46	20·10	9·28
IV		2·57	5·30	22·89	7·84

Source: Brown and Longbrake, 1968, Tables 14 and 16.

to get to a certain destination from a given origin (for example, there would be an average of 4 moves for someone from a type I area before he reached a type II: see Brown, 1970). This latter step makes several unreal assumptions if it is interpreted in a dynamic fashion as representing a long-term migration process: its main value is as a descriptive device for indicating the amount of movement between areas.

Although most moves may not have been direct to such neighbourhoods, the type I areas were clearly most in demand, and the average mover would sooner or later get to a type I district before one similar to that which he originally left. This suggests that the main catalyst for movement was changing family circumstances, since type I areas were characterised by high familism and their suburban location. Type IV areas were characterised by individuals starting the family cycle as well as retired people, type III were peculiar in the concentration of pre-child families there, and the middle and late stages of the cycle were represented in type II and I areas respectively. Migration generally followed this sequence, except that there was little movement between IV and III, most proceeding straight to I, and there was much more movement within the type I areas than from them to the socially more desirable type II. Finally, the high mobility in type IV areas fitted their 'peculiar facilities for serving transients, unmarrieds, retireds, and young adults in the early phases of their life cycle' (Brown and Longbrake, 1968, 20).

Aggregation of the sixty-four tracts into five neighbourhood types over-simplified the residential structure, since many tracts were not particularly representative of their types and were not very homogeneous in their characteristics. Brown and Longbrake thus repeated their analysis for the 'hard core', or most representative members of each type only, and the resulting Mean First Passage Time Matrix (Table VII.6D) illustrated the migration process very clearly. The trek out to the suburban type II areas stands out, as does the relative isolation of the type III neighbourhoods. The latter was ascribed by Brown and Longbrake to the small number of vacancies there, and the better social amenities and modern housing which made types I and II more attractive. The type III districts offered good-quality, relatively cheap rental accommodation, but did not seem to be attractive to the majority. Instead they were apparently inhabited by lower-status groups with limited aspirations and low-mobility levels; they were perhaps Cedar Rapids' 'urban villages'.

316

A final feature of Brown and Longbrake's matrices to be noted here was the movement from type II to type I areas, suggesting considerable downward mobility and downward filtering. This was accounted for in a small survey of individual migrants which indicated considerable heterogeneity in the type II districts (Kunkel and Zanarini, 1968). Almost a quarter of the migrants from these upper-middle-class, late-life-cycle areas in fact had the middle-class, middle-life-cycle characteristics of the type I neighbourhoods, while a further 25 percent had type III characteristics. These people tended to move to type I areas, and many of those going to a type II area may have moved to type I vacancies (which were estimated to form about 36 percent of the vacancies there).

Goldstein and Mayer's smaller study used a large population, and Brown and Longbrake worked on small samples, so too much cannot be inferred from the two sets of results. In addition, there are many problems in such analyses because of the heterogeneity of neighbourhoods, and the variety of causes which could produce the same patterns. Nevertheless, the evidence reviewed here strongly suggests the validity of the family-cycle mobility model, although it also indicates parallel filtering in terms of housing quality.

Moves in Physical Space

Irrespective of the community types at the origin and destination, the great weight of available evidence indicates that short-distance moves predominate within cities; Simmons claimed that 'the most powerful regularity is the tendency to relocate near the origin' (Simmons, 1968, 648–649). Geographers have generally ascribed this to the 'friction of distance' on human spatial behaviour. People are more aware of their immediate environs in a large city, having more and better information on neighbouring than on distant areas. With regard to residence change, the potential mover will obtain other information from mass media, real-estate agents and other third parties (see Brown and Moore, 1968). However, since most people are more aware of their adjacent neighbourhoods (Horton and Reynolds, 1969; Cox, 1969), they are better able to evaluate information referring to such areas.

It would appear, then, that urban residents have mental maps of their cities on which the desirability of various suburbs is charted, and that these desirability ratings are negatively related with distance from origin. In addition, there should be a directional bias within such mental maps because, except in the case of moves between the familism and non-familism housing markets, residents are likely to find outer suburban areas beyond their home more desirable than those older districts closer to the city centre (Figure VII.2; Adams, 1969). Preliminary investigations of such mental maps have shown a main correlation between desirability and an area's ascribed socio-economic status with a sectoral pattern accounting for much of the residual variation from this relationship (Johnston, 1971c). Working on a sample of movers in Cedar Rapids, Iowa, for whom they had information on the former residence, the present residence, and all other vacancies considered during the search for a new home, Brown and Holmes (1970) found no evidence to support a hypothesis of directional and sectoral biases in search behaviour. Similarly, Horton and Reynolds (1970) found a general distance bias only in the awareness spaces of two Cedar Rapids samples, with marked differences between the suburban and central city respondents.

The role of distance and information fields has been demonstrated in studies of Christchurch. Clark (1969) suggested that day-to-day activities such as shopping are important contributors to building up a person's spatial information field, and he constructed such information fields from data on shopping trips in Christchurch. These were used to simulate possible migration patterns, and compared with a sample of 365 moves. Similarities between the two were considerable (on both a 1·5 mile square grid (Clark, 1968) and a finer framework (Clark, 1969) of concentric circles at 0·5 mile radius intervals from the origin).

As well as distance effects in intra-urban migration, directional biases can also be suggested. The filtering, family-cycle, and invasion and succession models all have their migration streams directed away from the city centre. There should be more outward than inward moves, therefore, and the former should be more widely spread (Johnston, 1969b). This greater diffusion of out-migrants will result partly from the decreasing

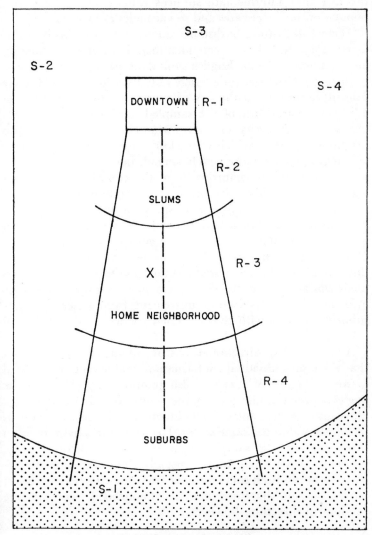

VII.2 The Sectoral Mental Map of an Urban Resident. A resident of X
will have a much sharper image of zones R–1 to R–4 in his own
sector (S–1) than of other parts of the city. *Source:* Adams, 1969.

housing densities away from the city centre, and partly from the fact that intermediate suburbs usually have the lowest population turnover rates and so vacancies are fewer.

These two features of distance and directional bias in intra-urban migration have been identified in studies of London and Melbourne. In the English capital the amount of movement towards the CBD was on average only two-thirds of that away from it, according to the flows between seventy-three pairs of adjacent areas. Most of the sampled local government areas also drew a majority of their intra-urban in-migrants from neighbouring areas which were closer to the city centre. Their out-migrants were more widely spread, however, though there were still more going further from the conurbation than towards it (data difficulties prevented a complete test on this point; Johnston, 1969b). The study of movements within Melbourne had to deal with a much coarser pattern of areal units, but the data were 'very suggestive of the dominance of short-distance moves' (Johnston, 1969a, 44). Addition of the directional factor showed that most of this short-distance movement was away from the city centre, although there was some evidence of longer-distance movement from inner to outer suburbs—in line with the hypothesis of wider dispersal than capture.

Another test of directional bias by Adams (1969) suggested that since an individual's information field should be sectoral in form (Figure VII.2: see also Johnston, 1971c), then the angle between a line joining the origin and destination of a move and the city centre should be small as the person proceeds outwards within the same sector. His tests of this hypothesis on three Minneapolis samples indicated such directional bias, particularly with long moves (usually those into the suburbs from an origin itself some distance from the city centre). Short moves, within the immediate neighbourhood, were mainly random in direction, however.

CHOOSING A HOME

The studies reviewed so far have generally confirmed the various propositions concerning the patterns of migration among communities and over intra-urban space, and also have suggested that the family-cycle model of residential mobility within cities is more important than the filtering concept in accounting for movement. In many cases, however, the latter conclusion has only been inferred; even in Rossi's work there was much inference and relatively slender evidence. An interest among researchers in the actual factors which affect the choice of a home has developed recently, however, in many cases as tests of the accessibility models (such as Alonso, 1964) which are generally employed to account for the spatial patterns in cities.

Research by Weiss and others has developed as part of their general interest in urban development patterns (Kaiser and Weiss, 1969b). They suggested nine groups of factors which might contribute to the home purchase decision (in all, thirty-nine factors were specified), as follows:

City-wide accessibility.
Proximity to neighbourhood facilities.
Physical characteristics of neighbourhoods.
Site features.
Service and facility provision.
The social environment.
Neighbourhood amenities.
Features of the dwelling.
Financial considerations.

A sample of 180 new home purchasers were then asked which of these factors were important to them in choosing their present home, and which would be in any future choice (Weiss, Kenney and Steffens, 1966, 9).

Two tabulations from these data gave slightly different results. Considerations of the number of times a factor was mentioned showed features of the dwelling itself to be most important, notably the amount and arrangement of internal space, followed by physical and social features of the district— quality and character of its homes, the presence of paved streets, quietness, and neighbourhood reputation and prestige, in that order. A similar ranking occurred for future choices. Tabulation of the number of times a factor was ranked first, however, showed the quality of homes in an area to be as important as the interior space. On the other hand, the accessibility factors were unimportant in the present and future choices, and, of the proximity measures, only nearness to schools proved a significant factor for many.

Daly (1968) also reported that accessibility was relatively unimportant in the making of residential decisions, this time in Newcastle, NSW. The most important factor to his 676 respondents was freedom from industrial nuisances, and other environmental values, such as a bush setting, good views, a good atmosphere for children, and the availability of sewerage reticulation, were more significant choice factors than those suggested by economic rent theory, such as accessibility to work and CBD, and those proposed by many sociologists, such as proximity to friends and relatives.

Daly also attempted to determine differences between various population groups in their choice syndromes, with mixed results. He found, for example, positive associations between occupational status and 'bush surroundings, good views, and sewerage provision' (Daly, 1968, 46). More importantly, his results contradicted the economic rent theories, for it was generally those with higher incomes and occupational status who placed a premium on closeness to employment (Table VII.7), as well as on the aesthetic environmental qualities. Weiss, Kenney and Steffens made similar tests, although the findings are difficult to interpret, and concluded that their preliminary analyses 'tend to confirm the hypothesis that a broad array of choice variables contribute to the home purchase decision depending on varying degrees of association with identifiable household characteristics' (Weiss, Kenney and Steffens, 1966, 12).

Although these studies have dealt only with small samples, and then of recent home-buyers, and have only investigated the importance of previously identified factors, they suggest the role of two sets of major influences:

1. The desire for a pleasant environment, especially the physical environment, but often the social environment also. Wilson's (1962) study of the most prized environment qualities showed that the following five were already sufficient in his

TABLE VII.7

MAJOR FACTORS IN HOME CHOICE: NEWCASTLE, N.S.W., 1964

OCCUPATION	NUMBER	Employment Proximity	Close to Shops	Distance from High-density Housing	Bush Setting[1]	Good Views	Available Sewerage	Public Transport
				Percent Choosing[1]				
Miner	21	86	23	14	45	59	41	82
Unskilled Manufacturing	185	26	18	1	13	21	26	18
Skilled Manufacturing	184	25	21	14	23	26	36	17
Professional	58	39	22	17	58	60	39	25
Managerial	26	94	88	50	50	50	94	38
Clerical	38	41	22	16	44	48	30	22
Other Tertiary	164	28	24	28	37	29	82	30

[1] More than one factor could be chosen.

Source: Daly, 1968, 45.

respondents' neighbourhood; friendliness, homeyness, quietness, greenery and cleanliness. On the other hand, the desired
qualities that were most missing were: beauty, exclusiveness,
a country-like character, and spaciousness. These findings were
generated by the use of photographs, and in a similar study by
Peterson (1967) respondents were also asked to rate a series of
photographs of housing according to: preference, greenery,
open space, age, expensiveness, safety, privacy, beauty, closeness to nature, photograph quality. The last nine variables
were reduced to four via principal components analysis, and
were correlated against the preference values. The physical
quality of an area, reflected by its age, proved to be the best
predictor of preferences for it, followed by a harmony with
nature factor (greenness, privacy, open space, closeness to
nature) and then a noise factor.

2. The need for a dwelling which will fit household requirements. In particular this refers to the space factor and the
need for a home in which children can be raised, as shown in
Bell's work. Greenbie's survey of stable, middle-class neighbourhoods in Madison, Wisconsin, found that the main reason
for moving to the present home was the need for a larger house;
neighbourhood quality affected only about a sixth of the
respondents. He was testing a hypothesis that people

> are interested primarily in improving their dwellings as
> contrasted with their neighborhood, and they would replace
> their dwelling in its original site and remain in their original
> neighborhood if it were financially and otherwise feasible to
> do so (Greenbie, 1969, 360).

In general, he found this hypothesis to be valid; in a suburban
area, for example, over one-third of residents liked location best
about their previous home but only one-fifth liked it best about
their present dwelling, suggesting that

> while obtaining housing space is important as a motive for
> moving, neighborhood is an equally important consider-
> ation for staying (Greenbie, 1968, 362).

As Clark (1966) found in Toronto, so the people who moved
to suburbia in Madison were those who required housing
space above all else, had no strong kinship or community ties

in the city centre, and could not afford the expensive high-class spacious housing of the older residential districts. Daly's results suggest a similar conclusion, with higher-income people wishing for a home close to their work as long as it had an acceptable environment. The demand for space—the family-cycle model—is a prime determinant of moving therefore, but it is economic status which determines where that move is to.

The Journey to Work & Residential Location

The relative insignificance of workplace location as an influence on residential location has been indicated several times in the preceding paragraphs. Yet this factor has been a keystone of many theories of urban structure, including the multi-nuclei concept which was supposed to bring the zonal and sectoral concepts closer to reality. Indeed, studies by Kain (1962) of Detroit, Wheeler (1967) of Pittsburg, Taafe, Garner and Yeates (1963) and Duncan and Duncan (1960) of Chicago, and Hoover and Vernon (1960) in New York, have all, among many others, suggested the viability of this notion. They have followed Carroll's (1952) pioneer work in this field and suggested that major suburban employment centres act as nodes for lower socio-economic status residential areas within the general zonal pattern organised around the CBD. Higher-income, white-collar groups, on the other hand, place neighbourhood type above workplace accessibility in choosing a residence.

A recent statement by Logan has suggested the breakdown of metropolitan areas into a number of relatively independent employment fields, one based on the CBD and the others on suburban industrial nodes. Although claiming that 'the simple constructs of urban form summarised in the concentric ring, sectoral and multiple nuclei notions are no longer adequate' (Logan, 1968, 165), he presented what was in effect a multiple nuclei model. No detailed tests were employed, but he claimed that journey-to-work data for Sydney supported his contention which was clearly based on the accessibility factor.

In the societies under review, however, accessibility now seems to be an inferior good for a majority of householders, and it has been claimed that

325

Large numbers of suburban families do not have to trade off accessibility for savings in location rent: they can have both. Since households are able to move freely throughout the metropolitan housing stock, suburban locations become the most rational residential choices (Stegman, 1969, 22).

This conclusion was drawn from a nationwide survey in the United States, which showed that:

1. A large number of recent movers to suburbs were more concerned with neighbourhood quality than with accessibility.
2. Similar proportions of city and suburban householders drive to work, invalidating the usual assumption that central city locations are preferred because cheap public transport can be used.
3. Expressways leading to the CBD and fringe employment areas make the latter more accessible to suburban than to city centre residents.

These findings were based on more recent surveys than the classic transport studies of Chicago and Detroit of a decade or more ago, which provided data for the other American studies cited above. Thus they may indicate recent trends, but are probably rather too sweeping in dismissing the role of access in residential location. Nevertheless, rather similar conclusions have been drawn in a detailed study of Vancouver whose findings

suggest that distance from work has little effect as a determinant of residential location in Vancouver, except for limited groups of workers.

1. Females employed in clerical occupations downtown would seem to prefer relatively expensive apartment-living close to downtown. Even in this case, apartment living may be valued for other reasons than that it permits a short journey to work.

2. Married women who are employed, on the average travel short distances to work; this fact is not indicative of residential location being chosen close to employment, but rather of the wife's employment being sought close to home.

3. More significantly, a clustering of workers was observed about peripheral workplaces . . . Clustering occurs only

among plant workers and is strongest in areas in which the costs of housing are uniformly low. No clustering is observed for office workers in peripheral workplaces who tend, if anything, to favor high-cost residential locations at some distance from the place of work (Wolforth, 1966, 75).

The last of these groups seems to agree with the Chicago and Detroit findings, but Wolforth pointed out that it was not superimposed on the existing residential structure when the suburban industrial areas developed. A prior, sectoral spatial pattern had already developed, and workers at the various new plants had to choose within it according to their means (see also Duncan and Duncan, 1960).

Whether a change of workplace is associated with a change of residence is at present only a matter of speculation. Holmes (1965) has suggested that many long-time residents in a community are unable or unwilling to leave it and substitute long-distance commuting for migration. He was dealing with rather special cases of mining towns with declining employment opportunities, however, and in any case found that for many people long-distance commuting was only the prelude to a migration. Goldstein and Mayer (1964a) also pointed out that much residential mobility occurs without a change in job location, and many people change their job but not their home.

In an as yet only slightly tested model, Getis (1969) has suggested that there is a zone of indifference around workplace locations for most workers. He demonstrated this by fitting a more complex expression to a number of scattergrams of number of workers against distance from workplace, to which linear distance-decay models had previously been applied (Figure VII.3). Undoubtedly, the width of this zone will vary with the status of the workers; studies to date have suggested that it is not particularly valid for central city workplaces, and there are probably sectoral differences within the zone. In any case, as several studies have shown, higher-status groups are free from such ties, although 'a larger proportion of members of the lowest status groups who move to the suburbs also hold jobs in the suburbs' (Goldstein and Mayer, 1964b, 287). Some groups, usually of low status, are restricted to certain residential areas irrespective of workplace location and must

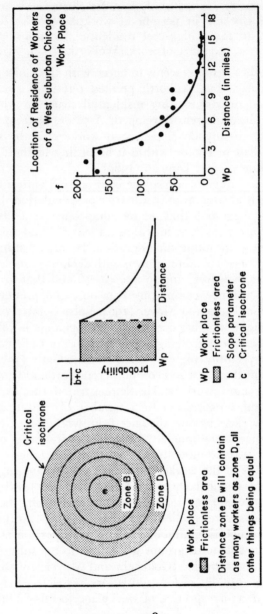

VII.3   Residence–Workplace Relationships. *Source:* Getis, 1969.

commute long distances whether they like it or not; Wheeler (1968) has shown this to be so for Negro ghetto residents, but it may apply to many low-income residents of central cities whose employment opportunities there are dwindling rapidly.

CONCLUSIONS

The amount of residential change within cities is clearly very considerable. There is much spatial order to it, however, both in terms of movement among communities and in movement over physical distance. Most of the observed migration takes place independently of any neighbourhood changes, districts often retaining their characteristics despite very considerable turnover of population. Apart from large amounts of movement within the central city rental-housing market, for which no single explanation exists, it would seem that most intra-urban migrations are the result of changing family circumstances which demand a different home. Most movers seek a satisfactory dwelling in a pleasant residential environment, but the evidence suggests that they are not motivated by socio-economic status considerations. Nevertheless, the latter undoubtedly play a large part both in determining who among the potential movers will move, and in the decision on where to move to. Few moves are made solely for socio-economic status reasons (at least in an upward direction; investigations have generally ignored downward social mobility), and the general consensus is that the family-cycle model provides the best account of the present patterns and processes.

CHAPTER VIII

The Changing Residential Mosaic:
Towards an Integrated Model

VARIOUS HYPOTHESES concerning the changing residential mosaic of cities have been tested in Chapters IV–VI. Each of these discussions dealt with a single dimension of urban society in virtual isolation, however, despite their obvious interrelationships. In Chapter VII, residential mobility within and between the various social areas was discussed, in an attempt to isolate the major processes operating within the framework of neighbourhoods. So far, however, no attempt has been made to integrate the findings of the earlier chapters. The present chapter aims at this and is in three parts; the first two review various studies which have attempted to assess the total spatial pattern, and the third uses these as a basis for a tentative integrated model of the city's residential mosaic.

THE PATTERN AT ONE POINT IN TIME

The first attempt to evaluate simultaneously the relevance of the zonal and sectoral models used four American medium-sized cities (Akron, Dayton, Indianapolis, and Syracuse). A sample of sixteen census tracts was chosen for each, based on a grid of four concentric circles and four equally-spaced radials centred on the CBD. The Shevky-Bell (1955) socio-economic and family status scores for each tract were computed (the third dimension of ethnic status was omitted because, perhaps surprisingly, 'the distribution of Negroes within the large U.S. city is known not to fit either of these [zonal and sectoral] patterns well': Anderson and Egeland, 1961, 394; see also

Anderson, 1962). Zonal and sectoral patterns of these scores were tested for with complex analysis of variance, and it was found that family status was zonally distributed in each city and socio-economic status was only sectorally patterned (except in Indianapolis, where it was both zonal and sectoral).

A similar approach was used in McElrath's studies of Chicago and Rome. He found in the latter that each of the two constructs (socio-economic status and family status) was both zonally and sectorally patterned. The lowest socio-economic status and family status areas were on the urban periphery (McElrath, 1962), and Murdie has observed that 'This finding is consistent with our knowledge of urban differentiation in relatively unindustrialized societies' (Murdie, 1969, 25).

McElrath and Barkey (1963) investigated the spatial patterns in Chicago of both the Shevky–Bell constructs and their constituent measures (see page 53). The SMSA was divided into ten zones and ten sectors by concentric rings and equally-spaced radials, which gave a sample of sixty-eight tracts at the intersections within the built-up area. Analyses of variance indicated clear zonal patterns of family status, and also a significant difference between sectors on this construct and two of its three components (for percent of working women and for multi-unit dwellings, but not fertility). Surprisingly, however, the tests indicated that the socio-economic construct 'clearly is zonal' but '*not* distributed by sectors' (McElrath and Barkey, 1964, 10). This latter conclusion contradicted many of the studies cited earlier, but may have been spurious because:

1. Hoyt did not suggest that the residential pattern would fit into such a rigid geometric framework (indeed McElrath's Rome study defined sectors on the basis of main roads, as Hoyt suggested).

2. Ten sectors were probably too many, and inspection of the data has suggested that their amalgamation to three would result in a significant sectoral pattern (Johnston, 1970).

Finally, the test for the minority-group dimension showed that 'The spatial distribution of sub-areas ordered by proportion non-white is *not* zonal and the hypothesis of sectorial distribution is barely supported' (McElrath and Barkey, 1964, 15);

331

again, this finding—especially its second part—could have been influenced by the sampling framework.

Murdie's (1969) study of Toronto used a similar geometrical framework of six zones and six sectors but:

1. All tracts were analysed, and within-zone, within-sector and within-cell (zone within sector) variations were investigated as well as those between zones and between sectors.

2. The Shevky-Bell measures were replaced by the component scores from prior factorial ecologies. 1951 and 1961 data were analysed separately, within each case six components replacing the original 109 variables.

There was only one insignificant zonal and one insignificant sectoral pattern at each date in the variance analyses of these component scores. The sectoral deviations were not especially important (Table VIII.1), but both insignificant zonal distributions were for economic status components.

According to the relative statistical significance of the zonal and sectoral distributions, Murdie classified each set of component scores as one of: primarily sectoral, primarily zonal, more sectoral than zonal, more zonal than sectoral, both sectoral and zonal (Table VIII.1).

The results confirmed his initial hypotheses that:

1. Economic status was primarily sectoral.

2. Family status was primarily zonal.

3. Recent growth was mainly zonal, as were components of service employment and certain household characteristics (which seem to represent middle-class familism).

4. Ethnic status was mainly sectoral, although two of the three had important zonal elements, also agreeing with Anderson's (1962) suggested 'clumping' in which the ethnic zones were only in certain sectors and the sectors did not extend through all zones.

A Critique

The studies cited so far in this chapter claimed to be testing hypotheses taken from the Burgess and Hoyt models. But was this so? Some used small samples and ignored within-zone and

TABLE VIII.1

SPATIAL PATTERNS WITHIN THE CITY:
TORONTO, 1951–1961
(variance test[1])

COMPONENT	SECTORAL	ZONAL	PATTERN
1951			
Economic Status	0·01	NS	Primarily sectoral
Family Status	0·05	0·01	Primarily zonal
Ethnic Status	0·01	0·01	Both sectoral and zonal
Recent Growth	0·05	0·01	Primarily zonal
Service/Clerical Employment	NS	0·01	More zonal than sectoral
Household Characteristics	0·01	0·01	Primarily zonal
1961			
Economic Status	0·01	NS	Primarily sectoral
Italian Ethnic Status	0·01	0·01	More sectoral than zonal
Household/Employment Characteristics	NS	0·01	Primarily zonal
Family Status	0·01	0·01	Primarily zonal
Jewish Ethnic Status	0·01	0·05	Primarily sectoral
Recent Growth	0·01	0·01	More zonal than sectoral
1951–1961			
Suburbanisation	0·01	0·01	Primarily zonal
Ethnic Change	0·01	0·01	Primarily sectoral
Urbanisation	0·01	0·01	Both sectoral and zonal
Changing Residential Stability	NS	0·01	Primarily zonal
Changing Employment Characteristics	0·01	0·05	More sectoral than zonal
Eastern European Ethnic Changes	0·01	0·01	More sectoral than zonal

[1] 0·01, 0·05—significant at those levels: NS—not statistically significant.

Source: Murdie, 1969, 161–165.

within-sector patterns (the degree of homogeneity within districts), but four major criticisms suggest that in fact the classical models have not been properly assessed.

First, are the rigid geometrical sampling frameworks valid? The number of zones would be unimportant if, as Burgess implied, they were merely used as convenient representations of continuous gradients. But it was shown in Chapter III that linear gradients may be atypical, in which case more careful zonal definition may be necessary for proper pattern identification. More importantly, Hoyt did not indicate that a random selection of a (perhaps random) number of sectors would adequately represent his model. Thus, both McElrath's Rome study and the Melbourne investigation (Johnston, 1969d) attempted to fit their sectors to the socio-economic reality, and the latter work found some evidence of sectoral patterns on other than socio-economic status. It did not affirm Hoyt's suggestion of zones within sectors, however, though this may have been a product of poor data on socio-economic status.

The second criticism is of the use of analysis of variance to test the hypotheses. Where sectoral differences in socio-economic status are very significant and large, then adjacent parts of the same zone should be very dissimilar. Over the whole city this could produce intra-zone heterogeneity which would obscure important between-zone differences within individual sectors (especially if there are no linear gradients within sectors). Thus Murdie found no zonal patterns of economic status in 1951, but re-working of the data for the individual sectors suggested significant between-zone differences in three of them (Johnston, 1970). Hoyt's hypothesis might be correct after all (Murdie (1970) has confirmed this impression: see also Rees, 1970b, 372–4).

Thirdly, most of the statistical tests of zonal and sectoral differences paid little or no attention to the actual form of the zonal gradients. Anderson and Egeland did not discuss this aspect, and Murdie provided only descriptive discussions of his maps, except for presentation of zonal means of economic status in 1951 which indicated increasing status only as far as the third zone. McElrath and Barkey also indicated that zonal gradients were not regular in Chicago; family status only increased away from the CBD as far as zone seven, socio-economic status increased to zone five (see pages 169–176).

In re-working Murdie's 1951 economic status figures, the mapped pattern was also submitted to more detailed scrutiny (Johnston, 1970). Each zone within each sector was classified according to its mean economic status, with the following resultant patterns:

1. The highest-status cells were in intermediate zones.

2. There was great similarity between the outer zones of all six sectors, suggesting a relatively homogeneous middle-class suburbia (as in Clark, 1966; a similar pattern was produced by a classification of the 105 districts in the Melbourne study, Johnston, 1966c).

The final criticism is that although the tests reported here used a technique which was supposed to assess the relative validity of two spatial hypotheses, they did it separately for each dimension of the urban society. It has already been suggested in this book that, despite the correlation and principal component analyses reported here, the various dimensions are neither structurally nor spatially independent; for example Bell's San Francisco data were used in Chapter V to argue for a relationship between socio-economic and family status there (see page 229).

Extension of analyses such as that of Bell's data can be achieved by the classification of observation units on the basis of their values for the various constructs. If the latter are independent, then all possible types should emerge, but this was not the case with the Melbourne study. Four neighbourhood types emerged, each with a significant spatial pattern (Johnston, 1966c):

1. A low socio-economic status, average family status type, with large proportions of immigrants. These areas were concentrated in the low-status sector and in its inner zones, though several were located in outer suburbs.

2. An average socio-economic status, high family status type with relatively few immigrants. The constituent areas were all in the outer zones, in all sectors.

3. A high socio-economic status, low family status type with very few immigrants. Districts in this type were concentrated in the intermediate zones of the high-status sector.

4. Above-average socio-economic and low family status areas, with few immigrants; the areas were again concentrated in the inner zones, and mainly in the high-status sector.

These results suggest that family status differentials occur only among the middle classes and above, and that lower socio-economic status districts cannot be categorised according to their family status; all are very similar. Also, the outer suburbs are generally not just areas of high family status; in almost all cases they are areas of middle-class, high family status.

A later, more detailed study of Melbourne produced similar results. Instead of a small sample of districts, Jones (1969) aggregated all of them into 611 quasi-tracts and classified these according to their scores on three components from a factorial ecology (identified as socio-economic status/ethnicity, familism, and northwestern European settlers). His classification produced three main groups, made up of twenty sub-groups (Table VIII.2). In general the main groups can be categorised as:

1. High socio-economic status, average family status and low-immigrant proportions. The largest subgroup (1202) included the middle-class suburbs which all but ringed the city (Figure VIII.1), and the other large subgroup contained the highest socio-economic status tracts with below-average familism, located in the intermediate suburbs.

2. High familism, low socio-economic status, with variable proportions of immigrants. The characteristic locations for these groups were the outer industrial suburbs of Melbourne's west and southeast.

3. Low familism, high immigrant proportions and variable socio-economic status, which features were peculiar to the inner zones, where they displayed a sectoral pattern of socio-economic status (Table VIII.2 and Figure VIII.1). One of the groups (1196) suggests at first glance that there was a large number of districts with low socio-economic and family status, in contradiction to the above arguments and the earlier study of Melbourne. However, these ninety-one districts had very high immigrant proportions, and the familism values (low proportions of children, and of private houses, small population changes, high percentages of single persons and of employed females, and high population densities) may have represented the characteristic demographic structure of the migrant communities.

While the first impression of Table VIII.2 may be that all types of area existed, further examination suggests otherwise

TABLE VIII.2

PROFILES OF SOCIAL AREAS: MELBOURNE, 1961

COMPONENT

GROUP		Socio-economic Status	Family Status	Ethnicity	Areas
I	1202	+	+	−	183
	1168	+ +	+ +	− −	14
	114	+ +	+	− −	1
	1197	+ +	−	−	81
	1193	−	−	− −	4
	1176	−	+	− −	3
II	1201	− −	+ +	+	8
	1173	− −	+ +	+	41
	1143	−	+ +	+	3
	1192	− −	+ +	+ +	14
	1191	− −	+ +	+ +	5
	65	− −	+ +	+ +	1
	1200	− −	+ +	− −	6
	1167	− −	+	− −	5
III	1198	+ +	− −	+	7
	1180	+ +	− −	+	47
	1185	−	− −	+ +	27
	1196	− −	− −	+ +	94
	1174	−	−	+	66
	218	− −	− −	+ +	1

+ + very high   + above average   − below average   − − very low

Source: Jones, 1969, 99.

(Johnston, 1971a). Omission of the groups characterised by very high ethnic status scores gives the following distribution of tracts:

Socio-Economic Status	Family Status		
	Very Low	Average	Very High
Very High	54	82	14
Average		256	3
Very Low		5	55

This indicates a very clear association between the two constructs, with the socio-economic status of areas presumably

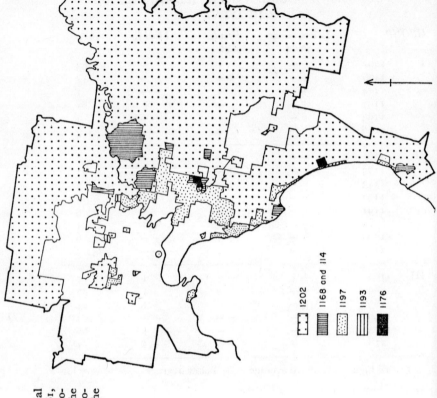

VIII.I   Distribution of various social areas in Melbourne, 1961, showing (A) the high socio-economic status types, (B) the high familism/low socio-economic status types, and (C) the high ethnicity types.

Source: Jones, 1969.

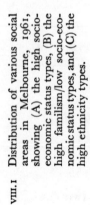

1202

1168 and 114

1197

1193

1176

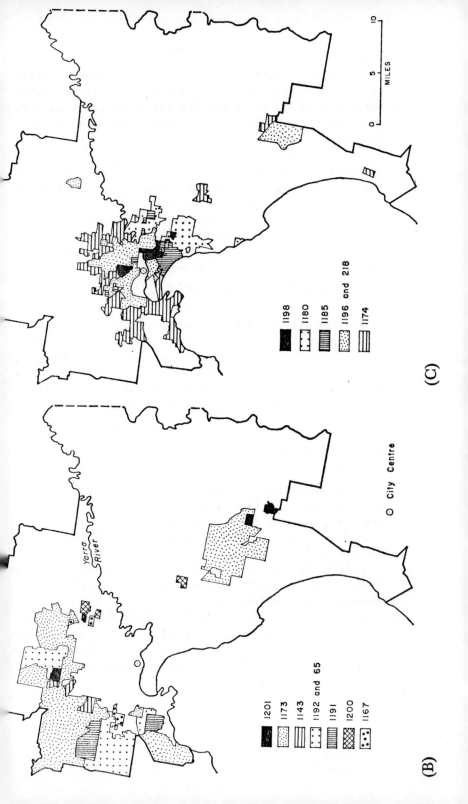

Yarra River

| 1201 |
| 1173 |
| 1143 |
| 1192 and 65 |
| 1191 |
| 1200 |
| 1167 |

○ City Centre

(B)

| 1198 |
| 1180 |
| 1185 |
| 1196 and 218 |
| 1174 |

(C)

0   5   10
MILES

being the main determinant of the residential mosaic. (Ethnic status is presumably a special case of socio-economic status, since none of the 611 tracts had very high values on both and only fifty-four with above-average immigrant proportions had very high socio-economic ratings.)

Thus, it is claimed that the tests of the total residential pattern of the city completed to date have been largely unsuccessful, more through their methodology than their actual results. More detailed, if as yet incomplete, analyses have suggested that the spatial patterns are akin to those suggested by Hoyt, except for the location of the highest socio-economic status areas, and that in producing this pattern, the various societal dimensions are not independent.

SPATIAL PATTERNS OF NEIGHBOURHOOD CHANGE

Few research efforts have assessed neighbourhood changes over time on all of the societal dimensions, mainly because of the lack of data. Two recent studies have attempted this, however.

Murdie (1969) was able to obtain data for fifty-six comparable variables in the 1951 and 1961 Census data for tracts in Toronto. He produced a data matrix of relative change quotients which compared changes in each tract for each variable with the relevant changes over the whole metropolitan area. Principal components analysis of this suggested the following six dimensions:

1. Suburbanisation, a component isolating the peripheral areas of rapid population growth. Increasing incomes suggested the development of a largely middle-class suburbia.

2. Ethnic change, identifying the areas of Italian and Roman Catholic invasion and succession.

3. Urbanisation, a bi-polar component separating suburban areas of increasing familism from inner-zone tracts with more apartments and working women.

4. Changes in residential stability, which identified districts in which relatively more people had lived in the same house for more than four years than in the city as a whole, but for which other variables 'do not produce consistent interpretations' (Murdie, 1969, 137).

5. Changes in employment characteristics, mainly due to a takeover of neighbourhoods by high-occupational-status Jews.

6. Eastern European ethnic changes, another invasion and succession component.

All three model patterns (filtering, expansion of non-familism areas, and invasion and succession) were identified in the outward growth of Toronto, therefore, with the lack of much evidence on filtering being ascribed to a paucity of variables which measured socio-economic characteristics. Analyses of variance for the component scores showed very strong zonal and sectoral elements in the distribution of most of the processes, with invasion and succession being mainly sectoral, filtering zonal, and urbanism both (Table VIII.1). All six variance analyses produced statistically significant interaction effects, however, indicating that considerable proportions of the patterns were not accounted for by the zonal and sectoral framework (and perhaps suggesting growth around a number of nuclei).

From a similar analysis of changes in a sample of 108 census tracts in Chicago over the decade 1950–1960, Brown and Horton (1968) indentified the following five components:

1. Occupational polarisation, which differentiated between areas with increasing proportions of higher occupational-status persons (and also more households in the later stages of the family cycle), and those experiencing decline in their socio-economic status.

2. Occupancy tenure, which contrasted tracts with more young families and lower income and education levels against those in which home ownership increased.

3. Income profile, a component that isolated areas of increasing and decreasing income levels.

4. Life-cycle profile, at one end of which were increases in crowding, renting and young families, while at the other end were increasing numbers in the middle sections of the family cycle.

5. Ethnic composition, contrasting Negro increases against increasing socio-economic status.

This study thus also isolated aspects of invasion and succession, filtering, and family-cycle changes. Within the filtering process, it seems that changes in income (component 3),

341

education (component 2) and occupation (component 1) were spatially uncorrelated, while the occupational changes were associated with some family-cycle changes.

The spatial patterns of these changes were only assessed visually. Brown and Horton suggested zonal dimensions for each component, especially those of occupational polarisation and occupancy tenure, but that within the zonal arrangement were prongs or sectors of more rapid change. No dominant sectoral patterns were identified, however, and for the last three components there was considerable evidence that the changes were emanating from a number of nuclei. Brown and Horton concluded that:

> This most likely stems from the diminished role of the CBD as a major factor in the change process and the increased accessibility of all urban area locations. The latter occurrence permits change to 'jump' from one location to another, rather than to proceed in step by step fashion. Nevertheless, the existence of sectorial type patterns of change emanating from one or several nuclei or the periphery of a concentric zone suggests that this pattern of change remains relevant but in a context different from that portrayed by Hoyt (1939). This observation suggests that some threshold function exists such that change occurs in some ordered spatial pattern if the threshold is not crossed, and that change 'jumps' otherwise (Brown and Horton, 1968, 8).

Both Murdie's and Brown and Horton's studies indicated change in neighbourhood characteristics over time, with attendant spatial patterns. (Note, however, that different change measures were used: Brown and Horton merely expressed change between 1950 and 1960 as a percentage of the 1950 value, but Murdie held constant city-wide changes by dividing such a percentage by the city percentage.) The criticisms made in the preceding section (page 333) also apply here; in addition, because data must be standardised before a principal components analysis, no indication of the *amount* of change in any part of the city was given. Nevertheless, within these, and the data, constraints, the investigations have indicated that the nature and spatial pattern of neighbourhood change have been somewhat as the 'classical' models predicted.

342

TOWARDS AN INTEGRATED MODEL

A feature of almost all the studies reviewed in this book has been their lack of a comprehensive approach to the question of urban residential patterns. Even if a division into static and dynamic approaches is accepted, neither the models discussed in Chapter III nor the many empirical studies quoted since have provided a complete view of the structure and processes of the city's residential pattern.

Building on a review of studies such as those discussed here, Berry and Rees (1969) have recently presented a useful framework for a comprehensive model. It was based on an assumption that a city's social structure contains two major dimensions, socio-economic status and stage in the life cycle. Household units are arranged along the first of these according to their education, occupation, and income, while on the second they are differentiated according to the number of children in their family. Together, these independent dimensions produce the urban social space (Figure VIII.2), which can be mapped into a housing space. In this, the socio-economic dimension is reflected in the price or rent of housing, its size and quality, and the life-cycle dimension correlates with housing type, with the childless families choosing apartments and those with several children preferring single-family houses.

Each individual household unit thus has a social position which is associated with the type of home it occupies, and since people of different types tend to live in similar areas, this produces a community space (Figure VIII.2C). Districts are then recognised by both socio-economic status and family characteristics. Those in the upper left quadrant are of high-income people living in high-quality apartments, in the upper right are high-income families with children occupying relatively large and luxurious single-family homes, while the lower quadrants contain communities of blue-collar workers living in less spacious quarters.

Finally, the various communities can be assigned to a location in the city's physical space, organised around the central business district. This takes the form of a series of zones and sectors. When the city is relatively small, the high socio-

343

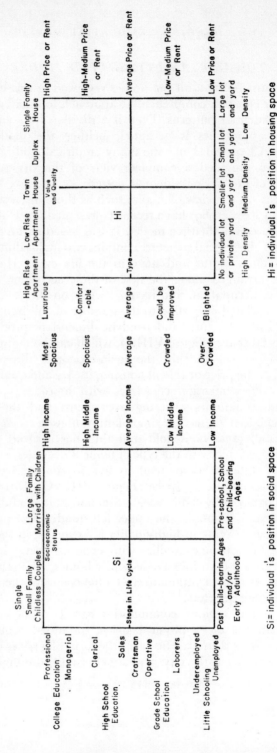

A. SOCIAL SPACE Units: Individual or Families

B. HOUSING SPACE Units: Dwellings

C. COMMUNITY SPACE Units: Tracts or Larger Sub-areas

D. LOCATIONAL OR PHYSICAL SPACE
Units: Tracts or Larger Sub-areas

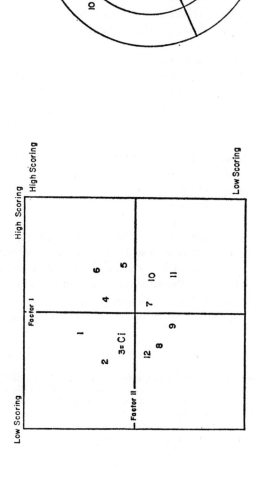

Ci = the community in which i's home is located

Li = the zone in the community in which i's home is located

VIII.2 The Residential Location Process. Household S_i is just below average in size, and just above average in socio-economic status (A). It occupies a similar position H_i in the housing space (B), which can be found in a community type C_i at 3 in the community space (C). These communities are located at L_i in the physical space of the city (D). [Note that Berry and Rees omitted type 10 from their community space diagram.] *Source:* Berry and Rees, 1969.

economic status groups pre-empt the most desirable residential districts, ensuring their exclusive use of them through economic, social and, sometimes, legal constraints. The other sectors are occupied by the other status groups. Within each sector, there is a zonal pattern of life-cycle position, determined by the requirements of communities at the right-hand side of the diagram (Figure VIII.2C) for low-density housing, which is provided on the cheaper land of the urban periphery. Thus, the community space of Figure VIII.2C can be divided into three columns representing family-cycle stages which form the three zones of Figure VIII.2D, and into four rows of similar socio-economic status which produce the four sectors in the physical space.

The model so far is built on the two dimensions of socio-economic and family status, but Berry and Rees showed that two important distorting factors also usually operate, leading to a more complex pattern. The first of these concerns the distribution of minority groups, usually—but not always—relatively low in socio-economic status and living in highly-segregated communities. As socio-economic status groups they generally occupy sectoral settlement patterns, within which there will be zonal differences that, while conforming to the same organisational principles as in the other sectors, are not spatially parallel with zonal patterns in the latter, producing what Berry and Rees termed 'tear faults'. Secondly, complexity is increased by the introduction of secondary workplaces which act as minor nuclei around which communities cluster, as they do around the CBD. Add to this the fact that there is no uniform transportation plain, as Quinn demonstrated, but rather a star-shaped city, and the resulting pattern is as shown in Figure VIII.3.

VIII.3 An Integrated Spatial Model of Urban Residential Areas, based on Chicago. A, B, and C show the socio-economic status, family status and racial patterns respectively; D amalgamates the three into 9 area types. E indicates differences in zonal patterns between white and Negro areas: F and G show how these are distorted by an uneven process of urban growth: and H and I introduce further distortions based on the location of workplaces. *Source:* Berry and Rees, 1969.

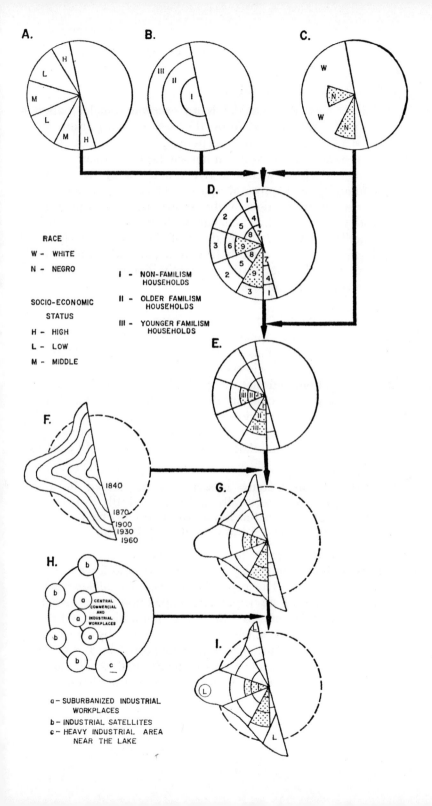

A.

B.

C.

RACE

W - WHITE

N - NEGRO

SOCIO-ECONOMIC STATUS

H - HIGH

L - LOW

M - MIDDLE

I - NON-FAMILISM HOUSEHOLDS

II - OLDER FAMILISM HOUSEHOLDS

III - YOUNGER FAMILISM HOUSEHOLDS

D.

E.

F.

1840
1870
1900
1930
1960

G.

H.

b

b

a

CENTRAL COMMERCIAL AND INDUSTRIAL WORKPLACES

a

b

a

b

c

a - SUBURBANIZED INDUSTRIAL WORKPLACES

b - INDUSTRIAL SATELLITES

c - HEAVY INDUSTRIAL AREA NEAR THE LAKE

I.

L

L

Some Alterations & Additions

Berry and Rees' model is an excellent amalgamation of research findings to date on the *static* spatial pattern of the 'Western' city (with some exceptions), but it omits any mention of the *dynamics*, inferring that households make their residential location decision within a given, unchanging framework of community and physical spaces. Thus, a complete model requires incorporation of the known processes operating to produce neighbourhood change, with the consequent patterns, as well as some of the findings of the present study which disagree with the generally held views, and which indicate the major directions for further research. The more important of these are outlined below.

I. ZONAL PATTERNS OF SOCIO-ECONOMIC STATUS

Although many apparently objective analytical studies have denied it, there seems really to be little doubt that in most cities the various socio-economic status sectors contain zonal differentiation, and that the spatial form of this differentiation varies between sectors in the same city. Each sector is not homogeneous in its socio-economic characteristics, as the Berry and Rees model suggests, but is also zonally patterned. (Note that Rees recognised that this may be so when he hypothesised that

> socio-economic status is sectorally distributed in smaller cities, but both sectorally and concentrically distributed in larger cities with the lowest status occupying most of the inner part of the central city (Rees, 1969, 69).)

Within the highest-status sectors such zoning has emerged as a result of both endogenous and exogenous forces acting on the community. The expansion of commercial landuses and the pressures of an expanding population have forced the highest-status groups to shift their communities away from the central city, a process which has been assisted by developments in transportation technology and supported by the residents' dissatisfaction with their present homes and neighbourhoods. Filtering thus occurred, with the older housing handed down the social scale. Generally, both internal and external forces were necessary for continued movement of communities. In cities which ceased growing, this produced a zonal pattern with the most prestigious districts on the city's edge; where expansion continued but the elite communities saw little reason to move, the middle classes took up the urban fringe, their rising real incomes allowing them to enjoy the freedom of movement which previously only the higher groups could afford.

Similar processes occurred lower down the social scale in some of the other sectors. For many middle-income households there was the choice of following their social betters and attempting to live near to them by occupying their discarded dwellings, or else building their own new, if more modest, homes in less-desirable locations on the edge of lower-status sectors, where land was cheaper. Zonal patterns thus emerged although in some sectors the availability of new suburban housing to the lower classes (perhaps by Government building or financing) produced the socio-economic homogeneity that some observers have suggested.

2. THE SUPPOSED INDEPENDENCE OF THE MAJOR DIMENSIONS

Not one but two zonal patterns are superimposed on each other in the city, therefore, for there can be little dispute about the existence of such distribution of the family-cycle dimension. But the possibility that the two major dimensions are not unrelated has been discussed several times during this book, it being claimed that statistical non-correlation has been confused with conceptual independence. Evidence has suggested that the higher the socio-economic status the greater the choice of life style, and thus the wider the range of housing types. Relatively few households fall into the lower left quadrant of Berry's social space (Figure VIII.2A): this does not imply that there are no blue-collar households in the pre- and post-child ages or consisting of single persons, but that these people generally are much less likely to postpone, or even forego, child-rearing. Single persons in these income groups are also less likely to leave the parental home before marriage, except when moving between cities. More importantly, there are few dwellings in the lower left quadrant of the housing

349

space (Figure VIII.2B): apartments (except those built by Governments) are usually built for higher income groups, and their large-scale development has been relatively recent so that there has been little filtering of them.

A further problem in the interpretation of Berry and Rees' diagrams is that they termed their dimension stage in life cycle, so that, as their Chicago findings indicated, there are 'old' neighbourhoods. But many studies have shown the separate existence of family-cycle and life-cycle (urbanisation) dimensions, with the 'old' neighbourhoods occupying the intermediate rather than the inner zones. In the middle-class sectors this would arise via the following process. From the original development, outward growth would take place as young families built a new home on the city's edge. Many of these would not move again, and so the area ages, while further outer zone development sees the growth of newer young suburbs. In the original inner district the demand for different types of accommodation occasioned by greater life style choice is met by apartment construction, so a zonal dichotomy develops between the single-family home suburbs and the central city apartments, with the former area divided according to its occupants' ages.

Lower-status sectors may display little zonal pattern on the life-style dimension and be dominated only by the family cycle or age pattern. But here the interdependence of family and socio-economic status introduces further complexity. Most households follow not only a family cycle but also a career cycle (irrespective of any social mobility), and it is only at certain stages in their careers, which may never be reached, that they can aspire to certain portions of the housing space. For example, many members of the lowest occupational groups are never able to purchase their own home, and so even at the maximum-size states of the family cycle they are unlikely to live in a low-density outer suburban single-family dwelling, few of which are available for rent (unless provided by public housing agencies). They must remain in the poorer property which is available for rental, and this is usually relatively old and high-density inner-city housing, which has been filtered down the social scale. Other families, slightly higher in the occupational hierarchy, may be able to purchase a single-family home, though only a fairly cheap and probably old one, recently vacated by families who have completed their life cycles. These might be slightly more distant from the CBD, in the oldest parts of suburbia proper.

In the type of urban society discussed in this book, therefore, zonal patterns of socio-economic status and of family status may occur independently of each other, because certain parts of the housing space are not available to households in parts of the social space. Thus, the physical space—especially its zonal patterns—is an amalgam of two separate community structures. In a low-status sector, the inner zones contain the older residents in the family cycle's final stages, still living in dwellings they occupied when the whole area was perhaps a lower-middle-class outer suburb, plus younger families with children, which cannot afford the more desirable housing further out. These two may form separate community types, apparently differentiated on family status though really by socio-economic status, but they are more likely to be inter-mixed. Beyond them will be another mixed zone of late middle-aged, geographically immobile families plus younger house-holds on the move towards outer suburbia. The outer zone will be characterised by its young families, but although family requirements may be the cause of them wanting to be there, economic situation will be the reason that they are.

Higher-status sectors will similarly have an amalgam of two or even three community structures. First, there will be the rough zonal division between inner-city apartment areas and the outer, family-oriented suburbs. The latter will be zoned according to stage in the family cycle, with youth a major characteristic of the outer areas, but socio-economic status will also be represented with a transition from relatively low through high to middle class as one moves towards the open country. Again, family requirements will be the reason for wanting to move into suburbia, but socio-economic status will determine where this move will terminate.

3. THE ROLE OF THE DISTORTING FACTORS

Although some factorial ecologies have suggested otherwise, analysis and interpretation indicate that the residential patterns of minority groups are not independent of those of socio-econo-mic status groups. The two dimensions are uncorrelated because although most minority-group residential areas are also low in socio-economic status, all districts with the latter characteristics are not minority neighbourhoods. As with the socio-economic status/family status association, the distribution is triangular, and traditional correlation methods are not suited to these. Thus, it may be that the distribution of various minority groups does not 'distort' the general pattern in any marked way, providing that they are treated for what they are—separate distributions. They follow the general pattern and live in the relevant zones of relevant sectors according to their socio-economic position: either because they are forced to or because they wish it. They develop their own patterns within these 'ghettoes' or 'villages', and in this way they may be different from the patterns for the wider society. And although they expand into neighbouring districts, much of this is not invasion as it was initially conceived, but merely rapid replace-ment as a consequence of very high rates of intra-urban geographical mobility.

The importance of workplace location in determining resi-dential patterns is difficult to assess. Certainly, many researchers have reported a clustering of homes around workplaces, especially those away from the CBD and its associated employ-ment collar, and higher-grade homes tend to avoid industrial districts. But in reporting where they would like to live, most people attach little importance to the length of the journey-to-work, a symptom of increased personal mobility in modern cities. Thus it would seem that people choose their home dis-tricts on aesthetic, social, and cost criteria which pay little heed to accessibility levels but if, as Adams has pointed out, their mental maps and movement patterns are sectoral in form, no marked separation of job and home is likely to occur.

IN CONCLUSION

The discussion in this book has shown how the interaction of societal divisions, along lines of occupation, income, life style, age, race, religion and birthplace, to name some of the more important, leads to the development of complex patterns

of residential areas. It has suggested that perhaps the inter-
actions between these divisions are not quite what have been
accepted, with the result that the complexities are even harder
to unravel. And, of course, the models discussed here have
assumed that similar people act in the same way, but many
clearly deviate from the general in choosing their residence.
The complexity is thus great, and the present book, with its
over-simplified views of society and models of residential
patterns, is only a brief introduction to the problem of discovering the order in urban residential patterns.

The basic framework for the chapters on residential patterns
has been a number of models, most of which were conceived
several decades ago. Many workers have claimed that these
models are inappropriate to the present urban circumstances
in the countries studied, particularly with increasing levels of
affluence, accessibility, and government participation in the
housing market. But given a belief that there is spatial order to
the residential patterns and processes within a city, then the
only profitable method of elucidating this is via a model or
series of models. Indeed, the 'classical' conceptions of Burgess,
Hoyt and others have proven remarkably resilient and relevant
in this search for order. Certainly, one may have to agree with
Firey that in some situations the evidence is only just sufficient
to suggest the relevance of the models, and we have very little
understanding of the behavioural bases for many of the spatial
patterns and processes. But no better set of models has been
produced, and so the 'classical' set, with additions and alterations from the mass of evidence slowly being compiled, continue
to play a vanguard role in the search for spatial regularity:
a search towards whose goal this review is aimed.

Bibliography of Works Cited

Abu-Lughod, J. L. 1969. Testing the Theory of Social Area Analysis: The Ecology of Cairo, Egypt. *American Sociological Review*, 34, 198–212.

Adams, J. S. 1969. Directional Bias in Intra-Urban Migration. *Economic Geography*, 45, 302–23.

Alihan, M. M. 1938. *Social Ecology: A Critical Analysis*. Columbia University Press, New York.

Alonso, W. 1964. *Location and Land Use*. Harvard University Press, Cambridge, Mass.

Amato, P. W. 1969. Environmental Quality and Locational Behavior in a Latin American City. *Urban Affairs Quarterly*, 4, 83–101.

Amato, P. W. 1970. Elitism and Settlement Patterns in the Latin American City. *Journal of the American Institute of Planners*, 36, 96–105.

Anderson, T. R. 1962. Social and Economic Factors Affecting the Location of Residential Neighborhoods. *Papers and Proceedings, Regional Science Association*, 9, 161–70.

Anderson, T. R. 1966. *The Spatial Organization of Metropolitan Housing in the United States*. Clearing House for Sociological Literature, Milwaukee.

Anderson, T. R. and Bean, L. L. 1961. The Shevky-Bell Social Areas: Confirmation of Results and a Reinterpretation. *Social Forces*, 40, 119–24.

Anderson, T. R. and Egeland, J. A. 1961. Spatial Aspects of Social Area Analysis. *American Sociological Review*, 36, 392–99.

Ashworth, W. 1964. Types of Social and Economic Development in Suburban Essex. In Centre for Urban Studies (1964), 62–87.

Baltzell, E. D. 1953. 'Who's Who in America' and 'The Social Register': Elite and Upper Class Indexes in Metropolitan America. In Bendix and Lipset, 1953, 172–85.

Baltzell, E. D. 1966. *Philadelphia Gentlemen*. The Free Press, New York.

Barber, G. and Bourne, L. S. 1969. *Structure and Process in Small Urban Centres: A Test of Some Preliminary Hypotheses*. Center for Urban and Community Studies, Research Paper 17, University of Toronto, Toronto.

Beckmann, M. J. 1969. On the Distribution of Urban Rent and Residential Density. *Journal of Economic Theory*, 1, 60–7.

Bedarida, F. 1968. Discussion of L. F. Schnore's 'Problems in the Quantitative Study of Urban History'. In Dyos, 1968, 212–13.

355

Bell, W. 1953. The Social Areas of the San Francisco Bay Region. *American Sociological Review*, 18, 39-47.

Bell, W. 1955. Economic, Family and Ethnic Status: An Empirical Test. *American Sociological Review*, 20, 45-52.

Bell, W. 1958a. The Utility of the Shevky Typology for the Design of Urban Sub-Area Field Studies. *Journal of Social Psychology*, 47, 71-83.

Bell, W. 1958b. Social Choice, Life Styles and Suburban Residence. In Dobriner, 1958, 225-47.

Bell, W. 1968. The City, The Suburb and a Theory of Social Choice. In Greer *et al.*, 1968, 132-68.

Bell, W. 1969: Urban Neighborhoods and Individual Behavior. In Meadows and Mizruchi, 1969, 120-46.

Bell, W. and Greer, S. 1962. Social Area Analysis and Its Critics. *Pacific Sociological Review*, 5, 3-9.

Bell, W. and Moskos, C. C. 1964. A Comment on Udry's 'Increasing Scale and Spatial Differentiation'. *Social Forces*, 42, 414-17.

Bendix, R. and Lipset, S. M. (editors). 1953. *Class, Status and Power: A Reader in Social Stratification*. The Free Press, New York.

Bergel, E. E. 1953. *Urban Sociology*. McGraw Hill Book Company, New York.

Berger, B. M. 1960. *Working-Class Suburb*. University of California Press, Berkeley and Los Angeles.

Berger, B. M. 1968. Suburbia and the American Dream. In Fava, 1968, 434-44.

Berry, B. J. L. 1961. Basic Patterns of Economic Development. In Ginsburg, 1961, 110-19.

Berry, B. J. L. 1963. *Commercial Structure and Commercial Blight*. University of Chicago, Department of Geography, Research Paper 85, Chicago.

Berry, B. J. L. 1965. Research Frontiers in Urban Geography. In Hauser and Schnore, 1965, 403-30.

Berry, B. J. L. 1969. Relationships between Regional Economic Development and the Urban System: The Case of Chile. *Tijdschrift voor Economische en Sociale Geografie*, 60, 283-307.

Berry, B. J. L. (editor) 1971. *Classification of Cities: New Methods and Evolving Uses*. International City Managers Assoc. and Resources for the Future, Washington, D.C.

Berry, B. J. L. and Horton, F. E. (editors) 1970. *Geographic Perspectives on Urban Systems*. Prentice-Hall Inc., Englewood Cliffs, New Jersey.

Berry, B. J. L. and Rees, P. H. 1969. The Factorial Ecology of Calcutta. *American Journal of Sociology*, 74, 445-91.

Beshers, J. M. 1962. *Urban Social Structure*. The Free Press, New York.

Beteille, A. (editor) 1969. *Social Inequality*. Penguin Books, Harmondsworth, Middlesex.

Beynon, E. D. 1936. Social Mobility and Social Distance among Hungarian Immigrants in Detroit. *American Journal of Sociology*, 41, 423-34.

Blumenfeld, H. 1949. On the Concentric-Circle Theory of Urban Growth. *Land Economics*, 25, 209-12.

Bogue, D. J. (editor) 1953. *Needed Urban and Metropolitan Research*. Scripps Foundation, Oxford, Ohio.

Bogue, D. J. 1963. *Skid Row in American Cities*. University of Chicago Press, Chicago.

Booth, C. 1889–1902. *Life and Labour of the People in London*. Macmillan and Co., London (17 volumes).

Bourne, L. S. 1967. *Private Redevelopment of the Central City*. University of Chicago, Department of Geography Research Paper 112, Chicago.

Bourne, L. S. 1968. Comments on the Transition Zone Concept. *The Professional Geographer*, 20, 313–16.

Bourne, L. S. 1969. Location Factors in the Redevelopment Process: A Model of Residential Change. *Land Economics*, 45, 183–93.

Bowen, E. G., Carter, H. and Taylor, J. A. (editors) 1968. *Geography at Aberystwyth*. University of Wales Press, Cardiff.

Bracey, H. E. 1964. *Neighbours: Subdivision Life in England and the United States*. Louisiana State University Press, Baton Rouge.

Brown, L. A. 1968. *Diffusion Processes and Location*. Regional Science Research Institute, Bibliography Series Number Four, Philadelphia.

Brown, L. A. 1970. On the Use of Markov Chains in Movement Research. *Economic Geography*, 46, 393–403.

Brown, L. A. and Holmes, J. 1970. *Search Behavior in an Intra-Urban Migration Context: A Spatial Perspective*. Ohio State University, Department of Geography Research Paper 13, Columbus.

Brown, L. A. and Horton, F. E. 1968. *Social Area Change: An Empirical Analysis*. Unpublished Paper, Department of Geography, Ohio State University.

Brown, L. A. and Longbrake, D. B. 1968. *Migration Flows in Intra-Urban Space: An Ecological Approach to Place Utility*. Unpublished Paper, Department of Geography, Ohio State University.

Brown, L. A. and Longbrake, D. B. 1969. On the Implementation of Place Utility and Related Concepts: The Intra-Urban Migration Case. In Cox and Golledge, 1969, 169–96.

Brown, L. A. and Moore, E. G. 1968. *Intra-Urban Migration: An Actor Oriented Framework*. Unpublished Paper, Department of Geography, Ohio State University.

Brown, L. A. and Moore, E. G. 1970. The Intra-Urban Migration Process: A Perspective. *Geografiska Annaler*, 52B.

Burgess, E. W. 1924. The Growth of the City: An Introduction to a Research Project. *Publications, American Sociological Society*, 18, 85–97.

Burgess, E. W. 1927. The Determination of Gradients in the Growth of the City. *Publications of the American Sociological Society*, 21, 178–84.

Burgess, E. W. 1928. Residential Segregation in American Cities. *Annals of the American Academy of Political and Social Science*, 140, 105–15.

Burgess, E. W. 1929. Urban Areas. In Smith and White, 1929, 114–23.

Burgess, E. W. 1930. The New Community and Its Future. *Annals of the American Academy of Political and Social Science*. 149, 157–64.

Burgess, E. W. 1953. The Ecology and Social Psychology of the City. In Bogue, 1953.

Burgess, E. W. and Bogue, D. J. 1967. Research in Urban Society: A Long View. In Burgess and Bogue, 1967, 1–14.

357

Burgess, E. W. and Bogue, D. J. (editors) 1967. *Urban Sociology*. The University of Chicago Press (Phoenix Books), Chicago.

Butler, E. W. and Barclay, W. J. 1967. A Longitudinal Examination of Two Models of Urban Spatial Differentiation: A Case Study of Los Angeles. *Research Previews* (University of North Carolina), 14, 2–25.

Butler, E. W., Sabagh, G. and Van Arsdol Jr., M. D. 1963. Demographic and Social Psychological Factors in Residential Mobility. *Sociology and Social Research*, 48, 139–54.

Butlin, R. A. 1965. The Population of Dublin in the Late Seventeenth Century. *Irish Geography*, 5, 51–66.

Caplan, E. and Wolf, E. P. 1960. Factors Affecting Racial Change in Two Middle-Income Housing Areas. *Journal of Intergroup Relations*, 1.

Caplow, T. and Forman, R. 1950. Neighborhood Interaction in a Homogeneous Community. *American Sociological Review*, 15, 357–66.

Carroll, Jr. J. D. 1952. The Relationship of Home to Work and the Spatial Pattern of Cities. *Social Forces*, 30, 271–82.

Centre for Urban Studies 1964. *London: Aspects of Change*. MacGibbon and Kee, London.

Chapin, F. S. and Brail, R. K. 1969. Human Activity Systems in the Metropolitan United States. *Environment and Behavior*, 1, 107–30.

Chapin, F. S. and Hightower, H. C. 1966. *Household Activity Systems—A Pilot Investigation*. Centre for Urban and Regional Studies, University of North Carolina.

Chapin F. S. and Weiss, S. F. (editors) 1962. *Urban Growth Dynamics*. John Wiley and Sons, New York.

Chorley, R. J. and Haggett, P. (editors) 1965. *Frontiers in Geographical Teaching*. Methuen and Company, London.

Clark, C. 1940. *The Conditions of Economic Progress*. Macmillan and Co., London.

Clark, C. 1951. Urban Population Densities. *Journal of the Royal Statistical Society*, 114, 110–16.

Clark, C. 1967. *Population Growth and Land Use*. Macmillan, London.

Clark, S. D. 1966. *The Suburban Society*. University of Toronto Press, Toronto.

Clark, W. A. V. 1968. *Measurement and Explanation in Intra-Urban Population Mobility*. Unpublished Paper, Department of Geography, University of Wisconsin.

Clark, W. A. V. 1969. Information Flows and Intra-Urban Migration: An Empirical Analysis. *Proceedings, Association of American Geographers*, 1, 38–42.

Clignet, R. and Sween, J. 1969. Accra and Abidjan: A Comparative Examination of the Theory of Increase in Scale. *Urban Affairs Quarterly*, 4, 297–324.

Coleman, J. S. 1964. *Introduction to Mathematical Sociology*. The Free Press of Glencoe, New York.

Collison, P. and Mogey, J. M. 1959. Residence and Social Class in Oxford. *American Journal of Sociology*, 54, 599–605.

Comhaire, J. and Cahnman, W. J. 1959. *How Cities Grew: The Historical Sociology of Cities*. Florham Park Press, Madison, New Jersey.

Coulson, M. R. C. 1968. The Distribution of Population Age Structures in Kansas City. *Annals, Association of American Geographers*, 58, 155–76.

Cox, K. R. 1969. The Genesis of Acquaintance Field Spatial Structures A Conceptual Model and Empirical Test. In Cox and Golledge, 1969, 146–68.

Cox, K. R. and Golledge, R. G. (editors) 1969. *Behavioral Problems in Geography: A Symposium*. Northwestern University, Department of Geography, Studies in Geography 17.

Cressey, P. F. 1938. Population Succession in Chicago: 1898–1930. *American Journal of Sociology*, 44, 59–69.

Crowe, P. R. 1938. On Progress in Geography. *Scottish Geographical Magazine*, 54, 1–19.

Curson, P. H. 1967a. The Changing Demographic Structure of Auckland. In Whitelaw, 1967, 22–39.

Curson, P. H. 1967b. Age-Sex Analysis within Auckland. *Pacific Viewpoint*, 8, 181–5.

Curson, P. H. 1968. Some Demographic Aspects of Cook Islanders in Auckland. *Proceedings, Fifth New Zealand Geography Conference*, 67–75.

Curson, P. H. 1970. Polynesians and Residence in Auckland. *New Zealand Geographer*, 26, 162–73.

Dahrendorf, R. 1969. On the Origin of Inequality among Men. In Beteille, 1969, 16–44.

Daly, M. T. 1967. Land Value Determinants: Newcastle, New South Wales. *Australian Geographical Studies*, 5, 30–9.

Daly, M. T. 1968. Residential Location Decisions: Newcastle, New South Wales. *Australian and New Zealand Journal of Sociology*, 4, 18–35.

Davie, M. R. 1938. The Pattern of Urban Growth. In Murdoch, 1938, 131–61.

Davies, R. J. 1964. Social Distance and the Distribution of Occupational Categories in Johannesburg and Pretoria. *South African Geographical Journal*, 46, 24–39.

Davis, J. T. 1965. Middle Class Housing in the Central City. *Economic Geography*, 41, 238–51.

Davis, K. 1942. A Conceptual Analysis of Stratification. *American Sociological Review*, 7, 309–21.

Davis, K. 1965. The Urbanisation of the Human Population. *Scientific American*, 213 (3), 40–53.

Davis, K. and Blake, J. 1956. Social Structure and Fertility: An Analytical Framework. *Economic Development and Cultural Change*, 4, 211–35.

Davis, K. and Moore, W. E. 1945. Some Principles of Stratification. *American Sociological Review*, 10, 242–9.

Davison, R. B. 1963. The Distribution of Immigrant Groups in London, *Race*, 5, 56–69.

Davison, R. B. 1966. *Black British*. Institute of Race Relations, London.

Dickinson, G. C. 1962. The Development of Suburban Road Transport in Leeds, 1840–95. *Journal of Transport History*, 8, 214–23.

Dickinson, R. E. 1964. *City and Region*. Routledge and Kegan Paul. London.

Dobriner, W. (editor) 1958. *The Suburban Community*. Geo Putnam, New York.

Dobriner, W. 1963. *Class in Suburbia*. Prentice-Hall Inc., Englewood Cliffs, New Jersey.

Dogan, M. and Rokkan, S. (editors) 1969. *Quantitative Ecological Analysis in the Social Sciences*. The M.I.T. Press, Cambridge, Mass.

Du Bois, W. E. 1899. *The Philadelphia Negro*. University of Pennsylvania, Philadelphia.

Duhl, L. J. (editor) 1963. *The Urban Condition*. Basic Books, New York.

Duncan, B. 1956. Factors in Work-Residence Separation: Wage and Salary Workers, Chicago, 1951. *American Sociological Review*, 21, 48–56.

Duncan, B. and Duncan, O. D. 1960. The Measurement of Intra-City Locational and Residential Patterns. *Journal of Regional Science*, 2, 37–54.

Duncan, B. and Hauser, P. M. 1960. *Housing a Metropolis—Chicago*. University of Chicago Press, Chicago.

Duncan, B., Sabagh, G. and Van Arsdol, Jr., M. D. 1962. Patterns of City Growth. *American Journal of Sociology*, 47, 418–29.

Duncan, O. D. 1966. Methodological Issues in the Analysis of Social Mobility. In Smelser and Lipset, 1966, 51–97.

Duncan, O. D., Cuzzort, R. P. and Duncan, B. 1961. *Statistical Geography*. The Free Press, New York.

Duncan, O. D. and Duncan, B. 1955. Occupational Stratification and Residential Distribution. *American Journal of Sociology*, 50, 493–503.

Duncan, O. D. and Duncan, B. 1957. *The Negro Population of Chicago*. University of Chicago Press, Chicago.

Duncan, O. D. and Lieberson, S. 1959. Ethnic Segregation and Assimilation. *American Journal of Sociology*, 64, 364–74.

Duncan, O. D. and Schnore, L. F. 1959. Cultural, Behavioral and Ecological Perspectives in the Study of Social Organisation. *American Journal of Sociology*. 65, 132–46.

Dyos, H. J. (edit.) 1968. *The Study of Urban History*. Edward Arnold, London.

Elias, N. 1965. *The Established and the Outsiders*. Frank Cass, London.

Fairbairn, K. 1963. Population Movements within the Christchurch Urban Area, 1959. *New Zealand Geographer*, 19, 142–59.

Faris, R. E. L. and Dunham, H. W. 1939. *Mental Disorders in Urban Areas*. University of Chicago Press, Chicago.

Fava, S. F. (editor) 1968. *Urbanism in World Perspective: A Reader*. Cromwell, New York.

Firey, W. 1945. Sentiment and Symbolism as Ecological Variables. *American Sociological Review*, 10, 140–8.

Firey, W. 1947. *Land Use in Central Boston*. Harvard University Press, Cambridge, Mass.

Firey, W. 1950. Residential Sectors Re-Examined. *The Appraisal Journal*, 27, 451–4.

Foote, N. N., Abu-Lughod, J., Foley, M. M. and Winnick, L. 1960. *Housing Choices and Constraints*. McGraw Hill Book Co., New York.

Ford, R. G. 1950. Population Succession in Chicago. *American Journal of Sociology*, 56, 151–60.

Forrest, J. 1970. Land Elevation, Dwelling Age, and Residential Stratification in a New Zealand Town. *New Zealand Geographer*, 26, 83–7.

Forster, J. (editor) 1969. *Social Processes in New Zealand*. Longmans Paul, Auckland.

Franklin, S. H. 1969. The Self-Employed Society. *Pacific Viewpoint*, 10, 29–56.

Franklin, S. H., Gibson, B., Treeby, B. 1963. Demographic Structure within a New Zealand Metropolitan Area. *Pacific Viewpoint*, 4, 194–8.

Frazier, E. F. 1937. Negro Harlem: An Ecological Study. *American Journal of Sociology*, 43, 72–88.

Frazier, E. F. 1967. The Negro Family in Chicago. In Burgess and Bogue, 1967, 224–38.

Freedman, R. 1967. City Migration, Urban Ecology, and Social Theory. In Burgess and Bogue, 1967, 92–114.

Freeman, T. W. 1962. The Manchester Conurbation. In *Manchester and its Region*. British Association, Manchester, 47–60.

Fried, M. 1963. Grieving for a Lost Home. In Duhl, 1963, 151–71.

Fried, M. 1967. Functions of the Working Class Community in Modern Urban Society: Implications for Forced Relocation. *Journal of the American Institute of Planners*, 33, 90–103.

Fried, M. and Gleicher, P. 1961. Some Sources of Residential Satisfaction in an Urban Slum. *Journal of the American Institute of Planners*, 27, 305–15.

Gans, H. J. 1961. Planning and Social Life: Friendship and Neighbor Relations in Suburban Communities. *Journal of the American Institute of Planners*, 27, 134–40.

Gans, H. J. 1962a. Urbanism and Suburbanism as Ways of Life: A Reevaluation of Definitions. In Rose, 1962, 625–48.

Gans, H. J. 1962b. *The Urban Villagers*. The Free Press, New York.

Gans, H. J. 1967. *The Levittowners*. Allen Lane—The Penguin Press, London.

Gans, H. J. 1969. Planning for People, Not Buildings. *Environment and Planning*, 1, 33–46.

Getis, A. 1969. Residential Location and the Journey from Work. *Proceedings, Association of American Geographers*, 1, 55–9.

Ginsburg, N. S. (editor) 1961. *Atlas of Economic Development*. University of Chicago, Chicago.

Gittus, E. 1964. The Structure of Urban Areas. *Town Planning Review*, 35, 5–20.

Glass, D. V. (editor) 1954. *Social Mobility in Britain*. Routledge and Kegan Paul, London.

Glass, D. V. and Hall, J. R. 1954. Social Mobility in Great Britain: A Study of Inter-Generational Changes in Status. In Glass, 1954, 177–217.

Glazer, N. and Moynihan, D. P. 1963. *Beyond the Melting Pot*. The M.I.T. Press, Cambridge, Mass.

Glick, P. C. 1957. *American Families*. John Wiley and Son, New York.

Goddard, J. B. 1968. Multivariate Analysis of Office Location Patterns in the City Centre: A London Example. *Regional Studies*, 2, 69–85.

Goldsmith, H. F. and Lee, S. Y. 1966. Socioeconomic Status within the Older and Larger 1960 Metropolitan Areas. *Rural Sociology*, 31, 207–15.

BIBLIOGRAPHY OF WORKS CITED

Goldsmith, H. F. and Stockwell, E. G. 1969. Interrelationship of Occupational Selectivity Patterns Among City, Suburban and Fringe Areas of Major Metropolitan Centers. *Land Economics*, 45, 194–205.

Goldsmith, H. F. and Stockwell, E. G. 1969b. Occupational Selectivity and Metropolitan Structure. *Rural Sociology*, 34, 387–95.

Goldstein, S. 1954. Repeated Migration as a Factor in High Mobility Rates. *American Sociological Review*, 19, 536–41.

Goldstein, S. 1958. *Patterns of Mobility 1910-1950: The Norristown Study*. University of Pennsylvania Press, Philadelphia.

Goldstein, S. and Goldscheider, C. 1968. *Jewish Americans*. Prentice-Hall, Inc., Englewood Cliffs, New Jersey.

Goldstein, S. and Mayer, K. B. 1961. *Metropolitanization and Population Change in Rhode Island*. Rhode Island Development Council, Providence.

Goldstein, S. and Mayer, K. B. 1964a. Migration and the Journey to Work. *Social Forces*, 42, 472–81.

Goldstein, S. and Mayer, K. B. 1964b. Migration and Social Status Differentials in the Journey to Work. *Rural Sociology*, 29, 278–87.

Goldstein, S. and Mayer, K. B. 1964c. Population Decline and the Social and Demographic Structure of an American City. *American Sociological Review*, 29, 48–54.

Goldstein, S. and Mayer, K. B. 1965a. The Impact of Migration on the Socio-Economic Structure of Cities and Suburbs. *Sociology and Social Research*, 50, 5–35.

Goldstein, S. and Mayer, K. B. 1965b. Demographic Correlates of Status Differences in a Metropolitan Population. *Urban Studies*, 2, 67–84.

Goode, W. J. 1963. Industrialization and Family Change. In Hoselitz and Moore, 1963, 237–55.

Gordon, G. 1966. The Evolution of Status Areas in Edinburgh. Institute of British Geographers, Study Group in Urban Geography, *The Social Structure of Cities*, Liverpool, 27–37.

Gordon, M. M. 1964. *Assimilation in American Life*. Oxford University Press, New York.

Greenbie, B. B. 1968. New House or New Neighborhood? A Survey of Priorities among Home Owners in Madison, Wisconsin. *Land Economics*, 45, 359–65.

Greer, S. 1962. *The Emerging City: Myth and Reality*. The Free Press, New York.

Greer, S., McElrath, D. C., Minar, D. W. and Orleans, P. (editors) 1968. *The New Urbanization*. St. Martin's Press, New York.

Gregory, S. 1963. *Statistical Methods and the Geographer*. Longmans, London.

Griffin, D. W. and Preston, R. E. 1966. A Restatement of the Transition Zone Concept. *Annals, Association of American Geographers*, 56, 339–50.

Grigsby, W. G. 1963. *Housing Markets and Public Policy*. University of Pennsylvania Press, Philadelphia.

Gutman, R. 1966. Review of L. F. Schnore, *The Urban Scene*. *American Sociological Review*, 31, 282–3.

Haggett, P. 1965. *Locational Analysis in Human Geography*. Edward Arnold, London.

362

BIBLIOGRAPHY OF WORKS CITED

Hammond, S. B. 1954. Attitudes to Immigration. In Oeser and Hammond, 1954, 51–65.

Handlin, O. 1951. *The Uprooted*. Little, Brown and Co., Boston.

Handlin, O. 1959. *The Newcomers*. Harvard University Press, Cambridge, Mass.

Handlin, O. and Burchard, J. 1963. *The Historian and the City*. The M.I.T. Press and Harvard University Press, Cambridge, Mass.

Harris, B. 1968. Quantitative Models of Urban Development: Their Role in Metropolitan Policy-Making. In Perloff and Wingo, 1968, 363–412.

Harris, C. D. and Ullman, E. L. 1945. The Nature of Cities. *Annals of the American Academy of Political and Social Science*, 242, 7–17.

Hart, J. F. 1960. The Changing Distribution of the American Negro. *Annals, Association of American Geographers*, 50, 242–66.

Hartman, C. W. 1963. The Limitations of Public Housing. *Journal, American Institute of Planners*, 29, 283–96.

Hartshorne, R. 1939. *The Nature of Geography*. Association of American Geographers, Lancaster, Pennsylvania.

Hauser, F. L. 1951. The Ecological Pattern of Four European Cities and Two Theories of Urban Expansion. *Journal of the American Institute of Planners*, 16, 111–29.

Hauser, P. M. and Schnore, L. F. (editors) 1965. *The Study of Urbanization*. John Wiley and Sons, New York.

Hawley, A. H. 1950. *Human Ecology*. The Ronald Press, New York.

Hawley, A. H. 1956. *The Changing Shape of Metropolitan America*. The Free Press, New York.

Hawley, A. H. and Duncan, O. D. 1957. Social Area Analysis: A Critical Appraisal. *Land Economics*, 33, 227–45.

Heberle, R. 1948. Social Consequences of the Industrialization of Southern Cities. *Social Forces*, 27, 29–37.

Heenan, L. D. B. 1967. Rural-Urban Distribution of Fertility in South Island, New Zealand. *Annals, Association of American Geographers*, 57, 713–35.

Herbert, D. T. 1967. Social Area Analysis: A British Study. *Urban Studies*, 4, 41–60.

Herbert, D. T. 1968. Principal Components Analysis and British Studies of Urban-Social Structure. *The Professional Geographer*, 20, 280–3.

Herbert, D. T. and Rodgers, H. B. 1967. Space Relationships in Neighbourhood Planning. *Town and Country Planning*, 35, 196–9.

Holmes, J. H. 1965. The Suburbanization of Cessnock Coalfield Towns, 1954–1964. *Australian Geographical Studies*, 3, 105–28.

Hoover, E. M. and Vernon, R. 1962. *Anatomy of a Metropolis*. Doubleday and Company (Anchor Books), New York.

Horne, D. 1965. *The Lucky Country*. Penguin Books, Harmondsworth, Middlesex.

Horton, F. E. and Reynolds, D. R. 1969. An Investigation of Individual Action Spaces: A Progress Report. *Proceedings, Association of American Geographers*, 1, 70–5.

Horton, F. E. and Reynolds, D. R. 1970. *Intra-Urban Migration and the Perception of Residential Quality*. Ohio State University, Department of Geography Research Paper 13, Columbus.

Hoselitz, B. F. and Moore, W. E. (editors) 1963. *Industrialization and Society*. UNESCO—Mouton, New York.

Hoyt, H. 1933. *One Hundred Years of Land Values in Chicago*. Chicago University Press, Chicago.

Hoyt, H. 1939. *The Structure and Growth of Residential Neighborhoods in American Cities*. Federal Housing Administration, Washington, D.C.

Hoyt, H. 1950. Residential Sectors Revisited. *The Appraisal Journal*, 27, 455–50.

Hoyt, H. 1963. The Residential and Retail Patterns of Leading Latin American Cities. *Land Economics*, 39, 449–54.

Hoyt, H. 1964. Recent Distortions of the Classical Models of Urban Structure. *Land Economics*, 40, 199–212.

Hurd, R. M. 1924. *Principles of City Land Values*. The Record and Guide, New York.

Inkeles, A. and Rossi, P. 1956. National Comparisons of Occupational Prestige. *American Journal of Sociology*, 61, 329–39.

Jackson, J. A. 1964. The Irish. In Centre for Urban Studies, 1964, 293–308.

Jakle, J. A. and Wheeler, J. O. 1969a. The Dutch and Kalamazoo, Michigan: A Study of Spatial Barriers to Acculturation. *Tijdschrift voor Economische en Sociale Geografie*, 60, 249–54.

Jakle, J. A. and Wheeler, J. O. 1969b. The Changing Residential Structure of the Dutch Population in Kalamazoo, Michigan. *Annals, Association of American Geographers*, 59, 441–60.

James, J. 1948. A Critique of Firey's *Land Use in Central Boston*. *American Journal of Sociology*, 54, 228–34.

Janson, C. G. 1969. Some Problems of Ecological Factor Analyses. In Dogan and Rokkan, 1969, 301–41.

Johnston, R. J. 1966a. The Location of High Status Residential Areas. *Geografiska Annaler*, 48B, 23–35.

Johnston, R. J. 1966b. The Population Characteristics of the Urban Fringe: A Review and Example. *Australian and New Zealand Journal of Sociology*, 2, 79–93.

Johnston, R. J. 1966c. *Residential Structure and Urban Morphology*. Unpublished Ph.D. Thesis, Monash University.

Johnston, R. J. 1968. An Outline of the Development of Melbourne's Street Pattern. *The Australian Geographer*, 10, 453–65.

Johnston, R. J. 1969a. Some Tests of a Model of Intra-Urban Population Mobility: Melbourne, Australia. *Urban Studies*, 6, 34–57.

Johnston, R. J. 1969b. Population Movements and Metropolitan Expansion: London 1960–1. *Transactions, Institute of British Geographers*, 46, 69–91.

Johnston, R. J. 1969c. Processes of Change in the High Status Residential Districts of Christchurch, 1951–1964. *New Zealand Geographer*, 25, 1–15.

Johnston, R. J. 1969d. Zonal and Sectoral Patterns in Melbourne's Residential Structure: 1961. *Land Economics*, 45, 463–7.

Johnston, R. J. 1969e. Towards an Analytical Study of the Townscape: The Residential Building Fabric. *Geografiska Annaler*, 51B, 20–32.

Johnston, R. J. 1970. On Spatial Patterns in the Residential Structure of Cities. *The Canadian Geographer*, 14.

Johnston, R. J. 1971a. On Factorial Ecologies and Social Area Analysis. *Economic Geography*, 47.

Johnston, R. J. 1971b. The Factorial Ecology of New Zealand Urban Areas: A Comparative Study.

Johnston, R. J. 1971c. Mental Maps of the City: Suburban Preference Patterns. *Environment and Planning*, 3.

Johnston, R. J. forthcoming. Intra-Societal Patterns of Increasing Scale: A Pilot Study.

Jonassen, C. T. 1949. Cultural Variables in the Ecology of an Ethnic Group. *American Sociological Review*, 14, 32–41.

Jones, E. 1960. *The Social Geography of Belfast*. Oxford University Press, Oxford.

Jones, E. and Sinclair, D. J. 1968. *Atlas of London*. Pergamon Press, London.

Jones, F. L. 1964. Italians in the Carlton Area: The Growth of an Ethnic Concentration. *Australian Journal of Politics and History*, 10, 83–95.

Jones, F. L. 1967a. Ethnic Concentration and Assimilation: An Australian Case Study. *Social Forces*, 45, 412–23.

Jones, F. L. 1967b. A Social Ranking of Melbourne Suburbs. *Australian and New Zealand Journal of Sociology*, 3, 93–110.

Jones, F. L. 1968. Social Area Analysis: Some Theoretical and Methodological Comments illustrated with Australian Data. *British Journal of Sociology*, 19, 424–44.

Jones, F. L. 1969. *Dimensions of Urban Social Structure: The Social Areas of Melbourne, Australia*. Australian National University Press, Canberra.

Jones, P. N. 1967. *The Segregation of Immigrant Communities in the City of Birmingham*. University of Hull, Department of Geography, Occasional Paper 7.

Jones, R. 1962. Segregation in Urban Residential Districts: Examples and Research Problems. *Lund Studies in Geography*, B24, 433–47.

Kain, J. F. 1962. The Journey-to-Work as a Determinant of Residential Location. *Papers and Proceedings, Regional Science Association*, 9, 137–60.

Kaiser, E. J. and Weiss, S. F. 1969a. Some Components of a Linked Model for the Residential Development Decision Process. *Proceedings of the Association of American Geographers*, 1, 75–9.

Kaiser, E. J. and Weiss, S. F. 1969b. Decision Agent Models of the Residential Development Process—A Review of Recent Research. *Traffic Quarterly*, 23, 597–630.

Katz, A. M. and Hill, R. 1958. Residential Propinquity and Marital Selection: A Review of Theory, Method, and Fact. *Marriage and Family Living*, 58, 27–35.

Keyfitz, N. 1965. Political-Economic Aspects of Urbanisation in South and Southeast Asia. In Hauser and Schnore, 1965, 265–309.

Kiang, Y–C. 1968. The Distribution of Ethnic Groups in Chicago. *American Journal of Sociology*, 74, 292–5.

Knights, P. R. 1969. Population Turnover, Persistence, and Residential Mobility in Boston, 1830–1860. In Thernstrom and Sennett, 1969, 258–74.

Knos, D. S. 1962. *The Distribution of Land Values in Topeka*, Kansas. Centre for Research and Business, Lawrence, Kansas.

Kosa, J. 1956. Hungarian Immigrants in North America: Their Residential Mobility and Ecology. *Canadian Journal of Economics and Political Science*, 22, 358–70.

Kunkel, R. and Zanarini, R. 1968. A Note on a Classification of Intra-Urban Migrants. Department of Geography, University of Iowa.

Lampard, E. E. 1955. The History of Cities in the Economically Advanced Areas. *Economic Development and Cultural Change*, 3, 81–102.

Lampard, E. E. 1963. Urbanisation and Social Change; on Broadening the Scope and Relevance of Urban History. In Handlin and Burchard, 1963, 225–48.

Lampard, E. E. 1968. The Evolving System of Cities in the United States: Urbanization and Economic Development. In Perloff and Wingo, 1963, 81–140.

Lansing, J. B., Clifton, C. V. and Morgan, J. N. 1969. *New Homes and Poor People*. Survey Research Center, University of Michigan, Ann Arbor.

Laserwitz, B. 1960. Metropolitan Community Residential Belts, 1950 and 1956. *American Sociological Review*, 25, 245–52.

Laurenti, L. 1960. *Property Values and Race*. University of California Press, Berkeley.

Lee, E. S. 1966. A Theory of Migration. *Demography*, 3, 47–57.

Lees, L. H. 1969. Patterns of Lower-Class Life: Irish Slum Communities in Nineteenth Century London. In Thernstrom and Sennett, 1969, 359–85.

Leiffer, M. R. 1933. A Method for Determining Local Urban Community Boundaries. *Proceedings, American Sociological Society*, 26, 137–43.

Lenski, G. 1966. *Power and Privilege: A Theory of Social Stratification*. McGraw Hill Book Co., New York.

Leslie, G. 1968. *The Spatial Distribution of Christchurch Land Values, 1914–1964*. Unpublished M.A. Thesis, University of Canterbury.

Leslie, G. R. and Richardson, A. H. 1961. Life-Cycle, Career Pattern, and the Decision to Move. *American Sociological Review*, 25, 894–902.

Lewis, O. 1965. The Folk-Urban Ideal Types. In Hauser and Schnore, 1965, 491–503.

Lieberson, S. 1961. The Impact of Residential Segregation on Ethnic Assimilation. *Social Forces*, 40, 52–7.

Lieberson, S. 1963a. *Ethnic Patterns in American Cities*. The Free Press, New York.

Lieberson, S. 1963b. The Old-New Distinction and Immigrants in Australia. *American Sociological Review*, 28, 550–65.

Lipman, V. D. 1964. Social Topography of a London Congregation. *Jewish Journal of Sociology*, 6, 69–74.

Lipset, S. M. and Bendix, R. 1959. *Social Mobility in Industrial Society*. University of California Press, Berkeley.

Little, K. L. 1965. *West African Urbanization*. Cambridge University Press, Cambridge.

Litwak, E. 1960a. Occupational Mobility and Extended Family Cohesion. *American Sociological Review*, 25, 9–21.

Litwak, E. 1960b. Geographic Mobility and Extended Family Cohesion. *American Sociological Review*, 25, 385–94.

Loewenstein, L. K. 1965. *The Location of Residences and Workplaces in Urban Areas*. The Scarecrow Press, New York.

Logan, M. I. 1968. Work-Residence Relationships in the City. *Australian Geographical Studies*, 6, 151–66.

Lowry, I. S. 1960. Filtering and Housing Standards: A Conceptual Analysis. *Land Economics*, 36, 362–70.

Mabry, J. H. 1968. Public Housing as an Ecological Influence in Three English Cities. *Land Economics*, 44, 393–8.

McElrath, D. C. 1962. The Social Areas of Rome: A Comparative Analysis. *American Sociological Review*, 27, 376–91.

McElrath, D. C. 1965. Urban Differentiation: Problems and Prospects. *Law and Contemporary Problems*, 30, 103–10.

McElrath, D. C. 1968. Societal Scale and Social Differentiation: Accra, Ghana. In Greer, McElrath, Minar and Orleans, 1968, 33–52.

McElrath, D. C. and Barkey, J. W. 1964. *Social and Physical Space: Models of Metropolitan Differentiation*. Unpublished paper, North-western University.

McGee, T. G. 1962. Indian Settlement in New Zealand: 1900–1956. *New Zealand Geographer*, 18, 203–23.

McGee, T. G. 1967. *The Southeast Asian City*. G. Bell and Sons, London.

McGee, T. G. 1969. The Social Ecology of New Zealand Cities: A Preliminary Investigation. In Forster, 1969, 144–83.

McKenzie, R. D. 1926. The Scope of Human Ecology. *American Journal of Sociology*, 32, 141–54.

McKenzie, R. D. 1924. The Ecological Approach to the Study of the Human Community. *American Journal of Sociology*, 23, 60–80.

Maisel, S. J. 1966. Rates of Ownership, Mobility and Purchase. In *Essays in Urban Land Economics*, University of California Press, Berkeley, 76–107.

Mann, P. H. 1965. *An Approach to Urban Sociology*. Routledge and Kegan Paul, London.

Mayer, H. M. and Kohn, C. F. (editors) 1959. *Readings in Urban Geography*, University of Chicago Press, Chicago.

Meadows, P. and Mizruchi, E. H. 1969. *Urbanism, Urbanization, and Change: Comparative Perspectives*. Addison-Wesley Publishing Co: Reading, Mass.

Mehta, S. K. 1961. A Comparative Analysis of the Industrial Structure of the Urban Labor Force of Burma and the United States. *Economic Development and Cultural Change*, 9, 164–79.

Metge, A. J. 1952. The Maori Population of Northern New Zealand. *New Zealand Geographer*, 8, 104–24.

Metge, A. J. 1964. *A New Maori Migration*. University of London Press, London.

Michelson, W. 1967. Potential Candidates for the Designers' Paradise: A Social Analysis from a Nationwide Survey. *Social Forces*, 46, 190–6.

Miller, A. R. 1967. The Migration of Employed Persons to and from Metropolitan Areas of the United States. *Journal of the American Statistical Association*, 62, 1418–32.

Minghi, J. V. (editor) 1966. *The Geographer and the Public Environment*. Tantalus Publications, Vancouver.

Mittelbach, F. G. 1963. *The Changing Housing Inventory, 1950–1960*. Profile of the Los Angeles Metropolis Series, University of California, Los Angeles.

Mogey, J. M. 1956. *Family and Neighbourhood*. Oxford University Press, Oxford.

Molotch, H. 1969. Racial Change in a Stable Community. *American Journal of Sociology*, 75, 226–38.

Moore, E. G. 1969. The Structure of Intra-Urban Movement Rates: An Ecological Model. *Urban Studies*, 6, 17–33.

Moore, E. G. and Brown, L. A. 1969. *Spatial Properties of Urban Contact Fields: An Empirical Analysis*. Department of Geography, Northwestern University, Research Report 52, Evanston.

Moore, W. E. 1963. *Social Change*. Prentice-Hall Inc., Englewood Cliffs, New Jersey.

Moore, W. E. 1966. Changes in Occupational Structures. In Smelser and Lipset, 1966, 194–212.

Morrill, R. L. 1965. The Negro Ghetto: Problems and Alternatives. *Geographical Review*, 55, 339–61.

Morris, R. N. 1968. *Urban Sociology*. George Allen and Unwin, London.

Morrison, P. A. 1967. Duration of Residence and Prospective Migration: The Evaluation of a Stochastic Model. *Demography*, 4, 553–61.

Moser, C. A. and Scott, W. 1961. *British Towns: A Statistical Study of their Social and Economic Differences*. Oliver and Boyd, Edinburgh.

Mowrer, E. R. 1958. The Family in Suburbia. In Dobriner, 1958, 147–64.

Munby, L. M. (editor) 1968. *East Anglian Studies*. W. Heffer, Cambridge.

Murdie, R. A. 1969. *Factorial Ecology of Metropolitan Toronto, 1951–1961*. University of Chicago, Department of Geography Research Paper 116, Chicago.

Murdie, R. A. 1970. A Reply to 'On Spatial Patterns in the Residential Structure of Cities'. *Canadian Geographer*, 14.

Murdock, G. P. (editor) 1938. *Studies in the Science of Society*. Yale University Press, New Haven.

Murphy, R. E. 1966. *The American City*. McGraw Hill and Co., New York.

Muth, R. F. 1961. The Spatial Structure of the Housing Market. *Papers and Proceedings, Regional Science Association*, 7, 207–20.

Muth, R. F. 1968. Urban Residential Land and Housing Markets. In Perloff and Wingo, 1968, 285–333.

Muth, R. F. 1969. *Cities and Housing*. University of Chicago Press, Chicago.

Myers, J. K. 1950. Assimilation to the Ecological and Social Systems of a Community. *American Sociological Review*, 15, 367–72.

Myrdal, G. 1957. *Rich Lands and Poor*. Harper and Row, New York.

Neutze, G. M. 1968. *The Suburban Apartment Boom*. Resources for the Future Inc., Washington, D.C.

Newling, B. E. 1969. The Spatial Variation of Urban Population Densities. *Geographical Review*, 59, 242–52.

Oeser, O. A. and Hammond, S. B. (editors) 1954. *Social Structure and Personality in a City*. Routledge and Kegan Paul, London.

Olsson, G. 1965. *Distance and Human Interaction: A Review and Bibliography*. Regional Science Research Institute, Bibliography Series Number Two, Philadelphia.

Orleans, P. 1966. Robert Park and Social Area Analysis: A Convergence in Urban Sociology. *Urban Affairs Quarterly*, 1, 5–19.

Pahl, R. E. 1965. *Urbs in Rure*. Department of Geography, London School of Economics, Occasional Paper 2.

Pahl, R. E. 1968. Newcomers in Town and Country. In Munby, 1968, 174–200.

Park, R. E. 1936a. Human Ecology. *American Journal of Sociology*, 42, 1–15.

Park, R. E. 1936b. Succession, An Ecological Concept. *American Sociological Review*, 1, 171–9.

Park, R. E. and Burgess, E. W. 1921. *Introduction to the Science of Society*. University of Chicago Press, Chicago.

Patterson, S. 1960. A Recent West Indian Immigrant Group in Britain. *Race*, 1, 27–39.

Patterson, S. 1965. *Dark Strangers*. Penguin Books, Harmondsworth, Middlesex.

Peach, G. C. K. 1966. Factors affecting the Distribution of West Indians in Great Britain. *Transactions, Institute of British Geographers*, 38, 151–63.

Peach, G. C. K. 1968. *West Indian Migration to Britain*. Institute of Race Relations, London.

Peattie, L. R. 1969. *The View from the Barrio*. University of Michigan Press, Ann Arbor.

Penalosa, F. 1967. Ecological Organisation of the Transitional City: Some Mexican Evidence. *Social Forces*, 46, 221–9.

Perlman, M. (editor) 1963. *Human Resources in the Urban Economy*. Resources for the Future Inc., Washington, D.C.

Perloff, H. S. and Wingo, Jr., L. (editors) 1968. *Issues in Urban Economics*. Johns Hopkins Press, Baltimore.

Peterson, G. L. 1967. A Model of Preference: Quantitative Analysis of the Visual Appearance of Residential Neighbourhoods. *Journal of Regional Science*, 7, 19–32.

Pfautz, H. W. 1967. *Charles Booth on the City*. University of Chicago Press, Chicago.

Pollins, H. 1964. Transport Lines and Social Divisions. In Centre for Urban Studies, 1964, 29–61.

Pool, D. I. 1961. Maoris in Auckland. *Journal of the Polynesian Society*, 70, 43–66.

Powers, M. G. 1964a. Age and Space Aspects of City and Suburban Housing. *Land Economics*, 40, 381–7.

Powers, M. G. 1964b. Socio-Economic Heterogeneity in New England Metropolitan Residential Areas. *The Canadian Review of Sociology and Anthropology*, 1, 129–37.

Powers, M. G. 1966. Socio-economic Status and the Fertility of Married Women. *Sociology and Social Research*, 50, 472–82.

Pred, A. 1965. Industrialization, Initial Advantage, and American Metropolitan Growth. *Geographical Review*, 55, 158–85.

Pred, A. R. 1966. *The Spatial Dynamics of US Urban-Industrial Growth, 1800–1914, Interpretive and Theoretical Essays*. The M.I.T. Press, Cambridge Mass.

Price, C. A. 1963. *Southern Europeans in Australia*. Melbourne University Press, Melbourne.

Quinn, J. A. 1940a. The Burgess Zonal Hypothesis and Its Critics. *American Sociological Review*, 5, 210–18.

Quinn, J. A. 1940b. Topical Summary of Current Literature on Human Ecology. *American Journal of Sociology*, 46, 191–226.

Quinn, J. A. 1950. *Human Ecology*. Prentice-Hall Inc., Englewood Cliffs, New Jersey.

Ramsøy, N. R. 1966. Assortative Mating and the Structure of Cities. *American Sociological Review*, 31, 773–86.

Rapkin, C. W. and Grigsby, W. G. 1960a. *Residential Renewal in the Urban Core*. University of Pennsylvania Press, Philadelphia.

Rapkin, C. W. and Grigsby, W. G. 1960b. *The Demand for Housing in Racially Mixed Areas*. University of California Press, Berkeley.

Ravenstein, E. G. 1885. The Laws of Migration. *Journal of the Royal Statistical Society*, 48, 168–227.

Ravenstein, E. G. 1889. The Laws of Migration. *Journal of the Royal Statistical Society*, 52, 241–301.

Reeder, D. W. 1968. A Theatre of Suburbs: Some Patterns of Development in West London, 1801–1911. In Dyos, 1968, 253–71.

Rees, P. H. 1969. *Residential Patterns in American Cities*. Ph.D. Dissertation Proposal: University of Chicago.

Rees, P. H. 1970a. The Urban Envelope: Patterns and Dynamics of Population Density. In Berry and Horton, 1970, 276–305.

Rees, P. H. 1970b. Concepts of Social Space: Toward an Urban Social Geography. In Berry and Horton, 1970, 306–94.

Rees, P. H. 1971. Factorial Ecology: An Extended Definition, Survey and Critique of the Field. *Economic Geography*, 47.

Rees, P. H. forthcoming. Factorial Ecology—An Orderly Basis for Intra-Metropolitan Community Studies. In Berry, 1971.

Richards, J. M. 1963. The Significance of Residential Preferences in Urban Areas. In Perlman, 1963, 123–36.

Rimmer, P. J. 1967. The Altona Petro—Chemical Complex. *The Australian Geographer*, 10, 211–12.

Robson, B. T. 1966. An Ecological Analysis of the Evolution of Residential Areas in Sunderland. *Urban Studies*, 3, 120–42.

Robson, B. T. 1968. New Techniques in Urban Analysis. In Bowen, Carter and Taylor, 1968, 235–52.

Robson, B. T. 1969. *Urban Analysis*. Cambridge University Press, Cambridge.

Rodgers, H. B. 1962. Victorian Manchester. *Journal of the Manchester Geographical Society*, 58, 1–12.

Rodwin, L. 1950. The Theory of Residential Growth and Structure. *The Appraisal Journal*, 27, 295–317.

Rodwin, L. 1961. *Housing and Economic Progress*. Harvard University Press, Cambridge, Mass.

Rose, A. M. (editor) 1962. *Human Behavior and Social Processes*. Houghton Mifflin and Co., Boston.

Rose, H. M. 1964. Metropolitan Miami's Changing Negro Population, 1950–1960. *Economic Geography*, 40, 221–38.

Rose, H. M. 1969. *Social Processes in the City: Race and Urban Residential Choice*. Association of American Geographers, Commission on College Geography, Resource Paper Number 6, Washington, D.C.

Rose, H. M. 1970. The Development of an Urban Subsystem: The Case of the Negro Ghetto. *Annals, Association of American Geographers*, 60, 1–17.

Rossi, P. H. 1955. *Why Families Move*. The Free Press, New York.

Rowland, D. T. 1971. Maori Migration to Auckland. *New Zealand Geographer*, 27.

Rummell, R. J. 1967. Understanding Factor Analysis. *Journal of Conflict Resolution*, 40, 440–80.

Runciman, W. G. 1969. The Three Dimensions of Social Inequality. In Beteille, 1969, 45–63.

Sabagh, G., Van Arsdol Jr., M. D. and Butler, E. W. 1969. Some Determinants of Intra-Urban Residential Mobility: Conceptual Considerations. *Social Forces*, 48.

Sauer, C. O. 1931. Cultural Geography. *Encyclopaedia of the Social Sciences*, 6, 621–4.

Saunders, D. A. L. 1967. Three Factors Behind the Form of Melbourne's Nineteenth Century Suburbs. In Troy, 1967, 1–18.

Schietinger, E. F. 1951. Racial Succession and Values of Small Residential Properties. *American Journal of Sociology*, 57, 833–8.

Schmid, C. F. 1950. Generalizations Concerning the Ecology of the American City. *American Sociology Review*, 15, 264–81.

Schmid, C. F., MacCannell, E. H. and Van Arsdol, Jr. M. D. 1958. The Ecology of the American City: Further Comparison and Validation of Generalizations. *American Sociological Review*, 23, 392–401.

Schmid, C. F. and Tagashira, K. 1965. Ecological and Demographic Indices: A Methodological Analysis. *Demography*, 1, 194–211.

Schnore, L. F. 1957a. Metropolitan Growth and Decentralization. *American Journal of Sociology*, 63, 171–80.

Schnore, L. F. 1957b. The Growth of Metropolitan Suburbs. *American Sociological Review*, 22, 165–73.

Schnore, L. F. 1957c. Satellites and Suburbs. *Social Forces*, 36, 121–7.

Schnore, L. F. 1961. The Statistical Measurement of Urbanization and Economic Development. *Land Economics*, 37, 229–46.

Schnore, L. F. 1962a. Municipal Annexations and Decentralization, 1950–1960. *American Journal of Sociology*, 57, 406–17.

Schnore, L. F. 1962b. City-Suburban Income Differentials in Metropolitan Areas. *American Sociological Review*, 27, 252–5.

Schnore, L. F. 1963a. The Social and Economic Characteristics of American Suburbs. *Sociological Quarterly*, 4, 122–34.

Schnore, L. F. 1963b. The Socioeconomic Status of Cities and Suburbs. *American Sociological Review*, 28, 76–85.

Schnore, L. F. 1964. Urban Structure and Suburban Selectivity. *Demography*, 1, 164–76.

Schnore, L. F. 1965a. On the Spatial Structure of Cities in the Two Americas. In Hauser and Schnore, 1965, 347–98.

Schnore, L. F. 1965b. *The Urban Scene*. The Free Press, New York.

Schnore, L. F. 1966. Measuring City-Suburban Status Differences. *Urban Affairs Quarterly*, 1, 95–108.

Schnore, L. F. 1968. Problems in the Quantitative Study of Urban History. In Dyos, 1968, 189–208.

Schnore, L. F. and Evenson, P. C. 1966. Segregation in Southern Cities. *American Journal of Sociology*, 72, 58–67.

Schnore, L. F. and Jones, J. K. O. 1969. The Evolution of City-Suburban Types in the Course of a Decade. *Urban Affairs Quarterly*, 4, 421–42.

Schnore, L. F. and Palen, J. J. 1965. Color Composition and City-Suburban Status Differences: A Replication and Extension. *Land Economics*, 41, 87–91.

Schnore, L. F. and Pinkerton, J. R. 1966. Residential Redistribution of Socioeconomic Strata in Metropolitan Areas. *Demography*, 3, 491–9.

Scott, P. 1959. The Australian CBD. *Economic Geography*, 35, 290–314.

Seeley, J. R., Sim, A. R. and Loosley, E. W. 1956. *Crestwood Heights*. Basic Books, New York.

Shaw, C. R. 1929. *Delinquency Areas*. University of Chicago Press, Chicago.

Shevky, E. and Bell, W. 1955. *Social Area Analysis*. Stanford University Press, Stanford, California.

Shevky, E. and Williams, M. 1949. *The Social Areas of Los Angeles*. University of California Press, Los Angeles.

Sibley, D. E. 1962. The Italian and Indian Populations in Bedford—A Contrast in Assimilation. *Northern Universities Geographical Journal*, 3, 48–52.

Simirenko, A. 1964. *Pilgrims, Colonists, and Frontiersmen*. The Free Press, New York.

Simmons, J. W. 1968. Changing Residence in the City: A Review of Intraurban Mobility. *Geographical Review*, 58, 622–51.

Sjoberg, G. 1960. *The Preindustrial City: Past and Present*. The Free Press, New York.

Smailes, A. E. 1964. Greater London—The Structure of a Metropolis. *Geografische Zeitschrift*, 52, 163–89.

Smelser, N. J. and Lipset, S. M. (editors) 1966. *Social Structure and Mobility in Economic Development*. Aldine Publishing Company, Chicago.

Smith, J., Form, W. H. and Stone, G. P. 1954. Local Intimacy in a Middle-Sized City. *American Journal of Sociology*, 60, 276–84.

Smith, P. J. 1966. Rural Interests in the Physical Expansion of Edinburgh. In Minghi, 1966, 55–68.

Smith, T. V. and White, L. D. (editors) 1929. *Chicago: An Experiment in Social Science Research.* University of Chicago Press, Chicago.

Smith, W. F. 1966. The Income Level of New Housing Demand. In *Essays in Urban Land Economics.* University of California Press, Berkeley, 143–78.

Spectorsky, A. C. 1955. *The Exurbanites.* Lippincott and Co., Philadelphia.

Steel, R. W. and Lawton, R. (editors) 1967. *Liverpool Essays in Geography.* Longmans, London.

Stegman, M. A. 1969. Accessibility Models and Residential Location. *Journal of the American Institute of Planners,* 35, 22–9.

Stein, M. R. 1960. *The Eclipse of Community.* Princetown University Press, Princeton.

Stimson, R. J. 1968. Quantitative Analysis of the Distribution of Migrant Groups in the Melbourne Metropolitan Area, 1947–1961. Paper presented to Section P, ANZAAS, Conference, Christchurch. Published as Patterns of Immigrant Settlement in Melbourne, 1947–1961. *Tijdschrift voor Economische en Sociale Geografie,* 61, 1970, 114–26.

Straits, B. C. 1968. *Racial Residential Succession.* Paper presented at the Population Association of America Meetings, Boston.

Sweetster, F. L. 1965a. Factorial Ecology: Helsinki, 1960. *Demography,* 2, 372–85.

Sweetster, F. L. 1965b. Factor Structure as Ecological Structure in Helsinki and Boston. *Acta Sociologica,* 8, 205–25.

Sweetster, F. L. 1969. Ecological Factors in Metropolitan Zones and Sectors. In Dogan and Rokkan, 1969, 413–56.

Taafe, E. J., Garner, B. J. and Yeates, M. H. 1963. *The Peripheral Journal to Work: A Geographical Consideration.* Northwestern University Press, Evanston.

Taeuber, K. E. 1968. The Effect of Income Redistribution on Racial Residential Segregation. *Urban Affairs Quarterly,* 3, 5–14.

Taeuber, K. E. and Taeuber, A. F. 1964. White Migration and Socio-Economic Differences between Cities and Suburbs. *American Sociological Review,* 29, 718–29.

Taeuber, K. E. and Taeuber, A. F. 1965a. The Changing Character of Negro Migration. *American Journal of Sociology,* 70, 429–41.

Taeuber, K. E. and Taeuber, A. F. 1965b. *Negroes in Cities.* Aldine Publishing Company, Chicago.

Thernstrom, S. and Sennett, R. (editors) 1969. *Nineteenth-Century Cities: Essays in the New Urban History.* Yale University Press, New Haven.

Thomas, C. J. 1966. Some Geographical Aspects of Council Housing in Nottingham. *East Midland Geographer,* 4, 88–98.

Thomlinson, R. 1969. *Urban Structure,* Random House, New York.

Thomson, K. W. 1967. Dutch Migrants in the Economy of New Zealand. *New Zealand Geographer,* 23, 95–105.

Thomson, K. W. and Trlin, A. D. (editors) 1970. *Immigrants in New Zealand.* Massey University Press, Palmerston North.

Tilly, C., Jackson, W. D. and Kay, B. 1965. *Race and Residence in Wilmington, Delaware*. Teachers' College, Columbia University, New York.

Timms, D. W. G. 1965. Quantitative Techniques in Urban Social Geography. In Chorley and Haggett, 1965, 239–65.

Trlin, A. D. 1968. Yugoslav Settlement in New Zealand, 1890–1961. *New Zealand Geographer*, 24, 1–22.

Troy, P. N. (editor) 1967. *Urban Redevelopment in Australia*. Research School of Social Sciences, Australian National University, Canberra.

Tryon, R. C. 1955. *Identification of Social Areas by Cluster Analysis*. University of California Press, Berkeley.

Tryon, R. C. 1967. Predicting Group Differences in Cluster Analysis: The Social Area Problem. *Multivariate Behavioral Research*, 2, 453–75.

Tryon, R. C. 1968. Comparative Cluster Analysis of Social Areas. *Multivariate Behavioral Research*, 3, 213–32.

Tunnard, C. and Pushkarev, B. 1963. *Man-Made America*. Yale University Press, New Haven.

Turner, J. C. 1968. Housing Priorities, Settlement Patterns, and Urban Development in Modernizing Countries. *Journal of the American Institute of Planners*, 34, 354–363.

Udry, J. R. 1964. Increasing Scale and Spatial Differentiation: New Tests of Two Theories from Shevky and Bell. *Social Forces*, 42, 404–13.

Udry, J. R. and Butler, E. W. 1968. A Longitudinal Examination of Changing Urban Spatial Differentiation in Four Southern Cities. *Research Previews*, 14, 34–43.

Ullman, E. L. 1953. Human Geography and Area Research. *Annals, Association of American Geographer*, 43, 54–66.

Uyeki, E. S. 1964. Residential Distribution and Stratification, 1950–1960. *American Journal of Sociology*, 69, 491–8.

Van Arsdol Jr., M. D., Camilleri, S. F. and Schmid, C. F. 1958a. An Application of the Shevky Social Area Indexes to a Model of Urban Society. *Social Forces*, 37, 26–32.

Van Arsdol, Jr., M. D., Camilleri, S. F. and Schmid, C. F. 1958b. The Generality of Urban Social Area Indexes. *American Sociological Review*, 23, 277–84.

Van Arsdol, Jr., M. D., Camilleri, S. F. and Schmid, C. F. 1961. An Investigation of the Utility of Urban Typology. *Pacific Sociological Review*, 4, 26–32.

Van Arsdol, Jr., M. D. Camilleri, S. F. and Schmid, C. F. 1962. Further Comments on the Utility of Urban Typology. *Pacific Sociological Review*, 5, 9–13.

Van Arsdol Jr., M. D., Sabagh, G. and Butler, E. W. 1968. Retrospective and Subsequent Metropolitan Residential Mobility. *Demography*, 5, 249–57.

Vance, J. E. 1966. Housing the Worker: The Employment Linkage as a Force in Urban Structure. *Economic Geography*, 42, 294–325.

Vance, J. E. 1967. Housing the Worker: Determinative and Contingent Ties in Nineteenth Century Birmingham. *Economic Geography*, 43, 95–127.

Vereker, C. and Mays, J. B. 1961. *Urban Redevelopment and Social Change*. Liverpool University Press, Liverpool.

Vidal de la Blache, P. 1913. Les Caracteres Distinctifs de la Geographie *Annales de Geographie*, 22, 299.

Ward, D. 1962. The Pre-Urban Cadaster and the Urban Pattern of Leeds. *Annals of the Association of American Geographers*, 52, 150–66.

Ward, D. 1968. The Emergence of Central Immigrant Ghettoes in American Cities: 1840–1920. *Annals, Association of American Geographers*, 58, 343–59.

Ward, D. 1969. The Internal Spatial Structure of Immigrant Residential Districts in the Late Nineteenth Century. *Geographical Analysis*, 1, 327–53.

Warner, S. B. 1962. *Streetcar Suburbs: The Process of Growth in Boston, 1870–1900.* The M.I.T. Press, Cambridge, Mass.

Warner, W. L., Meeker, M. and Eels, K. 1960. *Social Class in America.* Harper and Row (Harper Torchbooks), New York.

Wattell, H. L. 1958. Levittown: A Suburban Community. In Dobriner, 1958, 287–313.

Webber, M. M. 1964. Culture, Territoriality, and the Elastic Mile. *Papers, Regional Science Association*, 13, 59–70.

Weber, M. 1930. *The Protestant Ethic and the Spirit of Capitalism.* Scribners, New York.

Weiss, S. F., Kenney, K. B. and Steffens, P. C. 1966. Consumer Preferences in Residential Location: A Preliminary Investigation of the Home Purchase Decision. *Research Previews* (University of North Carolina), 13, 1–32.

Wendt, P. F. 1962. *Housing Policy: The Search for Solutions*, University of California Press, Berkeley.

Wesolowski, W. 1962. Some Notes on the Functional Theory of Stratification. *The Polish Sociological Review*, 3–4, 28–38.

Westergaard, J. H. 1964. The Structure of Greater London. In Centre for Urban Studies, 1964, 91–143.

Wheatley, P. 1967. Proleptic Observations on the Origins of Urbanism. In Steel and Lawton, 1967, 315–45.

Wheeler, J. O. 1967. Occupational Status and Work-Trips: A Minimum Distance Approach. *Social Forces*, 45, 508–15.

Wheeler, J. O. 1968. Work-Trip Length and the Ghetto. *Land Economics*, 44, 107–12.

Whitehand, J. W. R. 1967. The Settlement Morphology of London's Cocktail Belt. *Tijdschrift voor Economische en Sociale Geografie*, 58, 20–7.

Whitelaw, J. S. (editor) 1967. *Auckland in Ferment.* New Zealand Geographical Society, Auckland.

Whitney, V. M. and Grigg, C. M. 1958. Patterns of Mobility among a Group of Families of College Students. *American Sociological Review*, 23, 643–52.

Whittlesey, D. 1929. Sequent Occupance. *Annals, Association of American Geographers*, 19, 162–5.

Whyte, W. 1960. *The Organization Man.* Penguin Books, Harmondsworth, Middlesex.

Wilkinson, R. and Merry, D. M. 1965. A Statistical Analysis of Attitudes to Moving. *Urban Studies*, 2, 1–14.

Williams, W. M. and Herbert, D. T. 1962. The Social Geography of Newcastle-under-Lyme. *North Staffordshire Journal of Field Studies,* 2, 108–26.

Willmott, P. and Young, M. 1960. *Family and Class in a London Suburb.* Routledge and Kegan Paul, London.

Wilson, G. and Wilson, M. 1945. *The Analysis of Social Change.* Cambridge University Press, Cambridge.

Wilson, R. L. 1962. Livability of the City: Attitudes and Urban Development. In Chapin and Weiss, 1962, 359–99.

Wingo, Jr. L. 1961. *Transportation and Urban Land.* Resources for the Future Inc., Washington, D.C.

Wirth, L. 1938. Urbanism as a Way of Life. *American Journal of Sociology* 44, 1–24.

Wirth, L. 1956. *The Ghetto.* University of Chicago Press (Phoenix Books), Chicago.

Wolf, E. P. 1957. The Invasion-Succession Sequence as a Self-Fulfilling Prophecy. *Journal of Social Issues,* 13, 7–20.

Wolf, E. P. 1960. Racial Transition in a Middle-Class Area. *Journal of Intergroup Relations,* 1, 75–81.

Wolf, E. P. 1963. The Tipping Point in Racially Changing Neighborhoods. *Journal of the American Institute of Planners,* 29, 217–22.

Wolf, E. P. 1965. The Baxter Area: A New Trend in Neighborhood Changes?, *Phylon,* 26, 344–53.

Wolforth, J. R. 1966. *Residential Location and the Place of Work.* Tantalus Publications, Vancouver.

Yeates, M. H. 1966. Some Factors affecting the Spatial Distribution of Chicago Land Values, 1910–1960. *Economic Geography,* 42, 57–70.

Young, M. and Willmott, P. 1962. *Family and Kinship in East London.* Penguin Books, Harmondsworth, Middlesex.

Zorbaugh, H. W. 1929. *The Gold Coast and the Slum.* University of Chicago Press, Chicago.

Zubrzycki, J. 1960. *Immigrants in Australia: A Demographic Survey based on the 1954 Census.* Melbourne University Press, Melbourne.

Index

Abu-Lughod, J. L., 36, 62, 67, 231–2; with Foley, M. M., 103–10, 169, 306
Accessibility, 73–4, 79, 100, 102, 321–9
Adams, J. S., 318–19
Address, as status symbol, 39, 167
Age structures, 201, 203–10; changes in, 207–10
Akron, 330
Alihan, M. M., 76–7
Alonso, W., 79, 100–1, 122, 222, 321
Amato, P. W., 139, 141, 185
Anderson, T. R., 174–5, 331; with Bean, L. L., 57–8, 114; with Egeland, J. A., 330–1
Apartments, 45–7, 101, 215–18, 220–1, 229–34, 241
Ashworth, W., 165–6, 186
Assimilation, 33–4, 49–52, 112, 243–6, 274–90, 293
Attrition, of housing demand, 262–5
Auckland, 204–6, 207–10, 287–90
Australia, 17, 195, 246

Baltzell, E. D., 146, 176–7
Barber, G. and Bourne, L. S., 39
Beckmann, M. J., 79
Bedarida, F., 139
Belfast, 162–3
Bell, W., 30, 53, 56, 229–31, 235, 335; and Greer, S., 56; and Moskos, C. C., 58
Bergel, E. E., 49–50, 275

Berger, B. M., 170, 236
Berry, B. J. L., 16, 38, 222; and Rees, P. H., 36, 59, 292, 343–52; Simmons, J. W. and Tennant, R. J., 225
Beshers, J. M., 41, 59, 272
Beynon, E. D., 283
Blumenfeld, H., 121
Bogue, D. J., 117
Booth, C., 32, 164–5
Boston, 89–90, 157, 188–90, 234, 281–2
Bourne, L. S., 77, 215–18, 231
Bracey, H. E., 40, 236
Brisbane, 306
Brown, L. A., 16, 315; and Holmes, J. H., 318; and Horton, F. E., 341–2; and Longbrake, D. B., 313–17; and Moore, E. G., 40, 295, 317
Burgess, E. W., 65–79, 114, 120–1; and Bogue, D. J., 65–6
Butler, E. W., and Barclay, W. J., 212–14; Sabagh, G. and van Arsdol, M. D. Jr., 311
Butlin, R. A., 157

Caplan, E. and Wolf, E. P., 265
Caplow, T. and Forman, R., 40
Careerism, 30–1, 229
Carroll, J. D. Jr., 325
Cedar Rapids, 313–16, 318
Central city dwellers, 228–34; migration rates, 303–6
Centralisation, index for socio-economic status groups, 121–6

Chain migrations, 48, 112, 246
Chapin, F. S. and Brail, R. K.,
31; and Hightower, H. C., 232;
and Weiss, S. F., 218–19
Chicago, 43–5, 48–52, 65, 70, 75,
120–4, 180–1, 222–4, 227–8,
247–50, 269–72, 273, 325, 331,
340
Christchurch, 149–54, 224, 295
Circulation of elites, 182
Clark, C., 21, 225
Clark, S. D., 171, 234–5, 237, 240,
324–5, 335
Clark, W. A. V., 306, 318
Class: see Social stratification
Cleveland, 121–4
Clignet, R. and Sween, J., 36
Coleman, J. S., 35, 62
Collison, P. and Mogey, J. M.,
44, 158
Comhaire, J. and Cahnman, W. J.,
138
Commonwealth, immigrants to
U.K., 245
Consumerism, 32, 229
Coulson, M. R. C., 206–7
Council housing: see State housing
Cox, K. R., 40, 317
Cressey, P. F., 245, 247
Crowe, P. R., 16
Curson, P. H., 204–6, 207–10, 246,
287–90

Dahrendorf, R., 26
Daly, M. T., 222, 322
Davie, M. R., 69–71, 94, 121, 162
Davies, R. J., 124–6
Davis, J. T., 177–8, 184
Davis, K., 25, 32; and Blake, J.,
35; and Moore, W. E., 25–6
Davison, R. B., 245, 285
Dayton, 330
Detroit, 169, 265–6, 283, 325
Dickinson, G. C., 194
Dickinson, R. E., 16
Distance, role in social relations,
40–2, 43–5, 317–20; time and
cost, 72–4
Division of labour: see Specialisation
Divisions of society, 19–37;
number of, 24–37, 55;

independence of, 35, 55, 62,
115–17: see also Family status;
independence of socio-economic
status
Dobriner, W., 170
Du Bois, W. E., 258
Duncan, B., 122; and Hauser,
P. M., 45; Sabagh, G. and van
Arsdol, M. D. Jr., 210
Duncan, O. D., 27; and Duncan,
B., 43–5, 62, 91, 121–4, 251–61,
270–2, 325, 327; and Hawley,
A. H., 58, 63; and Schnore,
L. F., 139
Dutch, in Kalamazoo, 275–9; in
New Zealand, 290

Ecological complex, 139
Edinburgh, 157–8
Education, city-suburban
differences, 129–32; changing
city-suburban differences, 134–7;
of American population, 178–9;
patterns in Melbourne, 143–5
Elias, N., 44
Elite residential areas, 141–56, 167,
169–76; stability of, 176–9;
migration of, 150–4
Environmental requirements, of
households, 102, 294, 306–11,
321–5
Evolutionary sequence, urban
socio-economic status patterns,
137–41, 184–95

Factor analysis, 55, 59–60
Factorial ecology, 57, 59–62, 160,
267–8, 332, 336
Fairbairn, K., 180
Familism, 30, 229
Family, as economic and social
unit, 22, 29–31, 41
Family cycle, 31–2, 103–10, 197–
241; and migration, 293–4,
297–303, 306–11, 312–17, 341
Family status, 29–32, 35, 45–7,
335–340; independence of socio-
economic status, 36–7, 55, 62,
101, 221, 303, 349–51; in
ghetto, 270

Fertility, 35–6, 57–8, 199–200, 210–14, 297–303
Filtering, 87–8, 96–8, 154, 176, 190–1, 294, 306–11, 312–17, 341, 348–9
Firey, W., 89–93, 114, 147, 157, 162, 281–2
Foote, N. N. et al, 103–10, 176
Ford, R. G., 247–8
Forrest, J., 139, 161
Franklin, S. H., 143, 203–4
Frazier, E. F., 269–70
Freedman, R., 47, 180–1
Freeman, T. W., 157
Fried, M., 41, 234; and Gleicher, P., 41, 234

Gans, H. J., 40, 190, 233–4, 235–6, 282
Getis, A., 327–9
Ghetto, 111–14, 242–3, 293, 329; expanding, 251–72; patterns within, 267–72, 287; simulation, 266–7; stable, 272–4
Gittus, E., 77
Glass, D. V. and Hall, J. R., 27, 28
Glazer, N. and Moynihan, D. P., 114, 272
Glick, P. C., 107
Goldsmith, H. F. and Lee, S. Y., 171, 173; and Stockwell, E. G., 171–3
Goldstein, S., 303–4; and Goldscheider, C., 52, 273–4, 292; and Mayer, K. B., 181, 240, 312–13, 317, 327
Goddard, J. B., 95
Goode, W. J., 30, 31–2
Gordon, G., 158
Gordon, M. M., 33–4
Greeks, in Wellington, 290
Greenbie, B. B., 324
Greer, S., 59
Gregory, S., 59
Grief, for home, 41, 234
Griffin, D. W. and Preston, R. E., 80, 87
Grigsby, W. G., 96–7, 190, 297–300
Gutman, R., 138

Haggett, P., 16
Hammond, S. B., 50
Handlin, O., 114, 245
Harris, B., 79, 226–7
Harris, C. D. and Ullman, E. L., 83, 94–6
Hart, J. F., 245
Hartman, C. W., 234
Hartshorne, R., 16
Hauser, F. L., 165
Hawley, A. H., 127
Heberle, R., 138
Heenan, L. D. B., 246
Herbert, D. T., 55, 61, 141; and Rodgers, H. B., 40
Holmes, J. H., 327
Home ownership, 45, 103, 167
Hoover, E. M. and Vernon, R., 170–1, 210–14, 221, 325
Horne, D., 167
Horton, F. E. and Reynolds, D. R., 317
Housing, age, 102–3; choice, 99, 320–9; space requirements, 45–7
Hoyt, H., 79–94, 138, 140, 147, 168, 220, 342
Hungarians, in Detroit, 283; in Toronto, 283
Hurd, R. M., 65, 222

Income groups, city-suburban differences, 132–4, 170–1
Index, of centralisation, 121; of dissimilarity, 43; of sector concentration, 124–6; of segregation, 43
Indianapolis, 330
Industry, location in city, 71, 73, 163
Inkeles, A. and Rossi, P. H., 26
Integration, 33
Invasion and succession, 68–9, 115, 180–2, 251–66, 285–7, 294, 318, 341
Irish, in U.K., 245, 284; in New Zealand, 246; in Birmingham, 285–6
Italians, in Boston, 281–2; in Chicago, 48; in New Haven, 282

Jackson, J. A., 245, 284

Jakle, J. A. and Wheeler, J. O., 114, 275–9
James, J., 90
Janson, C-G., 35, 62
Johannesburg, 124–6
Johnston, R. J., 35, 37, 62, 63, 116, 117, 141, 142–54, 180, 199–203, 284, 287, 303, 318, 320, 331, 334–5, 337
Jonassen, C. T., 282
Jones, E., 141, 162–3; and Sinclair, D. J., 165
Jones, F. L., 46, 52, 58–9, 60–1, 114, 142, 146, 246, 287, 336–40
Jones, P. N., 285–7
Jones, R., 39, 161, 192
Journey to work, 102, 122, 167, 186, 192–5, 325–9

Kain, J. F., 325
Kaiser, E. J. and Weiss, S. F., 219–20, 221, 321–2
Kansas City, 206–7
Katz, A. M. and Hill, R., 41
Keyfitz, N., 21
Kiang, Y-C., 247–50, 292
Kinship, 31–2, 33, 47–8, 112, 234, 282, 324
Knights, P. R., 304
Knos, D. S., 100, 222
Kosa, J., 283
Kunkel, R. and Zanarini, R., 317

Lafayette, 309–10
Lampard, E. E., 19–20
Land values, 44, 79, 99–101, 222–4
Lansing, J. B., Clifton, C. V. and Morgan, J. N., 300–3
Laserwitz, B., 173
Latin American cities, 138–9, 141
Laurenti, L., 264–5
Lee, E. S., 293
Lees, L. H., 284
Leiffer, M. R., 71
Lenski, G., 26
Leslie, G., 224
Leslie, G. R. and Richardson, A. H., 309–10
Levittowns, 190, 310
Lewis, O., 22, 24, 47

Lieberson, S., 49, 52, 61, 246; and Duncan, O. D., 50–2, 250
Life style, 29–32, 45–7, 98–110, 197–241: see also Family status
Lipman, V. D., 274
Lipset, S. M. and Bendix, R., 27–9
Little, K. L., 48
Litwak, E., 32, 112
Loewenstein, L. K., 77
Logan, M. I., 325
London, 163–6, 284–6, 295, 320
Los Angeles, 190, 212–14, 305, 310
Lowry, I. S., 96–7

Mabry, J. H., 161
Madison, 324
Maisel, S. F., 300, 305, 306
Manchester, 157
Mann, P. H., 77, 163–4
Maori, 48, 246, 289
Marriage, and distance, 41–2, 272
Mayer, H. M. and Kohn, C. F., 84
McElrath, D. C., 36–7, 242, 331; and Barkey, J. W., 331–2, 334
McGee, T. G., 17, 154–6, 246
McKenzie, R. D., 65, 68
Mehta, S. K., 22
Melbourne, 46, 50, 52, 60–1, 141–9, 199–203, 233, 240–1, 287–8, 295, 320, 335, 336–40
Mental maps, 317–20
Metge, A. J., 48
Michelson, W., 45
Middle class, 92; housing, 187–95; housewives attitudes, 238–9; in central city, 177–8; in suburbia, 170, 175–6, 234–9
Migration, 32–4, 47–52, 293–329; directions, 318–20; international, 33, 47, 180, 245; intra-urban, 115–17, 293–329; matrices, 297–300; movers and stayers model, 303–6; rates, 32, 115, 295–6, 297, 303–11; retrospective and subsequent, 305; sequences, 300–3; in community space, 311–17; in physical space, 317–20
Migrant zones in Chicago, 180
Miller, A. R., 182

Minneapolis, 279–80, 320
Minority groups, 32–4, 47–52;
    residential clustering of, 48–52,
    110–14, 242–92, 352
Mittelbach, F. G., 190
Mogey, J. M., 41
Molotch, H., 264, 266
Moore, E. G., 305–6
Moore, W. E., 21–2
Morrill, R. L., 266–7
Morris, R. N., 23, 24, 94
Morrison, P. A., 304
Mortgages, 103, 188–90, 192–3
Moser, C. A. and Scott, W., 38
Mowrer, E. R., 40, 237
Multi-nucleated city, 73, 94–5, 325
Murdie, R. A., 331, 332–3, 334,
    341–2
Muth, R. F., 225, 227–8
Myers, J. K., 242
Myrdal, G., 19

Negro, 50, 68–9, 245, 300, 330; in
    Chicago, 251–6; ghetto, 251–74,
    329
Neighbourhood change, 340–2; in
    London, 165–6; in Manchester,
    157; in Chicago, 341–2; in New
    York and Los Angeles, 210–14;
    in San Francisco, 296; in
    Toronto, 340–1; in United
    States, 179–82; patterns in U.K.,
    156–66; types in Cedar Rapids,
    313; types in Melbourne,
    335–40; stability in United
    States, 176–9
Neutze, G. M., 220–1, 239
New Haven, 71, 282
New York, 169, 170–1, 210–12,
    282, 325
New Zealand, 48; housing loans,
    192–3; immigration to, 246;
    urban residential patterns,
    154–6, 195
Newcastle (NSW), 222, 322
Newling, B. E., 225
Newmarket (NZ), 207–10
Norristown, 303–4

Occupational selectivity, in US
    SMAs, 171–3

Olsson, G., 40
Orleans, P., 65

Pahl, R. E., 163, 238–9
Park, R. E., 65, 68, 73
Patterson, S., 245, 287
Peach, G. C. K., 245
Peattie, L. R., 30
Penalosa, F., 141
Peterson, G. L., 324
Pfautz, H. W., 164
Philadelphia, 121, 176–7, 261–4,
    297–300, 304, 307–9
Pittsburg, 325
Pollins, H., 165, 194
Polynesians, in Auckland, 287–90
Pool, D. I., 246
Population densities, 225–8
'Port-of-entry' model, 69, 258, 267,
    289, 297
Powers, M. G., 35, 173–4
Pred, A. R., 19, 20
Pretoria, 124–6
Price, C. A., 48
Property values, 264–5
Providence, 240, 273–4, 312–13

Quinn, J. A., 71–6, 77, 78, 127,
    220, 346

Ramsøy, N. R., 42
Rapkin, C. W. and Grigsby, W. G.,
    232, 262–4
Ravenstein, E. G., 32
Reeder, D. W., 165
Rees, P. H., 56, 59, 62, 114, 224,
    348
Repletion of neighbourhoods, 149,
    154
Residential development process,
    218–20
Residential preferences, 321–5
Residential segregation, 35; in
    Chicago, 43–5, 48–52; of
    minority groups, 49–50
Richards, J. M., 102
Rimmer, P. J., 95
Robson, B. T., 61, 141, 159–61,
    192

Rodgers, H. B., 157
Rodwin, L., 90–3, 143, 188–90, 192
Rome, 331
Rose, H. M., 111, 114, 257, 266–7
Rossi, P. H., 307–11
Rowland, D. T., 246, 289–90
Rummel, R. J., 60
Runciman, W. G., 25, 26–7
Russians in Minneapolis, 279–80

Sabagh, G., van Arsdol, M.D. Jr. and Butler, E. W., 293–5
San Francisco, 54, 296, 335
Sauer, C. O., 16
Saunders, D. A. L., 188
Schietinger, E. F., 264
Schmid, C. F., 36; MacConnell, E. H. and van Arsdol, M. D. Jr., 36; and Tagashira, K., 60, 114–17
Schnore, L. F., 16, 19, 78–9, 126–41, 169–70, 178–9, 184, 270; and Evenson, P. C., 127; and Jones, J. K. O., 133–7; and Palen, J. J., 132; and Pinkerton, J. R., 136–7
Scott, P., 95
Seattle, 60, 117
Sector, definition, 91; model, 79–94; model related to zonal model, 330–40; mental maps, 318–20; pattern in ghettoes, 111–14, 251–6; pattern of apartments, 215–18; patterns, 122–4, in Belfast, 162–3, in Edinburgh, 157–8, in London, 163–6, in Melbourne, 143–6, in Sunderland, 159–61
Seeley, J. R., Sim, A. R. and Loosley, E. W., 236
Sentiment and symbolism, 89–90, 147–8, 154, 176–8, 294
Sex ratios, 117
Shaw, C. R., 69, 120
Shevky, E. and Bell, W., 23, 24, 35–6, 53–9, 115, 229–30, 330
Sibley, D. E., 245
Simirenko, A., 279–80
Simmons, J. W., 307, 312, 317
Sjoberg, G., 138

Skid Row, 117
Smailes, A. E., 165
Smith, J., Form, W. H. and Stone, G. P., 40
Smith, P. J., 158, 163
Smith, W. F., 190
Social area analysis, 53–9, 296
Social interaction, 40–2, 294
Social mobility, 27–9, 41, 110; downward, 300; related to migration, 294, 309–11
Social stratification, 25–7, 91–2
Socio-economic status, 25–9; city-suburban differences, 126–7; of neighbourhoods, 38–45, 65–98, 119–96: see also under Family status
Space preferences, 79, 102, 104–10, 226–7
Specialisation, 19–20; concomitants and consequences, 21–4; prerequisites, 21
Spectorsky, A. C., 236
State housing, 160–1, 192, 195, 234, 289, 349
Stegman, M. A., 326
Stein, M. R., 235
Stimson, R. J., 287
Straits, B. C., 258, 261, 263
Street patterns, 72–4, 149
Suburban, sadness, 235; types, 127, 136
Suburbia, 234–9
Sunderland, 159–61
Sweetster, F. L., 59, 292
Sydney, 34, 325
Syracuse, 330

Taaffe, E. J., Garner, B. J. and Yeates, M. H., 325
Taeuber, K. E., 50, 243; and Taeuber, A. F., 43, 180–2, 258–9, 263, 272, 297
Thomas, C. J., 161
Thomlinson, R., 16
Thomson, K. W., 246, 290; and Trlin, A. D., 246, 290
Tilly, C., Jackson, W. D. and Kay, B., 261, 265
Timms, D. W. G., 44
Toledo, 57–8, 267–8

Toronto, 215–18, 231, 283, 324–5, 332–3, 341–2
Trlin, A. D., 48, 246
Tryon, R. C., 296
Tunnard, C. and Pushkarev, B., 210
Turner, J. C., 99

Udry, J. R., 36, 58; and Butler, E. W., 37
Ullman, E. L., 94–6
United Kingdom, neighbourhood patterns, 156–66
Urban villages, 111–12, 233–4, 281–4
Urbanism, 23–4
Uyeki, E. S., 44, 123–4

van Arsdol, M. D. Jr., Camilleri, S. F. and Schmid, C. F., 36, 55–6
van Arsdol, M. D. Jr., Sabagh, G. and Butler, E. W., 305–6
Vance, J. E. Jr., 187
Vancouver, 326–7
Vereker, C. and Mays, J. B., 41, 234
Vidal de la Blache, P., 16

Ward, D., 114, 192, 275
Warner, S. B., 186–8
Warner, W. L., Meeker, M. and Eels, K., 38
Wattell, H. L., 310
Webber, M. M., 52
Weber, M., 21
Weiss, S. F., Kenney, K. B. and Steffens, P. C., 321–2
Wellington, 203–4, 290
Wendt, P. F., 192
Wesolowski, W., 25
West Indians, in Birmingham, 285–7; in London, 284–6, 287

Westergaard, J. H., 165–6
Wheatley, P., 21
Wheeler, J. O., 325, 329
Whitehand, J. W. R., 141, 165
Whitney, V. M. and Grigg, C. M., 310
Whittlesey, D., 16
Who's Who, 146–54
Whyte, W. H., 40, 170, 182, 236, 239, 304
Wilkinson, R. and Merry, D. M., 304
Williams, W. M. and Herbert, D. T., 141
Willmott, P. and Young, M., 165
Wilmington, 261
Wilson, G. and Wilson, M., 22
Wilson, R. L., 322–4
Wingo, L. Jr., 100
Winnick, L., 176
Wirth, L., 23–4, 35, 39, 47, 65, 233, 272–3
Wolf, E. P., 265–6
Wolforth, J. R., 326–7

Yeates, M. H., 222–4
Young, M. and Willmott, P., 41, 234

Zonal model, 66–78, 93–4, 136–7; versus gradients, 76–7; relation to sectoral model, 330–40; pattern in Melbourne, 143–6
Zones, of education groups, 129–32, 134–6; of family status/life cycle, 197–241; of housing types, 98–110; of income groups, 132–4; of indifference, 327; of socio-economic status, 348–9; within Negro ghetto, 269–72; within sectors, 88, 348–9, 350
Zorbaugh, H. W., 39, 40–1, 247
Zubrzycki, J., 52, 246